This book has two main goals: the re-establishment of a rule-based phonology as a viable alternative to current non-derivational models, and the rehabilitation of historical evidence as a focus of phonological theory. Although Lexical Phonology includes several constraints, such as the Derived Environment Condition and Structure Preservation, intended to reduce abstractness, previous versions have not typically exploited these fully. The model of Lexical Phonology presented here imposes the Derived Environment Condition strictly; introduces a new constraint on the shape of underlying representations; excludes underspecification; and suggests an integration of Lexical Phonology with articulatory phonology. Together, these innovations ensure a substantially more concrete phonology. The constrained model is tested against a number of well-known processes of English, Scottish and American accents, including the Vowel Shift Rule, the Scottish Vowel Length Rule, and [r]-Insertion, and draws interesting distinctions between what is derivable by rule and what is not. Not only can this Lexical Phonology model the development of low-level variation to phonological rules, and ultimately to dialect differentiation in the underlying representations; but a knowledge of history also makes apparently arbitrary synchronic processes quite natural. In short the phonological past and present explain one another.

April McMahon is Lecturer in Phonology and Historical Linguistics in the Department of Linguistics at the University of Cambridge.

CAMBRIDGE STUDIES IN LINGUISTICS

General Editors: S. R. ANDERSON, J. BRESNAN, B. COMRIE,
W. DRESSLER, C. J. EWEN, R. HUDDLESTON, R. LASS,
D. LIGHTFOOT, J. LYONS, P. H. MATTHEWS, R. POSNER,
S. ROMAINE, N. V. SMITH, N. VINCENT

In this series

LEXICAL PHONOLOGY AND THE HISTORY OF ENGLISH

APRIL McMAHON

Department of Linguistics
University of Cambridge

PUBLISHED BY THE PRESS SYNDICATE OF THE UNIVERSITY OF CAMBRIDGE
The Pitt Building, Trumpington Street, Cambridge, United Kingdom

CAMBRIDGE UNIVERSITY PRESS
The Edinburgh Building, Cambridge CB2 2RU, UK   www.cup.cam.ac.uk
40 West 20th Street, New York, NY 10011–4211, USA   www.cup.org
10 Stamford Road, Oakleigh, Melbourne 3166, Australia

First published 2000

Printed in the United Kingdom at the University Press, Cambridge

Typeset in Times 10/13pt.   [CE]

A catalogue record for this book is available from the British Library

Library of Congress Cataloguing in Publication data
McMahon, April M. S.
  Lexical Phonology and the history of English / April McMahon.
    p.   cm. – (Cambridge studies in linguistics; 91)
  Includes bibliographical references and index.
  ISBN 0 521 47280 6 hardback
    1. English language – Phonology, Historical. 2. English language –
History. 3. Lexical Phonology.   I. Title.   II. Series.
PE1133.M37   2000
421′.5 – dc21   99–28845 CIP

ISBN 0 521 47280 6 hardback

For Aidan and Fergus, who make life so much fun

Contents

Acknowledgements

Most of this book was written during a sabbatical leave from the University of Cambridge, and a term of research leave awarded by the Humanities Research Board of the British Academy, which I acknowledge with gratitude and in the absolute certainty that I couldn't have done the job otherwise. Heinz Giegerich, who was my PhD supervisor longer ago than either of us would really like to believe, has been unstintingly generous with his time and ideas and a reliable dispenser of concise and effective pep-talks. Colleagues too numerous to mention have listened to talks based on chunks of the book, shared information and made useful comments; and Paul Foulkes, Francis Nolan, Peter Matthews and Laura Tollfree have read drafts of various sections and helped reravel unravelling arguments. Roger Lass has waded through the lot at various stages, and been unfailingly constructive; and the thought of the ouch factor in his comments has saved me from all sorts of excesses I might otherwise have perpetrated. And last but not least, my heartfelt thanks to Rob, Aidan and Fergus for being there (albeit two of them from only part-way through the project).

Selwyn College, Cambridge

1 *The rôle of history*

1.1   Internal and external evidence

Any linguist asked to provide candidate items for inclusion in a list of the slipperiest and most variably definable twentieth-century linguistic terms, would probably be able to supply several without much prompting. Often the lists would overlap (*simplicity* and *naturalness* would be reasonable prospects), but we would each have our own idiosyncratic selection. My own nominees are *internal* and *external evidence.*

In twentieth-century linguistics, types of data and of argument have moved around from one of these categories to the other relatively freely: but we can identify a general tendency for more and more types of evidence to be labelled *external*, a label to be translated 'subordinate to internal evidence' or, in many cases, 'safe to ignore'. Thus, Labov (1978) quotes Kuryłowicz as arguing that historical linguistics should concern itself only with the linguistic system before and after a change, paying no attention to such peripheral concerns as dialect geography, phonetics, sociolinguistics, and psycholinguistics. Furthermore, in much Standard Generative Phonology, historical evidence finds itself externalised (along with 'performance factors' such as speech errors and dialect variation), making distribution and alternation, frequently determined by introspection, the sole constituents of internal evidence, and thus virtually the sole object of enquiry. In sum, 'If we study the various restrictions imposed on linguistics since Saussure, we see more and more data being excluded in a passionate concern for what linguistics is *not'* (Labov 1978: 275–6).

Labov accepts that 'recent linguistics has been dominated by the drive for an autonomous discipline based on purely internal argument', but does not consider this a particularly fruitful development, arguing that 'the most notorious mysteries of linguistic change remain untouched by such abstract operations and become even more obscure' (1978: 277). He consequently pleads for a rapprochement of synchronic and diachronic study, showing that advances in phonetics and sociolinguistics, which have illuminated many aspects of change in progress, can equally explain completed changes, provided that we accept the uniformitarian principle: 'that is, the forces which operated to produce the historical record are the same as those which can be seen operating today' (Labov 1978: 281). An alliance of phonetics, sociolinguistics, dialectology and formal model-building with historical linguistics is, in Labov's view, the most promising way towards understanding the linguistic past. We must first understand the present as fully as possible: 'only when we are thoroughly at home in that everyday world, can we expect to be at home in the past' (1978: 308).

Labov is not, of course, alone in his conviction that the present can inform us about the past. His own approach can be traced to Weinreich, Labov and Herzog's (1968: 100) emphasis on 'orderly heterogeneity' in language, a reaction to over-idealisation of the synchronic system and the exclusion of crucial variation data. However, integration of the synchronic and diachronic approaches was also a desideratum of Prague School linguistics, as expressed notably by Vachek (1966, 1976, 1983). Vachek uses the term 'external evidence' (1972) to refer solely to the rôle of language contact and sociocultural factors in language change; this work has informed and influenced both contact linguistics and Labovian sociolinguistics. Although Vachek accepts external causation of certain changes, however, he still regards the strongest explanations as internal, involving the language's own structure. This leads to attempts to limit external explanation, often via circular and ultimately unfalsifiable statements like Vachek's contention (1972: 222) that 'a language system ... does *not* submit to such external influence as would be incompatible with its structural needs and wants'. For a critique of the internal/external dichotomy in this context, see Dorian (1993), and Farrar (1996).

More relevant to our discussion here is Vachek's argument that synchrony is never truly static: 'any language system has, besides its solid central core, its periphery, which need not be in complete accordance with the laws and tendencies governing its central core' (1966: 27). Peripheral elements are those entering or leaving the system, and it is vital that they should be identified, as they can illuminate trends and changes in the system which would not otherwise be explicable, or even observable. Peripheral phonemes, for instance, might be those perceived as foreign; or have a low functional yield; or be distributionally restricted, like English /h/ or /ŋ/ (Vachek 1976: 178). A dynamic approach is therefore essential: the synchronically peripheral status of certain elements allows us to understand and perhaps predict diachronic developments, while the changes which have produced this peripherality can in turn explain irregularities in the synchronic pattern. This is not to say that Vachek collapses the two; on the contrary, his review of Chomsky and Halle (1968) is particularly critical of 'the lack of a clear dividing line that should be drawn between synchrony and diachrony' (1976: 307). Vachek considers Chomsky and Halle's extension of the Vowel Shift Rule from peripheral, learned forms like *serene ~ serenity*, to non-alternating, core forms like *meal*, an unjustified confusion of synchrony and diachrony: by in effect equating sound changes and synchronic phonological rules, Standard Generative Phonology in practice significantly reduces the useful conclusions which can be drawn about either.

Although Vachek seems to regard synchronic and diachronic data and analysis as mutually informing, the relationship is seen rather differently in Bailey's time-based or developmental linguistics. Bailey (1982: 154) agrees that 'any step towards getting rid of the compartmentalization of linguistics into disparate and incompatible synchronic, diachronic, and comparative or dialectal pursuits must ... be welcomed', and proposes polylectal systems sensitive to diachronic data. He coins the term 'yroëth' (which is theory spelled backwards) for 'something claiming to be a *theory* which may have a notation and terminology but fails to achieve any deep-level explanation ... All synchronic–idiolectal analysis is yroëthian, since deep explanation and prediction are possible only by investigating and understanding how structures and other phenomena have developed into what they have become' (Bailey 1996: 378). It is therefore scarcely surprising that Bailey regards the influence of diachronic on synchronic analysis as one-way, arguing that historical linguists are fundamentally misguided in adopting synchronic frameworks and notions for diachronic work: in doing so, they are guilty of analysing out the variation and dynamism central to language change by following the 'nausea principle': 'if movement makes the mandarins seasick, tie up the ship and pretend it is part of the pier and is not meant to sail anywhere' (Bailey 1982: 152).

We therefore have four twentieth-century viewpoints. The standard line of argumentation focuses on synchrony; historical evidence here is external, and is usable only as in Chomsky and Halle (1968), where sound changes appear minimally recast as synchronic phonological rules.

Vachek, conversely, argues that synchronic and diachronic phonology are equally valid and equally necessary for explanation. Labov argues that the present can tell us about the past, and Bailey the reverse. My own view is closest to Vachek's: if we are really to integrate synchrony and diachrony, the connection should cut both ways. That is, the linguistic past should be able to help us understand and model the linguistic present: since historical changes have repercussions on systems, an analysis of a synchronic system might sometimes benefit from a knowledge of its development. Perplexing synchronic phenomena might even become transparent in the light of history. But in addition, a framework originally intended for synchronic analysis will be more credible if it can provide enlightening accounts of sound change, and crucially model the transition from sound change to phonological rule without simply collapsing the two categories.

This book is thus intended as a contribution to the debate on the types of evidence which are relevant in the formulation and testing of phonological models, and has as one of its aims the discussion and eventual rehabilitation of external evidence. There will be particular emphasis on historical data and arguments; but issues of variation, which recent sociolinguistic work has confirmed as a prerequisite for many changes (Milroy and Milroy 1985; Milroy 1992), will also figure, and some attention will also be devoted to the phonetic motivation for sound changes and phonological rules.

However, although these arguments are of general relevance to phonologists, they are addressed here specifically from the perspective of one phonological model, namely Lexical Phonology. In short, the book also constitutes an attempt to constrain the theory of Lexical Phonology, and to demonstrate that the resulting model can provide an illuminating analysis of problematic aspects of the synchronic phonology of Modern English, as well as being consistent with external evidence from a number of areas, including diachronic developments and dialect differences. I shall focus on three areas of the phonology in which the unenviable legacy of Standard Generative Phonology, as enshrined in Chomsky and Halle (1968; henceforth SPE) seriously compromises the validity of its successor, Lexical Phonology: these are the synchronic problem of abstractness; the differentiation of dialects; and the relationship of sound changes and phonological rules. I shall show that a rigorous application of the principles and constraints inherent in Lexical Phonology permits an enlightening account of these areas, and a demonstration that generative models need not necessarily be subject to the failings and infelicities of their predecessor. Finally, just as the data discussed here are drawn from the synchronic and diachronic domains, so the constraints operative in Lexical Phonology will be shown to have both synchronic and diachronic dimensions and consequences.

1.2   Lexical Phonology and its predecessor

Lexical Phonology (LP) is a generative, derivational model: at its core lies a set of underlying representations of morphemes, which are converted to their surface forms by passing through a series of phonological rules. It follows that LP has inherited many of the assumptions and much of the machinery of Standard Generative Phonology (SGP; see Chomsky and Halle 1968). LP therefore does not form part of the current vogue for monostratal, declarative, non-derivational phonologies (see Durand and Katamba 1995, Roca (ed.) 1997a), nor is it strictly a result of the recent move towards non-linear phonological analyses, with their emphasis on representations rather than rules (see Goldsmith 1990, and the papers in Goldsmith (ed.) 1995). Although elements of metrical and autosegmental notation can readily be incorporated into LP (Giegerich 1986, Pulleyblank 1986), its innovations have not primarily been in the area of phonological representation, but rather in the organisational domain.

The main organisational claim of LP is that the phonological rules are split between two components. Some processes, which correspond broadly to SGP morphophonemic rules, operate within the lexicon, where they are interspersed with morphological rules. In its origins, and in the version assumed here, the theory is therefore crucially integrationist (but see Hargus and Kaisse (eds.) 1993 for discussion, and Halle and Vergnaud 1987 for an alternative view). The remainder apply in a postlexical, postsyntactic component incorporating allophonic and phrase-level operations. Lexical and postlexical rules display distinct clusters of properties, and are subject to different sets of constraints.

As a model attempting to integrate phonology and morphology, LP is informed by developments in both these areas. Its major morphological input stems from the introduction of the lexicalist hypothesis by Chomsky (1970), which initiated the re-establishment of morphology as a separate subdiscipline and a general expansion of the lexicon. On the phonological side, the primary input to LP is the abstractness controversy. Since the advent of generative phonology, a certain tension has existed between the desire for maximally elegant analyses capturing the greatest possible number of generalisations, and the often unfounded claims such analyses make concerning the relationships native speakers perceive among words of their language. The immensely powerful machinery of SGP, aiming only to produce the simplest overall phonology, created highly abstract analyses. Numerous attempts at constraining SGP were made (e.g. Kiparsky 1973), but these were never more than partially successful. Combating abstractness provided a second motivation for LP, and is also a major theme of this book.

The problem is that the SPE model aimed only to provide a maximally simple and general phonological description. If the capturing of as many generalisations as possible is seen as paramount, and if synchronic phonology is an autonomous discipline, then, the argument goes, internal, synchronic data should be accorded primacy in constructing synchronic derivations. And purely internal, synchronic data favour abstract analyses since these apparently capture more generalisations, for instance in the extension of rules like Vowel Shift in English from alternating to non-alternating forms. However, as Lass and Anderson (1975: 232) observe, 'it just might be the case that generalizations achieved by extraparadigmatic extension are specious'; free rides, for instance, 'may just be a property of the model, rather than of the reality that it purports to be a model of. If this should turn out to be so, then any "reward" given by the theory for the discovery of "optimal" grammars in this sense would be vacuous.' In contrast, I assume that if LP is a sound and explanatory theory, its predictions must consistently account for, and be supported by, external evidence, including diachronic data; the facts of related dialects; speech errors; and speaker judgements, either direct or as reflected in the results of psycholinguistic tests. This coheres with Churma's (1985: 106) view that '"external" ... data ... must be brought to bear on phonological issues, unless we are willing to adopt a "hocus pocus" approach ... to linguistic analyses, whereby the only real basis for choice among analyses is an essentially esthetic one' (and note here Anderson's (1992: 346) stricture that 'it is important not to let one's aesthetics interfere with the appreciation of fact'). The over-reliance of SGP on purely internal evidence reduces the scope for its validation, and detracts from its psychological reality, if we accept that 'linguistic theory ... is committed to accounting for evidence from all sources. The greater the range of the evidence types that a theory is capable of handling

satisfactorily, the greater the likelihood of its being a "true" theory'
(Mohanan 1986: 185).

These ideals are unlikely to be achieved until proponents of LP have
the courage to reject tenets and mechanisms of SGP which are at odds
with the anti-abstractness aims of lexicalism. For instance, although
Mohanan (1982, 1986) is keen to stress the relevance of external evidence,
he is forced to admit (1986: 185) that his own version of the theory is
based almost uniquely on internal data. Elegance, maximal generality
and economy are still considered, not as useful initial heuristics, but as
paramount in determining the adequacy of phonological analyses (see
Kiparsky 1982, Mohanan 1986, and especially Halle and Mohanan
1985). The tension between these relics of the SPE model and the
constraints of LP is at its clearest in Halle and Mohanan (1985), the most
detailed lexicalist formulation of English segmental phonology currently
available. The Halle–Mohanan model, which will be the focus of much
criticism in the chapters below, represents a return to the abstract
underlying representations and complex derivations first advocated by
Chomsky and Halle. Both the model itself, with its proliferation of
lexical levels and random interspersal of cyclic and non-cyclic strata, and
the analyses it produces, involving free rides, minor rules and the full
apparatus of SPE phonology, are unconstrained.

Despite this setback, I do not believe that we need either reject
derivational phonology outright, or accept that any rule-based
phonology must inevitably suffer from the theoretical afflictions of SGP.
We have a third choice; we can re-examine problems which proved
insoluble in SGP, to see whether they may be more tractable in LP.
However, the successful application of this strategy requires that we
should not simply state the principles and constraints of LP, but must
rigorously apply them. And we must be ready to accept the result as the
legitimate output of such a constrained phonology, although it may look
profoundly different from the phonological ideal bequeathed to us by the
expectations of SGP.

In this book, then, I shall examine the performance of LP in three
areas of phonological theory which were mishandled in SGP: abstractness; the differentiation of related dialects; and the relationship of
synchronic phonological rules and diachronic sound changes. If LP,
suitably revised and constrained, cannot cope with these areas adequately, it must be rejected. If, however, insightful solutions can be
provided, LP will no longer be open to many of the criticisms levelled at

SGP, and will emerge as a partially validated phonological theory and a promising locus for further research.

The three issues are very clearly connected; let us begin with the most general, abstractness. SGP assumes centrally that the native speaker will construct the simplest possible grammar to account for the primary linguistic data he or she receives, and that the linguist's grammar should mirror the speaker's grammar. The generative evaluation measure for grammars therefore concentrates on relative simplicity, where simplicity subsumes notions of economy and generality. Thus, a phonological rule is more highly valued, and contributes less to the overall complexity of the grammar, if it operates in a large number of forms and is exceptionless.

This drive for simplicity and generality meant exceptions were rarely acknowledged in SGP; instead, they were removed from the scope of the relevant rule, either by altering their underlying representations, or by applying some 'lay-by' rule and a later readjustment process. Rules which might be well motivated in alternating forms were also extended to non-alternating words, which again have their underlying forms altered and are given a 'free ride' through the rule. By employing strategies like these, a rule like Trisyllabic Laxing in English could be made applicable not only to forms like *divinity* (~ *divine*) and *declarative* (~ *declare*), but also to *camera* and *enemy*; these would have initial tense vowels in their underlying representations, with Trisyllabic Laxing providing the required surface lax vowels. Likewise, an exceptional form like *nightingale* is not marked [−Trisyllabic Laxing], but is instead stored as /nɪxtVngǽl/; the voiceless velar fricative is later lost, with compensatory lengthening of the preceding vowel, to give the required tense vowel on the surface.

The problem is that the distance of underlying representations from surface forms in SGP is controlled only by the simplicity metric – which positively encourages abstractness. Furthermore, there is no linguistically significant reference point midway between the underlying and surface levels, due to the SGP rejection of the phonemic level. Consequently, as Kiparsky (1982: 34) says, SGP underlying representations 'will be at *least* as abstract as the classical phonemic level. But they will be more abstract whenever, and to whatever extent, the simplicity of the system requires it.' This potentially excessive distance of underliers from surface forms raises questions of learnability, since it is unclear how a child might acquire the appropriate underlying representation for a non-alternating form.

A further, and related, charge is that of historical recapitulation: Crothers (1971) accepts that maximally general rules reveal patterns in linguistic structure, but argues that these generalisations are non-synchronic. If we rely solely on internal evidence and on vague notions of simplicity and elegance to evaluate proposed descriptions, we are in effect performing internal reconstruction of the type used to infer an earlier, unattested stage of a language from synchronic data. Thus, Lightner (1971) relates *heart* to *cardiac* and *father* to *paternal* by reconstructing Grimm's Law (albeit perhaps not wholly seriously), while Chomsky and Halle's account of the *divine ~ divinity* and *serene ~ serenity* alternations involves the historical Great Vowel Shift (minimally altered and relabelled as the Vowel Shift Rule) and the dubious assertion that native speakers of Modern English internalise the Middle English vowel system. I am advocating that historical factors should be taken into account in the construction and evaluation of phonological models; but the mere equation of historical sound changes and synchronic phonological rules is not the way to go about it.

Here we confront our second question: how are sound changes integrated into the synchronic grammar to become phonological rules? In historical SGP (Halle 1962, Postal 1968, King 1969), it is assumed that a sound change, once implemented, is inserted as a phonological rule at the end of the native speaker's rule system; it moves gradually higher in the grammar as subsequent changes become the final rule. This process of rule addition, or innovation, is the main mechanism for introducing the results of change into the synchronic grammar: although there are occasional cases of rule loss or rule inversion (Vennemann 1972), SGP is an essentially static model. The assumption is that underlying representations will generally remain the same across time, while a cross-section of the synchronic rule system will approximately match the history of the language: as Halle (1962: 66) says, 'the order of rules established by purely synchronic considerations – i.e., simplicity – will mirror properly the relative chronology of the rules'. Thus, a sound change and the synchronic rule it is converted to will tend to be identical (or at least very markedly similar), and the 'highest' rules in the grammar will usually correspond to the oldest changes. SGP certainly provides no means of incorporating recent discoveries on sound change in progress, such as the division of diffusing from non-diffusing changes (Labov 1981).

It is true that some limited provision is made in SGP for the restructuring of underlying representations, since it is assumed that children will learn the optimal, or simplest, grammar. This may not be identical to the grammar of the previous generation: whereas adults may only add rules, the child may construct a simpler grammar without this rule but with its effects encoded in the underlying representations. However, this facility for restructuring is generally not fully exploited, and the effect on the underliers is in any case felt to be minimal; thus, Chomsky and Halle (1968: 49) can confidently state:

> It is a widely confirmed empirical fact that underlying representations are fairly resistant to historical change, which tends, by and large, to involve late phonetic rules. If this is true, then the same system of representation for underlying forms will be found over long stretches of space and time.

This evidence that underlying representations are seen in SGP as diachronically and diatopically static, is highly relevant to our third problem, the differentiation of dialects. The classical SGP approach to dialect relationships therefore rests on an assumption of identity: dialects of one language share the same underlying representations, with the differences resting in the form, ordering and/or inventory of their phonological rules (King 1969, Newton 1972). Different languages will additionally differ with respect to their underlying representations. The main controversy in generative dialectology relates to whether one of the dialects should supply underlying representations for the language as a whole, or whether these representations are intermediate or neutral between the realisations of the dialects. Thomas (1967: 190), in a study of Welsh, claims that 'basal forms are *dialectologically mixed*: their total set is not uniquely associated with any total set of occurring dialect forms'. Brown (1972), however, claims that considerations of simplicity compel her to derive southern dialect forms of Lumasaaba from northern ones.

This requirement of a common set of underlying forms is extremely problematic (see chapter 5 below). Perhaps most importantly, the definition of related dialects as sharing the same underlying forms, but of different languages as differing at this level, prevents us from seeing dialect and language variation as the continuum which sociolinguistic investigation has shown it to be. Furthermore, the family tree model of historical linguistics is based on the premise that dialects may diverge across time and become distinct languages, but this pattern is obscured by the contention that related dialects are not permitted to differ at the underlying level, while related languages characteristically do. It is not at all clear what conditions might sanction the sudden leap from a situation where two varieties share the same underlying forms and differ in their rule systems, to a revised state involving differences at all levels. These theoretical objections are easily swept aside, however, in a model like SGP where the central assumptions require maximal identity in the underlying representations.

The three areas outlined above are all dealt with unsatisfactorily in SGP; moreover, these deficiencies are due in all cases, directly or indirectly, to the insistence of proponents of the SPE model on a maximally simple, exceptionless phonology. The use of an evaluation measure based on simplicity, the lack of a level of representation corresponding to the classical phonemic level, and the dearth of constraints on the distance of underlying from surface representations all encourage abstractness. Changes in the rule system are generally preferred, in such a system, to changes in the underlying forms, which are dialectally and diachronically static. Rules simply build up as sound changes take effect, with no clear way of encoding profound, representational consequences of change, no means of determining when the underliers should be altered, and no link between sound changes and phonological rules save their identity of formulation. This historical recapitulation contributes to further abstractness, and means that, in effect, related dialects *must* share common underlying forms. King (1969: 102) explicitly states that external evidence, whether historical or from related dialects, may play no part in the evaluation of synchronic grammars; this is presented as a principled exclusion, since speakers have no access to the history of their language or to the facts of related varieties, but is equally likely to be based on the clear inadequacies of SGP when faced with data beyond the synchronic, internal domain.

I hope to show in the following chapters that LP need not share these deficiencies, and that its successes in the above areas are also linked. Working with different varieties of Modern English, I shall demonstrate that the abstractness of the synchronic phonology can be significantly restricted in LP. In general, the strategy to be pursued will involve imposing and strengthening the constraints already existing in LP, most notably the Strict Cyclicity Condition or Derived Environment Condition, and assessing the analyses which are possible, impossible, or required within the constrained model. Because maximally surface-true analyses will be enforced for each variety, we will be unable to consistently derive related dialects from the same underlying representations, and the underliers will also be subject to change across time. Sound changes and related phonological rules will frequently differ in their formulation, and new links between diachrony and synchrony will be revealed.

Of course, this is not the first time that questions have been raised over aspects of SGP: for instance, I have already quoted Lass and Anderson (1975), a Standard Generative analysis of Old English phonology incorporating an extremely eloquent and perceptive account of the difficulties which seemed then to face SGP, a model which had seemed so 'stable and unified' (1975: xiii) in 1970, when their account of Old English was first drafted. Lass and Anderson set out to test SGP against a particular set of data. They discover that the theory makes particular predictions; that it permits, or even requires, them to adopt particular solutions. These solutions are sometimes fraught with problems. Lass and Anderson could, of course, have made use of the power of SGP to reformulate the areas where they identify problems and weaknesses; instead, they include a final section explicitly raising doubts about the theory, and the issues they identify have been crucial in remodelling phonological theory ever since.

The conclusion, more than twenty years on, is that these difficulties cannot be solved within SGP: the simplicity metric, the overt preference (without neurological support) for derivation over storage, and the denial of 'external' evidence, mean that many of the generalisations captured are simply over-generalisations. The model must be rejected or very radically revised.

LP is one result. But the revisions have so far not been radical enough. I shall show in the following chapters that it is possible to maintain the core of the generative enterprise in phonology (namely, that alternating surface forms may be synchronically derived from a common underlier) without a great deal of the paraphernalia which was once thought to be crucial to the goal of capturing significant generalisations, but in practice encouraged the statement of artefactual and insignificant ones. Thus, we shall reject the SGP identity hypothesis on dialect variation; rule out free rides; prohibit derivation in non-alternating morphemes; revise the feature system; and exclude underspecification, which has recently become an expected ingredient of LP, but is in fact quite independent from it.

In the rest of the book, then, I shall follow much the same route as Lass and Anderson: we shall begin with a phonological model, in this case LP, and assess its performance given a particular set of data, here the vowel phonology, loosely defined, of certain accents of Modern English. The model is characterised by a number of constraints; I shall argue that these should be rigorously applied, and indeed supplemented with certain further restrictions. We can then examine what is possible within the model, and what solutions it forces us to adopt. If we are forced to propose analyses which seem to conflict with internal or external evidence, being perhaps apparently unlearnable, or counter-historical, or without phonetic or diachronic motivation, we must conclude that the model is inadequate. Likewise, the model may never make decisions for us: in other words, any analysis may be possible. Such a theory clearly makes no predictions, and is unconstrained, unfalsifiable and uninteresting. On the other hand, we may find that the predictions made are supported by internal and external evidence; that the phonology becomes more concrete, and arguably more learnable than the standard model; that phonetics and phonology can be better integrated, and the relationship between them better understood; and that a more realistic model of variation and change can be proposed.

So far, I have introduced LP only in the broadest terms. A number of outlines of LP are available (Kiparsky 1982, 1985; Mohanan 1982, 1986; Pulleyblank 1986; Halle and Mohanan 1985). However, most aspects of LP, including its central tenets, are still under discussion (see Hargus and Kaisse (eds.) 1993, Wiese (ed.) 1994). Available introductions therefore tend to be restricted to presenting the version of LP used in the paper concerned (Kaisse and Shaw 1985 does provide a broader perspective, but is now, in several crucial respects, out of date). Consequently, it may be difficult for a reader not entirely immersed in the theory to acquire a clear idea of the current controversies, which become apparent only by reading outlines of LP incorporating opposing viewpoints. I shall conse-quently attempt in chapter 2 to provide an overview of LP, considering both its evolution, and current controversies within the theory which will be returned to in subsequent chapters. First, however, I must justify approaching the problems outlined above in a derivational model at all.

1.3   Alternative models

Sceptical observers, and non-generative phonologists, may see my pro-gramme as excessively idealistic, on the not unreasonable grounds that generative phonology is by its very nature far too flexible to allow adequate constraint. In other words, given phonological rules and under-lying forms, an analysis can always be cobbled together which will get the right surface forms out of the proposed underliers: if the first attempt doesn't do the trick, you can alter the underliers, or the rules, until you find a set-up that works. And since LP is generative, and phonologists are no less ingenious now than in the heyday of SGP, the new model is open to precisely the same criticism as the old one. Here again, Lass and Anderson (1975: 226) ask: 'But is the mere fact that a phonological solution works any guarantee that it is correct?' Of course not: it is precisely because we cannot rely purely on distribution and alternation that we need extra, 'external' evidence. The analyses I shall propose in subsequent chapters will look peculiar in SGP terms; but I hope to show that they are coherent with evidence of a number of different kinds, and that they allow interesting predictions to be made. For instance, we shall see that my analysis of the English Vowel Shift specifies a principled cut-off point between what can be derived, and what cannot, giving a partial solution to the determinacy problem. A typical progression from sound changes to phonological rules will also be identified, giving a certain amount of insight into variation and change, as well as the embedding of change in the native speaker's grammar. These impli-cations and conclusions lend support to LP, and suggest, if nothing else, that the model should be pursued and tested further. Phonetics, phon-ology, variation and change cannot be integrated in this way in SGP. I have not yet seen similar clusterings of evidence types in non-generative phonologies, either.

Arguments of this kind give me one reason for adopting LP, and attempting to constrain generative phonology, rather than rejecting a derivational model altogether. Nonetheless, questions will undoubtedly be raised concerning the relevance of this work, given the current move towards monostratal, declarative, and constraint-based phonologies. I cannot fully address these issues here, but the rest of the book is intended as a partial answer; and I also have some questions of my own.

1.3.1   *Rules and constraints*

Let us begin with the issue of rules versus constraints (see Goldsmith (ed.) 1993a, and Roca (ed.) 1997a). There seems to be a prevailing opinion in current phonology that it is somehow more respectable to work with constraints only, than to propose rules and then constrain their application, however heavily. For instance, Government Phonology

(Kaye, Lowenstamm and Vergnaud 1985, Kaye 1988) includes principles and parameters, but no destructive operations, while Optimality Theory (Prince and Smolensky 1993) incorporates only constraints.

We might assume that positing constraints *per se* is uncontroversial, as they are part of all the phonological models surveyed here: but they are still criticised when they are part of theories which also contain rules, like LP. For instance, Carr (1993: 190–1) accepts that LP may in principle be highly constrained and therefore relatively non-abstract, but argues that 'The crucial issue here is whether such constraints (if they are desirable) come from within the theory or have to be imposed from outside. If the latter is the case, then the LP theory itself is, for those seeking a non-abstract phonology, in need of revision.' How are we to assess whether constraints are 'imposed from outside'? Is the condition against destructive operations in Government Phonology not 'imposed from outside'? Why should the specification of the number of vowel or consonant elements, or the assumption that reference should be made to universal, innate principles, have the status of internally determined, intrinsic aspects of the theory, while the constraints of LP should not? For example, I shall argue below that the main constraint on LP is the Strict Cyclicity Condition (SCC), which does follow from the architecture of the model, insofar as it is restricted to the (universally cyclic) first lexical level. Moreover, it is quite possibly derivable from the arguably innate Elsewhere Condition, and may not therefore require to be independently stated. Even so, why should this be seen as such a conclusive advantage? If we consider language change, we see that purely formal attempts to explain developments have rarely been very successful. For instance, in the domain of word order change, scholars like Lehmann (1973) and Vennemann (1974) attempted to account for the correlations of certain logically independent word order properties, and the fact that the change of one often seemed to have repercussions for others, in terms of the principle of natural serialisation; this would probably be interpreted today as a principle or a parameter (see Smith 1989). However, this principle is not, on its own, explanatory (Matthews 1981): it is only when issues of parsing and learnability (see Kuno 1974) are invoked that we begin to understand why change should proceed so regularly in a particular direction. It seems highly likely that the same should be true of phonology: synchronically or diachronically, we need external evidence to explain why certain patterns occur and recur. Thus, the SCC is not purely a formal constraint. Instead, like Kiparsky's

Alternation Condition (Kiparsky 1973), which it is partially intended to formalise, it is a learnability constraint: grammars violating either condition will be harder to learn. This means that, for instance, a grammar ordering rules on Level 1, within the domain of SCC, should be easier to acquire than a similar grammar with the same rules permitted to apply on Level 2, where they will not be controlled by SCC.

However, there is one crucial difference between the constraints of LP and those of Optimality Theory, for instance: the former restrict rule applications, whereas the latter replace rules. The next question, then, is whether rules are required at all. There are two considerations here, which relate in turn to the question of transparency in the synchronic grammar, and to the importance accorded to universality.

Anderson (1981), in a study of 'Why phonology isn't "natural"', argues that the effects of sound changes may build up in a language over time so that ultimately extremely opaque phonological processes may be operating synchronically. For instance, in Icelandic, Velar Fronting operates in a synchronically highly peculiar environment, giving back velars before the front vowels [y] and [ø], and front velars before the diphthong [ai], with a back first element. However, once we know that historically, the problematic front vowels are from back [u] and [ɔ], while the difficult diphthong was earlier front [æ:], we can see that Velar Fronting applies in the context of historically front vowels. Anderson points out that a synchronic grammar must nonetheless contain a description of these facts, and that this synchronic rule will not be phonetically motivated, or universal. The synchronic state is simply the result of language-specific history, and the fact that we have a historical explanation means the synchronic rule need provide no more than a description.

Everyday, work-horse descriptive work of this language-particular kind is what phonological rules are for, and it is my contention that phonological theories need them, whether their proponents are happy to admit it or not. For instance, Goldsmith's introduction to his (1993) collection of papers, entitled *The Last Phonological Rule*, argues that rules and derivations should not be part of a theory of phonology. However, Hyman's (1993) paper, despite setting out to find cases where extrinsic rule ordering will not work, comes to the conclusion that it is, in fact, a viable approach, while other papers (notably Goldsmith's and Lakoff's) involve language-specific constraints, such as Lakoff's (1993: 121) statement that 'When C precedes ?# at level W, an /e/ absent at level

W intervenes at level P', which is surely an epenthesis rule by any other name. As Padgett (1995) notes, these papers also include sequential, extrinsic level-ordering of constraints, and are therefore scarcely free of the apparatus of derivational phonology.

Similarly, Coleman (1995: 344) argues that 'Far from being a rule free theory completely unlike the SPE model, as its proponents claim, Government-based phonological analyses employ various derivational devices which are transformational rules in all but name ... Government Phonology is therefore as unconstrained as the models it seeks to replace.' For instance, Coleman points out that, to model the ostensibly prohibited deletion of segments, Government Phonology can first delete each marked element in turn, which the theory will permit; this will ultimately leave only the single 'cold' element which can be removed by the Obligatory Contour Principle (OCP) (see also 1.3.2 below). Furthermore, many of the principles invoked in Government Phonology seem language-specific; for instance, as we shall see in chapter 6, Harris (1994) argues that the loss of [r] in non-rhotic English dialects results from the innovation of the Non-Rhoticity Condition, which allows the R element to be licensed only in onsets. This condition allows an accurate description of the synchronic situation: the question is why such a constraint should become operative in the grammar of a particular dialect or set of dialects at a particular time. We might be dealing with a parameter resetting; but then, of course, we would have to ask why the resetting happened. Principles and parameters theory is faced with similar difficulties in historical syntax; thus, Lightfoot (1991: 160) remarks that, at the point when a parameter is reset, 'an abrupt change takes place, but it was preceded by gradual changes affecting triggering experiences but not grammars'. So, Lightfoot recognises 'piecemeal, gradual and chaotic changes' in the linguistic environment; these can affect, for instance, the frequency of a construction, and may be introduced for reasons of contact, or for stylistic effect. These changes are not amenable to systematic explanation; but they are important in creating the conditions for parameter resetting, which *is* intended to be explicable in terms of Lightfoot's theory of grammar. It is quite unclear where the language change actually begins, and what the status of these preparatory changes is. Of course, a rule-based theory has no particular advantages here; a rule of [r]-deletion would simply be written as a response to the loss of a segment which was present before, and we would seek out reasons for the loss in, for instance, phonetics or sociolinguistics. But we would not be taking the portentous step of labelling this variety-specific behaviour as a condition or a constraint, or falsely implying universality.

Finally, and most controversially, we turn to Optimality Theory (OT). In this theory, Universal Grammar for phonology consists of two components, a function Gen, and a set of universal constraints on representational well-formedness. Gen (for 'generate') takes a particular input, which will be a lexical entry, and generates *all possible outputs* – an infinite set of possible candidate analyses, which is then evaluated by the list of constraints. These constraints are universal, but crucially ordered differently for each language, to give the different attested surface results. Most theories of constraints in phonology have held that constraints are exceptionless. In OT, every constraint is potentially violable. This means that the 'winning', or maximally harmonic representation will not necessarily be the one which satisfies every constraint. It will be the one which violates fewest. More accurately, since constraints are ranked, it will be the candidate parse which violates fewest high-ranking constraints.

Prince and Smolensky (1993: 101) accept that 'Any theory must allow latitude for incursions of the idiosyncratic into grammar.' However, they argue that idiosyncratic behaviour is not modellable using rules, but rather by '(slightly) modified versions of the universal conditions on phonological form out of which core grammar is constructed ... [which] interact with other constraints in the manner prescribed by the general theory' (ibid.). This assumption has various consequences. First, constraints may be too low-ranked in particular languages to have any discernible effect. This is not taken to affect learnability adversely, since the strong assumption of universality means the constraints do not have to be learned, only their ranking; note, however, that acquisition is non-trivial given the explosion of constraints to be ranked in recent versions of the theory: Sherrard (1997) points out that only five constraints will give 120 possible grammars, while ten will allow 36 million. Contrast this with a rule-based approach, where a rule is written only where it captures phonological behaviour in the language concerned; we would not write, for instance, a universal version of the Vowel Shift Rule with effects tangible only in English and concealed elsewhere. To do so would be against every requirement of learnability, and would also unacceptably blur the distinction between the universal and the language-specific.

However, the question also arises of quite how different a constraint-based theory like OT is from a rule-based one. Prince and Smolensky's contention that constraints can be language-specifically modified leads to formulations like the now notorious Lardil FREE-V (1993: 101), which states that 'word-final vowels must not be parsed (in the nominative)', and again seems a static recasting of a very language-specific deletion rule. In similar vein, Prince and Smolensky (1993: 43), in considering the constraint NONFINALITY, note that 'It remains to formulate a satisfactory version of NONFINALITY for Latin.' What this means is that, logically, the issue is not solely one of determining the place of constraint C in the hierarchy of Language X. The formulation of C may also differ, and it is not clear how appreciably, between Languages X and Y. More generally, there is an issue of extrinsic ordering here, since while many constraints must be ranked language-specifically, there are others which are never violated, and which must therefore be placed universally at the top of the hierarchy. Prince and Smolensky (1993: 46) argue that this is acceptable since 'we can expect to find principles of universal ranking that deal with whole *classes* of constraints'. If ordering is acceptable when it refers to classes of ordered items, a rule-based model should be equally highly valued provided that it involved level-ordering, or ordering all lexical before all postlexical rules, for instance.

Even closer to the core of OT, the definition of the function Gen is itself controversial. Although Prince and Smolensky (1993: 79) advocate a parallel interpretation, they concede that Gen can also be understood serially, in which case its operation is much closer to a conventional derivation:

> some general procedure (DO-α) is allowed to make a certain single modification to the input, producing the candidate set of all possible outcomes of such modification. This is then evaluated; and the process continues with the output so determined. In this serial version of grammar, the theory of rules is narrowly circumscribed, but it is inaccurate to think of it as trivial.

However, this serial interpretation of Gen may be necessary; Blevins (1997) argues strongly that, without it, there is no way of verifying constraint tableaux, as each tableau will contain the allegedly maximally harmonic parse plus a random set of other candidates, but will not contain all possible parses, and therefore crucially does not contain all the evidence necessary to permit evaluation.

The perceived advantage of an OT account is the absence of specific processes; but it is unclear why such a theory, with vast overgeneration courtesy of Gen, should be seen as more parsimonious than a derivational theory with a finite number of non-overgenerating language-specific rules. Of the papers in Roca (ed.) (1997a), which focus on the rules–constraints debate, a surprising number contend that rules and derivations are still necessary, while Roca himself notes that 'OT is stretching its original formal fabric in ways that closer scrutiny may reveal are nothing but covert rules, and perhaps even derivations' (1997b: 39). Indeed, some work in OT is entirely open about the addition of rules: McCarthy (1993: 190) includes an epenthesis rule to account for the distribution of English /r/, and states quite explicitly that 'By a "rule" here I mean a phonologically arbitrary stipulation: one that is outside the system of Optimality.' As Halle and Idsardi (1997: 337–8) argue, 'Conceptually, reliance on an arbitrary stipulation that is outside the system of Optimality is equivalent to giving up on the enterprise. Data that cannot be dealt with by OT without recourse to rules are fatal counter-examples to the OT research programme.' At the very least, this introduction of rules alongside constraints removes the alleged formal superiority of OT, making it just as theoretically heterogeneous as LP, for instance, in containing both categories of statement.

1.3.2   Modelling sound changes
We return now more specifically to diachronic evidence. Proponents of some recent phonological models explicitly exclude historical processes from their ambit; Coleman (1995: 363), for instance, working within Declarative Phonology, refuses to consider one of Bromberger and Halle's (1989) arguments for rule ordering because of 'its diachronic nature. The relevance of such arguments to synchronic phonology is highly controversial, and thus no basis on which to evaluate the transformational hypothesis.' I reject this curtailment of phonological theory for two reasons. First, more programmatically, theorists should not be able to decide *a priori* the data for which their models should and should not account. It is natural and inevitable that a model should be proposed initially on the basis of particular data and perhaps data types, but it is central to the work reported below that the model subsequently gains credence from its ability to deal with quite different (and perhaps unexpected) data, and loses credibility to the extent that it fails with respect to other evidence. Secondly, and more pragmatically, no absolute distinction can be made between synchronic and diachronic phonology. Variation is introduced by change, and in turn provides the input to further change; and even if we are describing a synchronic stage, we must

unavoidably contend with the relics of past changes and the seeds of future ones. Furthermore, synchronic and diachronic processes have much in common; yesterday's speech error or low-level phonetic process may be today's sound change, and is quite likely to be tomorrow's morphophonemic alternation. And different time-zones cross-cut the domain of any particular language, so discerning exactly where we are in that simplistic typology of yesterday, today and tomorrow is not always straightforward.

To take a slightly different tack, those phonologists working in non-derivational theories are often precisely those most interested in phonological universals. It must be important to test hypotheses involving universals on as wide a range of systems as possible, ideally from genetically, areally and typologically distinct languages, and also dialects, which in time may well diverge into distinct languages. Since variation and change are intimately connected, it seems unreasonable to accept the input and output for sound change, but to sideline or ignore the changes themselves. Similarly, if we want to explain phonological processes, and perhaps more accurately, to define and delimit possible process types, then it is extremely important to include sound changes: why should comparison across space be legitimate but not across time, in the search for universals? This is particularly incoherent given that the types of processes to be found in change overlap substantially with those operating to create synchronic alternations. That is to say, a synchronic fast speech process may become a categorical insertion or deletion change cross-generationally; or an automatic, phonetically motivated process can be phonologised, perhaps in different ways in different dialects, to give a synchronic phonological rule; we shall see examples of such interaction in the following chapters. However, this does not mean that we can automatically subsume historical processes in the set of synchronic ones: even if a theory can model a synchronic process in an enlightening way, it is by no means a foregone conclusion that it can similarly deal with a historical analogue of the process.

With this in mind, we shall now move on to see how two allegedly non-derivational theories, Government Phonology and Optimality Theory, fare when confronted with certain generic types of sound change.

We turn first to Government Phonology (Kaye, Lowenstamm and Vergnaud 1985, 1990; Harris 1990, 1992), in which phonology is taken to consist of a system of universal principles, and a set of parameters set on a language-specific basis. There are no phonological rules. Segments are

composed of elements, which are autonomous and independently interpretable (Durand and Katamba (eds.) 1995). The defining property of
each element is a feature with a marked value, the hot feature: this is the
only component contributed by the operator, as opposed to the head, in
fusion. The only element lacking a hot feature is the cold vowel.
Government itself is a relationship holding between adjacent positions in
a phonological string, and holds at three different levels of analysis:

(1) within the constituents onset, nucleus and rhyme, where government is strictly local and left to right:

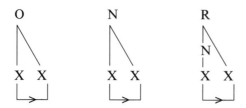

(2) at the interconstituent level, where e.g. an onset will govern a
preceding rhymal complement; again we have strict locality and directionality, but here the direction is right to left:

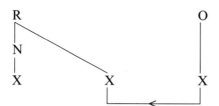

(3) at the level of nuclear projection, directionality is parametric:

Government is partly determined by whether segments are positively,
negatively or neutrally 'charmed' (although charm theory seems to play a
less prominent part in more recent formulations of Government Phonology). The Projection Principle is adopted, ruling out underspecification,

default rules and resyllabification. Finally, phonological processes all involve elemental composition or decomposition, seen as spreading or delinking of elements. Furthermore, such processes are local and non-arbitrary, in that there must be a clear connection between a process and its environment. Not only does there have to be a local source for a spreading element, for instance, but it also seems that some principle or parameter should generally be identifiable as providing motivation for the process in question to happen where it does. In Kaye's (1995: 301) words, 'Events take place where they must.'

Our first sound change type is assimilation, which perhaps predictably involves elemental composition, with one locally present element spreading from its own segment onto another. Take, for instance, the case of Korean umlaut discussed in Kaye, Lowenstamm and Vergnaud (1990), and shown in (1.1).

(1.1)	Korean:	*radical*	*causative*		
		cɑp-ta	cap-hi		'to take'
		sum-ta	sym-ki		'to hide'
		radical	*subject*		
		pɑm	pam-i		'night'
		tɑm	tam-i		'wall'
		pɑ:m	pɑ:m-i	*pa:m-i	'chestnut'

Kaye, Lowenstamm and Vergnaud argue that the element I spreads from the suffix vowel in the causative or subject forms onto the stem vowel: fusion of the A and I elements will give the observed low front [a] vowel. The process cannot give equivalent results for the long vowel because the conditions for proper government (see Kaye, Lowenstamm and Vergnaud 1990) are not met with this configuration. This makes the interesting prediction that long vowels and heavy diphthongs should never in fact be affected by umlaut or harmony. There are, as Kaye, Lowenstamm and Vergnaud note, exceptions to this prediction, notably the case of umlaut in German. However, they say (1990: 226) that 'the nature of German umlaut is still a subject of debate, in particular, as regards its current synchronic status. By contrast, Korean umlaut is totally productive.' While it might seem reasonable to rule out unproductive processes from consideration, German umlaut was at a certain historical period almost exceptionless, and it is unclear how Government Phonology could model that process, in the phonology of that period. To look at the problem from a rather different angle, it is not absolutely certain that we have resolved the problem of why Korean umlaut happens in the context where it does. Indubitably, we can model the process as the spread of the I element; and the I element is allowed to spread because it properly governs the nucleus on its left. But why, in fact, does it spread? Is it *forced* to spread because of the configuration in which it appears? If so, then we face clear difficulties in attempting to model any previous stage of Korean where the umlaut sound change had not yet operated: we would have to assume that at this earlier stage, the environment was different; or we predict that the earlier stage could not have existed at all. Conversely, if the spreading is not obligatory in this configuration, then the account is not really non-arbitrary, and Kaye's (1995: 301) maxim that 'Events take place where they must' is not adhered to.

Similar difficulties arise with deletion. In Government Phonology, it is only possible to delete certain things, and only under certain circumstances. In general, the deletion of skeletal positions seems very highly constrained. One case, discussed in Kaye, Lowenstamm and Vergnaud (1985) and shown in (1.2), involves the vowel system of Kpokolo, an eastern Kru language spoken in the Ivory Coast.

(1.2)   Kpokolo: *singular*   *plural*
dɔ́bʊ̀   dɤ́bɪ̀   'duck'
gɔ̄lʊ̄   gɤ̄lɪ̄   'dugout'
dɔ̀gbʊ   dɤ̀gbɪ   'electric fish'

In the singular (see (1.3)), the rounding of the stem vowel, which is lexically represented as simply the element A, is taken to be a function of the suffix vowel, from which the rounding element, U, spreads.

(1.3)   BACK/ROUND   –   –   –   –   U   –   –

HIGH   –   –   A   –   v   –   –

x   x   x   x
[g]   [ɔ]   [l]   [ʊ]

However, when the suffix vowel is added in the plural as shown in (1.4), the final rounded vowel is no longer permitted, since there cannot be two adjacent nuclei in a word, an effect Kaye, Lowenstamm and Vergnaud tentatively ascribe to the OCP. This means the bracketed position is deleted, leaving the U element floating. They argue that U cannot reassociate to either of the remaining vowels, since this element needs to be licensed by a rounded governor. Consequently the U element is not phonetically realised, and the stem vowel surfaces as unrounded.

(1.4)   BACK/ROUND   –   –   v   –   U   I

```
BACK/ROUND      –   –   v   –   U   I
                        |       |
HIGH            –   –   A   –   v   v
                        |           |
                x   x   x  (x)      x
               [g] [ɜ] [l]        [ɪ]
```

However, in other cases in Kpokolo, similar rounding alternations arise without any loss of a skeletal slot. Kpokolo has three back unrounded vowels, which alternate with the rounded vowels in brackets, as shown in example (1.5). The unrounding is accomplished by dissociating the U element and replacing it with the cold vowel. The question is why the U is allowed to be dissociated here. It gives the right results; but it is presented simply as part of the description, without any reference to a principle which might control the dissociation. The conclusion at present must be that the deletion of segmental positions is better regulated than the deletion of single elements.

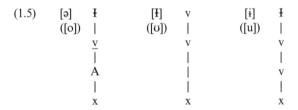

(1.5)

Apparent segmental insertion in Government Phonology typically involves spreading some locally present element, as in Broadbent's (1991) work on glide formation in West Yorkshire English, where [j] is found after high front vowels, and [w] after high back ones; this can be analysed as the spread of the I or U element respectively (see (1.6)).

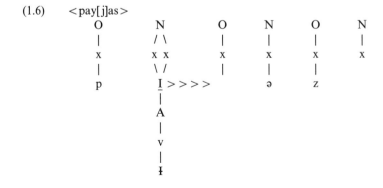

(1.6)   <pay[j]as>

< go[w]ing >
```
        O         N          O    N    O    N
        |        / \         |    |    |    |
        x        x x         x    x    x    x
        |        \ /         |    |    |
        g         U >>>>      I    n
                  |
                  A
                  |
                  v
                  |
                  ɨ
```

There are, however, some less clear cases of insertion of elements which do not have a local source, including Charette's (1990) account of vowel–zero alternations in French. In Moroccan Arabic, empty nuclei which are not properly governed surface as [ɨ], the independent realisation of the cold vowel. However, in French, the alternation instead involves schwa, which has the A element as well as the cold vowel. Charette regards this as parametric variation, arguing that (1990: 235) 'languages vary as to whether they choose the element A, I, U or simply nothing to add to the internal representation of the empty nucleus which contains as its only content the cold vowel'. This addition seems similar to the proposal in Kaye, Lowenstamm and Vergnaud (1990: 228) that 'ambient elements', such as the positively charmed ATR element ɨ, might sometimes have to be added to an expression to satisfy the requirements of charm theory. Durand (1995: 287) accepts that 'it is probably the case that a number of operations postulated by Government Phonology (e.g. ambient elements) should not be countenanced. Their arbitrariness is at least apparent whereas arbitrary insertions/deletions are the norm in the classical SPE framework.' However, if Government Phonologists have been proposing ambient elements, and must now choose not to countenance them, then the theory must sanction them, and is therefore not as constrained as it is claimed to be. In that case, there is rather little distance between this model and one like LP, where process types are unlimited but their *application* is limited by the constraints of the theory and the facts of the language itself. That is, an 'arbitrary' deletion or insertion rule will simply reflect the fact that a particular segment is absent from or present in a particular context in a particular language. The only arbitrariness here results from history, which may render an earlier, transparent process opaque. In that case, searching for universal motivation in the

Government Phonology sense is arguably misguided; indeed, if such motivation can always be found, this might in itself be the sign of an over-powerful theory, where spurious principles can be invented at will.

There is one further consequence of treating vowel–zero alternations as reflecting underlying empty nuclei. To quote Charette (1990: 252, fn. 17), 'It ... follows from the Projection Principle that positions cannot be inserted. That is, new governing relations may not be created in the course of a derivation. Consequently, the theory denies vowel epenthesis as a phonological process.' Presumably this means that if a vowel which was not present on the surface at some earlier historical period becomes apparent at some later period, then we have to conclude that the empty nucleus was always there structurally, but not realised phonetically. So for instance, in cases like Latin *schola* to Spanish *escuela* or French *école*, the empty nucleus is realised in the daughter languages but absent in the parent. The problem is working out the conditions for this: why should the empty nucleus be properly governed in the first case but not in the second, when in all cases there is a full vowel in the next syllable?

Lenition in Government Phonology involves elemental decomposition, or reduction in segmental complexity. To take one fairly straightforward example (1.7), the case of Korean /p/ → [w] and /t/ → [r] can be seen as the delinking of the occlusion element.

(1.7)   Korean: /p/ → [w] and /t/ → [r]

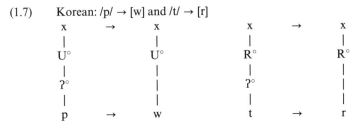

It is also possible (Harris 1990) to regard trajectories of lenition as the progressive decomposition of elements; (1.8) shows a typical sequence from /t/ to /s/ to /h/ to zero.

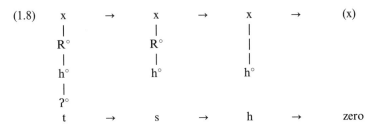

One of the most interesting aspects of the Government work on lenition is Harris's (1992) work on prime lenition sites, which informally are word-final, preconsonantal and intervocalic: these are unified by inheriting their a-licensing potential, which determines the segmental material they can tolerate, from a position which is itself licensed; thus, such positions can support a smaller range of less complex segments. The difficulty here lies perhaps in deciding which elements to delink in a particular prime lenition site, and indeed how many. Is there a parameter for the reduction process? And if so, how was it reset? If the parameter can only be reset on the basis of what people are already doing, this is not really explanatory, and we may still need an external, perhaps phonetic, account of why the change happened in the first place.

Similar problems arise with respect to other deletion changes, such as Brockhaus's (1990) account of German final devoicing, which she characterises as loss of the L element (slack vocal cords, or voicing in a complex segment) after a branching nucleus or rhyme, and before an empty nucleus. In some dialects, only final empty nuclei trigger the process, and Brockhaus claims that this is defined parametrically. Again, however, we encounter a difficulty when we see final devoicing in historical perspective, since we know from written records that at an earlier stage of German, final devoicing did not operate, at least phonologically. Before devoicing, were there then no empty nuclei? If there were, why did they not cause final devoicing? Furthermore, to what extent is the association of process and context here really non-arbitrary; in other words, why is it the L element that disappears? Of course, L must delink to produce the right results on voicing, but this is purely descriptive, not explanatory. It is quite true, as Brockhaus points out, that final devoicing takes place in the context of an empty nucleus, and that it is always L that is delinked, but this does not tell us what property of the empty nucleus makes L in particular go away.

Finally, there is little in the Government Phonology literature about fortition. Harris (1990) points out that, logically, if lenition is elemental decomposition, then fortition should be composition, and analyses the Sesotho case shown in (1.9) as spreading of the occlusion element.

(1.9)   Sesotho: /f/ → /p/, /r/ → /t/ after nasals
            = spreading of occlusion element ʔ° from nasal.

However, this analysis is entirely counter-historical: Bantuists seem to agree that the sound change involved was in fact a straightforward lenition except in the protected environment following a nasal (Bruce Connell personal communication, Guthrie 1967–71, Janson 1991–2). Worse still, Foulkes (1993), in a rigorous cross-linguistic survey of /p/ > /f/ (> /h/) changes, fails to find a single case of the reverse shift. It must be a matter of concern that Government Phonology, as a theory intended to be restrictive in the sense of only dealing with attested process types, can with such facility model a change which in all probability did not, and perhaps could not, happen.

Furthermore, Harris notes that he cannot model what he calls 'spontaneous' fortition, notably Latin *maior* → Italian *maggiore*. Again, this might reflect spread of the occlusion element, but this time there is no immediate source. Harris suggests that this is perhaps not of great concern, as the change is so sporadic: but there are numerous cases where the same [j] to [dʒ] change happens between Latin and Italian, as shown in (1.10). Indeed, there seem to be no cases with the same conditions where the supposedly sporadic fortition fails; so this may in fact be a real problem for Government Phonology, especially as such fortitions are repeated elsewhere in Romance (for instance in River Plate Spanish, where [j] from <-ll>, Castilian [ʎ], has regularly become [ʒ], or initial [dʒ] alternating with medial [ʒ]).

(1.10) Latin [j] > Italian [dʒ]:

iam	>	già	'now' > 'already'
iunius	>	giugno	'June'
iacere	>	giacere	'lie'
iocus	>	gioco	'toy, game'
maius	>	maggio	'May'
maiorem	>	maggiore	'greater'
peiorem	>	peggio	'worse'

(Nigel Vincent, personal communication)

Some rather similar problems arise in OT, although very few cases of sound change are discussed in the OT literature to date, and I therefore limit my comments here to cases of apparent insertion and deletion. As we have seen, OT involves the generation of candidate parses from a lexical entry; these are then evaluated by a language-specifically ranked set of universal constraints, and the maximally harmonic parse, which violates the fewest high-ranking constraints, is selected. This evaluation process can be represented in the type of constraint tableau shown in (1.11) for the two constraints ONS and HNUC and Imdlawn Tashlhiyt Berber, where any segment can be a syllable nucleus. Given a sequence /ul/, either the first segment will be parsed as nuclear, or the second. The harmonic parse is the latter, with the lateral nuclear. Therefore we assume that ONS must dominate HNUC in Imdlawn Tashlhiyt Berber. In constraint tableaux, * signals a 'black mark' assigned by a violated constraint, while ! indicates that the violation is fatal to that parse.

(1.11)   ONS: syllables must have an onset
          HNUC: Nuclear Harmony Constraint. Higher sonority nuclei are more harmonic.

          Imdlawn Tashlhiyt Berber: possible syllabifications of /ul/:

Candidates	ONS	HNUC
☞ .wL.		|l|
.Ul.	*!	|u|

Constraint interaction also accounts for phonological behaviour which has generally been analysed by means of processes. In cases of apparent insertion or deletion, the constraints involved are crucially FILL and PARSE, outlined in (1.12). If these faithfulness constraints are globally respected, then clearly FILL will ban insertion, and PARSE will ban deletion; but they may be violated because of higher-ranking constraints.

(1.12)   FILL: outputs must be based on inputs, i.e. empty nodes are banned. All nodes must be properly filled.
          PARSE: all underlying material must be analysed, or attached to a node. Unparsed material (i.e. unfilled nodes, and underlying lexical material not attached to nodes) is phonetically unrealised. (This has equivalent effects to Stray Erasure in other frameworks.)

In more recent versions of OT (see Roca (ed.) 1997a), FILL and PARSE are replaced by the correspondence constraints DEP-IO and MAX-IO (whereby every element of the input is an element of the output, and vice versa); however, their effects seem sufficiently similar to allow illustration using FILL and PARSE.

Let us first take two schematic cases: language (1.13a) requires onsets, and (1.13b) forbids codas. In (1.13a), for an input structure consisting of a single V, syllabification gives two options. We can violate PARSE by simply not parsing this vowel; that means the vowel cannot be realised phonetically, so this option results effectively in vowel deletion (although we are really leaving the structure floating or unattached, rather than deleting it *sensu stricto*). Alternatively, we can violate FILL by creating an empty onset slot, giving consonant epenthesis. Turning to (1.13b), an

input string of /CVC/ cannot be syllabified without violating the prohibition on codas, unless we again violate PARSE or FILL. This time,
violating PARSE gives effective consonant deletion by leaving the final C
unparsed, while violating FILL creates an empty nuclear slot and hence a
second syllable; feature fill-in of some sort instantiates a vowel, giving a
percept of vowel epenthesis.

(1.13)   a.   Obligatory onsets: input = /V/
         (i)   *PARSE – null parse: leave unparsed and hence unrealised. V
               deletion.
         (ii)   *FILL – parse as .□V. C epenthesis.

         b.   No codas: input = /CVC/
         (i)   *PARSE – leave final C unparsed. C deletion.
         (ii)   *FILL – parse as .CV.C□. V epenthesis.

A real-language example from Arabic, where onsets are obligatory, is
shown in (1.14). If there is no onset, a glottal stop is supplied, and this is
a violation of FILL. We conclude that ONS dominates FILL.

(1.14)   Arabic: /al-qalamu/ 'the-pen' (nom.)

Candidates	ONS	FILL
☞ .□al.qa.la.mu.		*
.al.qa.la.mu.	*!	
.□al.qa□.la.mu.		**!
.□al.qal.□a.mu.		**!
.□al.qa□.la□.mu.		**!*
.□al.qa□.la□.mu□		**!**

A second case is from Lardil, where short noun stems are
augmented and long ones truncated in the nominative. Augmentation
(see (1.15)) involves a further violation of FILL: the optimal parse
supplies an empty nuclear slot, and phonetic material is supplied.
Truncation is slightly more difficult; relevant data appear in (1.16).
Here, PARSE is violated – the final vowel is left unparsed and
therefore unrealisable, and because of restrictions on the coda in
Lardil, preceding consonants are typically also lost, as in the 'termite'
example. PARSE is violated here due to the higher-ranking (and
language-specific; see 1.3.1 above) constraint, FREE-V, shown in
(1.17).

(1.15)   Lardil:

nominative	*non-future accusative*	*gloss*
yaka	yak-in	'fish'
ɻelka	ɻelk-in	'head'

(1.16)   *nominative*   *non-future accusative*   *gloss*
          mayař   mayařa-n   'rainbow'
          yukař   yukařa-n   'husband'
          ŋawuŋa   ŋawuŋawu-n   'termite'

(1.17)   FREE-V:
          'Word-final vowels must not be parsed (in the nominative).'
          (Prince and Smolensky 1993: 101)

The OT account of insertion and deletion is problematic in several respects. First, there is an issue of restrictiveness. Prince and Smolensky argue that epenthesis can take place only in an onset where the nucleus is filled, or in a nucleus where the onset is filled, so ruling out (1.18).

(1.18)   *.(□)□C.
          'No syllable can have Cod as its only filled position.'
          (Prince and Smolensky 1993: 95)

However, epentheses of this kind do seem to occur, as in the well-known Romance *schola* > *école* cases. Prince and Smolensky admit this, and say 'we must argue ... that other constraints are involved' (1993: 96), but give no indication of *what* other constraints. We also face the problem of supplying the right phonetic material in epenthetic positions. If overparsed nodes are 'phonetically realized through some process of filling in default featural values' (1993: 88), it follows that the glottal stop should be the default, or maximally underspecified, or unmarked Arabic consonant. Similarly, we assume from the Lardil data that the default Lardil vowel is /a/. For French initial vowel epenthesis, like *école*, *étoile*, presumably the same conclusion follows for /e/, although (Durand 1990) typically several French vowels are analysed as more underspecified than /e/, including /i/, /a/, /u/ and schwa. Similarly with PARSE violation, underlying segments may be unrealised, or underlying long vowels shortened because moras are unparsed, but this may have phonetic consequences, for instance on vowel quality, and it is not clear how we are to account for these.

Assuming we can produce the correct parse, and provide (or dispose of) the appropriate phonetic material, there is still the issue of why the old form was harmonic then, and the new one is now. If change reflects constraint re-ordering, we are faced with much the same options and problems as the principles and parameters approach of Government Phonology, since there are the same questions of how re-ranking occurs, and what motivates it. Finally, as we have already seen, issues around the type, number, ordering and variant cases of constraints are still to be addressed.

In returning now to a rule-based model, I do not pretend to have answered all the questions which might be raised by proponents of alternative phonologies. This section is also in a sense incomplete, since I have not shown how LP can model the types of sound change surveyed above. To some extent, this is a non-issue: we might say that it can model anything, which is at the heart of the problem for any model with parochial rules. I hope to show below that these unwelcome abilities can be limited for LP. Secondly, whether such changes can be modelled sensibly depends in large part on the feature system; there are long-standing difficulties with the binary features generally associated with the SPE model, and hence with LP, and I return to these in chapter 6 below. Needless to say, if the model of LP I propose here turns out to perform badly, in the analysis of synchronic alternations and in the other domains discussed above, it cannot reasonably be maintained on the grounds that no-one else is doing any better. On the other hand, I hope I have raised enough questions to justify at least considering the performance of a radically revised generative model. Once the investigation is under way, the results will speak for themselves.

1.4   The structure of the book

In chapter 2, I shall appraise the lexical model of Modern English morphology and phonology proposed by Halle and Mohanan (1985), highlighting the abstract and unconstrained nature of this version of LP and arguing for a restriction of the model to two lexical levels. The relationship of the SCC to the Elsewhere Condition, and to Kiparsky's Alternation Condition, will also be discussed. Further invocation of the SCC and other constraints in chapter 3 will lead to a reanalysis of certain central rules of the English vowel phonology, in particular the Vowel Shift Rule, and a general appraisal of the appropriateness of the resulting framework for Received Pronunciation (RP) and various American accents. In chapter 4, I introduce a further reference accent, Scottish Standard English (SSE), and give a synchronic and diachronic outline of this and non-standard Scots dialects. I shall concentrate here on the synchronic status of the Scottish Vowel Length Rule, assessing whether it applies lexically or postlexically, and also consider its history, thereby establishing a possible 'life-cycle' for sound changes and phonological rules. In chapter 5, I focus on dialect variation in a Lexical Phonology, with particular emphasis on the impact of radical underspecification on the analysis of dialect differences. Finally, in chapter 6, I return to the tension between synchrony and diachrony in phonological theory, considering English /r/ and its present-day and historical interactions with preceding vowels; strengthening the hypotheses put forward earlier on the lexicalisation of phonological rules; and indicating that the modelling of rules and changes can perhaps best be dealt with by integrating Articulatory Phonology with Lexical Phonology.

2 Constraining the model: current controversies in Lexical Phonology

2.1 Lexical Phonology and Morphology: an overview

Current models of Lexical Phonology vary markedly in their approaches to certain central areas of debate. In this chapter, I shall identify these controversial areas and outline the assumptions I shall make in the model of LP developed in the rest of the book. Some of these are shared with other current versions of LP; others are new. Before proceeding to these reassessments, however, I shall provide a historical outline of LP, highlighting its inheritance in terms of both phonology and morphology, which will provide a shared background for the discussion below.

2.1.1 Morphology

As Aronoff (1976: 4) observes, 'Within the generative framework, morphology was for a long time quite successfully ignored. There was a good ideological reason for this: in its zeal, post-*Syntactic Structures* linguistics saw syntax and phonology everywhere, with the result that morphology was lost somewhere in between.' The inclusion of the traditional substance of morphology within syntax meant that, in the *Aspects* (Chomsky 1965) model, no distinction was drawn between word-building and sentence-building operations: all distributional regularities were necessarily captured using transformational rules, which derived related surface structures from a common Deep Structure. This methodology, and the large number of surface relations between words and constructions to be accounted for, had two results: the Deep Structures became progressively more remote from these surface representations, and the transformations became more and more complex and unconstrained.

Chomsky's 'Remarks on nominalization' (1970) is a first attempt to simplify and reduce the power of the transformational component, at the cost of more complex base rules and an enriched lexicon. The paper focuses on derived nominals, such as *criticism, reduction, transmission, recital*, although it is clear that these should be regarded as a test-case, and that Chomsky's proposals generalise to all derivational morphology. Chomsky argues that these nominals are unsuited to transformational derivation, since, for example, the processes involved are characteristically unproductive, while the nominals themselves are semantically idiosyncratic. Chomsky concludes that T-rules should be used only to effect fully regular relationships; processes like nominalisation, which have lexical exceptions, should instead be handled in the lexicon. In the *Aspects* model, the lexicon had been seen as simply a repository for idiosyncratic information on lexical items; it was now extended and equipped with lexical rules intended to cope with subregularities. Verbs like *criticise, reduce* and their derived nominals, *criticism* and *reduction*, could then be base-generated, and their lexical entries related using these lexical rules.

Chomsky's (1970) suggestions for the structure of this revised lexicon are extremely sketchy; in retrospect, it is clear that 'the significance of "Remarks" lies less in what it says itself than in what it caused others to say' (Hoekstra, van der Hulst and Moortgat 1981: 1). The removal of derivational morphology from the scope of the transformations facilitated the reintroduction of morphology as a linguistic subdiscipline separate from phonology and syntax; and the location of morphological processes in the lexicon also gave rise to lexicalist syntaxes (Hoekstra, van der Hulst and Moortgat 1981, Bresnan 1982), and eventually to LP.

However, it is clear that base-generating and storing all word-forms would introduce high levels of redundancy into the grammar. Consequently, most morphological work after 'Remarks' (Halle 1973, Siegel 1974, Aronoff 1976, Allen 1978) has proposed that word-formation rules perform morpheme concatenations rather than linking independent lexical entries. The next innovation involves the organisation of these word-formation processes in the lexicon. Siegel (1974) observes that derivational affixes in English fall into two classes; Class I affixes include *in-, -ity*, Adjective-forming *-al, -ic* and *-ate*, while Class II includes *un-, -ness, -er*, Noun-forming *-al* and *-hood*. The former set corresponds to the +-boundary affixes of SPE, and the latter to #-boundary affixes. This class division rests on the morphological behaviour of the affixes, as well as having phonological consequences (see 2.1.2).

First, as shown in (2.1), Class I affixes are free to attach to roots, while Class II affixes attach only to words.

(2.1)   inert   *unert
              intrepid   *untrepid
              insipid   *unsipid
              immaculate   *unmaculate
              (from Allen 1978)

Secondly, in multiple affixation, Class I affixes appear nearer the stem, so that a Class II affix can be added 'outside' a Class I affix, but not *vice versa* (2.2).

(2.2)   1 1   1 2
           atomicity   atomicness
              2 2   2 1
           hopelessness   *hopelessity

Siegel proposes that all Class I affixations precede all Class II affixations. This idea is developed and extended by Allen (1978: 6), who reinterprets Siegel's classes as levels, arguing that 'the "level" designation indicates that the morphology is partitioned into blocks of rules, each block having different morphological characteristics. Furthermore ... the morphology is level-ordered. That is, the levels of rule operation are ordered with respect to each other, although no ordering is imposed on individual rules of word-formation.'

Derivational word-formation rules attaching Class I affixes will therefore be ordered on Level, or Stratum 1 of the lexicon, while Class II affixations will take place on Level 2, as shown in (2.3). Underived stems are acceptable on Level 1, but only words on Level 2. Bound stems must therefore undergo some affixation process on Level 1, or will be ineligible to pass to subsequent levels.

(2.3)   Underived lexical entries

	[ert]	[graph]	[hope]
STRATUM 1	[in[ert]]	–	–
	–	[[graph]ic]	–
STRATUM 2	–	–	[[hope]less]
	–	[[graphic]ness]	[[[hope]less]ness]
	[inert]	[graphicness]	[hopelessness]

                   in- Prefixation: Level 1
                   -ic Suffixation: Level 1
                   -less Suffixation: Level 2
                   -ness Suffixation: Level 2

The diagram in (2.3) incorporates a number of more or less controversial assumptions on the organisation of the lexicon, especially concerning the storage and attachment of affixes. There are two opposing views here, represented by Lieber (1981) and Mohanan (1982, 1986) on one hand, and Kiparsky (1982; partly after Aronoff 1976) on the other.

Lieber argues that both stems and affixes are lexically stored, with appropriately specified features and labels: thus, the suffix -*ness* would be labelled $]_A -]_N$, showing that it is added to an adjective to create a noun, while the verbal suffix -*ed* would carry the label $]_V -]_V$ and the feature [+ past]. Unlabelled binary branching trees, generated by a single context-free rewrite rule, represent the internal structure of words. Formatives are inserted from the lexicon under the terminal nodes of these trees, and features are transferred to higher nodes by Feature Percolation Conventions. In Lieber's model, affixes are heads, and the final affix determines the category and features of the word (2.4).

(2.4)

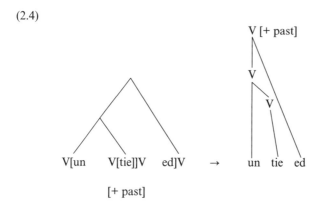

Mohanan (see 1986: 16) appears to accept a version of Lieber's proposal. He assumes that stems and affixes are stored in a single morpheme list, and are undifferentiated in terms of bracketing. This lack of differentiation extends also to compounding and affixation, as shown in (2.5); note that the single] bracket of LP replaces the + and # boundaries of SPE.

(2.5)   [happy]   stem
         [un], [ness]   affixes
         [[happy][ness]] affixation
         [[green][house]] compounding

Mohanan (1986: 16–17) further suggests that the information given for each affix in the morpheme list includes a specification of the domain of application for the rule attaching that affix: this domain may be a single stratum, or a set of continuous strata.

On the other hand, Kiparsky (1982) proposes that stems alone should be stored, and that affixes are introduced by word-formation rules, which again will be marked for their domain of application: 'affixes will not then be lexical entries, and they will have no lexical features either inherently or by percolation' (1982: 6). Restrictions on the environment in which the affix may be attached, corresponding to Lieber's subcategorisation frame and categorial specification, are instead construed as contextual restrictions on the affix-insertion rules, as shown in (2.6).

(2.6)   General affixation rule: Insert A in env. $[Y\text{-}Z]_X$

      Plural:
             Insert *-en* in env. $[\text{ox-}]_{N, +Pl.}$
             Insert *-s* in env. $[X\text{-}]_{N, +Pl.}$

Kiparsky also distinguishes stems (which are stored) from affixes (which are not) by bracketing, and in his model, the outputs of affixation and compounding will also be distinct in terms of bracket configurations, as (2.7) shows. For the moment, I follow Kiparsky's assumptions on bracketing and affix insertion: I shall justify this decision more fully, and make some revisions, in 2.3.2 and 2.3.3 below.

(2.7)   [happy]   stem
        [un[happy]]   prefixed form
        [[happy]ness]   suffixed form
        [[green][house]]   compound

Finally, Mohanan and Kiparsky agree that, although word-internal structure is relevant within the stratum on which it is created, it should not be accessible to rules on subsequent strata. A Bracket Erasure Convention therefore removes all word-internal brackets at the end of each level: this 'opacity principle' (Mohanan 1982: 7) will be further justified in 2.1.2 below in terms of the interaction of phonological and morphological processes.

The extension of the lexicalist hypothesis since Chomsky (1970) has led to the inclusion of morphological processes other than derivation in the expanded lexicon. Allen (1978) proposes that compounding, as well as derivational affixation, should be regarded as lexical, and introduces a third morphological stratum for compounding processes. Halle had already argued that a generative model of morphology should not be limited to derivation, but that 'facts that traditionally have been treated under the separate heading of inflectional morphology must be handled in completely parallel fashion' (1973: 6); Lieber (1981) follows this lead and adds inflectional affixation to the inventory of lexical processes, on the grounds that inflectional stem allomorphs may form the input to derivation and compounding, so that all these word-formation processes should take place in the same component. The assumption that *all* morphology is lexical is one shared by most proponents of LP, including Kiparsky (1982, 1985), Mohanan (1982, 1986) and Halle and Mohanan (1985). There have been attempts to argue that inflection should be regarded as syntactic (and therefore postlexical); Anderson (1982), for instance, presents an analysis of Breton verb agreement which relies on the interaction of inflectional morphology and syntax. However, Anderson's proposals are countered by Jensen and Stong-Jensen (1984), and further persuasive arguments for parallel treatment of inflectional and derivational morphology can be found in Halle (1973) and Miller (1985). I shall therefore adopt the view that processes of inflection, derivation and compounding all take place within the lexicon. To indicate the composition of such a morphological model, I give in (2.8) the lexical organisation proposed in Kiparsky's early (1982) work on English; note that this is included simply for illustration, and will be amended later.

(2.8)	LEXICON	
		Underived lexical entries
	LEVEL 1:	Class I derivation, e.g. *-ic, -al*$_A$, *in-* Irregular inflection, e.g. *oxen, indices, kept*
	LEVEL 2:	Class II derivation, e.g. *-ness, -hood, un-* Compounding
	LEVEL 3:	Regular inflection, e.g. plural *-s*, past *-d*
	SYNTAX	

Kiparsky (1982) has thoroughly investigated the morphological consequences of the level-ordering hypothesis. We have already mentioned the phenomenon of stacking (the fact that affixes from a later stratum may be attached only 'outside' those attached earlier in the lexicon, not nearer the stem; this has become known as the Affix Ordering General-isation (Selkirk 1982a)), and also the ability of Level 1 affixes alone to attach to bound stems. I shall consider one further example of the morphological predictions of the lexicalist model, namely blocking.

The blocking effect, which Aronoff (1976) calls 'pre-emption by synonymy', has two subcases:

(1) Forms may not usually receive two alternative affixes with the same semantic content. So, we have *feet* and *oxen* but not additionally **foots*, **oxes*, and zero-derived *guide, spy*, but not **guider, *spier*.

(2) Lexical items with some inherently marked morphological feature do not additionally acquire an affix which marks this feature. Thus, *people*, which is already inherently [+ plural], does not receive plural -*s*. Linked to this is the failure of semantically equivalent affixes to accumulate on a single stem; so, *oxen* does not undergo regular plural suffixation to give **oxens*. This generalisation does sometimes break down: English *children*, Dutch *kinderen, lammeren* and Afrikaans *kinders, eiers* would all be exceptions at least historically.

Kiparsky (1982) argues that these blocking phenomena can be readily explained within the lexicalist model, by two slightly different strategies.

(a) Doublets are prohibited by making morphological rules obligatory in the unmarked case: so, *ox*, if it carries the feature [+ plural], is marked to undergo a special Level 1 rule attaching -*en*. The form is not then eligible to undergo the Level 3 regular plural rule. In cases where doublets *do* obtain, as with *indices–indexes*, Kiparsky assumes that the special rule is exceptionally speaker-specific. The system for blocking derivational doublets is identical (although less rigid): the deverbal agent noun *spy* is zero-derived on Level 1, and may not also acquire the functionally identical Level 2 agentive marker -*er*. Blocking is therefore seen as 'pre-emption by prior application' (Kiparsky 1982: 8). Kiparsky uses these facts to support a number of hypotheses on the organisation of the lexicon: notably, he argues that when a set of processes is involved in a blocking relationship, special rules with restricted applicability must precede general, regular processes. Hence rules on later levels are more productive, and more semantically uniform, than those higher in the lexicon.

(b) The exclusion of functionally equivalent stacked affixes and double marking of features is rather more complex, and requires the introduction of one of the principal constraints of LP, the Elsewhere

Condition (henceforth EC). The EC governs disjunctive application of rules, and is given in (2.9).

(2.9)   Rules A, B in the same component apply disjunctively to a form Φ if and only if
(i) The structural description of A (the special rule) properly includes the structural description of B (the general rule).
(ii) The result of applying A to Φ is distinct from the result of applying B to Φ. In that case, A is applied first, and if it takes effect, then B is not applied. (Kiparsky 1982: 8)

Kiparsky makes the further assumption that every lexical entry, and the output of every layer of derivation, is an identity rule L, where the structural description and structural change of L are both L. The lexical entry for *people* is then inherently marked [+ plural], so that L = $[people]_{+N, +Pl}$. L in this case is disjunctive with the regular plural rule by (2.9): the rule $[people]_{+N, +Pl}$ properly includes the structural description $[X -]_{+N, +Pl}$, and the outputs, *people* and *peoples*, are distinct. The identity rule, as the special rule, then takes precedence. Similarly, **oxens* is impossible, since the Level 1 derived lexical entry $[oxen]_{+N, +Pl}$ is again disjunctive with the regular plural rule. The EC has had profound consequences for the development of lexicalist theory, and we shall return to it during the next section.

2.1.2   Phonology

The organisation of the morphological component of the lexicon assumed in LP should now be clear. However, the morphology is not the sole inhabitant of the lexicon; rather, there is considerable interaction with the phonology.

Siegel (1974) did not motivate her division of English derivational affixes into Classes I and II solely by reference to morphological factors, but adduced additional evidence from their phonological behaviour. In particular, Siegel notes that Class I suffixes shift the stress of the stem, while Class II affixes are stress-neutral (2.10). However, Class II affixes may have constraints on their insertion, governed by the position of stress on the stem; thus, $-al_N$ attaches only to verbs with final stress. Such constraints do not affect Class I affixes (2.11).

(2.10)   válid   valídity   válidness
          átom   atómic   átomise
          párent   paréntal   párenthood

(2.11)   arríve   arrival
          refúse   refusal
          édit   *edital
          depósit   *deposital

Siegel consequently proposes that cyclic phonological rules, including word-stress assignment, should operate between Class I and Class II affixation in the lexicon; Class I affixes will then be added before stress-placement, so that the position of stress on an underived base and on a Class I affixed form may be calculated differently by the stress rules. Class II affixation will occur too late to influence stress assignment, but may be sensitive to the already determined position of stress.

Allen (1978) observes that this interaction of morphology and pho-nology is not limited to the stress rules, and suggests that on each stratum a particular boundary will be assigned to structures derived on that stratum: the boundary will be + on Level 1, and # on Level 2. Phonological rules may then be formulated to apply across + but not #. Subsequently, Mohanan (1982) and Kiparsky (1982) translate these preliminary observations into a much more integrative model. The central assumption of LP is that each lexical level constitutes the domain of application for a subset of the phonological rules, as well as certain word-formation processes. The phonological rules do not apply between the morphological strata, as Siegel suggested, but are assigned to them. The output of every morphological operation is passed back through the phonological rules on that level; this builds cyclicity into the model, and allows for the progressive and parallel erection of phonological and morphological structure, as shown in (2.12).

(2.12)   Underived lexical entries

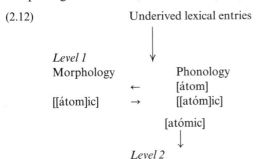

Level 1
Morphology   Phonology
                  ←   [átom]
[[átom]ic]   →   [[atóm]ic]
                              [atómic]
        Level 2

This model also removes the need for distinct boundary symbols such as + and #. Instead, the distinct boundaries of SPE are replaced by a single bracket, 'which is actually nothing more than the concatenation operator on both the morphological and syntactic levels' (Strauss 1979: 394), and their effects are captured by level ordering.

We can now turn to the second major input to LP, the abstractness controversy, perhaps best introduced with reference to Kiparsky's (1982) account of Trisyllabic Laxing (TSL) in English.

TSL (2.13) laxes (or shortens) any vowel followed by at least two vowels, the first of which must be unstressed.

(2.13) $V \rightarrow [- \text{tense}] / \_\_ C_0 V_i C_0 V_j$
where V_j is not metrically strong
(Kiparsky 1982: 35)
declare ~ declarative   divine ~ divinity   table ~ tabulate

TSL was problematic for the SGP model because of the presence of the two classes of exceptions exemplified in (2.14).

(2.14)   a. mightily   bravery   weariness
          b. ivory   nightingale   Oberon   Oedipus

In LP terms, the first set of exceptions all include Class II suffixes, while the forms undergoing TSL in (2.13) all have Class I affixes; thus, we simply order TSL on Level 1. The forms in (2.14a) will only become trisyllabic on Level 2, beyond the domain of TSL. The exceptions in (2.14b) are more problematic. The SGP methodology would involve adjusting the underlying representations of forms like *nightingale, ivory* so that the structural description of TSL is not met. For instance, Chomsky and Halle assigned *nightingale* the underlying form /nɪxtVngæl/; further rules were then required to transform /ɪx/ into surface [aɪ]. However, this stratagem promotes abstractness, and is *ad hoc*, non-generalisable, and non-explanatory.

Kiparsky also notes the existence of a further problematic set of words (2.15), which 'have two possible derivations, while only one is ever needed' (1982: 35).

(2.15)   camera   pelican   enemy

These words could be derived from underlying representations with a short, lax vowel in the first syllable, but the more likely SGP derivation would involve positing underlyingly long, tense vowels, and giving these non-alternating forms a 'free ride' through the TSL rule. The drive for maximal generality of rules, and the attendant principle that surface irregularity should stem from underlying regularity, thus add considerably to the abstractness of the model.

Kiparsky claims that, within LP, a single constraint can explain the non-application of TSL in the forms in (2.14b), and prohibit the derivation of the words in (2.15) from remote underliers. Kiparsky refers to work on the strict cycle in phonology (Kean 1974, Mascaró 1976, Rubach 1984), where it is claimed that cyclic rules are only permitted to apply in derived environments. The Strict Cyclicity Condition (SCC), which effects this restriction, is formulated in (2.16).

(2.16)   SCC: Cyclic rules apply in derived environments. An environment is
         derived for rule A in cycle (i) iff the structural description of rule A is
         met due to a concatenation of morphemes at cycle (i) or the operation
         of a phonological rule feeding rule A on cycle (i).

TSL, as a cyclic rule subject to SCC, will be permitted to apply in *declarative*, *divinity*, etc. due to the prior application of a Level 1 affixation rule on the same cycle. However, it will not be applicable in *ivory* and *nightingale*; these happen to meet the structural description of TSL at the underlying level, but they are not trisyllabic by virtue of any concatenation operation, nor do they undergo any phonological rule feeding TSL. Their underliers can therefore be listed as equivalent to their surface forms, and their apparent exceptionality with respect to TSL follows automatically from the SCC.

Likewise, the mere assignment of a tense vowel to the first syllable of forms like *pelican*, *enemy* and *camera* will no longer enable these to be passed through TSL, since they will constitute underived environments for the laxing rule: the appropriate surface form [ɛnəmi] is no longer derivable from [ēnɛmɪ], if we assume the validity of SCC and accept that TSL is a cyclic rule.

In the earliest versions of LP (Mohanan 1982, Kiparsky 1982) it was assumed that all lexical rules were cyclic, as shown in the model for English given in (2.17) (adapted from Kiparsky 1982: 5).

(2.17)   Underived lexical entries
                                ↓
         Irregular inflection   ←   Stress   LEVEL 1
         Class I derivation   →   Laxing

         Class II derivation   ←   Compound   LEVEL 2
         Compounding   →   stress

         Regular inflection   ←   Sonorant   LEVEL 3
                                →   resyllabification

                  SYNTAX

In such a model, the domain of SCC would be the entire lexicon, and all lexical phonological rules would be restricted to derived environments. This early, strong claim has been somewhat weakened since, so that it is now generally accepted that not all cyclic rules are subject to SCC, and that not all lexical rules are cyclic.

First, it appears that rules which build structure rather than changing it should not be subject to SCC (Kaisse and Shaw 1985), to allow stress rules, and syllabification rules erecting metrical structure, to apply on the first cycle in underived environments. Stems like *atom* will then be eligible for stress assignment and syllabification without undergoing previous morphological or phonological processes. Kiparsky (1985) further suggests that an initial application of a structure-building rule should not be accepted as creating a derived environment for a subsequent structure-changing rule.

Secondly, Halle and Mohanan (1985) claim that there are a number of phonological rules which, due to their interaction with morphological processes and other rules of the lexical phonology, should themselves apply in the lexicon, but which do not obey SCC. For instance, Velar Softening is clearly sensitive to morphological information, since it applies in Class II derived forms like *magi[ʃ]ian*, but not medially in compounds, as in *magi*[k] *eye*. Since Velar Softening must be ordered before Level 2 Palatalisation, Halle and Mohanan argue that it should also apply on Level 2. However, Velar Softening also applies in underived forms like *reduce* and *oblige*, although this should be prohibited by the SCC if Velar Softening is a cyclic rule. Halle and Mohanan produce similar arguments for a number of the core rules of English vowel phonology, including the Vowel Shift Rule; again, they propose that Vowel Shift should be ordered on Level 2 of the lexicon, but again this rule is said to apply, in apparent contravention of SCC, in underived forms like *divine*, *sane* and *verbose*.

These findings have provoked various limitations of the power of SCC. Kiparsky (1985) suggests that rules on the last lexical level are exempt from SCC, although he does not explicitly state whether he believes rules on this 'word level' to be cyclic or non-cyclic. A far more radical solution is adopted by Halle and Mohanan (1985) and Mohanan (1986), who argue that 'the cyclicity of rule application in Lexical Phonology ... is a stipulation on the stratum' (Halle and Mohanan 1985: 66); thus, cyclic and non-cyclic strata may be interspersed. Mohanan (1986: 47) even proposes that all lexical strata are non-cyclic in the unmarked case, reversing Kiparsky's earlier hypothesis on the relationship between cyclicity and lexical application.

The lexical structure which Halle and Mohanan (1985) propose for English is shown in (2.18). There are four lexical levels; three are cyclic, but Level 2, the domain of Velar Softening and the Vowel Shift Rule, is non-cyclic. On cyclic strata, forms pass through the phonology, then to the morphology, and are resubmitted to the phonology after every morphological operation. On non-cyclic strata, however, all appropriate morphological rules apply first, and the derived form then passes through the phonological rules on that level once only.

(2.18)   Underived lexical entries
         ↓

Irregular inflection	←	Stress	LEVEL 1
Class I derivation	→	Shortening ...	
Class II derivation	→	Vowel Shift	LEVEL 2
		Velar Softening ...	
Compounding	←	Compound	LEVEL 3
	→	stress	
Regular inflection	←	Sonorant	LEVEL 4
	→	syllabification	

The matter of the number of cyclic and non-cyclic strata is inextricably linked with the problem of limiting the overall number of strata. Kiparsky, as we have seen, proposed three levels for English; Halle and Mohanan (1985) argue for four. The lack of any principled limitation on the number of lexical levels proposed has cast serious doubts on the validity of LP; it would be theoretically possible, for instance, to propose a level for every rule, or some arbitrary number of levels with all rules applying on all levels. Even if individual analysts refrain from positing unrealistically high numbers of levels, the potential for unconstrained stratification remains, making a lexicalist model potentially unconstrainable; and in any case, we have no criteria to tell us what number of strata would *be* unrealistically high.

Recent emendations to LP by Booij and Rubach (1987) aim to provide a universal lexical organisation, a constrained number of strata, and a principled division of cyclic from non-cyclic levels. On the basis of evidence from Dutch, Polish, French and English (admittedly a restricted corpus), Booij and Rubach restrict the lexical component to one cyclic and one postcyclic level. This model, applied to English, gives the lexical organisation shown in (2.19). I shall simply accept this restrictive model for the moment, returning to it in 2.3 below and in the following chapters.

(2.19)   Underived lexical entries
                                    ↓
    Irregular inflection ← Stress   LEVEL 1
    Class I derivation   → Laxing...

    Class II derivation   Vowel Shift   LEVEL 2
    Compounding   →   Compound Stress
    Regular inflection   Palatalisation...

Finally, not all phonological rules in LP are lexical; some apply in a postlexical component, located after the syntax. If the lexical phonology corresponds roughly to the morphophonemic rules of SGP, the post-lexical rules may be thought of as allophonic, an equation supported by the strong similarity of the 'lexical level' of representation, the output of the lexicon, to the classical phonemic level. The two types of rules are characterised by different syndromes of properties, which can be used to determine the component in which a given rule applies. For instance, there are considerations of ordering: if a rule necessarily applies before a rule which must, for independent reasons, be lexical, then it must itself be lexical. Similarly, a process which crucially follows a postlexical rule will be postlexical. If a rule can be shown to be cyclic, it must also be lexical; more specifically, in Booij and Rubach's (1987) model, it must apply on Level 1. Further evidence must, however, be adduced to decide whether a non-cyclic rule is postcyclic or postlexical. For instance, any rule which is conditioned or blocked by the presence of brackets, exception features, or morphological features such as [± Latinate] in the string, is necessarily lexical. The expected sensitivity of lexical phonological rules to word-internal structure follows from their interaction with the morphology, while the opacity of such internal structure for postlexical processes is a natural result of bracket erasure at the end of each level. Conversely, it follows from ordering with respect to syntactic concatenation that only postlexical phonological rules may apply across word boundaries.

Lexical rules may also have lexically marked exceptions, but post-lexical ones apply wherever their structural description is met. Bresnan (1982) similarly argues that only lexical syntactic rules may have excep-tions; perhaps the correlation of lexical application with exceptionality reflects the early transformational–generative characterisation of the lexicon as a store of idiosyncratic information. Furthermore, it was the irregular, exceptional tendencies of derivational morphology which prompted Chomsky (1970) to move it into the lexicon, initiating the lexical expansion which has led to LP. Finally, postlexical rules may create novel segments and structures, but lexical rules are structure preserving, and may not create any structure which is not part of the underlying inventory of the language. I give Borowsky's (1990: 29) definition of Structure Preservation in (2.20).

(2.20)   Structure Preservation: Lexical rules may not mark features which are non-distinctive, nor create structures which do not conform to the basic prosodic templates of the language.

Structure Preservation (SP) is the third major constraint of LP, after the EC and the SCC and, like the other two, is rather controversial. I shall return to it below.

Mohanan (1986) regards the postlexical component as bipartite. He suggests that forms exit the lexicon and enter first a syntactic submodule, including phonological rules which make necessary reference to syntactic information, such as the rule governing the *a ~ an* alternation in English. This submodule creates a syntactico-phonological representation of phonological phrases; these then pass into a postsyntactic submodule, where phonetic implementation rules 'spell out the details of the phonetic implementation of a phonological representation in terms of *gradient* operations' (Mohanan 1986: 151). In other words, Mohanan, like Chomsky and Halle (1968), argues that binary features become scalar late in the derivation, although again like Chomsky and Halle, he gives no details of how this transition is to be achieved. For instance, Mohanan notes that the degree of aspiration of voiceless stops in English depends on the degree of stress, so that scalar values are required in the phonetic implementation submodule. Mohanan emphasises that these implementational rules are not universal and purely physiological, but low-level and language-specific; for instance, the dependence of aspiration on stress does not hold in Hindi or Malayalam.

Mohanan further argues that 'mappings in the implementational module may dissolve phonological segments' (1986: 173). At the eventual phonetic level, the derivation will then produce features which are assigned scalar values and aligned independently with a timer. The potential for overlap which this alignment provides seems promising for the treatment of coarticulation and timing; we shall return to this issue, from a rather different angle, in chapter 6.

Finally, rules may apply both lexically and postlexically: for instance, Palatalisation in English (2.21) must, for reasons of ordering and interaction with the morphology, apply on Level 2 of the lexicon, but it also operates between words.

(2.21)   Level 2:
            [res]
            [[res]jəl]   *-ial* suffixation
            [[reʃ]jəl]   Palatalisation

            Postlexical:
            I'll race you [resjə] or [reʃjə]

Kiparsky (1985) extends this notion of application in two components, proposing that a process which appears to apply in a gradient fashion may be a postlexical reflex of a rule which also applies categorically in the lexicon.

2.2   Why constraints? Halle and Mohanan (1985)

The most extensive and comprehensive lexicalist account of English vowel phonology currently available is Halle and Mohanan (1985), and my attempts below to constrain the framework and mechanisms of LP will focus on this version of the theory. The critique developed here is applicable also to Mohanan (1986), which shares many of the assumptions of Halle and Mohanan (1985). Although Halle and Mohanan are working within the letter of LP, their analyses frequently fail to cohere with the spirit of the lexicalist enterprise, if we take that spirit to include the reduction of abstractness and the removal of unwarranted machinery and unmotivated derivation. In the sections below, and in chapter 3, I shall return in detail to the Halle and Mohanan model, considering many of their analyses in depth. For the moment, I intend only to demonstrate that their model cannot be seen as a significant advance over SGP.

First, let us turn to the general architecture of the model. As noted above, the Halle and Mohanan model comprises four lexical strata, as against Kiparsky's (1982) three and Booij and Rubach's (1987) two, as well as one postlexical level. If the number of levels proposed for a language is in principle unbounded, the theory loses any claim to explanatory adequacy, since an analysis would be possible in which each word-formation rule or phonological process were assigned to a separate stratum, or every rule to every stratum. Moreover, allowing random interspersal of cyclic and non-cyclic strata, as Halle and Mohanan also do, further compromises LP in that the operation or suspension of constraints will be purely a matter of stipulation. Nor do they strictly adhere to the four lexical strata they declare; their model also incorporates a so-called Loop, which allows compounded forms derived on their Level 3 to cycle back into Level 2 affixation. Since there is no principled limit to the levels between which loops could be proposed, the way would in principle be open for such morphological interaction between every pair of strata. In Halle and Mohanan's model, the concept of morphological level-ordering is effectively dead in the water.

There are similar problems of permissiveness in their specific phonological analyses. Halle and Mohanan are primarily concerned with General American, although they claim the underlying vowel system they propose (see (2.22)) is also appropriate for RP; this assignment of a single underlying phonological system to related dialects was a characteristic of SGP which Halle and Mohanan carry over into LP.

(2.22)   *short*
/ɪ/ bit	/i/ ven*ue*	/ʊ/ put
/ɛ/ bet	/ʌ/ but	/o/ baud, shot
/æ/ bat	/a/ balm	/ɔ/ bomb

long
/ī/ divine	/ī/ profound	/ō/ pool
/ē/ serene	/ʌ̄/ cube	/ɔ̄/ verbose
/ǣ/ sane		

If we were looking for a predominantly surface-true vowel system, we would not find it here. The SPE account of Vowel Shift is retained, with the tense vowels shifting in *sane*, *serene*, *divine*, and free rides in parallel non-alternating *plain*, *mean*, *pine*. A single underlying representation is proposed for the vowel in *balm*, and one for *bomb*, although the realisations vary widely across British and American accents, and indeed the two are homophonous for many speakers. Absolute neutralisation is rife, with [jū] in *cube* and [jū] in *venue* derived from distinct underlying vowels.

For the moment, I consider only one further example: the Modern English strong verbs (see further chapter 3). On the principle of 'can do, will do' familiar from SPE, Halle and Mohanan elect to derive alternating pairs like *seek ~ sought*, *choose ~ chose* and *blow ~ blew* from single underlying forms. This requires, of course, the whole panoply of SGP derivational techniques, as illustrated in (2.23).

(2.23)   *seek ~ sought*

	Pres.	*seek*	Past
Underlying:		/sēk/	
/t/-Suffixation:	–		sēk]t
x-Formation:	–		sext
Cluster Shortening:	–		sɛxt
Backing Ablaut:	–		soxt
x-Deletion:	–		sot
VSR/Diphthongisation:	sīyk		–
o-Tensing:	–		sōt
o-Lowering:	–		sɔt
Output:	[sīyk]		[sɔt]

choose ~ chose (marked [−t/d suffixation])

	Pres.	*choose*	Past
Underlying:		/tʃōz/	
Lowering Ablaut:	–		tʃɔz
VSR/Diphthongisation:	tʃūwz		tʃōwz
Output:	[tʃūwz]		[tʃōwz]

blow ~ blew (marked [−t/d suffixation])

	Pres.	*blow*	Past
Underlying:		/blī/	
Lowering Ablaut:	blæ		–
Backing Ablaut:	blɔ		blɨ̄
Shortening Ablaut:	–		blɨ
i-Lengthening:	–		blɨ̄
i-Rounding:	–		blū
VSR/Diphthongisation:	blōw		blūw
Output:	[blōw]		[blūw]

Connoisseurs of untrammelled generative analysis will find all their old favourite tricks here. We have non-surface-true underliers; special diacritic marking; a whole complex of ablaut and related rules which are required only for these strong verbs, and yet are presented as if equivalent to productive processes; abuses of extrinsic ordering involving 'lay-by' procedures; and 'Duke-of-York' derivations, which involve the production, destruction and re-derivation of the desired output, as in *chose*.

In the face of examples like these (and there are plenty to choose from), it must be clear that LP is in serious danger of losing sight of its founding aims. Lexical Phonologists are not, of course, alone in their weaknesses here; there is a recurring tendency in phonology to invent constraints or conditions, then see these as some panacea which means entirely unrestrained derivation is somehow all right. Take Brand X, drink anything you like, and you won't have a hangover. Except that 10-to-1 you still will, and Brand X will have wreaked its own havoc on your system in the meantime. And you still behaved like an idiot.

It should go without saying, but doesn't, that constraints are useless unless they are imposed and taken seriously. There is no point in formulating restrictions if we then devote all our intellectual energies to finding ways to defuse and disarm them; as we shall see below, the use of underspecification to get round SP, and the ordering of rules on Level 2 to evade SCC are excellent examples of precisely this strategy. Identifying circumstances in which the constraints fail does not occasion congratulations. At best, it is a signal that we must find the underlying principle or factor which explains the non-application of the constraint. We shall see later that such explanations may in fact be historical rather than synchronic.

2.3 Current controversies

It should be clear from the examples reviewed above that LP is in urgent need of constraint; or put slightly differently, that we need to look again at the constraints available in LP to strengthen them and maximise their application. This re-examination will be one aim of this section, in which I shall consider, and state my position on a number of current controversies in the theory. These are the distinction of lexical from postlexical rules; the interaction of morphology and phonology; stratification within the lexicon; the formulation and interrelations of the major constraints of LP; and the associated matter of underspecification.

2.3.1 Lexical and postlexical rules

In SGP, the drive to construct the simplest possible phonology (where simplicity is calculated with reference to feature counting and maximal rule application) led to the rejection of the classical phonemic level of representation or any equivalent to it, with the result that SGP lost any ready way of encoding surface contrast or the speaker intuitions which seem to relate to it, and it became impossible to restrict the distance of underlying representations from the surface. However, LP has three linguistically significant levels of phonological representation. It shares the underlying representations of individual morphemes, and the phonetic representation (the output of the morphology, phonology and syntax, which contains near-surface forms of phrases), with the SPE model. But LP also includes the lexical representation (Mohanan 1986: 10), the output of the phonological derivation at the end of the lexicon, which involves neither morphemes nor phrases, but words.

The lexical representation is not necessarily identical with the phoneme level, although it equally allows LP to refer easily to surface contrast, and equally is relevant in language acquisition, perception and production. Mohanan (1982: 12–13; 1986: ch.7) discusses a number of phenomena which seem to have the lexical representation as their locus: these include speaker judgements on whether sounds are the same or different, and speech errors which permute segments, while secret code languages like Pig Latin seem to perform a coding operation on the lexical representation, then apply the postlexical rules. Mohanan (1986: 194) also proposes that speakers enter words in the mental lexicon in their lexical representations: 'underlying representations of the constituent morphemes of a word are arrived at as and when the speakers come across morphologically related words which provide evidence for the underlying forms'.

All this, however, rests on a clear distinction between lexical and postlexical rules or rule applications; and that clear distinction seems in some respects to be breaking down. We have already seen that Mohanan (1986) proposes two 'levels' of postlexical rules, challenging the association of level-ordering with the lexicon; Kaisse argues similarly that 'postlexical rule application is a more complex phenomenon than the simple across-the-board matter we once thought it might be' (1990: 127). Some postlexical rules may also show properties hitherto seen as lexical: for instance, Carr (1991) discusses the postlexical neutralisation rule of Tyneside Weakening, whereby /t/ → [ɹ] in word-final intervocalic position, as in *not a chance, put it down, delete it.* Carr notes that Weakening does not affect feet like *putty, fitter,* which are formed in the lexicon, but only those created postlexically by cliticisation, and concludes that we require a notion of postlexical derived environment. Carr also shows that Weakening is in an Elsewhere relationship with the later, more general and across-the-board rule of Glottalisation, as shown by the application of Weakening and not Glottalisation in *fit her.* Finally, Carr argues that Weakening is Structure Preserving, although as we have seen, SP has generally been seen as a property of lexical rules, and that it is undergoing lexical diffusion; we return to lexical diffusion, which is a vital ingredient in LP accounts of sound change, in chapter 4.

Essentially, then, Carr's paper challenges the restriction of Structure Preservation, the Elsewhere Condition, derived environment effects and lexical diffusion to the lexicon. There is a growing awareness in LP that the lexical–postlexical division may be gradient: thus Kaisse (1990: 130) observes that 'the most lexical of lexical rules occur at Stratum 1, while less lexical characteristics emerge as one travels "down" towards the word level and the postlexical level(s)', and that, equally, we might expect those postlexical rules nearer the lexicon to share some lexical properties. A similar contention is found in Pandey (1997: 92), who identifies 'a property of interfacing modules, namely, polarity, which is the presence of different properties of representation and rule application at its opposite ends'. That is to say, lexical rules may become progressively less lexical in character as we approach the postlexicon; and conversely, early postlexical rules may exhibit some properties of the lexical syndrome. This might then account both for Carr's observations on Tyneside Weakening, and the possible suspension of, for example, SP at Level 2 of the lexicon, to be discussed in 2.3.4. There are obvious difficulties with Pandey's claim, which is not yet well worked out: for instance, if SP did not operate at Level 2 of the lexicon, it is hard to see how it could percolate into the high postlexicon; and Tyneside Weakening may remain problematic, since Carr does not characterise it as an early postlexical rule, but as part of a group operating between the post-syntactic and across-the-board processes. More centrally, Pandey's approach of proposing a 'Polarity Principle' may not be the right way of dealing with what is clearly a variable and gradient situation; and it is unclear what Pandey means by the 'ends' of a component (in a two-level lexicon, both Level 1 and Level 2 may be 'ends', and the whole lexicon is therefore 'polar' in his terms). Nonetheless, this work is symptomatic of a realisation that the dividing line between lexical and postlexical rules may not be a rigid one, and that, again, we must begin to look instead at where and why particular properties are suspended or activated.

2.3.2 *Integration of phonology and morphology*
One vital choice for LP is whether or not the model should be interactionist, with morphological and phonological operations inter-spersed. This interaction was one of the major motivations for the

development of LP, and remains for many phonologists an attractive feature of the model; but it is not without its problems.

Some of these difficulties seem relatively minor. For instance, certain affixes appear to display properties of both Class I and Class II; thus, *-ism* is stress-shifting in *Cathólicism* from *Cátholic*, but stress-neutral in *Prótestantism* from *Prótestant*. Other morphological concerns are less tractable; thus, the existence of so-called bracketing paradoxes (like the famous *ungrammaticality*; see Badecker 1991) has led to Aronoff and Sridhar's (1983) contention that the Affix Ordering Generalisation is invalid, and morphological level-ordering untenable. Further critiques of the same sort are included in Sproat (1985) and Szpyra (1989). Halle and Vergnaud (1987), for example, consequently adopt a non-interactionist model, with a separate morphological module which precedes all phonology, and contact between the two components limited to the fact that 'morphology ... creates the objects on which the rules of phonology operate' (1987: 78).

We can respond to these developments in two ways. First, we might agree with Badecker (1991: 131) that 'there is substantial content to the role of morphology in Lexical Phonology even when Level Ordering is subtracted out'; and indeed, Halle and Vergnaud (1987) still find it necessary to account for the behaviour of stress-neutral versus stress-sensitive suffixes, for instance. On the other hand, we might wish to maintain an integrationist approach, with level ordering retained and respected for both morphology and phonology; this stronger version of LP is more in keeping with the origins of the model, and is the approach I adopt here. Hargus (1993), in a defence of interactionism, demonstrates that phonology must precede morphology in some cases, since morphology may necessarily refer to a derived phonological property, often stress. Furthermore, the domain of phonological rules may exclude material reflecting a morphological process: thus, spirantisation in Luiseño fails to apply to reduplicative structures, while nasal harmony in Sundanese must precede and follow plural infixation. Hargus argues that, although some cases previously seen as supporting interaction have been reanalysed, not all can be. Giegerich (in press) also argues strongly for interaction, albeit in a model of base-driven stratification rather different from standard LP. Giegerich highlights failures of the Affix Ordering Generalisation, and the large number of affixes with at least potentially dual membership of Levels 1 and 2, but claims that these are only problematic when the stratal distinction is driven by affix behaviour.

If we assume instead that properties of the base are predominantly at issue, with Level 1 being the domain of roots and Level 2 of words, we can derive stratification while allowing dual membership as the norm for derivational suffixes in English, for instance. There are many consequences of this change in perspective, some of which I shall discuss in 2.3.5. Others, for instance Giegerich's argument that morphology on Level 1 will effectively involve listing, with each root being stored along with the list of Level 1 affixes it can potentially attract (from which follows the unproductive and semantically idiosyncratic nature of Level 1 morphology), cannot be fully developed here. Nonetheless, morphological developments of this kind, as well as the arguments given earlier, may justify retaining an integrated model.

2.3.3   Stratification

The topic of stratification covers both the question of how the domain of application is to be stated for particular rules, and the related and more complex matter of the number of lexical levels. We have seen that, although Booij and Rubach (1987) attempt to limit the lexicon to two levels, Halle and Mohanan (1985) propose four strata. Any limitation will depend on the shape of affixation processes and the possibility of reference by phonological rules to morphological boundaries.

2.3.3.1   Domain assignment

The facts of English phonology, where the majority of phonological rules apply on only one level, motivated Kiparsky's (1982) hypothesis that 'the phonological rules at each level of the lexicon and in the postlexical component constitute essentially independent mini-phonologies' (1985: 86). Each rule is assigned to a particular level or component, and each level in turn is defined by the rules which are located there. Although this model is perhaps suitable for English phonology in the unmarked case, processes which must apply in more than one component, like Palatalisation, would have to appear twice or more in the grammar, in this approach.

Mohanan (1982) and Mohanan and Mohanan (1984) argue that such a model is untenable for Malayalam, a language with much more overlap between lexical levels and between the postlexical and lexical components. Rather than multiply listing each rule, Mohanan (1982, 1986) proposes that the rules should each be listed once, but that each should carry a domain specification. Mohanan claims that this notion of phonological modularity parallels developments in syntax. In early transformational–generative syntax (Chomsky 1965), rules 'belonged to' individual modules; in Government and Binding theory (Chomsky 1981), however, rules are essentially independent of modules, so that 'the same set of rules is allowed to apply in multiple modules, with different consequences' (Mohanan 1986: 13). Kiparsky (1985) accepts this revision of domain assignment, and suggests that the marking of rules for application on particular levels may be more restricted than Mohanan's model implies, because the constraints of LP, which operate differently in different modules, may themselves restrict rule operation; consequently, apparently quite different processes may be recognised as lexical and postlexical applications of the same rule, with distinct inputs and outputs determined by the differential application of principles like SCC and SP in the two components.

Kiparsky tentatively concludes that 'it may, in fact, be possible to restrict the marking of domains to specifications of the form "rule R does not apply after level n"' (1985: 87). A more extreme statement of the same kind of view is Borowsky's (1990: 3) Strong Domain Hypothesis, which states that 'all rules which are marked for a particular domain of application apply at Level 1 only'. All other rules are available throughout the phonology, and apparent restrictions to certain levels result from the principles of the theory, not from any rule-specific stipulation.

In Borowsky's model, the unmarked mode of application would involve operation both lexically and postlexically, and at all lexical levels. Note, however, that Borowsky's hypothesis refers to *potential* application, with *actual* application often severely restricted by the constraints of LP. Her proposal cannot therefore be invalidated simply by observing that there are apparently few, if any, rules which do apply on all levels and in both components. Mohanan (1986: 46–7) takes a different, and weaker view; his principles of domain assignment (given in (2.24)) make postlexical application only the unmarked option. Evidence on the relationship of sound changes and phonological rules in chapters 4–6 will suggest that the postlexical level is the unmarked domain for newly introduced rules; lexicalisation may then proceed.

(2.24)   In the absence of counterevidence, choose the minimum number of strata as the domain of a rule.
In the absence of counterevidence, choose the lowest stratum as the domain of a rule.
The domain of a rule may not contain nonadjacent strata.

2.3.3.2   Limiting lexical levels

One major problem for Lexical Phonology has been the proliferation of lexical levels, as evidenced especially in recent analyses of English like Halle and Mohanan (1985). However, Booij and Rubach (1987) advocate a restrictive, principled division of the English lexicon into one cyclic and one postcyclic level (2.25), plus postlexical rules.

(2.25)   LEVEL 1:   Class I derivation, irregular inflection
                    Cyclic phonological rules

         LEVEL 2:   Class II derivation, compounding, regular inflection
                    Postcyclic phonological rules

This model of lexical organisation is claimed to be readily generalisable to Dutch and Polish, and may even be universal, although further investigation is clearly required. However, languages may vary along certain parameters; for instance, English has both morphological and phonological rules on Level 2, whereas Dutch and Polish seem to require all word-formation rules to be ordered on cyclic Level 1. Such limited cross-linguistic variation can easily be accommodated within the revised model.

It is clear that such a principled limitation of the number of strata is desirable. However, Halle and Mohanan (1985) have produced data which, they claim, necessitates the four-way division of the lexicon shown in (2.26). In view of this evidence, can a reduction to two lexical levels be achieved?

(2.26)   LEVEL 1:   Class I derivation, irregular inflection
                    Stress, Trisyllabic Shortening . . .

         LEVEL 2:   Class II derivation
                    Vowel Shift, Velar Softening . . .

         LEVEL 3:   Compounding
                    Stem-Final Lengthening and Tensing

         LEVEL 4:   Regular inflection
                    /l/-Resyllabification

The arguments presented by Halle and Mohanan (1985) and Mohanan (1986) involve the supposed cyclicity of Strata 1, 3 and 4 in English, as against non-cyclic Stratum 2, and the existence of four phonological rules which appear to require a four-stratum lexicon to ensure correct application. This evidence is exclusively phonological, already a tacit admission of defeat in a supposedly integrational theory. Morphological evidence for a division of Class I from Class II derivational affixes is very strong (Siegel 1974, Allen 1980), but similar evidence for a division of Class II derivation, compounding and regular inflection is at best tenuous and at worst non-existent. For instance, Kiparsky (1982) classed compounding and Class II derivation together as Level 2 phenomena, on the grounds that each could provide input to the other process (see (2.27)).

(2.27)   [[[neighbour]hood][gang]]
         = affixation → compounding

         [re[[air][condition]]]
         = compounding → affixation

This mutual feeding relationship is recognised by Halle and Mohanan who, however, wish to differentiate Strata 2 and 3 for phonological reasons. They consequently propose that Class II derivation takes place on Stratum 2 and compounding on Stratum 3, but introduce a device, the Loop, which 'allows a stratum distinction for the purposes of phonology, without imposing a corresponding distinction in morphological distribution' (1985: 64). Thus, compounds may be looped back into the Level 2 morphology to acquire Class II affixes.

The separation of compounding from regular inflection (Level 2 versus 3 in Kiparsky 1982, 3 versus 4 in Halle and Mohanan) was originally justified by the assumption that inflections like plural /S/ appear only 'outside' compounds, i.e. on the final stem, as shown in (2.28).

(2.28)   *motorsway service station
         *motorways service station
         *motorway services station
         motorway service stations

However, it is now clear that this assumption was mistaken: the plural inflection appears 'inside' compounds (2.29), albeit under limited circumstances (Sproat 1985). Sproat proposes that compounding and inflection should occupy a single stratum, and that 'The left member of a compound must be unmarked for number, unless the plural is interpreted collectively or idiosyncratically.'

(2.29)   systems analyst   human subjects committee
         ratings book   parts department

Since compounding and Class II derivation must be allowed to be interspersed, and compounding and regular inflection also interact, there seems to be no morphological motivation for a Stratum 2 versus 3 versus 4 distinction for English. If compounding, inflection and Class II derivation are to share a single stratum, however, how are regular inflections to be restricted to word-final position, with no Class II derivational suffixes attaching to their right?

Borowsky (1990: 254) notes that sequences of regular inflection plus Class II suffix may, in fact, be permissible in certain forms, like *yearningly* and *lovingly*; these could be generated in Halle and Mohanan's model only by proposing a second loop, this time from Level 4 to Level 2. In cases where a restriction holds on the position of regular inflections within the word, appropriate sequencing constraints would have to be formulated. Such constraints will be independently necessary in any case, as Giegerich (in press) also argues, since certain Class II derivational affixes do not appear outside others; *-ful* cannot follow *-ness*, for example (*wearinessful*, *happinessful*). Consequently, the solution need not lie in a stratal distinction.

We now return to Halle and Mohanan's phonological arguments for a four-level lexicon, beginning with cyclicity. Their Stratum 1 is clearly cyclic, like the initial level in other lexical phonologies of English (Kiparsky 1982, 1985; Booij and Rubach 1987); some evidence for this is that the stress rules, which are situated on Level 1, are generally agreed to operate cyclically, and that rules like Trisyllabic Laxing/Shortening clearly obey the Strict Cyclicity Condition. Halle and Mohanan also provide evidence for the non-cyclic nature of Stratum 2. First, they argue that Stem-Final Tensing (which operates on Stratum 2 in their dialects A and B, although it is ordered on Stratum 3 for Dialect C – see below and also Halle and Mohanan 1985: 59–62) would produce the wrong output if applied cyclically. In Dialects A and B, Tensing occurs word-finally, before inflections, stem-finally in compounds, and before Class II derivational affixes, except *-ful* and *-ly*; Halle and Mohanan's Tensing rule is given in (2.30). It should be noted that this rule affects only tenseness: Halle and Mohanan generally separate lengthening and tensing processes, and regard length as the underlying dichotomising feature in their English vowel system, with tenseness introduced by a redundancy rule during the course of the derivation.

(2.30) $\begin{bmatrix} -\text{cons} \\ -\text{low} \end{bmatrix} \rightarrow [+\text{tense}] / \underline{\quad}]$

$\qquad\qquad\qquad\qquad |$

$\qquad\qquad\qquad\quad R$

except before *-ly*, *-ful*
(Halle and Mohanan 1985: 67)

Cyclic operation of Stem-Final Tensing would yield the derivation in (2.31).

(2.31)   [hæpɪ]   [lɪ]   Underlying
        [hæpī]   [lī]   Tensing
        [[hæpī][lī]]   Affixation
        *[hæpīlī]   Output
        (after Halle and Mohanan 1985: 67)

If, however, the Tensing rule is allowed to apply only after all Stratum 2 morphology, and thus after the affixation of -*ly*, the correct output, [hæpɪlī], will be produced. Halle and Mohanan conclude that, since in their view cyclicity is a property of strata and not of individual rules, Stratum 2 must be non-cyclic. The hypothesis that Stratum 2 is non-cyclic for English is supported by the fact that Stratum 2 phonological rules like Velar Softening and Vowel Shift, in their traditional SGP formulations, do not obey the SCC. Vowel Shift, for instance, affects *divine* and *serene*, while Velar Softening applies in *receive* and *oblige*, all non-derived environments.

The situation is less clear for Halle and Mohanan's Strata 3 and 4. If these levels were cyclic, they could hardly be merged with Stratum 2 to give a single postcyclic level like that suggested by Booij and Rubach (1987). Halle and Mohanan do state that 'stratum 2, unlike strata 1 and 3, is a non-cyclic stratum' (1985: 96); however, they produce no arguments for the cyclicity of Stratum 3, and do not even broach the subject with regard to Stratum 4. The only reason for assuming that they regard Strata 3 and 4 as cyclic is their remark that 'given that at least some strata have to be cyclic, the null hypothesis would be that all lexical strata in all languages are cyclic' (1985: 67); thus, evidence must be produced to establish the non-cyclic nature of a stratum, but not to establish that it is cyclic. Cyclicity is the default value for lexical strata.

In fact, however, there are good reasons to assume that neither Stratum 3 nor Stratum 4 is cyclic. Whereas a large number of English phonological rules seem to apply on Levels 1 and 2 (see Halle and Mohanan 1985: 100), Halle and Mohanan order only one rule, /l/-Resyllabification, on Level 4, and only two, Stem-Final Tensing (Dialect C) and Stem-Final Lengthening (Dialect B) on Level 3. Mohanan (1986) additionally argues for Sonorant Resyllabification on Level 4. There is certainly no evidence for cyclic application of /l/-Resyllabification, and an analogue of Stem-Final Tensing, Vowel Tensing, applies on non-cyclic Level 2 in Halle and Mohanan's Dialects A and B, without the discrepancies in operation that might be expected due to cyclic application in some dialects and non-cyclic operation in others. In addition, Stem-Final Tensing violates the SCC, which Halle and Mohanan regard as a constraint on all cyclic strata, by applying in *city, happy*, which are underived and will have undergone no previous processes on the same cycle as the Tensing rule. The same reasoning holds for Stem-Final Lengthening: if Stem-Final Tensing, which feeds the Lengthening rule, were cyclic, then it could create derived environments on the same cycle as Lengthening, which could then apply in *city, happy*. However, we have already established that Tensing is non-cyclic, so that it may not apply on Stratum 3 if this is a cyclic level. In that case, Stem-Final Lengthening also violates SCC, and consequently cannot be cyclic. If Levels 3 and 4 are indeed non-cyclic, this removes one argument against the incorporation of Halle and Mohanan's Strata 2–4 into a single postcyclic stratum.

However, the rules Halle and Mohanan (1985) order on Levels 3 and 4 might still necessitate a separation of Strata 2, 3 and 4, all *non*-cyclic, if they are to apply correctly. I shall now examine this possibility, beginning with Sonorant Resyllabification (2.32), the sole phonological occupant of Halle and Mohanan's Level 4.

(2.32)   cylinder   [sɪlɪndɽ̩]   cylindrical   [sɪlɪndrɪk]̩]

         prism   [prɪzm̩]   prismatic   [prɪzmætɪk]

         simple   [sɪmpl̩]   simply   [sɪmpli]

         twinkle   [twɪŋkl̩]   twinkling (N)   [twɪŋklɪŋ]

The generalisation behind (2.32) is that 'In all dialects of English, a syllabic consonant becomes nonsyllabic when followed by a vowel-initial derivational suffix, whether it is class 1 or class 2' (Mohanan 1986: 32). However, sonorants are not resyllabified across the stems of compounds: a syllabic /l/ surfaces in *double edged*. Mohanan therefore proposes that Stratum 3 (compounding) should be distinguished from Stratum 2 (Class II derivation), and that syllable formation should not reapply at Stratum 3. However, sonorants may resyllabify before vowel-initial inflectional suffixes, giving *doubling* as [dʌblɪŋ] or [dʌbl̩ɪŋ], and *twinkling* as [twɪŋklɪŋ] or [twɪŋkl̩ɪŋ]. Stratum 4 (regular inflection) must therefore be kept separate from Stratum 3 (compounding). Mohanan cannot account for this resyllabification by invoking the syllable formation rules, since these are inapplicable at Stratum 3 and 'the domain of a rule may not contain nonadjacent strata' (Mohanan 1986: 47), and must therefore introduce another rule, given in (2.33).

(2.33)   Sonorant Resyllabification (domain: Stratum 4. Optional)

V → C / __] V

|

[+ cons]

However, Kiparsky (1985: 134–5, fn.2) discusses the same data, but contends that the syllabification facts involving Class II derivational suffixes and inflections are identical: '*hinder#ing, center#ing* are trisyllabic (versus disyllabic level 1 *hindr+ance, centr+al*) to exactly the same extent as noun-forming derivational *-ing* and as the present participle suffix (*John's hindering of NP* and *he was hindering NP*)'.

Kiparsky does admit that speakers may contrast disyllabic *crackling* 'pork fat' with optionally trisyllabic *crackle#ing*, but holds that 'here again the abstract noun and inflectional *-ing* both work the same way and the disyllabic concrete noun in *-ing* is probably best regarded as an unproductive level 1 derivative' (1985: 135).

If Sonorant Resyllabification does operate equivalently with Class II derivational affixes and regular inflections, Mohanan's data can be generated in a model of the lexicon with only two strata, and using only one rule. However, this solution depends crucially on the maintenance of a distinction between affixes and stems in terms of brackets, and on the ability of phonological rules to refer to this distinction. In 2.1.2 above I simply stated that I would follow Kiparsky (1982), who assumes the structures in (2.34) for affixed forms and compounds.

(2.34)   [[...] ...]   = stem plus suffix
[... [...]]   = prefix plus stem
[[...][...]] = compound (stem plus stem)

Kiparsky further assumes that double 'back-to-back' brackets,][, block phonological rules unless they are mentioned in the structural description of the rule, although single brackets do not. I return to this issue below.

In the resulting two-stratum lexicon, compounds, Class II derivation and regular inflection will be ordered on postcyclic Stratum 2, and in terms of brackets, Class II derived items and inflected words will be classed together as against compounds; these alone will contain double internal brackets. If phonological rules are permitted to refer to bracketing configurations, we would expect them to apply to compounds alone, or to all items derived at Stratum 2, or to both types of affixed items, but not to compounds. Sonorant Resyllabification exhibits the last type of behaviour. This rule will apply at Stratum 2, but since the double brackets][will not be specified in its structural description, it will be unable to operate across the stems of compounds. Sonorant Resyllabification does not, then, require more than a two-stratum lexicon.

The same turns out to be true of /l/-Resyllabification, which moves non-syllabic /l/ from the coda of one syllable into the onset of the next. /l/-Resyllabification and /l/-Velarisation, a postlexical rule which 'darkens' /l/ in syllable rhymes, together govern the distribution of clear (palatalised) and dark (velarised) variants of /l/ in English. /l/-Resyllabification produces clear [l] in onset position, and thus bleeds /l/-Velarisation. Both Halle and Mohanan (1985: 65–6) and Mohanan (1986: 35) state that /l/-Resyllabification operates in compounds and across vowel-initial inflections, but not across words. The domain of /l/-Resyllabification must therefore be Stratum 4, in Halle and Mohanan's model.

Neither Halle and Mohanan (1985) nor Mohanan (1986) say whether /l/-Resyllabification applies before vowel-initial derivational suffixes, but informal observations, supported by the data in Bladon and Al-Bamerni (1975), indicate that /l/ is clear in *hellish, dealer, scaly*. If /l/-Resyllabification does operate in the context of Class II derivational suffixes, the process will be allowed to apply freely to all Level 2-derived forms, and all phonological motivation for Stratum 4 is removed.

The version of /l/-Resyllabification discussed above is not, however, the only one. Mohanan (1986: 35) notes that some British English speakers resyllabify /l/ before any vowel-initial suffix, derivational or inflectional, but not across the stems of compounds or across words, where the /l/ will be dark. Mohanan proposes that speakers of these dialects have a slightly different rule of /l/-Resyllabification, which still applies at Level 4, but which requires the presence of double morphological brackets; given Mohanan's system of bracketing, these double brackets will be present at Stratum 4 in inflected words, but will have been removed medially in compounds by Bracket Erasure at the end of Stratum 3.

However, Mohanan's rule also prevents /l/-Resyllabification from applying before vowel-initial derivational suffixes, since these are attached prior to Stratum 4 in Mohanan's model and their internal brackets will equally have been deleted. Unfortunately, Mohanan (1986: 35) actually says that /l/ is clear for these speakers before vowel-initial derivational suffixes. It is hard to see how this is to be resolved in a four-stratum lexicon, without proposing a domain for /l/-Resyllabification consisting of non-adjacent strata.

No such difficulties arise, however, within a two-stratum lexical model, provided that we allow phonological rules to be blocked by morphological bracketing and that compounds are differentiated from affixal formations in terms of bracketing configurations: these requirements were also necessary for the correct application of Sonorant Resyllabification. /l/-Resyllabification will then be a postcyclic, Level 2 rule which will apply in one set of English dialects in all forms derived at Level 2, i.e. in Class II derived, inflected and compound forms. In a second set of (British) English dialects, /l/-Resyllabification will be formulated so as to exploit the difference in morphological structure between derived and inflected forms on one hand and compounds on the other, and will not apply across the double internal brackets of compounds, since these will not be specified in the structural description of the rule.

We turn finally to Stem-Final Tensing and Lengthening, which Halle and Mohanan (1985: 59–62) use as evidence for the separation of Levels 2 and 3, and which are intended to account for the treatment of underlying /ɪ/ in four unidentified dialects (see (2.35)).

(2.35)	Dialect	A	B	C	D
word-final:	city	ī	īy	ī	ɪ
before inflections:	cities	ī	īy	ī	ɪ
stem-final in compounds:	city hall	ī	īy	ī	ɪ
before Class II affixes (not -ly, -ful):	happiness	ī	ī	ɪ	ɪ

In Dialect D, stem-final /ɪ/ is never tensed or lengthened. In Dialects A and B, Stem-Final Tensing takes place in all the environments in (2.35); Halle and Mohanan order this rule on Stratum 2 for these dialects. However, /ɪ/ does not tense in Dialect C before Class II derivational suffixes, and [ī] in Dialect B does not lengthen, or diphthongise, in this environment. Stem-Final Tensing (Dialect C) and Stem-Final Lengthening (Dialect B) cannot apply on Level 2, since they would then produce *[hæpīnɛs] and *[hæpīynɛs]. Halle and Mohanan assign these rules instead to Stratum 3, where the appropriate vowel before Class II derivational suffixes will no longer be constituent-final due to Bracket Erasure.

In a two-stratum lexical phonology, non-cyclic Stem-Final Lengthening and Tensing would be ordered on Level 2, and would thus be expected to apply in Class II derived forms, inflected words and compounds; or, if sensitive to bracketing differences, in both sets of affixed forms but not compounds; or in compounds alone. However, there is no way, in terms of brackets, to distinguish compounds and inflected forms from words with Class II derivational suffixes.

Although Halle and Mohanan take this problem as decisive evidence for the necessity of a Stratum 2 versus 3 distinction in English, the difficulty may not be as insurmountable as it seems. Borowsky (1990: 250), for instance, questions the motivation for proposing separate rules of Stem-Final Lengthening and Tensing. She notes that Halle and Mohanan separate these processes because tensed vowels supposedly need not lengthen; thus *theses*, [θīysīyz], with a long vowel in the final syllable, may contrast with *cities*, [sɪtīz], in which the second vowel has been tensed but not lengthened. Borowsky attributes this difference instead to 'a phonetic difference from the stress' (1990: 251) – the greater length of the second vowel of *theses* is due to the fact that this word has two stressed syllables, while *cities* has only one. Furthermore, Borowsky challenges Halle and Mohanan's assumption that, in their Dialect B, lengthening fails before Class II derivational suffixes, asserting instead that lengthening/tensing will operate in *happiness*, *city*, *cities* and *city hall*, but that 'perceptually the length is more salient in absolute word-final position, or preceding tautosyllabic voiced consonants, as in *cities*, where we know there is an independent phonetic lengthening effect' (1990: 253).

Borowsky also dismisses Halle and Mohanan's contention that the failure of Stem-Final Tensing in *happiness* in Dialect C necessitates a distinction between Level 2 (Class II derivation) and Level 3 (compounding). She points out that -*ly* and -*ful* are already exceptions to their rule, and suggests that 'dialect C is one in which a few more of the level 2 affixes block tensing' (1990: 252): -*ness* at least must be added to the list, although owing to the lack of information in Halle and Mohanan (1985) it is not possible to say whether all Level 2 derivational suffixes behave in this way in Dialect C.

Even if we do not accept Borowsky's reinterpretation, the facts of Stem-Final Tensing and Lengthening are clearly amenable to reanalysis: these two rules then constitute very meagre justification for a stratal distinction, especially one with such far-reaching consequences, since if Halle and Mohanan are right, we must accept that the number of strata in a language cannot be restricted in any principled way, and that cyclic and non-cyclic strata may be interspersed. In addition, Halle and Mohanan's data on Stem-Final Lengthening and Tensing are based only on 'an informal survey' (1985: 59); no experimental findings are presented and the four dialects discussed are never identified or localised. It is no wonder that Kaisse and Shaw (1985: 24) regard the rules involved as 'probably subject to alternative explanations or indeed to disagreement over the basic facts'.

Finally, Halle and Mohanan's account itself suffers from problems and inconsistencies. First, they assign Stem-Final Tensing (Dialect C) and Stem-Final Lengthening (Dialect B) to Stratum 3, although they consider Stratum 3 to be cyclic, and Stem-Final Lengthening and Tensing both violate SCC. Furthermore, they represent the output of Stem-Final Lengthening in Dialect B as [īy]; however, as a lengthening rule, this process should produce the long monophthong [ii]. The only rule which could then produce [īy] is Diphthongisation (Halle and Mohanan 1985: 79), which transforms long uniform vowels into vowel plus offglide structures. However, Halle and Mohanan argue that Diphthongisation is a Stratum 2 rule, and since they propose no phonological loop between Levels 2 and 3, it follows that, if Stem-Final Lengthening operates on Level 3, the correct output cannot be derived. If, on the other hand, we assume a two-stratum lexicon, Stem-Final Lengthening can apply on Level 2, feeding Diphthongisation (although in fact these rules will be much more radically revised in subsequent chapters).

It seems, then, that evidence adduced by Halle and Mohanan and Mohanan (1986) for a four-stratum lexical phonology and morphology of English can be refuted, and that the adoption of a two-stratum lexical model (along the lines of Booij and Rubach 1987) can be recommended. However, certain phonological rules in such a revised model will only apply correctly if compounds and affixed forms are differentiated in terms of brackets, and if the phonology is permitted to refer to these morphological distinctions.

Recall that Kiparsky (1982) assumes distinct morphological structures for prefixed forms, suffixed forms and compounds, as shown in (2.34). He also holds that morphological brackets may trigger or block phonological rules. However, Mohanan and Mohanan (1984), Halle and Mohanan (1985) and Mohanan (1986) all disagree with one or both of these assumptions, arguing that compounds and derived or inflected forms are identical in terms of bracketing, or that, even if there are different bracket configurations, phonological rules may not be blocked by them.

Before proceeding to a discussion of the main arguments for and against Kiparsky's position, we should look briefly at the sources of these competing theories of bracketing. In SPE, brackets marking morphosyntactic concatenation were seen as quite separate entities from the phonological boundaries +, # and =, which were units in the segmental string, distinguished from vowels and consonants only by the presence of the specification [−segment] in their distinctive feature matrices. Of the three SPE boundaries, + and # are said to be universal, and are inserted into representations by convention; the formative boundary, +, appears at the beginning and end of each morpheme, while #, the word boundary, borders lexical or higher categories. + and # thus coincide with morphosyntactic brackets. There are also language-specific boundary-weakening processes changing # to +, motivated for instance by inadequacies in the stress rules. The third boundary, =, appears only after the Latinate prefixes *de-*, *per-*, *con-*, *inter-* and so on, and 'is introduced by special rules which are part of the derivational morphology of English' (Chomsky and Halle 1968: 371), again due primarily to wrong predictions made by the stress rules. For instance, Chomsky and Halle represent the verbs *advocate* and *interdict* as [ad=voc+ate] and [inter=dict], and modify the Alternating Stress Rule to operate across = when it appears between the second and third syllables from the end of the word, but not when it separates the penultimate and final syllables.

As for the property of blocking and triggering phonological rules, Chomsky and Halle argue that all boundaries may trigger rules, and that + alone typically fails to block them, since any string in the structural description of a process which contains no instances of the formative boundary is taken as a schema for other strings identical but for the presence of any number of occurrences of +. Thus, the cycle in SPE operates within domains bounded by #＿#, disregarding any intervening +. In fact, the formative boundary may block rules, but to achieve this, 'we must resort to certain auxiliary devices ... thus adding to the complexity of the grammar' (Chomsky and Halle 1968: 67, fn.10).

The SPE theory of boundaries is clearly quite unconstrained; novel boundaries like = can be introduced on a language-specific basis, and boundaries can be interchanged to forestall problems in the rule system, while no account is taken of the fact that + and # coincide with morphosyntactic concatenation markers. Subsequent developments can be seen largely as attempts to remedy these shortcomings.

Siegel (1974, 1980) reduces the number of permitted boundaries to two, the word and morpheme boundaries. = is replaced by +, on the grounds that 'the real generalisation governing stress retraction in Latinate-prefixed verbs has nothing to do with the boundary with which the prefix is introduced. Rather, it seems to be the case that stress does not retract off stems in verbs where the stem is the final formative' (1974: 117).

Siegel correctly predicts that stress retraction will operate in *advocate* but not in *interdict*. She also, as we have seen, proposes a division into Class I, Latinate affixes which may attach to stems or words, affect stress placement, and are introduced with +; and Class II, predominantly Germanic affixes which attach only to words, are stress-neutral (but potentially stress-sensitive) and include # as part of their representation.

Siegel's account involves morphosyntactic brackets as well as phonological boundaries. However, following the introduction of level-ordering by Allen (1978), Strauss (1979) argues against any distinctions among phonological boundaries for English, since the ordering of Class I affixation and the stress rules on Level 1, and of Class II derivation on Level 2, now allows for the different interactions of the two sets of affixes with stress, without reference to word versus morpheme boundary. Strauss equates the single residual boundary with the morphosyntactic bracket. Finally, Strauss accepts Aronoff's (1976) system of bracketing, in which affixes are not independently bracketed, rather than Siegel's, in which affixes and stems are identically delimited by [], on the grounds that, in Aronoff's theory, ' "][" will be unambiguously interpreted as signifying a word-terminal position ... With the richer bracketing possibilities of Siegel's system, "][" can be interpreted as a juncture between *any* two formatives' (Strauss 1979: 395). Here we see the origin of the divergence of the two current bracketing theories, those of Siegel, Halle and Mohanan and Mohanan, versus Aronoff, Strauss and Kiparsky.

Mohanan and Mohanan (1984) accept Kiparsky's proposal that compounds differ from affixed forms morphologically, and that this difference can be encoded using brackets; and they agree that such brackets are preferable to the multiplicity of boundary symbols found in SPE. However, they argue that 'morphological brackets may trigger phonological rules, but not block them' (1984: 578): although brackets may be present in the structural description of a rule to cause it to operate, 'the effect of boundaries "blocking" phonological rules is achieved by stipulating the domain of the relevant rule to be a stratum prior to the morphological concatenation across which the rule is inapplicable' (1984: 598).

Mohanan and Mohanan present no evidence or arguments for this assertion that morphological bracketing is only partially accessible to the phonology, and the same is true of Halle and Mohanan (1985). Halle and

Mohanan do not distinguish compounds from affixed forms, proposing the structure [[...][...]] for both, but their only justification for dropping Kiparsky's distinction is that they 'see no reason to distinguish between compounding and affixation in terms of bracketing' (1985: 60). Halle and Mohanan's separation of Strata 2, 3 and 4 for English is a reminder that they do indeed see reason for such a distinction, albeit differently encoded.

Mohanan (1986), who, like Halle and Mohanan, uses the same bracketing for compounds and derived or inflected forms, provides the only real arguments against Kiparsky's and Strauss's proposal; but even these are not strong. Mohanan's arguments are intended to support two stipulations: first, he asserts that 'morphological brackets are incapable of blocking rules' (1986: 20) and secondly, that 'if a grammar has to distinguish between compounding and affixation, it may do so by making a stratal distinction, but not by making a distinction in terms of brackets' (1986: 128).

Mohanan's first two arguments are that a theory which does not distinguish X]Y from X][Y is more restrictive than one which does, and that, even given such a distinction, a theory allowing brackets to block phonological rules is less restrictive than one which disallows this. However, we have already seen that a two-stratum model of the lexicon, with only one cyclic and one postcyclic level, has various advantages over Mohanan's four-level model. If Mohanan is correct, we must accept that a theory allowing, in principle, an infinite number of lexical strata with cyclic and non-cyclic strata arbitrarily interspersed is more restrictive than one which permits only two lexical levels, but allows the phonology to make reference to independently necessary morphological brackets.

Mohanan's contention that brackets may not block phonological rules can be traced back to the SPE distinction of the non-blocking formative boundary from other boundaries, which could both trigger and block rules. Like Chomsky and Halle, Mohanan does not deny that boundaries may appear to block rules, but chooses to encode this blocking via stratification rather than allowing phonological processes to make direct reference to morphosyntactic brackets. The fact that Mohanan allows brackets to trigger but not block rules in this way is merely a stipulation which in no way follows from the tenets of the theory; this is amply demonstrated by the existence of a completely opposing situation in Natural Generative Phonology, where Hooper (1976: 15) asserts that non-phonological boundaries like the word and morpheme boundaries may block rules but not condition them. Mohanan (1986: 143) attempts a justification, claiming that 'saying that the presence of brackets, which represent the concatenation and hierarchical structure of forms, can block phonological rules ... is as conceptually incoherent as saying that the presence of features like [+ noun] can block the application of phonological rules unless mentioned by the structural description'. But this objection can also be countered, for two reasons. First, why should the presence of morphological brackets in a phonological rule be admissible if they are to trigger it, but 'conceptually incoherent' if they are to stop it? Secondly, it is clear that phonological rules must be able to refer to some kinds of morphological information – indeed, one of Mohanan's own criteria for the separation of lexical and postlexical rules is that lexical rules require access to such morphological information, while postlexical operations never do – and again it seems inexplicable that a phonological rule can be sensitive (as Halle and Mohanan's Velar Softening rule is) to the presence of a feature like [+ Latinate], which refers to an etymologically motivated division of the vocabulary peculiar to English, but not to morphological brackets, which encode a putatively universal distinction of stems from affixes.

Mohanan (1986: 21) points out that, given his stipulation that blocking involves ordering on an earlier level, it is impossible for Level 1 morpheme boundaries to block rules, capturing the SPE generalisation that the behaviour of + is different from that of other boundaries. However, Mohanan does not recognise separate boundaries like the + and # of SPE, but only morphosyntactic brackets, which are of the form] and [on all levels. He is then forced into the general statement that brackets may not block phonological rules, in effect making all brackets exceptional to accord with the exceptionality of brackets on Level 1.

It seems preferable to say that phonological rules may refer to morphological bracketing, which may either condition or block them at all levels of the lexicon, but with the proviso that Level 1 bracketing in English does not block rules. The effect of such blocking is actually achieved by the cyclic nature of Stratum 1 and the operation of the SCC, which in my model, like that of Booij and Rubach (1987), will be restricted to the earliest lexical level. This insight, however, is lost in Mohanan's framework, since he allows cyclic and non-cyclic strata to be randomly interspersed, and does not regard Level 1 as the sole cyclic level. At the moment, we have insufficient cross-linguistic data to verify that Level 1 brackets universally fail to block rules; this may relate to the putative universality of Booij and Rubach's model, which similarly is yet to be ascertained.

We return now to the question of whether prefixation, suffixation and compounding should be differentiated, as Kiparsky and Strauss advocate, or whether the representation [[...][...]] should be adopted for both affixation and compounding, as suggested by Halle and Mohanan (1985) and Mohanan (1986). Mohanan's argument here is that bracket notation encodes constituent structure, incorporating information on order of concatenation, linearity and categories: bracketing therefore corresponds to tree-diagram notation. Mohanan then notes that representations like [[[X]Y]Z] or [[X[Y]]Z] have no tree-structure counterparts, and argues that this 'means either that brackets are not a notational equivalent of trees, or that the representations ... are illegitimate' (1986: 129). Since Mohanan is committed to the equivalence of brackets and trees, he must draw the second conclusion; and since the potentially illegitimate representations match Kiparsky's notation for a stem with two suffixes (e.g. *hopelessness*) and a stem with one prefix and one suffix (e.g. *unsafeness*) respectively, Kiparsky's bracketing system must be abandoned if Mohanan's argument holds.

However, Mohanan's case rests on the assertion that Kiparsky's bracketing configurations have no tree-diagram equivalents; the provision of just such hierarchical representations by Strauss (1982) consequently robs it of much of its force. Strauss proposes representations like a., b. and c., in (2.36) below as the tree and bracket configurations corresponding to inflection, derivation and compounding respectively.

(2.36)   a. *inflection*
         suffixation

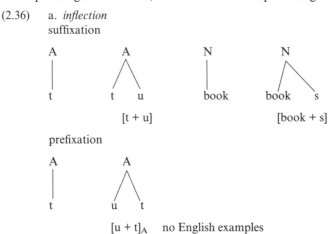

prefixation

[u + t]_A   no English examples

b. *derivation*
suffixation

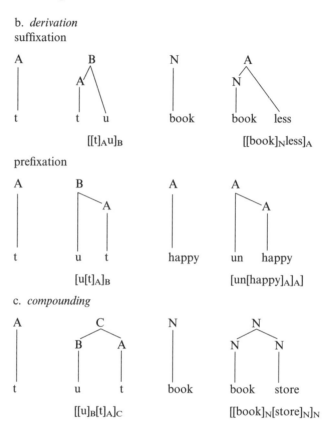

prefixation

c. *compounding*

If these correspondences are accepted, Kiparsky's bracketings [[[X]Y]Z] (*hopelessness*) and [[X[Y]]Z] (*unsafeness*), which Mohanan claimed cannot be assigned tree-diagram counterparts, can be paired with the hierarchical structures in (2.37).

(2.37)

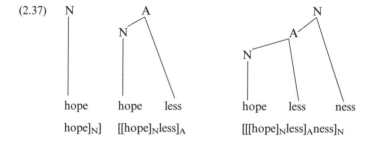

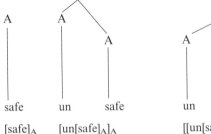

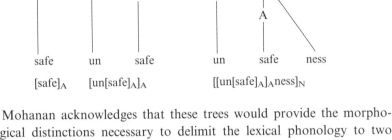

Mohanan acknowledges that these trees would provide the morphological distinctions necessary to delimit the lexical phonology to two levels, at least for English. However, he objects to Strauss's model, Lexicalist Phonology, and to his introduction of inflectional representations entirely lacking internal bracketing. The first objection is irrelevant here, as Strauss's hierarchical representations can be accepted in isolation from his framework. The second seems more justifiable. Strauss proposes bracketings like [book s] for *books*, to indicate both that *-s* is a bound element, like all derivational and inflectional affixes, and that it does not cause a category change; in Strauss's view, additional external brackets serve only to show a categorial reassignment. However, his representation loses the generalisation that stems and words, like *book* in this case, are always autonomously bracketed, and makes it necessary for him to include the symbol +, giving [book + s], simply to show that two formatives are present.

I propose that inflection and derivation should instead be represented equivalently, as b. in (2.36) above, and that the category-changing versus category-maintaining parameter should be regarded as less significant, since it is not the case that all derivational affixation entails an alteration of category; for instance, prefixation of *un-* to an adjective produces a (negative) adjective. The resulting tree and bracket notations, which are equivalent to those of Kiparsky (1982), are given in (2.38) below.

(2.38)   a. *affixation – derivational and inflectional*
         prefixation

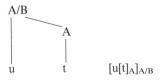

suffixation

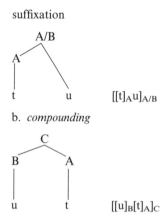

$[[t]_A u]_{A/B}$

b. *compounding*

$[[u]_B [t]_A]_C$

If this is not yet sufficiently conclusive, further evidence against Mohanan's representations of both compounding and affixation as [[…][…]] comes from Selkirk (1982a). Selkirk uses Kiparsky's system of bracketing, although she denies direct access of phonological rules to such brackets. Instead, affixes are marked with the special category label Af, while stems and words receive a lexical category symbol such as N, V or A. However, Selkirk's arguments equally support a theory which does permit the morphological concatenation operators to block and condition rules.

Selkirk argues that, for two main reasons, affixes and stems/words, and hence affixed items and compounds, must be differentiated in morphological structure, either using brackets and category labels, or brackets alone. First, she asserts that 'compound words do not have the same phonology as affixed words' (1982a: 123), a contention supported for English in respect of the rules discussed in 2.2.4 above, as well as the stress rules. Such rules, which 'apply to, or interpret, morphological structures … must "know" whether a morpheme is an affix or not'; and clearly, this difference can be encoded via bracketing.

Secondly, Selkirk (1982a: 123) argues that, if compounding and derivational affixation involved fundamentally the same word-formation process, 'the word-structure rules required for generating affixed words would be the same as those generating compound words'. For derivationally affixed forms, Selkirk proposes the rules shown in (2.39). In Mohanan's model, where affixes are effectively regarded as stems/words, these would have to be replaced by the rules in (2.40), to accord with those for compounding: but actual compounds of the form generable by the rules in (2.40) do not exist in English.

(2.39) a. $V \rightarrow N\ V_{Af}$ (e.g. atom-ise)
   $= [\ ]_N \rightarrow [[\ ]_N\ V_{Af}]_V$
   b. $V \rightarrow A\ V_{Af}$ (e.g. soft-en)
   $= [\ ]_A \rightarrow [[\ ]_A\ V_{Af}]_V$
   c. $A \rightarrow V\ A_{Af}$ (e.g. fidget-y)
   $= [\ ]_V \rightarrow [[\ ]_V\ A_{Af}]_A$

(2.40) a. $V \rightarrow N\ V$
   $= [\ ]_N \rightarrow [[\ ]_N[\ ]_V]_V$
   b. $V \rightarrow A\ V$
   $= [\ ]_A \rightarrow [[\ ]_A[\ ]_V]_V$
   c. $A \rightarrow V\ A$
   $= [\ ]_V \rightarrow [[\ ]_V[\ ]_A]_A$

Finally, Mohanan's morphological organisation follows Lieber (1981), who assumes that affixes are lexically stored with major word class categories, and are the heads of words, so that these categories will be transferred to the eventual word by feature percolation. However, Miller (1985) and Corbett, Fraser and McGlashan (1993) argue that the concept of head does not generalise easily from syntax to morphology, while Zwicky (1985) defends the traditional viewpoint of stems as major elements and affixes as minor markers of insertion rules, arguing that 'the apparently determinant formative in affixal derivation is merely a concomitant of the operation' (1985: 25). Lieber's system also arguably belongs to the Item-and-Arrangement school of morphology (Hockett 1954), and is therefore subject to the familiar criticisms of this model reiterated in Matthews (1974) and Miller (1985). For instance, feature percolation can cope reasonably well with linear, agglutinative operations, but Lieber is forced to introduce further powerful mechanisms in the form of string-dependent lexical transformations to deal with reduplication and other non-concatenative processes of word-formation; see Bauer (1990) for further limitations of percolation. Giegerich (in press) adopts a position intermediate between Mohanan and Kiparsky here, arguing that stems and affixes are lexically stored; that affixation on Level 2 is achieved by Kiparsky-type rules, but on Level 1 by listing; but that roots, prefixes and suffixes are crucially distinguished by bracketing. This has some repercussions for the constraints of LP, to be discussed in 2.3.5 below, but does not challenge my adoption of Kiparsky's bracketing representations, or the assumption that brackets may block and condition phonological rules. A two-stratum model of the lexicon, incorporating these assumptions, will be adopted in the chapters below.

2.3.4   *Structure Preservation and underspecification*

One of the major constraints originally proposed for the lexical component of LP is Structure Preservation, defined by Kiparsky (1985: 87) as

> the result of constraints operating over the entire lexicon. For example, if a certain feature is non-distinctive, we shall say that it may not be specified in the lexicon. This means that it may not figure in non-derived lexical items, nor be introduced by any lexical rule, and therefore may not play any role at all in the lexical phonology.

Borowsky (1990: 29) slightly redefines SP, to make it more obviously relevant to issues of syllabification, tone and other prosodic phenomena, rather than apparently limited to segmentals; her version was given in (2.20) above, repeated below as (2.41).

(2.41)   Structure Preservation:
Lexical rules may not mark features which are non-distinctive, nor create structures which do not conform to the basic prosodic templates of the language.

As Kaisse and Hargus (1993: 11) note, 'The basic concept of structure preservation is a simple one, though ... its proper technical instantiation may be anything but that.' Although it may seem straightforward to require that the underlying and lexical segment inventories and sets of prosodic structures should be isomorphic, with allophones and novel structures derived postlexically, this simple version of SP turns out not to be tenable. Notably, Borowsky (1989, 1990) and Harris (1987) present evidence that SP must switch off at the final lexical level. For instance, Borowsky (1989) argues that only two rhymal positions are permitted in syllables until the end of Level 1, thus necessitating CC shortening in *kept*, *dreamt*, *depth*, but not in Level 2 derived *dreamed*, *deeply*. Harris (1987) considers various South-Eastern Bantu languages, where half-close and half-open vowels are in regular harmonic alternation and thus non-distinctive, but the relevant vowel harmony rules must be lexical. Similarly, Kaisse and Hargus (1994) review arguments that assimilation rules creating linked structures are exempt from SP. However, they show that not all such rules violate SP, and that those which do are consistently word level rules. Hence, allowing SP to switch off at the final lexical level accounts for the cases raised by Borowsky, Harris, and Kaisse and Hargus. This coheres with Borowsky's (1990: 23–4) contention that Level 2 displays 'vaguely split loyalties'. If we accept the Booij and Rubach model, with Level 2 as non-cyclic, both SP and SCC will be limited to Level 1. Level 2 will then be a bridge between the maximally lexical Level

1, and the postlexicon: its lexical properties follow from its interaction with the morphology, while its phonological sympathies are postlexical. This does leave the problem raised in 2.3.1 above, that some postlexical rules have also been claimed to be structure preserving. In this context, and to test the assumption that SP switches off at Level 2, and the possible reasons for this, we shall return to SP from time to time below. Notably, in chapters 4–6, I shall present evidence which suggests that newly lexicalised rules may violate SP. Such violation of the constraint is therefore a diagnostic of a process which has recently progressed from postlexical to lexical application; and furthermore, it is possible that the reassertion of SP may dictate the future direction of change in such a case.

There remains, however, one serious challenge to SP – and indeed, to other constraints of the lexical component like SCC, the topic of the next section. This challenge is the use of underspecification.

Although underspecification and LP are technically independent of one another, many proponents of LP argue against fully specified lexical entries. As Kiparsky (1982: 53) observes, the assumption of under-specification will allow cyclic, lexical rules to apply on the first cycle to fill in feature specifications; this will not violate SCC, since such rules will introduce features rather than producing clashing feature specifica-tions. Redundancy rules and morpheme structure rules, given this hypothesis, are simply rules of the lexical phonology applying under special circumstances.

Underspecification has a great deal of unexplored potential; as Kaisse and Hargus (1993: 15) say, 'It is apparent that while no one is yet able to agree on exactly how underspecification works, it is a powerful tool.' Not all of this power will be welcome in a theory which is intended to impose and explore constraints on phonological abstractness. For instance, it appears that underspecification makes it extremely difficult to assess the operation of SP. Borowsky (1990: 30) claims that 'if the segment /x/ is not a phoneme of English, there is no occurrence of it, or a partially specified form of it, anywhere in the lexicon' (at least, as Borowsky's discussion makes clear, until SP switches off at Level 2). However, if underlying representations can be maximally underspecified, it is unclear how we can tell what is a partially specified form of /x/ and what is not, especially given Borowsky's assumption (1990: 106) that different par-tially specified underliers may merge on the surface once all features have been filled in. To check that SP is not about to be contravened, we would then have to take all potentially eligible underlying segments, put them through all phonological and default rules, and see if [x] appears as the output and on what level it is derived.

However, SP is not the only constraint defused by the use of underspecification. For example, Borowsky (1990: 49) considers the *ruki* rule of Sanskrit, where /s/ retroflexes after /r u k i/. Retroflexes do appear in underived environments, but the SCC is specifically designed to prevent free rides, and should stop the *ruki* rule from applying here. However, Borowsky makes use of the limitation of SCC to structure-changing rules, and of underspecification, to effectively neutralise the constraint: if the underlying representations of forms with surface retroflexes are left unspecified for [retroflex], a blank-filling version of *ruki* can apply without contravening SCC. Borowsky produces similar analyses of Velar Softening (1990: 130) and s-Voicing in English. She does concede that 'abstractness moves into the system by the use of partially specified segments' (1990: 54), but seems unconcerned by this. Indeed, considering the possibility that rules might be stopped from applying in underived environments, she notes that 'This is simply to miss a generalization from my point of view' (1990: 73). It is at best frustrating that we should impose constraints to force a non-abstract analysis, which can then almost infallibly be circumvented by underspecification. Borowsky has noticed this interaction, but her conclusion is that SCC should be done away with, on the grounds that it does so little work, as 'the use of underspecification removes many classic cases which motivated the SCC' (1990: 28). My view is that this is not an argument against SCC, but against underspecification as part of a Lexical Phonology.

I shall therefore exclude underspecification for the time being, and will return to a detailed account of its place in LP in chapter 5. For the moment, discussions of phonological rules will be clearer if it is obvious that I am dealing with feature-changing rather than blank-filling or default applications. Furthermore, since I shall be arguing for a model of LP in which the constraints, particularly SCC but also SP, are of central importance on synchronic and diachronic grounds, it makes no sense to assume underspecification, which bleeds the SCC and makes the operation of SP opaque. Let us first see what these constraints can achieve unimpeded.

2.3.5   *The Strict Cyclicity Condition*

Unquestionably the most important constraint of LP is the SCC, which restricts cyclic rules to derived environments, and therefore blocks free rides. However, the history of the SCC, and various problems with its formulation and operation, indicate that it may best be replaced by a modified version, in the form of the Derived Environment Condition, and perhaps supplemented by other, associated restrictions in LP.

The SCC originates in Kiparsky's (1973) Alternation Condition, which prohibited obligatory neutralisation rules from applying to all occurrences of a morpheme, hence limiting such rules to alternating forms. This condition, however, was not statable as a formal condition on grammars, so that the entire output of a grammar would have to be checked for coherence with it. Other, equally stipulative conditions with approximately the same intended force were proposed at around the same period. For instance, Lass and Anderson (1975: 231) attempt to 'define the constraints on permissible lexical abstractness and extra-paradigmatic rule extension' using the formal statement in (2.42) (which they say is based on a suggestion by Bob Stockwell).

(2.42) a. Let there be a class P of formatives containing the phones p_i, p_j (where $p_i \neq p_j$), of which it is true that $p_i \sim p_j$; and the rule R which produces the alternation $p_i \sim p_j$ is well motivated.
 b. Let there be potential classes, P_i, P_j, in which any morpheme $m_i \in P_i$ contains P_i, and any morpheme $m_j \in P_j$ contains p_j, and it is not true that $p_i \sim p_j$ in either class.
 c. If the classes P_i, P_j are empty, i.e. it is always the case that $p_i \sim p_j$, then there is only one lexical representation /p/ occurring in all formatives that are members of P, and the rule R is a function $R(p \rightarrow p_i)$ for some contexts, and a function $R(p \rightarrow p_j)$ for the others.
 d. If either P_i or P_j or both are non-empty, i.e. there is at least one class where p_i or p_j appears, but it is not true that $p_i \sim p_j$, then the non-empty class or classes must have separate lexical representations /p_i/ or /p_j/. And this is so even if the rule R which is well motivated for the alternation-class P could map some segment /p/ into p_i or p_j with no complication of the grammar.

As Lass and Anderson (1975: 231) paraphrase it, this condition means that 'if any phone appears in a non-alternating form, it must be lexical in that form. No segment then which appears in non-alternating forms may not be lexical.' This, they point out, is the inverse of Kiparsky's Strong Alternation Condition: whereas the Strong Alternation Condition prohibits segments which do not appear phonetically from underlying representations, Lass and Anderson's condition requires segments which appear in non-alternating surface forms to be present underlyingly in those forms, even if theoretically derivable by a free ride through a rule formulated for alternating forms.

Like the Alternation Condition, however, Lass and Anderson's proposal permits the single underlier in alternating forms, /p/, to be differentially derived to [pᵢ] and [pⱼ] in the two shapes of an alternating pair like, say, *divine* and *divinity*, where the underlier consequently need not be identical to either surface form. Kiparsky (1982) took a step towards more surface-true representations even in alternating forms by formulating the Revised Alternation Condition, which restricts neutralisation rules to derived environments; this is then further recast as the Strict Cyclicity Condition.

Kiparsky's main argument for the SCC is that it 'does not have to be stipulated in the theory. A version of it is deducible from the Elsewhere Condition' (Kiparsky 1982: 46). This deduction rests on the assumption that each lexical entry, as well as the output of every morphological process, is an identity rule. If we accept this, then, in the case of Trisyllabic Laxing (see 2.1.2 above), the rules /nītVngæl/ and TSL will be disjunctive by the EC: the structural description of the identity rule properly includes that of TSL, and the result of applying them would be different, since TSL would give a lax vowel where /nītVngæl/ specifies a tense one.

Kiparsky therefore argues that these two constraints are subsumed by 'the essentially trivial Elsewhere Condition, which may conceivably be reducible to a more general cognitive principle' (Kiparsky 1982: 58). Mohanan and Mohanan (1984), however, challenge this conclusion, on the grounds that Kiparsky's identity rules lack independent motivation. Furthermore, Kiparsky gives no reason why his identity rules should be limited to Level 1; unless this restriction applies, we would expect SCC to operate throughout the lexicon, while in fact it seems to be violated freely on Level 2.

A stratagem for deriving SCC from EC without badly motivated identity rules has now been promoted by Giegerich (1988, in press). Giegerich adopts Selkirk's (1982a) hypothesis that Stratum 1 affixation operates on roots, while Stratum 2 processes require words, and proposes a general Root → Word rule (2.43) which performs the conversion necessary to allow Stratum 1 forms to be input to Stratum 2.

(2.43)   [ ]ᵣ → [[ ]ᵣ]ᴸ   (where L = N, V, A)

Since roots are acceptable only on Level 1, Root → Word rules can apply only here; Giegerich argues that (2.43) will be the final process on Level 1. If Level 1 is the sole cyclic stratum, then the link of application in derived environments and cyclicity remains. However, this connection may be purely fortuitous: SCC may not be a property of cyclic rules at all, but of non-final strata. We might then choose to rechristen it the Derived Environment Condition (DEC).

This line of argument is also followed by Cole (1995), who points out that SCC has two components. First, there is the DEC. Secondly, there is what Cole (1995: 72) calls the Reaching Back Constraint, which 'prevents a cyclic rule R applying on cycle j from reaching back inside an earlier cycle i to apply to a string contained wholly within cycle i'. Cole points out that very few analyses in LP have made use of the Reaching Back Constraint, and argues that those which do are subject to reanalysis, or have been pre-empted by more recent phonological developments. Cole further argues that the DEC, the remaining portion of the earlier SCC, should be replaced by the earlier Revised Alternation Condition. This would capture the connection with derived environments, but would be a stronger constraint as it would not be limited to Level 1, or even to the lexicon, but might be expected to hold of all neutralisation rules throughout the phonology. As this condition seems too strong to deal with the behaviour of many postlexical rules, Cole proposes to limit the Revised Alternation Condition to the lexicon by exploiting the lexical interaction of morphology and phonology, and restricting neutralisation rules to *morphologically* derived environments. She accepts that this is stipulative, but points out that there is empirical support for the move, since 'in the two decades of research since the proposal of the Revised Alternation Condition, many examples have been cited in which rules apply only across a morpheme boundary, yet there have been no additional examples in which a derived environment can be created morpheme-internally by the prior application of a phonological rule' (1995: 76). I shall show in chapter 3 that the Vowel Shift Rules of Modern English constitute just such examples, so that the DEC will have to be stated independently of the Revised Alternation Condition (whether or not it is derivable from the EC). The question then is whether the DEC and some version of the Alternation Condition are both required, or whether we need only the former.

Giegerich (in press) argues that there is a place in LP for the Alternation Condition as well as the DEC. He follows Kiparsky (1982: 36), who sees the Alternation Condition as 'a strategy of language acquisition which says that a learner analyzes a form "at face value" unless he has encountered variants of it which justify a more remote underlying representation'. Anderson (1981: 530) makes a similar point when he claims that 'the language learner does not hypothesize an underlying form distinct from the observed surface form without some positive evidence to support doing so'. The Alternation Condition, in Giegerich's proposal, is still not a formal condition on grammars, but can be seen as an informal constraint imposed during acquisition. It will, however, be pre-empted by the stronger DEC on Level 1: the Alternation Condition limits neutralisation rules to alternating forms, but permits application in either the derived or underived member of an alternation. On the other hand, DEC enforces application in derived environments only. Thus, the Alternation Condition would allow Vowel Shift in either *divine* or *divinity*, precisely because both exist. As we shall see in the next chapter, DEC would limit Vowel Shift to derived *divinity*, were it to constrain the rule. All of this would mean that the optimally learnable grammar would be one with no structure-changing rules on Level 2. Giegerich (in press) argues that such rules will exist on a temporary basis, prior to relocation on Level 1, and we shall adduce further evidence for this idea in subsequent chapters.

In what follows, I shall assume the following constraints, which replace the SCC, extend some of its effects onto Level 2, and control the shape of possible underlying representations.

- The Derived Environment Condition limits Level 1 rules to derived environments.
- The Alternation Condition, although more stipulative, means we shall limit lexical rules to Level 1 wherever possible, rather than allowing them to apply in non-alternating forms. Level 2 application will be permitted only when there is positive evidence, for instance interaction with the Level 2 morphology.
- Finally, I propose to adopt and strengthen one aspect of Lass and Anderson's suggestion given in (2.42) above. Lass and Anderson assume that, in a class P where $[p_i]$ alternates with $[p_j]$, there will be a single underlier /p/, from which $[p_i]$ and $[p_j]$ will both be derived by rule. Bearing in mind Anderson's (1981: 530) argument that 'the language learner does not hypothesise an underlying form distinct from the observed surface form without some positive evidence to support doing so', and given that learners will generally encounter morphologically underived forms earlier, I assume as a working hypothesis that the underlying

representation for an alternating form will be equivalent to the lexical representation of the underived member of the alternating pair in the first instance. That is, factoring out the effects of postlexical rules, the underlier will necessarily be either /p$_i$/ or /p$_j$/ , whichever appears at the lexical level in the underived form. We will then explore the derivation of the surface forms from this underlier as an initial possibility, before entertaining the option that restructuring has taken place during acquisition to produce an underlier equivalent to the lexical representation of the derived form, or intermediate between the two.

The connection of this last restriction to the Alternation Condition follows from the invocation of learning strategies and the idea of an optimal grammar in acquisitional terms; its links with the DEC will be observed below, in that it will frequently result in the limitation of phonological rules to Level 1. To illustrate these connections, we turn to one of the best-known processes of Modern English segmental phonology, Vowel Shift.

3 Applying the constraints: the Modern English Vowel Shift Rule

3.1 Introduction

The last chapter attempted to strengthen the constraints usually assumed in Lexical Phonology, and to streamline the architecture of the lexical component, reducing it to two levels. However, these alterations were mainly made on general theoretical grounds, and were largely independent of actual phonological analyses. In this chapter, then, we turn to the application of the constraints. Specifically, I shall propose a revised account of the Modern English Vowel Shift Rule (VSR), which adheres to the principles that underlying and lexical representations should be identical in non-alternating and underived forms. This reanalysis will have implications for various other aspects of the English vowel phonology, including the analysis of surface diphthongs, and the derivation of the [jū] sequence, and will furthermore indicate that synchronic rules can differ markedly from the historical changes which originally caused the variation they describe, a hypothesis to be developed in the following chapters. Finally, even given the constraints of LP, dubious cases will inevitably arise. For instance, alternations may exist in a language, but the time depth from the creation of these alternating forms may be so great, and the forms involved so few, that speakers may be unable to discern a synchronically productive pattern. The adoption of a more concrete phonology may enforce a division between those alternations which are derivable by rule from a common underlier and those which are better treated as stored variants, and I shall show below that a less abstract formulation of VSR clarifies the difficult area of supposed 'regularity' for Modern English verbs.

Before turning to VSR, we revisit the vowel system of Halle and Mohanan (1985), which shows the main problems that a revised account of English vowel phonology must confront (see (3.1)).

(3.1)   *short*
          /ɪ/ bit   /ɨ/ venue   /ʊ/ put
          /ɛ/ bet   /ʌ/ but   /o/ baud, shot
          /æ/ bat   /a/ balm   /ɔ/ bomb

          long
          /ī/ divine   /ɨ̄/ profound   /ō/ pool
          /ē/ serene   /ʌ̄/ cube   /ɔ̄/ verbose
          /ǣ/ sane

Halle and Mohanan are primarily concerned with General American, but claim their underlying vowel system is also appropriate for RP; this assignment of a single underlying phonological system to related dialects was a characteristic of SGP which Halle and Mohanan carry over into LP, and which we shall challenge below. As a result of this assumption, Halle and Mohanan propose a single underlying representation for the vowel in *balm*, and one for *bomb*, despite considerable surface variation. Absolute neutralisation means that [jū] in *cube* and [jū] in *venue* are derived from distinct underlying vowels, while all underlyingly tense vowels take a free ride through VSR. The revision of Vowel Shift below will address all these issues, directly or indirectly.

Note first, however, that the terms 'RP' and 'General American' are both to some extent controversial. Gimson (1973: 116) describes RP as 'a somewhat fictional standard [that] has been in existence for centuries and was finally sanctified some forty years ago by the BBC's *Advisory Committee on Spoken English*'. This is of some concern to Ramsaran (1990: 180–1), who comments that 'Since RP is the only accent that I have ever spoken with, I have a subjective conviction that it exists. This is, of course, an indefensibly circular statement. More objectively, I could say that I discovered as an undergraduate that my native accent was fairly accurately described in Gimson (1962).' In a sense, both Gimson and Ramsaran are right. Ohala's (1974) assumption that individual speakers may have different underlying representations, for instance, will render 'somewhat fictional' any system not based on detailed observation of the usage of a single speaker. Yet to make our conclusions interesting and significant, we surely have to extrapolate beyond this detailed level. The fictionality of RP is also assured if we regard it as fixed; the truth is that RP is changing like any other variety, with more conservative versions having, for instance, [ɐ] in *blood and guts* while more innovative ones have [ʌ], and increasing glottalisation of stops among younger speakers contributing to the creation of a continuum with London English. With these caveats in mind, phonologists, phoneticians and sociolinguists still see RP as a useful idealisation: Nolan and Kerswill (1990: 316), for instance, define it as 'the prestige-accent of South East England which also serves as a prestige norm in varying degrees elsewhere in England.' I assume for RP the surface vowel system in (3.2) (excluding for the present vowels before historical /r/, which will be discussed fully in chapter 6), although I shall from time to time refer to other variants.

(3.2)   *short*
[ɪ] bit   [ʊ] put
[ɛ] bet   [ə] about   [ʌ] but
[æ] bat   [ɒ] bomb, frost

long
[i:] serene   [u:] pool   [aɪ] divine
[eɪ] sane   [oʊ] verbose   [aʊ] profound
                              [ɔ:] law   [ɔɪ] boy
                              [ɑ:] balm, glass   [ju:] cube

Similarly, I use 'General American' (GenAm) to refer to a variety with the surface vowel system in (3.3), again with some regional variants which will be discussed below. For the low vowels at least, the system in (3.3) is identical with that of Upstate New York/ Eastern Pennsylvania/ South Midland described by Kurath and McDavid (1961: 7).

(3.3)   *short*
[ɪ] bit   [ʊ] put
[ɛ] bet   [ə] about   [ʌ] but
[æ] bat, glass

long
[i:] serene   [u:] pool   [aɪ] divine
[e:] ~ [eɪ] sane   [o:] ~ [oʊ] verbose   [aʊ] profound
                              [ɔ:] law, frost   [ɔɪ] boy
                              [ɑ:] balm, bomb   [ju:] cube

3.2   The Vowel Shift Rule and the Derived Environment Condition

Chomsky and Halle (1968) first proposed that the phonology of Present-Day English incorporates a synchronic analogue of the Middle English Great Vowel Shift, namely the VSR. Although VSR has subsequently been the focus of much theoretical argument (Goyvaerts and Pullum 1975), and various changes in its formulation have evolved over the years (see Halle 1977, Rubach 1984, Halle and Mohanan 1985), the core of the original SPE rule remains in much post-SPE generative phonology.

In the light of increasingly serious attempts at constraining phonological rules, two major objections must be raised against the SPE version of VSR and its successors in the more recent literature, both involving allegations of excessive abstractness. First, non-surfacing vowels and rules of absolute neutralisation are frequently proposed to ensure the proper application of VSR; for instance, Halle and Mohanan use VSR to produce surface [jū] from back unrounded /ɨ ɨ̄ ʌ/. Secondly, VSR applies to non-alternating forms, which are given free rides through the rule. Thus *divine*, which alternates with *divinity*, will be listed with a remote underlying vowel, but so will non-alternating forms like *bee*, *house*, *pine*, *road*, *pain* and *cube*. Consequently, in SPE, *all* tense or long vowels are underlyingly distinct from their surface realisations. The plausibility of this assumption, which entails the hypothesis that children learning Modern English internalise what is basically a Middle English vowel system (with the addition of various underliers which equally did not surface in Middle English) has been questioned elsewhere (Goyvaerts and Pullum 1975, Zwicky 1970, 1974).

Although this version of VSR applies to all tense, stressed vowels, it is motivated only in alternating morphemes, given the principles discussed in chapter 2 above. So, the supposed output of VSR is observable in *divine* because of the existence of related *divinity*, where no shift has taken place. Similarly, the alleged operation of VSR in *sane*, *verbose*, *comedian* and *variety* is evidenced by the absence of its results in *sanity*, *verbosity*, *comedy* and *various*. There can be no analogous direct evidence of Vowel Shift in non-alternating forms like *bee*, *pain* and *road*, so there is no motivation for assigning them abstract underliers, and deriving the surface vowels via VSR.

If the problem of free rides is to be solved, then, we must crucially find some way of restricting VSR to members of alternating pairs of words like those in (3.4).

(3.4)	*a.*	*b.*
	various ~ variety	divine ~ divinity
	comedy ~ comedian	serene ~ serenity
	courage ~ courageous	sane ~ sanity
	study ~ studious	assume ~ assumption
	harmony ~ harmonious	verbose ~ verbosity
		(fool ~ folly; see 3.3.2)
		(profound ~ profundity; see 3.3.2)

As discussed in the previous chapter, this restriction might be effected via the Alternation Condition; this will limit VSR to alternating morphemes, but will still allow it to operate in underived forms like *divine*, *sane*, *verbose*. To restrict VSR maximally, we must turn to the DEC (3.5), which can be imposed on the grammar as a formal condition on the proper application of Level 1 rules, and is potentially derivable, as we have seen, from the more general Elsewhere Condition. DEC must be the obvious candidate for a suitable constraint on VSR.

(3.5)   DEC: Cyclic rules apply in derived environments. An environment is derived for rule A in cycle (i) iff the structural description of rule A is met due to a concatenation of morphemes at cycle (i) or the operation of a phonological rule feeding rule A on cycle (i).

Whatever the hypothetical desirability of constraining VSR using the DEC, however, this seems impracticable. Halle and Mohanan (1985) classify VSR as a non-cyclic, Level 2 process, precisely in order to exempt it from DEC, since the majority of forms traditionally supposed to undergo VSR constitute underived environments for it: they show no concatenation of morphemes, and no phonological rule feeding VSR has applied. But this is again to ignore the fact that VSR is only motivated in alternating pairs of words; if VSR could be restricted to the *derived* members of these pairs, it could be ordered on Level 1 within the domain of DEC, and the problem of free rides would disappear. Indeed, Borowsky's (1990) Principle of Domain Assignment, which allows free application of any rule not explicitly restricted to Level 1, will prevent the ordering of VSR solely on Level 2 on which Halle and Mohanan's analysis relies.

The restriction of VSR to derived environments is unproblematic for the forms in (3.4a). If VSR applies to tense, stressed vowels, the capitalised vowels in *varIous*, *comEdy*, *courAge*, *stUdy* and *harmOny* will be ineligible for shifting. However, in the right-hand forms in (3.4a), each of the corresponding vowels has undergone one of the tensing rules, which are triggered by affixation and in turn feed VSR (see (3.6)).

(3.6)		comedy	comedian	various	variety
	Underlying:	/ɛ/	/ɛ/	/ɪ/	/ɪ/
	Pre-V Tensing:	–	–	ī	ī
	CiV Tensing:	–	ē	–	–
	VSR:	–	ī	–	aɪ

In the alternating pairs in (3.4b), however, the underived forms contain tense, stressed vowels, while the derived forms have short or lax vowels. Relocation of VSR on Level 1, subject to DEC, therefore commits us to a fundamental revision of the Vowel Shift Rule: the single rule shifting tense vowels will be replaced by two rules, one for tense vowels (V̄SR) and the other for lax vowels (V̌SR). V̄SR will be fed by the tensing rules; similarly, derived environments for V̌SR will be created by the laxing rules – TSL in *divinity*, Suffix Laxing in *satiric*, and so on.

The possibility of shifting lax vowels is mentioned by McCawley (1986), who reports that Chomsky and Halle considered a lax-vowel VSR in the early 1960s, before replacing this with the tense-vowel VSR published in SPE. In their earlier version, 'tense vowels retain their underlying heights and lax vowels shift their heights (in the opposite direction from the shift that tense vowels undergo in ... SPE)' (McCawley 1986: 30). The derivations predicted by this VSR are given in (3.7), but will be amended below.

(3.7)	Tense vowels:	/æ	i	e	ɔ̄	u	ō/
	Diphthongisation:	æy	īy	ēy	ɔ̄w	ūw	ōw
	Other rules:	āy			āw		
	Lax vowels:	/æ	ɪ	ɛ	ɒ	ʊ	o/
	V̌SR (a):	ɛ	–	æ	o	–	ɒ
	V̌SR (b):	ɪ	ɛ	–	ʊ	o	–
	Other rules:				ʌ	ɒ	

Whereas Chomsky and Halle first proposed a vowel-shift rule for lax vowels, then adopted instead a rule shifting tense vowels, I assume that both V̄SR and V̌SR (formulated in (3.8)) are synchronic rules of Modern English; neither would be sufficient to account for the data in (3.4). The inevitable allegations of rule duplication and missed generalisations must be weighed against the solution to the problem of free rides which is supplied by splitting VSR and ordering both rules on Level 1, in the scope of DEC: some complication of the grammar is necessary in the interests of the principles of chapter 2. However, I believe that minor formal complications are far less important than the greater goal of producing a grammar which adheres to the principles and constraints of LP; in other words, the optimal grammar is not necessarily the simplest and most elegant, but the one which coheres best with both internal and external evidence, and in which the rules are bound by the constraints of the theory.

If we accept the bipartite VSR outlined above, all non-alternating forms, and the underived members of alternating pairs of words, will be represented underlyingly with their surface vowels: *pool* will be /pūl/, *bean* /bīn/, and *sane* /sēn/. Nor are we imputing an excess of computational mental agility to the Modern English speaker; we need only assume that speakers 'know' that certain patterns of alternation exist, involving certain pairs of surface vowels (so that, if [ī] alternates, it will be with [ɛ], and likewise [ō] with [ɒ] and [aɪ] with [ɪ]; leaving aside for the moment reduction to [ə] in some circumstances), and that the vowel selected as the appropriate underlier by the speaker is the surface vowel of the underived form. Related derived words will be subject to either tensing or laxing, and will then be eligible for the appropriate VSR.

(3.8)   a. V̄SR

$$
\begin{bmatrix} V \\ +\text{tense} \\ +\text{stress} \end{bmatrix} \rightarrow
\left\{
\begin{array}{l}
[-\alpha\,\text{high}] / \begin{bmatrix} \underline{\quad} \\ \alpha\,\text{high} \\ -\text{low} \end{bmatrix} \\[6ex]
[-\beta\,\text{low}] / \begin{bmatrix} \underline{\quad} \\ \beta\,\text{low} \\ -\text{high} \end{bmatrix}
\end{array}
\right\}
$$

b. V̌SR

$$
\begin{bmatrix} V \\ -\text{tense} \\ +\text{stress} \end{bmatrix} \rightarrow
\left\{
\begin{array}{l}
[-\alpha\,\text{low}] / \begin{bmatrix} \underline{\quad} \\ \alpha\,\text{low} \\ -\text{high} \end{bmatrix} \\[6ex]
[-\beta\,\text{high}] / \begin{bmatrix} \underline{\quad} \\ \beta\,\text{high} \\ -\text{low} \end{bmatrix}
\end{array}
\right\}
$$

Interestingly, the DEC makes precisely the correct predictions here, accounting for the absence of V̌SR in *damnable* and *solemnity* and V̄SR in *obesity* and *notify*, although these forms initially look problematic. Consider *solemn ~ solemnity*. If the underlying representation is /sɒlɛmn/, and if *solemnity* is derived from this by affixation on Level 1, it would be expected to be eligible for Level 1 rules, including VSR. However, if VSR did apply, the result would be *[sɒlæmnɪti]. Conversely, to produce [sɒlɛmnɪti] after V̌SR, the underlier would have to be /sɒlɪmn/, which would give the wrong surface vowel in the underived form. The same applies to *obesity*, which might be expected to surface as [ōbaɪsɪti] by V̄SR.

This apparent exceptionality in fact follows from the failure of *damnable*, *solemnity*, *obesity* and *notify* to undergo any tensing or laxing rules in the course of the derivation (contrast, for instance, *obese* ~ *obesity* with *obscene* ~ *obscenity*, with TSL only in the last form). To clarify this assertion, we must return to the notion of derived environment embodied in the DEC. Although both VSRs appear to operate consistently in morphologically complex environments, it is not the addition of a morpheme per se which sanctions VSR, since neither Vowel Shift Rule demands a structural description which can be satisfied by morpheme concatenation. Both 'ask for' a specific type of segment to apply to, but this environment is purely phonological – [+ tense] vowels for V̄SR, and [−tense] ones for V̆SR. In contrast, TSL and CiV Tensing require certain combinations of segments to follow the focus vowel; since these configurations can be provided by adding a Class I affix, DEC can be satisfied morphologically. Level 1 tensing and laxing rules will then feed the appropriate VSR by supplying the derived features [+ tense] or [−tense]. It follows that forms like *obesity*, *notify*, *damnable* and *solemnity*, which exceptionally fail to undergo tensing and laxing, will necessarily fail to meet the conditions for VSR.

The fact that both VSRs are clearly fed by preceding phonological rules makes these processes rather important theoretically: recall from chapter 2 that Cole (1995: 76) suggested the replacement of DEC with the Revised Alternation Condition on the grounds that 'there have been no ... examples in which a derived environment can be created morpheme-internally by the prior application of a phonological rule'. It is true that the tensing and laxing rules are triggered by affixation, and that the addition of a morpheme is crucial here, but the VSRs themselves are fed directly by tensing and laxing, and are co-morphemic with these rules. It follows that the DEC and any version of the Alternation Condition thought to be desirable must be stated independently, and that both clauses of the DEC must be retained.

In the rest of this chapter, I shall examine some potential problems for the account of Vowel Shift sketched above. In 3.3, problematic aspects of the lax-vowel V̆SR are discussed; these include the derivation of the *divine* ~ *divinity* alternation, the generation of the high and low back vowels, and the analysis of [jū]. In 3.4, I shall consider difficulties for Level 1 VSR, concerning interacting rules and the Modern English irregular verbs, which present a test case on how far the formulation of Vowel Shift proposed here itself limits the adoption of abstract underlying representations.

3.3   Problems for lax-vowel Vowel Shift Rule

3.3.1   The divine ~ divinity *alternation*

According to McCawley (1986), the underlying vowel of [aɪ] ~ [ɪ] in
divine ~ divinity is /æ/, giving the derivations shown in (3.9).

(3.9)		divine	divinity
	Underlying:	/æ/	/æ/
	TSL:	–	æ
	V̆SR:	–	ɪ
	Diphthongisation:	æy	–
	Backness Adjustment:	āy	–

/æ/ will not be adopted here as the underlier for the [aɪ] ~ [ɪ]
alternation, for the following reasons:

(1) This would be the only case (excluding *profound ~ profundity*,
which will be excluded from Vowel Shift in 3.3.2) in which the underlying
vowel never surfaces without a quality change: /ī ē ō/, the underlying
vowels of *serene, sane* and *verbose*, surface unchanged in these underived
forms (but for Diphthongisation in some accents), but /æ/ in *divine* must
invariably be diphthongised and generally also backed.

(2) Deriving [aɪ] from /æ/ commits us to the production of surface
diphthongs from underlying monophthongs; but there are good reasons
for rejecting this analysis.

The prohibition of underlying diphthongs dates from Chomsky and
Halle's assertion (1968: 192) that 'contemporary English differs from its
sixteenth- or seventeenth-century ancestor in the fact that it no longer
admits phonological diphthongs – i.e. sequences of tense low vowels
followed by lax high vowels – in its lexical formatives'. This declaration
has won widespread acceptance, despite the fact that Chomsky and Halle
fail entirely to cite any evidence or justification for it. Indeed, since
Modern English, like earlier stages of the language, has surface
diphthongs, it is hard to see why the language should have retained this
category phonetically, but opted for a phonological restructuring,
especially when no alternations are involved, and the learnability of the
restructured system must therefore be questioned.

Diphthongisation might be favoured as enabling a more 'elegant'
analysis, which remains plausible only if *all* surface diphthongs are
derived from monophthongal sources. It is unfortunate, then, that
Diphthongisation is not maximally general. For instance, in RP only the
long mid monophthongs /ē ō/ are realised consistently as the diphthongs

[eɪ], [oʊ]; the high and low vowels /ī ū ā ɔ̄/ may surface without offglides. Some American accents have diphthongs in *day*, *go*, but not all. In Scots and Scottish Standard English, varieties which we shall explore further in subsequent chapters, there is no Diphthongisation at all, and the long vowels of *bee*, *day*, *you*, *go* are phonetically monophthongal. In such dialects, a Diphthongisation rule could only derive surface [ʌi], [ʌu] and [ɔi] in *divine*, *profound* and *boy*, and forfeits its claim to be an independently motivated process which is simply extended to these cases.

A final problem for Diphthongisation is that, while it has proved relatively easy to derive [aɪ] and [aʊ] from shifted and diphthongised /ī/ and /ū/, finding an appropriate underlier for [ɔɪ] has been more taxing. Various contenders have been proposed, the most notorious being the /œ/ of SPE, whose adoption makes English unique among known languages in having a low front rounded vowel without the corresponding high and mid vowels. The major, and perhaps only, advantage of this choice is that it will regularly undergo Diphthongisation to become [œy], thus accounting for the appearance in [ɔy] of a front offglide after a back vowel. However, [ɔɪ] does not figure in alternations (the few apparent examples, such as *destroy* ~ *destruction*, are almost certainly allomorphic), and as a remote underlier for non-alternating forms like *boy*, *coin*, /œ/ is impermissible in the model proposed here.

Alternative derivations of [ɔɪ] are not markedly more successful. For instance, Zwicky (1974: 59) suggests underlying /x̄/; Halle (1977) tentatively proposes deriving [ɔɪ] from /ū/, via Vowel Shift, Diphthongisation and a Glide-Switching rule; while Halle and Mohanan (1985) are unable to choose between /ū/ and /ü/. Deriving [ɔɪ] from /ū/ would, as in Halle's account, involve Vowel Shift and Diphthongisation to [ɔw], and a further rule fronting the glide; Halle and Mohanan do not, however, propose to unround [w], and the final output will therefore be neither [ɔy] nor [ɔw], but some intermediate amalgamation. If /ü/ is preferred as a source vowel, Vowel Shift, Diphthongisation and a rule of Diphthong Backing will produce [ɔy], but Halle and Mohanan (1985: 102) are reluctant to adopt this ostensibly simpler derivation as 'it would require a special weakening of the principles that determine the feature complexes in the system of underlying vowels, since the system would now have to include instances of the somewhat marked category of rounded front vowels'.

This is scarcely a convincing objection, given that Halle and Mohanan include in their underlying Modern English vowel system /ɨ ɨ̄/ and /x̄/, three non-surfacing instances of the arguably even more marked category of back unrounded vowels. It is easy to sympathise with Rubach (1984: 35), who observes that 'the whole endeavour of deriving /ɔj/ may not be worth the trouble ... one might as well give up the generalisation that English has no underlying diphthongs, and so derive *boy* from //bɔj//'. If /ɔɪ/ is permitted underlyingly, it is a very small step to add /aɪ/ and /aʊ/, which also appear in non-alternating forms like *high, bright, fine* or *loud, round, crowd*.

I propose, then, that the underlying vowel system(s) of Modern English should contain at least the diphthongs /ɔɪ/, /aɪ/ and /aʊ/ (centring diphthongs like [ɪə], [ʊə] in RP *here, poor* will be discussed in chapter 6). Diphthongisation will be replaced by a rule lengthening tense vowels (except in Scots and SSE, where vowel length is governed by the Scottish Vowel Length Rule – see chapter 4). The various special rules associated with previous analyses will now be lost: however, V̄SR will produce long tense low front [æ] from tensed [ī] in *variety* and so on, and to convert this into surface [aɪ], one additional rule (3.10) is required. This will be ordered on Level 1 after V̄SR, which will feed it by providing the specification [+ low].

(3.10)

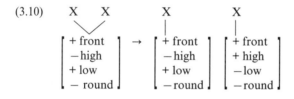

The diphthong [aɪ] therefore functions synchronically only as a target in Vowel Shift; no diphthongs shift themselves, although diphthongs were directly involved in the historical Great Vowel Shift. It also follows that the underlying vowel in *divine ~ divinity* must be the diphthong /aɪ/, the surface vowel in underived *divine*.

However, since the required surface vowel in *divinity* is [ɪ], and [ɪ] is derived from a [− back, − round, + low] vowel by V̄SR, such a vowel must result from Trisyllabic Laxing of /aɪ/. Halle and Mohanan (1985) propose that laxing and shortening should be differentiated, but since, at least in RP and GenAm, the only surface vowel-types are short-lax and long-tense, it is preferable to assume that one process implies the other. A laxed vowel will then lose one timing slot: long monophthongs will shorten, while diphthongs will monophthongise, and since [aɪ] is a falling diphthong, it is the less prominent, non-syllabic second element which will be lost (3.11). Further evidence for this analysis of diphthong laxing will be presented below and in chapter 4.

(3.11)

3.3.2 *Apparent exceptions*

A lax-vowel VSR of the type proposed by McCawley (1986) will produce the derivations in (3.12) for underlying high and low back vowels.

(3.12)

	/ʊ/	/ɒ/
V̆SRa:	–	o
V̆SRb:	o	ʊ
Other rules:	ɒ	ʌ

Although /ō/ will regularly lax to [o], and shift to [ɒ] in the *verbose ~ verbosity* alternation, V̆SR alone is insufficient to derive [aʊ] ~ [ʌ] and [ū] ~ [ɒ]: extra rules are needed to produce [ʌ], [ɒ] and [aʊ]. These two alternations were also problematic for 'traditional' VSR, and a very small number of alternating pairs is involved (see (3.13)).

(3.13)

[aʊ] ~ [ʌ]

profound ~ profundity		pronounce ~ pronunciation
announce ~ annunciation		denounce ~ denunciation
South ~ Southern	flower ~ flourish	tower ~ turret

[ū] ~ [ɒ]

shoot ~ shot	lose ~ lost	school ~ scholar
poor ~ poverty	fool ~ folly	food ~ fodder

It is surely questionable whether the members of these pairs are synchronically related by any productive phonological process, although they may be linked in morphological and/or semantic terms: I return to this point for the strong verbs, *lose ~ lost* and *shoot ~ shot*, in 3.4.2 below. In *profound ~ profundity* there is the additional problem of finding an appropriate underlying vowel. If we allow underlying diphthongs, the underlier should clearly be /aʊ/. However, the Vowel Shift derivation proposed above for /aɪ/ in *divine ~ divinity* is not going to work for /aʊ/ in *profound ~ profundity*: /aʊ/, like /aɪ/, would be expected to monophthongise when laxed by losing its second element, since it is a falling diphthong; it would then become [æ] (or [a]) and shift to [ɪ]. Even if, against all the principles of LP, we invented a short low back unrounded [ɑ] for this 'back' diphthong to monophthongise to, it would shift to [+ high, −low]. To derive [ʌ], we must stop the shift half-way, and to derive [ʊ], we need a rounding rule. What this may mean is that this alternation is not part of the Modern English Vowel Shift set. In fact, there are ways of testing this hypothesis.

In SPE, the *profound ~ profundity* and *fool ~ folly* alternations would result from shifting /u/ and /o/. It is interesting that in Older Scots and other Northern Middle English dialects, /ū/ and /ō/ did not participate in the Great Vowel Shift, suggesting that these may represent in some sense the 'weakest' subpart of the Vowel Shift. Psycholinguistic evidence certainly suggests that these alternations are not synchronically charac- terised using VSR. Several recent experiments which aimed to discover whether speakers 'know' the VSR and which alternations they include in the Vowel Shift set have concluded that, while the [aɪ] ~ [ɪ], [ī] ~ [ɛ], [ē] ~ [æ] and [ō] ~ [ɒ] alternations do have some measure of psychological reality for Modern English speakers, [aʊ] ~ [ʌ] and [ū] ~ [ɒ] apparently do not. For instance, in a productivity experiment carried out by Wang (1985), in which speakers were presented with nonsense words as adjectives and required to derive a related noun in -*ity*, with a shifted vowel, only the alternations [aɪ] ~ [ɪ], [ī] ~ [ɛ], [ē] ~ [æ] and [ō] ~ [ɒ] showed any strength. Similar results were obtained in a concept- formation experiment reported in Wang and Derwing (1986). Such experiments are designed to ascertain which elements informants perceive as part of a specific group. In this case, speakers were encouraged to form a Vowel Shift concept by answering 'yes' to the core Vowel Shift alternations given above, and 'no' to 'anti-vowel shift' (McCawley 1986) pairs like [aɪ] ~ [ɛ] and [ī] ~ [æ]. The informants were then asked to extend this classification to novel stimuli, and did not respond positively to tokens of the [aʊ] ~ [ʌ] and [ū] ~ [ɒ] alternations. In Jaeger's (1986) experiment, speakers' percentage acceptability responses for [aʊ] ~ [ʌ] were often lower than for alternations to which they had been trained to respond negatively (see (3.14)).

(3.14)   *% affirmative responses to examples of:*
Trained affirmative:
[aɪ] ~ [ɪ]   93
[ī]   ~ [ɛ]   88
[ē]   ~ [æ]   80
[ō]   ~ [ɒ]   87.5

Trained negative:

Tense–lax same height	25
Distinct lax vowels	8
Distinct tense vowels	20
Identical vowels	17
Other tense–lax pairs	13

Not included in training sessions:

[aʊ] ~ [ʌ]	9
[jū] ~ [ʌ]	75

Although the [aʊ] ~ [ʌ] alternation was historically a result of the Great Vowel Shift, at least in the South, the synchronic VSR may no longer include all those vowels that participated in the diachronic change. Wang and Derwing (1986) and McCawley (1986) argue that the Vowel Shift alternations [aɪ] ~ [ɪ], [ī] ~ [ɛ], [ē] ~ [æ] and [ō] ~ [ɒ] may be reinforced for Modern English speakers by their correspondence with the English Spelling Rule, since these pairs of vowels are normally spelt <i>, <e>, <a> and <o> respectively. The synchronic VSR would then be partially orthographically motivated. Jaeger (1986: 86) goes further here, claiming that 'the source of speakers' knowledge about these vowel alternations is a combination of orthography and the frequency with which given alternations occur'. If these are indeed the criteria for inclusion of alternations in the synchronic VSR, then [aʊ] ~ [ʌ] and [ū] ~ [ɒ] clearly fail, since the phonological members of the alternations do not correspond to a single letter in the orthography, and since there are so few examples of the alternations in Present-Day English. Since I argued above that the Modern English vowel system(s) should include underlying diphthongs, we can assume that *profound* has underlying /aʊ/, *profundity* /ʌ/, *fool* /ū/, and *folly* /ɒ/.

The *fool* ~ *folly* alternation brings us to a second contentious area for Vowel Shift, since the pronunciation of the low vowel in *folly*, and that of other low vowels in *glass*, *balm*, *frost* and *law*, varies considerably across accents of English. Although Halle and Mohanan (1985) propose common underlying long and short vowel systems for RP and GenAm, they require three special rules, a/o-Tensing, ɔ-Unrounding, and o-Lowering, to deal with the divergent realisations of the low vowels in words like *balm*, *bomb* and *baud*. All three rules operate in GenAm, giving the derivations shown in (3.15).

(3.15)   GenAm:

	balm	bomb	law/frost
	/a/	/ɔ/	/o/
a/o-Tensing:	a_t	–	o_t
ɔ-Unrounding:	–	a	–
o-Lowering:	–	–	$ɔ_t$

However, Halle and Mohanan contend that only a/o-Tensing applies in RP, producing the truncated derivations of (3.16).

(3.16)   RP:

	balm	bomb/frost	law
	/a/	/ɔ/	/o/
a/o-Tensing:	a_t	–	o_t

Halle and Mohanan's GenAm derivations in (3.15) preserve a surface contrast of *balm* [a_t] and *bomb* [a]. Wells (1982), however, assumes that underlying /ɒ/ in words of the *bomb* type is lengthened, tensed and unrounded to merge with the long low unrounded tense /ā/ of *balm* words. Wells also asserts that 'the result of the merger is phonetically usually a rather long vowel' (1982: 246), although Halle and Mohanan consider their [a_t] and [a] to be short. Furthermore, they (1985: 101) assign *shot* and *lost* underlying /o/, which will tense and lower to [$ɔ_t$] in GenAm, although phonetically these words have [ɑ]. This representation is also incorrect for RP, where *shot* and *lost* surface with [ɒ], not [o_t].

In contrast, I propose that, in RP, *balm* will have underlying and surface long tense /ā/ [ā], *bomb/frost* short lax /ɒ/ [ɒ], and *law* long tense /ɔ̄/ [ɔ̄]. Although Halle and Mohanan regard length as the underlying dichotomiser of the English vowel system, with tenseness introduced subsequently during the derivation, I consider long and tense, and short and lax, as present both underlyingly and on the surface (see chapters 4 and 5 below). In GenAm, *balm* will similarly have /ā/ [ā], and *law/frost*, /ɔ̄/ [ɔ̄] (although note that Kurath and McDavid (1961: 7) list various other possible low vowel systems for American varieties, and that diphthongs like [ɔə] may occur in *frost* words).

The derivation of *bomb* words in GenAm is not quite so straightforward. If the Halle and Mohanan/SGP assumption of identity of underlying representations is to be maintained, *bomb* words in GenAm must be assigned underlying /ɒ/, as is the case in RP, with a rule merging /ɒ/ with /ā/. American varieties in which *bomb* and *balm* words are kept distinct, such as the Eastern New England accent included in Kurath and McDavid's (1961: 7) table, will have this variation encoded in the form of the unrounding rule. However, complete underlying identity between RP and GenAm is in any case impossible, given the underlying distributional distinction regarding *cough, frost, dog* words, which belong with the /ɒ/ class in RP but have /ɔ/ in GenAm. Furthermore, absolute neutralisation is clearly involved, jeopardising the synchronic status of /ɒ/ in GenAm: it is more plausible to omit /ɒ/ from the modern GenAm vowel system, since all words which historically contained /ɒ/ [ɒ] now have either [ā] (like *bomb* and *stop*) or [ɔ̄] (like *cough* and *frost*) on the surface. The principle that underlying and lexical representations should be equivalent in non-alternating forms dictates that these lexical sets be represented underlyingly with /ā/ or /ɔ̄/ respectively.

The next question is whether underlying /ɒ/ is motivated in alternating forms like *verbose ~ verbosity* and *harmony ~ harmonious* for GenAm. Low back lax rounded /ɒ/ is involved in the derivation of these alternating forms in RP, as shown in (3.17).

(3.17)

	verbose	verbosity
Underlying:	/vɜ̄bōs/	/vɜ̄bōs/ /ɪti/
Affixation:	–	vɜ̄bōs]ɪti
TSL:	–	o
V̌SR:	–	ɒ
Surface:	[vɜ̄bōs]	[vɜ̄bɒsɪti]

	harmony	harmonious
Underlying:	/hāmɒni/	/hāmɒni/ /əs/
Affixation:	–	hāmɒni]əs
CiV Tensing:	–	ɔ̄
V̌SR:	–	ō
Surface:	[hāmɒni]	[hāmōniəs]

There are two points to make here. First, the relevant surface vowel in *harmony* is in fact reduced, although we might assume that comparison with *harmonic* justifies underlying /ɒ/. Giegerich (1994) goes further, proposing an underlyingly empty nucleus in alternating forms where the underived surface form has schwa; the appropriate full vowel can be supplied only by reference to independent orthographic representations, and the derivation depends crucially on a structure-building and structure-preserving Spelling Pronunciation rule. I will not pursue this analysis here; it assumes underspecification and is therefore not tenable in my model of LP, although a modified version with underlying schwa and a structure-changing Spelling Pronunciation rule would be compatible with my account of Vowel Shift. Secondly, in GenAm *harmonic* and *verbosity* have [ɑ]/[ā], although *verbose* and *harmonious* share surface [o]/

[oʊ] with RP. If we omit /ɒ/ from the GenAm vowel system in alternating forms, how will the Vowel Shift Rules operate?

Let us first turn to *verbose ~ verbosity*. The input vowel in RP is /ō/, and since this surfaces in both RP and GenAm in *verbose*, we can assume that /ō/ also underlies this alternation in GenAm. Only one derivational path through VSR is available to /ō/: suffixation of -*ity* will feed TSL, which in turn will feed V̄SR, producing [ɒ]. In American varieties lacking [ɒ], we must apply an unrounding rule (and subsequently a tensing rule for some subvarieties) to give [ɑ]/[ā]. This derivation involves [ɒ] only as an intermediate step (and note here Goldsmith's 1990: 224 contention that Structure Preservation may enforce further derivation if a rule application produces some form which does not exist at the underlying level).

If we assume underlying /ɒ/ for GenAm in *harmony ~ harmonious*, this will tense and shift to [ō] in *harmonious*, as in RP, while /ɒ/ in underived *harmony* must subsequently be unrounded and optionally tensed. This analysis is clearly impermissible in the model developed here, since absolute neutralisation is involved, and the underlying representation will not be equivalent to the lexical representation of the underived form. To maintain this principle, we must assume that the underlying vowel is /ɒ/ in RP, but has been restructured to /ɑ/ in GenAm. This is the only case of apparent cross-dialectal variation in the quality of the input vowel; interestingly, it is also the sole instance where alternative paths through VSR may be available, both producing the same output. The derivational path of /ɒ/ in RP is clear from (3.17); it is tensed in *harmonious* and subjected to V̄SR, giving [ō]. In GenAm, /ɑ/ would similarly tense to give intermediate [ā], feeding Vowel Shift as shown in (3.18), with a subsequent rounding rule required to produce surface [ō].

(3.18)		harmony	harmonious
	Underlying:	/ɑ/	/ɑ/
	CiV Tensing:	–	ā
	V̄SR:	–	ʌ̄
	ʌ̄-Rounding:	–	ō

We have not, however, exhausted the issue of the [ā] vowel of *balm*, *father* and, in some varieties of GenAm, *bomb*. The problematic derivation of this stressed vowel in *father*, *rather*, *Chicago*, *ga′rage* and *balm* is familiar from SPE: the *father* vowel is phonetically long and tense, but does not diphthongise or undergo Vowel Shift. Its underlier must therefore be convertible into the appropriate surface vowel, but also be exempt from VSR and Diphthongisation.

This challenge has produced solutions of varying degrees of credibility. Chomsky and Halle propose underlying tense low back unrounded /ā/, and remove it from the scope of Vowel Shift by restricting the input of this rule to vowels which are [α back, α round]; this condition also excludes /œ/, the SPE source for [ɔɪ]. However, in SPE /ā/ does undergo Diphthongisation, receiving a following /w/ glide, which is then vocalised, shifted and unrounded to produce [āʌ] (see (3.19)). This [ʌ] may then be realised as 'a centering glide of some sort or a feature of extra length' (Chomsky and Halle 1968: 205). The SPE analysis therefore extends the structural description of Rounding Adjustment and allows Vowel Shift, a process historically and otherwise synchronically confined to the long vowel system, to apply to a short lax vowel derived from an offglide; and its product is an exceptional representation whose realisation is ambiguous.

(3.19)	Underlying:	/fāðVr/
	Diphthongisation:	āw
	Glide Vocalisation (after /ā/):	āʊ
	Vowel Shift (extended to lax /ʊ/):	āo
	Rounding Adjustment:	āʌ

Since Halle (1977) does not allow lax vowels to undergo Vowel Shift, he cannot vocalise and shift glides. However, since *father* is not phonetically *[fāwðə(r)], Halle must make his underlying vowel an exception to both Vowel Shift and Diphthongisation. He does so by modifying the redundancy rule linking length and tenseness in English so that it 'admits both tense and lax varieties among long low vowels, but not elsewhere' (Halle 1977: 618). Halle then assigns the underlying long lax vowel /aₗ/ to *father*, *Chicago*, etc. Diphthongisation and Vowel Shift are both sensitive to tenseness, and hence neither will apply to [aₗ], although both will operate on the low tense unrounded vowel /aₜ/, as shown in (3.20). Halle also finds it necessary to reformulate the English Stress Rule so that long, rather than tense vowels will be stressed, to account for the stress on /aₗ/ in *Chicago*, *soprano* and so on.

(3.20)		father	volcano
	Underlying:	/aₗ/	/āₜ/
	Vowel Shift:	–	ē
	Diphthongisation:	–	ēy

Halle and Mohanan (1985) also exploit discrepancies between length and tenseness in their characterisation of the *father* vowel. However, whereas Halle (1977) proposed a long lax low unrounded vowel, Halle and Mohanan prefer a short tense one. More accurately, they assign short back low unrounded /a/ to *father*, *Chicago*, *balm* underlyingly, but /a/ is then subject to a/o-Tensing, and is said to surface as [ā$_t$] in both RP and GenAm. Since Halle and Mohanan restrict the VSR and Diphthongisation to long, rather than to tense vowels, /a/ will, as required, be exempted from these rules. They also claim that their analysis allows them to eliminate the feature [± tense] from underlying representations, but since they assume that the Main Stress Rule is also sensitive to length (1985: 76), they are forced to assign a diacritic feature [+ accented] to the penultimate syllable of *Chicago*, *sonata*, *soprano* and similar trisyllabic forms to account for their otherwise exceptional stress pattern.

I have already pointed out some difficulties inherent in the SPE account: as for the others, Halle (1977) seems to be using laxness merely as a diacritic to dichotomise instances of the same vowel into Diphthongising and Shifting versus 'static' sets, while Halle and Mohanan, by assigning a short lax underlying vowel to *father* and *Chicago*, create difficulties for their stress rules and are also forced to resort to diacritic marking. Furthermore, Halle and Mohanan cannot derive the long vowel pronunciations which are characteristic of the stressed vowel in *father*, *balm*, *spa* and others in American accents and in RP: although they do propose a rule of Long Vowel Tensing (1985: 73), which redundantly tenses all long vowels, they have no mechanism for lengthening tense vowels, and [a$_t$] is consequently predicted to surface short.

In revising these analyses, it is first important to observe that words like *father* surface with the back vowel assumed by Chomsky and Halle (1968), Halle (1977) and Halle and Mohanan (1985) in only some accents of English, including GenAm and RP. In many Scots varieties, Australian and New Zealand English, and certain areas of England such as West Yorkshire (see Wells 1982), the *father* vowel is phonetically front. In a SGP account, these two sets of realisations would be derived synchronically from a single underlying vowel, reflecting the probable historical origin of the divergent forms. However, in LP we are not tied to such an analysis, and I propose therefore that the *father* vowel should be assigned two distinct underliers: these will be back /ā/ in accents like RP and GenAm with a phonetically back vowel in *father* words, and front /æ/ in those accents where the surface vowel is front. Short lax /a/ (from Halle's system) and long lax /ɔ₁/, /a₁/ (from Halle and Mohanan's) will be eliminated from all underlying English vowel systems, and the

perfect correlation of length and tenseness which was disturbed by
Halle's and Halle and Mohanan's treatment of the *father* vowel will be
restored. Two sample systems are given in (3.21): the back unrounded
vowels /ɨ ɨ̄ ʌ̄/ which figure in Halle and Mohanan's system are omitted
until 3.4 below.

(3.21)   a. RP

	Lax vowels		Tense vowels	
	front	*back*	*front*	*back*
high	ɪ	ʊ	ī	ū
mid	ɛ	ʌ	ē	ō
low	æ	ɒ		ā ɔ̄

b. Scots (see chapters 4 and 5)

	Lax vowels		Tense vowels	
	front	*back*	*front*	*back*
high	ɪ		i	u
mid	ɛ	ʌ	e	o
low		a	æ	ɔ

Nor, in the model presented here, need these low vowels be exempted
from Vowel Shift or Diphthongisation. First, recall that I have argued
against the Diphthongisation rule; all varieties of English will now
include some underlying diphthongs, most generally /aɪ aʊ ɔɪ/. Furthermore, the revised lax- and tense-vowel VSRs will never affect underlying
vowels: that is, VSR can never be the first phonological rule to apply to a
vowel, since it must be fed by a tensing or laxing rule to satisfy DEC.
Underlying /æ/ will no longer appear in any word involved in a VSR
alternation: *sane ~ sanity* will have underlying /ē/, while *divine ~ divinity*
show [aɪ] ~ [ɪ] derived from /aɪ/. Underlying /æ/ or /ā/ in *father, Chicago,
spa* therefore require no special exclusion from V̄SR, since all the *father*
words will constitute underived environments for both Vowel Shift
Rules, so that the relevant vowel will be low underlyingly and throughout
the derivation. Only in some American accents might /ā/ appear in
suitable alternating forms like *harmonic ~ harmonious*; the resulting
derivation was outlined earlier in this section, and has no consequences
for the treatment of non-alternating *father*.

3.3.3   The derivation of [jū]

I now turn to the [jū] sequence of sounds and the related vowels [ū], [ʌ]
and [ʊ], a second area of English phonology which has occasioned
abstract analyses, to see whether [jū] is also amenable to a more concrete

reinterpretation. Some sample words with [jū], [ū], [ʌ], [ʊ] and the [jū] ~ [ʌ] alternation are shown in (3.22) and (3.23).

(3.22)
[jū]/[ū]	[jū]/[ū]	[ū]/[ʌ]
cube	tabular	reduce ~ reduction
avenue	angular	assume ~ assumption
issue	ambiguous	consume ~ consumption
venue	ambiguity	study ~ studious
accuse	habitual	Malthus ~ Malthusian
huge	credulous	Lilliput ~ Lilliputian
duke	credulity	
tube	architecture	

(3.23)
[ū]	[ʊ]	[ʌ]
juke-box	pull	profundity
acoustic	push	putt
chew	bush	but
blue	cushion	couple
rude	put	fund
woo	soot	pun

The main problems raised by [jū], [ū], [ʌ] and [ʊ] for a phonological description of RP and GenAm are the following:

1. What is the status of the [j] glide which appears before [ū]?

2. How can we capture the fact that [j] appears predominantly before [ū], but not before every instance of this vowel?

3. What are the most appropriate underlying vowels for [jū], [ū], [ʌ] and [ʊ]?

I shall first outline the answers given by Chomsky and Halle (1968), Halle (1977), Rubach (1984) and Halle and Mohanan (1985), then offer an alternative account.

3.3.3.1   Previous analyses of [jū]

As Halle and Mohanan (1985: 89) point out,

> It is well known that the sequence [Cy] in English is regularly followed by the vowel [uw] or its unstressed reduced reflex. Thus, although [kyuw] *Kew*, [kyut] *cute*, as well as [kwiyn] *queen*, [kwæk] *quack*, [kwam] *qualm*, [kwowt] *quote*, etc., are well-formed, *[kyiyn], *[kyæk], *[kyam], *[kyowt], etc., are not.

There are two possible ways of dealing with this observation in a phonological description: either [j] is nuclear, making [jū] a diphthong; or it is inserted by rule in the onset, before the vowel or vowels which eventually surfaces as [ū] (or [uw]). SPE, Halle (1977), Rubach (1984) and Halle and Mohanan (1985) all adopt the j-Insertion approach; we turn to the possibility of a diphthongal analysis in the next section.

Before considering the SPE analysis of [jū] in detail, I should point out that the sample words in (3.22) above can be split into four subsets. Some forms with surface [jū], like *tabular* and *angular*, alternate with base forms, in this case *table* and *angle*, in which there is no vowel corresponding to [jū] in the derived forms. In SPE, a rule inserting /ʊ/ in *tabular*, *angular* was proposed (see (3.24)); this procedure has generally been followed in subsequent studies.

(3.24)
$$\varnothing \rightarrow \upsilon \ / \ \begin{bmatrix} -\text{cont} \\ -\text{voc} \\ +\text{cons} \end{bmatrix} \ \text{—} \ 1 + \text{VC} \, [-\text{seg}]$$

(Chomsky and Halle 1968: 196)

In the second set of [jū] words, which includes *ambiguous*, *ambiguity*, *credulous*, *credulity* and *habitual*, the vowel surfacing as [jū] belongs underlyingly to a morpheme distinct from the stem. In Chomsky and Halle (1968: 195), this morpheme is taken to be the 'stem-forming augment' [+ ʊ], which is stored with certain lexical items and subsequently deleted word-finally but retained before affixes. The remaining words in (3.22) fall into two further classes; those in which [jū] alternates with [ʌ], as in *reduce* ~ *reduction* or *study* ~ *studious*, and non-alternating forms like *cube*, *argue*, *venue*, *huge* and *duke*.

In SPE, surface [jū] always corresponds to underlying high back lax rounded /ʊ/ (= /u/ in SPE). /ʊ/ undergoes a rule producing tense, unrounded [ɨ] (Chomsky and Halle 1968: 195), which provides the context for /j/-Insertion before being unconditionally rerounded; since [ɨ] is [+ back, − round], it will not undergo Vowel Shift. In order to meet the structural description of this rule, *reduce*, *cube*, *huge*, *venue* and so on have to be represented underlyingly as /re=dʊkɛ/, /kʊbɛ/, /hʊgɛ/ and /vɛnʊɛ/, with the final /ɛ/ being disposed of later in the derivation. In *tabular*, where [jə] may surface rather than [jū], a further rule laxing unstressed /ɨ/ is also necessary. In addition, to account for [ʌ] in *reduction* and *study*, Chomsky and Halle are forced to allow lax /ʊ/ to undergo Vowel Shift, and to extend the structural analysis of the Rounding Adjustment rule to convert the resulting [o] to [ʌ]. The same derivation, involving Vowel Shift, applies to [ʌ] in *profundity*, although here the underlying vowel is tense /ū/, which undergoes Vowel Shift, Rounding Adjustment and Backness Adjustment to [āw] in *profound*, but laxes, shifts and unrounds in *profundity*.

Chomsky and Halle still encounter problems with [jū], [ʌ] and [ʊ]. The extension of Vowel Shift to lax /ʊ/ will convert all underlying cases of this vowel (unless they are first tensed and unrounded to [ɨ]) into surface [ʌ]; and indeed, this strategy is used in SPE to derive *putt, fund, pun* and so on. However, in *push, pull, cushion, put* and *soot*, which have surface [ʊ], a complex 'lay-by' rule (Chomsky and Halle 1968: 204) unrounds certain cases of /ʊ/ to [ɨ] until Vowel Shift has operated, whereupon [ɨ] is re-rounded. Lay-by rules of this type have attracted a good deal of criticism (Goyvaerts and Pullum 1975); and quite apart from such general objections, the proposed rule 'does not cover several exceptional cases of unrounding' (Chomsky and Halle 1968: 204), including *put, pudding* and *cushion*.

The SPE analysis of [jū] and related vowels suffers from one final problem; [j] has to be deleted by a later rule in certain dialects after dentals and palato-alveolars (Chomsky and Halle 1968: 231), giving [nū] *new*, [dūk] *duke*, etc. Here, however, Chomsky and Halle are missing a generalisation; while some American English accents do indeed lack [j] after coronals (unless [ū] is unstressed), [j] *never* surfaces after /r w dʒ ʃ/, for instance, in *any* dialect. Some sample SPE derivations are given in (3.25).

(3.25)   SPE

	profound	profundity	reduce	reduction
Underlying:	/u/	/u/	/ʊ/	/ʊ/
Tensing/Unrounding:	–	–	ɨ	–
Trisyllabic Laxing:	–	ʊ	–	–
Vowel Shift:	ɔ̄	o	–	o
Rounding Adjustment:	ā	ʌ	–	ʌ
Diphthongisation:	āw	–	ɨw	–
y-Preposing:	–	–	yɨw	–
Re-rounding:	–	–	yūw	–
Surface:	āw	ʌ	yūw	ʌ

	cube/venue	ambiguity	ambiguous
Underlying:	/ʊ/	/ʊ/	/ʊ/
Tensing/Unrounding:	ɨ	ɨ	ɨ
Diphthongisation:	ɨw	ɨw	ɨw
y-Preposing:	yɨw	yɨw	yɨw
Re-rounding:	yūw	yūw	yūw

	tabular
Underlying:	Ø
Ø → ʊ:	ʊ
Tensing/Unrounding:	ɨ

Diphthongisation:	īw
y-Preposing:	yīw
Re-rounding:	yūw
u → [−tense]:	yʊ
Vowel Reduction:	yə

	push	pun
Underlying:	/ʊ/	/ʊ/
Unrounding:	ɨ	−
Vowel Shift:	−	o
Rounding Adjustment:	−	ʌ
Re-rounding:	ʊ	−
Surface:	ʊ	ʌ

Halle (1977) is largely a revision of the SPE analysis of [jū], [ʌ] and [ʊ]. Halle restricts the VSR to tense vowels, although these need not be stressed, and reformulates j-Preposing to operate before /x̄/, or lax /ʌ/ in an open syllable. Sample derivations are shown in (3.26).

(3.26)   Halle (1977)

	profound	profundity
Underlying:	/ɨ̄/	/ɨ̄/
Trisyllabic Laxing:	−	ɨ
ɨ → [−high]:	−	ʌ
Vowel Shift:	aₜ	−
Diphthongisation:	aₜw	−
Surface:	aₜw	ʌ

	reduce	reduction	cube/venue
Underlying:	/x̄/	/x̄/	/x̄/
-CC Laxing:	−	ʌ	−
y-Preposing:	yx̄	−	yx̄
Vowel Shift:	yɨ̄	−	yɨ̄
High Rounding:	yū	−	yū
Diphthongisation:	yūw	−	yūw
Surface:	yūw	ʌ	yūw

	study	studious	ambiguity	ambiguous
Underlying:	/ʌ/	/ʌ/	/ʌ/	/ʌ/
Pre-V Tensing:	−	−	x̄	
				x̄
CiV Tensing:	−	x̄	−	−
y-Preposing:	−	yx̄	yx̄	yx̄
Vowel Shift:	−	yɨ̄	yɨ̄	yɨ̄
High Rounding:	−	yū	yū	yū
Diphthongisation:	−	yūw	yūw	yūw
Surface:	ʌ	yūw	yūw	yūw

	tabular
Underlying:	Ø
ʌ-Insertion:	ʌ
y-Preposing (before lax ʌ in open σ):	yʌ
Vowel Reduction:	yə

	push	pun
	/ʊ/	/ʌ/
Underlying:		
= Surface:	ʊ	ʌ

Halle's underlying representations are in some cases more surface-true than those of SPE; in addition, he no longer requires the SPE Rounding Adjustment rule, and his derivations make more use of independently necessary tensing and laxing rules rather than specially formulated ones. On the other hand, he introduces two additional absolute neutralisation rules and two non-surfacing, abstract underlying vowels, /ǣ/ and /ʌ̄/ (which are additionally suspect in belonging to the cross-linguistically rare category of back unrounded vowels), in order to derive the *reduce ~ reduction, study ~ studious* and *profound ~ profundity* alternations via the Vowel Shift Rule. Halle also assumes that both *ambiguous* and *ambiguity* have underlying /ʌ/, which in both cases undergoes Prevocalic Tensing and Vowel Shift. This derivation is possible only if the Vowel Shift is generalised to all tense vowels, regardless of stress, since [jū] is stressed in *ambiguity* but not in *ambiguous*. However, Halle's revised formulation of Vowel Shift has one major drawback; this concerns forms like *various* and *managerial*. The SPE derivations for these are given in (3.27).

(3.27)	Underlying:	væri+ous	mænægér+i+æl
	Pre-V Tensing:	værī+ous	mænæger+ī+æl
	CiV Tensing:	vǣrī+ous	mænægēr+ī+æl
	Vowel Shift:	vērī+ous	mænægīr+ī+æl
	Diphthongisation:	vēyrīy+ous	mænægīyr+īy+æl

As SPE restricts VSR for tense vowels to those which are also [+ stress], Chomsky and Halle have no difficulty with the failure of /ī/ to shift in both *various* and *managerial*. Halle, on the other hand, does not indicate how these vowels are to be stopped from shifting. A late tensing rule might be suggested, but some cases of tensing must be ordered before Vowel Shift to provide a suitable input, as in *Canadian* or *variety*, and it does not seem feasible to extract any context from the main Tensing Rule and order it after Vowel Shift.

However, if the VSR is restricted to stressed vowels, Halle cannot derive [jū] from /ʌ/ in *ambiguous*. His account is further compromised by the difficulty of deriving [jū] in words like *habitude, credulity* and *credulous.* These have the same augment as *ambiguous* and *ambiguity,* so that the same underlying representation, /ʌ/, should be appropriate. However, neither CiV Tensing nor Prevocalic Tensing can operate in *credulity,* etc., so that /ʌ/ cannot be tensed and shifted. Nor can Halle deal adequately with items like *angular* and *tabular.* Here, /ʌ/ is inserted by rule and the second expansion of Halle's y-Preposing rule, which inserts /j/ (= /y/) before lax /ʌ/ in an open syllable, will then operate. Since no tensing rule is appropriate in such cases, and the /ʌ/ vowel is unstressed, Vowel Reduction subsequently produces [jə]. However, as Chomsky and Halle (1968: 197) observe, the pronunciation [tæbjələ(r)] is only one variant: we must also allow for 'fairly careful speech, in which the medial vowel is rounded'. Yet Halle has no way of deriving phonetic [tæbjʊlə(r)].

Finally, Halle's y-Preposing rule itself (Halle 1977: 621) is problematic. This rule inserts /j/ (Halle's /y/) before all instances of tense /ʌ̄/, and before lax /ʌ/ in an open syllable. The restriction to open syllables is intended to exclude *pun, luck, but* and so on from y-Preposing. However, *butter, fussy* and *mussel* arguably have /ʌ/ in an open syllable but no [j]. Rubach (1984: 36) observes that 'the only way to exclude these words from j-Preposing is to posit underlying geminates. This is hardly a solution, since the geminates would serve no purpose other than to block j-Preposing.'

As Halle (1977) based his treatment of [jū] and related vowels on SPE, so Rubach (1984) in turn attempts to improve on Halle's study. Rubach retains some elements of Halle's analysis, such as the underlying /ɨ/ vowel in *profound ~ profundity,* but also makes some significant departures from the earlier work.

Like Halle, Rubach proposes /ʌ/ as the underlying vowel in *study ~ studious* and *Lilliput ~ Lilliputian,* but /ʌ̄/ in *reduce ~ reduction, punish ~ punitive.* Rubach consequently formulates his j-Preposing rule (1984: 32) to operate before tense /ʌ̄/, inserting /j/ in *reduce, studious, Lilliputian* and *punitive,* but correctly excluding *reduction, study, Lilliput, punish, pun, cut* and so on. In addition, Rubach assumes that this rule will insert /j/ in certain non-alternating forms like *mute, cucumber.*

Rubach's main innovation concerns the augment in *ambiguous* and *ambiguity* and the inserted vowel in *tabular, angular.* Halle considers the augment to be /ʌ/; this will undergo Vowel Shift and High Rounding. For *tabular,* Halle proposes /ʌ/-Insertion, open-syllable y-Preposing, and

Vowel Reduction. We have seen that the derivation of *ambiguous* and *tabular* cause difficulties for Halle: he must extend Vowel Shift to unstressed vowels to account for surface [jū] in *ambiguous*, and cannot produce a rounded medial vowel in *tabular*. Rubach acknowledges these problems, and proposes that VSR be once again restricted to stressed tense vowels. However, he is then forced to assign underlying /ʊ/ to *ambiguous* and *ambiguity*, and to insert /ʊ/ in *tabular*, where Vowel Reduction may then optionally apply to give [jə] or [jʊ]. These uses of /ʊ/ rather than /ʌ/ present Rubach, in turn, with two problems. First, he must exclude /ū/ (and consequently /ō/) from the domain of VSR, to stop tensed, stressed /ʊ/ from shifting in *ambiguity*. The exclusion of /ū/ and /ō/ from Vowel Shift is of no great consequence: Rubach assigns *profound* ~ *profundity* underlying /ư̄/, and the *lose* ~ *lost*, *shoot* ~ *shot*, and *fool* ~ *folly*, *school* ~ *scholar*, *food* ~ *fodder* and *poor* ~ *poverty* sets of alternations are extremely small, and arguably unproductive. Furthermore, experimental evidence considered earlier (Jaeger 1986, Wang and Derwing 1986) suggests that Modern English speakers no longer perceive these [ūw] ~ [ɒ] alternations to be part of the synchronic Vowel Shift pattern.

Secondly, because Rubach's j-Preposing rule only applies before tense /ʌ̄/, [j] is generated in *ambiguous*, *ambiguity* and *tabular* by an additional rule of j-Insertion (Rubach 1984: 36) which applies before lax /ʊ/. The cyclic nature of this rule means it does not apply in underived *put*, *push*, *bullet*, *soot* and the like, but will insert /j/ in *ambiguous* and *ambiguity*, where /ʊ/ is an augment; in *architecture*, where /ʊ/ is part of the suffix /-ʊr/; and in *tabular* and *angular*, where /ʊ/ is inserted earlier in the derivation. Rubach's derivations are given in (3.28).

(3.28)   Rubach

	profound	profundity	
Underlying:	/ư̄/	/ư̄/	
Trisyllabic Laxing:	–	ɨ	
ɨ → [−high]:	–	ʌ	
Vowel Shift:	ā	–	
Diphthongisation:	āw	–	
Surface:	āw	ʌ	

	reduce	reduction	cube/venue
Underlying:	/ʌ̄/	/ʌ̄/	/ʌ̄/
-CC Laxing:	–	ʌ	–
j-Preposing:	jʌ̄	–	jʌ̄
Vowel Shift:	jɨ̄	–	jɨ̄

High Rounding:	jū	–	jū
Diphthongisation:	jūw	–	jūw
Surface:	jūw	ʌ	jūw

	study	studious
Underlying:	/ʌ/	/ʌ/
CiV Tensing:	–	ʌ̄
j-Preposing:	–	jʌ̄
Vowel Shift:	–	jɨ̄
High Rounding:	–	jū
Diphthongisation:	–	jūw
Surface:	ʌ	jūw

	ambiguous	ambiguity	tabular
Underlying:	/ʊ/	/ʊ/	Ø
ʊ-Insertion:	–	–	ʊ
j-Insertion:	jʊ	jʊ	jʊ
Pre-V Tensing:	jū	jū	jū
Vowel Reduction:	–	–	jə or jʊ
Diphthongisation:	jūw	jūw	–
Surface:	jūw	jūw	jə or jʊ

	push	pun
Underlying:	/ʊ/	/ʌ/
= Surface:	ʊ	ʌ

However, it is not clear how Rubach is to derive *blue*, *rude*, etc., which have the same surface [ūw] as *ambiguous*, *reduce* and *cube* but lack [j]. Conversely, Rubach admits that he is unable to generate [j] in words like *copula* and *population* (1984: 37), and has to assume that the glide is present lexically in these forms. Rubach also requires two rules, j-Preposing and j-Insertion, to perform what seems intuitively to be a single process, and his analysis still relies on absolute neutralisation and the non-surfacing vowels /ɨ/ and /ʌ̄/ in the derivation of *profound* ~ *profundity*, *reduce* ~ *reduction*, *mute*, *tutor* and *cucumber* (and presumably also *cube* and *venue*).

Halle and Mohanan (1985) retain substantially the same derivations as Rubach for the *profound* ~ *profundity*, *reduce* ~ *reduction* and *study* ~ *studious* alternations. They also derive [ʌ] in *gun*, *but*, etc. directly from /ʌ/, and [ʊ] in *put*, *push* from /ʊ/. However, their treatment of the [yūw]/ [jū] sequence in non-alternating forms like *cube*, *music*, *residue*, *avenue*, *statue* and *venue* departs considerably from previous analyses, primarily because their version of Vowel Shift is restricted to long, rather than tense vowels. Like Halle (1977), Halle and Mohanan drop the requirement that vowels should be stressed in order to shift; to account for *various* ~ *variety, impious* ~ *pious* and *maniac* ~ *maniacal*, they consequently propose an *ad hoc* rule of Prevocalic Lengthening (a process quite distinct from the remarkably similar Prevocalic Tensing), to lengthen the stressed vowel in certain lexically marked words. Halle and Mohanan also propose that the English Main Stress Rule should be made sensitive to vowel length: it follows that the presence or absence of stress can be one indicator of underlying vowel length, and therefore of the eligibility of a vowel for Vowel Shift (recall that Halle and Mohanan order VSR on Level 2, where it is not subject to DEC). Halle and Mohanan rely on this supposed interdependence of vowel length, stress and VSR to argue that the vowels which surface as [jū] in (3.29) and (3.30) 'cannot be identical in underlying representation, but become identical (save for stress)' due to Vowel Shift (1985: 90).

(3.29) | argue | issue | statue | venue |
|---|---|---|---|
| ague | tissue | virtue | menu |

(3.30) | cube | music | putrid | beauty |
|---|---|---|---|
| revenue | residue | avenue | |
| absolute | hypotenuse | substitute | |

The argument which leads to this unexpected conclusion runs roughly as follows. In (3.29), the word-final vowels are stressless and must therefore be underlyingly short; [jū] cannot, therefore, be derived via Vowel Shift, and the underlying vowel must be [+ high], since the surface vowel is [+ high]. Halle and Mohanan propose underlying /i/, which will subsequently undergo Stem-Final Lengthening and Tensing. However, in (3.30), the vowel surfacing as [jū] 'is long and must therefore have undergone Vowel Shift. Since [yūw] is [+ high], its pre-Vowel Shift source must be [− high]' (Halle and Mohanan 1985: 90). They conclude that, in (3.30), [yūw]/[jū] is derived from /ƛ̄/, which will shift to [ɨ]. y-Insertion (Halle and Mohanan 1985: 90) is formulated to operate before high back unrounded [ɨ] and [i]. Lax [ɨ] must then be lowered in closed syllables, to give surface [ʌ] in *sulphur, profundity* and so on, while lax [ɨ] in open syllables and tense [ɨ] in all cases are rounded. One final extra rule of i-Lengthening, which applies to stressed short /i/, is also posited to account for [jū] in *sulphuric*. Derivations for the *profound* ~ *profundity, reduce* ~ *reduction, study* ~ *studious* and *sulphur* ~ *sulphuric* alternations, and for *cube, revenue* and *venue*, are given in (3.31).

(3.31)   Halle and Mohanan (1985)

	study	studious	sulphur	sulphuric
Underlying:	/ʌ/	/ʌ/	/ɨ/	/ɨ/
CiV Lengthening:	–	ʌ̄	–	ɨ̄
Vowel Shift:	–	ɨ̄	–	–
ɨ-Lowering:	–	–	ʌ	–
ɨ-Lengthening:	–	–	–	ɨ̄
y-Insertion:	–	ȳi	–	yɨ̄
Diphthongisation:	–	yɨ̄w	–	yɨ̄w
ɨ-Rounding:	–	yūw	–	yūw
Vowel Reduction:	–	–	ə	–
Surface:	ʌ	yūw	ə	yūw

	profound	profundity
Underlying:	/ɨ̄/	/ɨ̄/
Trisyllabic Laxing:	–	ɨ
Vowel Shift:	ā	–
ɨ-Lowering:	–	ʌ
Diphthongisation:	āw	–
Surface:	āw	ʌ

	reduce	reduction	cube/revenue
Underlying:	/ʌ̄/	/ʌ̄/	/ʌ̄/
-CC Shortening:	–	ʌ	–
Vowel Shift:	ɨ̄	–	ɨ̄
y-Insertion:	yɨ̄	–	yɨ̄
Diphthongisation:	yɨ̄w	–	yɨ̄w
ɨ-Rounding:	yūw	–	yūw
Surface:	yūw	ʌ	yūw

	venue/statue
Underlying:	/ɨ/
y-Insertion:	yɨ
Stem-Final Tensing/Lengthening:	yɨ̄
ɨ-Rounding:	yū
Surface:	yū

Halle and Mohanan's account of [jū] and the alternations in which it is involved must surely be the most complex and least satisfactory of the post-SPE studies considered here. Halle and Mohanan's underlying vowel system contains more non-surfacing vowels, i.e. /ɨ/, /ɨ̄/ and /ʌ̄/, than those of either Halle (1977) or Rubach (1984), and Halle and Mohanan also require more additional rules, in the form of ɨ-Lowering, ɨ-Lengthening and ɨ-Rounding, to dispose of these non-surfacing segments. Their logic in assigning different final underlying vowels to *revenue*, *avenue* and *residue* on the one hand, and *venue* and *statue* on the other, also seems flawed, for two reasons. First, there seems no distinctive difference in stress between the final vowel of *venue* and that of *avenue*, yet stress is Halle and Mohanan's major motivation for arguing that the first is underlyingly short and the second long. Secondly, although Halle and Mohanan assert that the final vowels of *venue* and *avenue*, as well as the stressed vowel of *cube*, 'become identical (save for stress)' (1985: 90) during the course of the derivation, a careful consideration of their ordered list of rules (1985: 100) shows that this cannot be so: [yūw] can indeed be derived from /ʌ̄/ in *cube* and *avenue*, via Vowel Shift, y-Insertion, Diphthongisation and ɨ-Rounding, but there is no way of deriving [yūw] in *venue, statue*, etc.

The *venue* vowel can, however, surface in two different ways, according to dialect. In Halle and Mohanan's Dialect D, final /ɨ/ will undergo y-Insertion and postlexical ɨ-Rounding. However, since Dialect D shows no evidence of Stem-Final Tensing (Halle and Mohanan 1985: 59), /ɨ/ cannot be tensed. Nor can it be lengthened stem-finally, since Stem-Final Lengthening (Halle and Mohanan 1985: 61) affects only tense back vowels in dialects other than B. In Dialect D, then, the word-final vowel in *venue* will surface as short high lax [jʊ]. In Dialects A, B and C, /ɨ/ in *venue* will have [j] inserted, and will then be eligible for Stem-Final Tensing and Lengthening and postlexical ɨ-Rounding. However, although this will allow for surface [jū], the vowel cannot then undergo Diphthongisation to produce Halle and Mohanan's [yūw], since Stem-Final Lengthening is a Stratum 3 rule but Diphthongisation, which applies to long vowels, applies on Stratum 2.

It is clear, then, that Halle and Mohanan cannot derive [yūw] vowels, 'identical (save for stress)' (Halle and Mohanan 1985: 90) in *venue, statue, cube* and *avenue*. It seems also that they will find difficulty in deriving [yūw] in *ambiguous* and *ambiguity* (which they mention only very briefly) and in *tabular* (which they do not mention at all). To take *tabular* first; if /ʌ/ is inserted, this cannot undergo Vowel Shift to [ɨ] since the medial vowel is unstressed and must therefore be underlyingly short. If /ɨ/ is the vowel inserted, it can attract /y/ and undergo ɨ-Rounding, but cannot be lengthened, tensed or diphthongised. As for *ambiguous* and *ambiguity*, the only possible underlying vowel is again /ɨ/ (see (3.32)).

(3.32)		tabular	ambiguous	ambiguity
	Underlying/Inserted:	/ɨ/	/ɨ/	/ɨ/
	Pre-V Tensing:	–	ī	ī
	y-Insertion:	yɨ	yī	yī
	ɨ-Rounding:	yʊ	yū	yū

Again, [yūw] cannot be derived, since Diphthongisation affects only long vowels, and Halle and Mohanan propose a rule of Prevocalic *Lengthening* only in a few lexically marked words such as *variety*, *maniacal* and *pious*. Even if Prevocalic Lengthening were permitted, *ambiguity* would require underlying /ʌ/, since the tensed, stressed, long vowel otherwise resulting could not be excluded from Vowel Shift. It seems that the best we can do in Halle and Mohanan's system is to derive [jʊ] in *tabular* and [jū] in *ambiguous* and *ambiguity*, but as the surface facts demand [jū] (Halle and Mohanan's [yūw]) obligatorily in *ambiguity* and at least optionally in *ambiguous* and *tabular*, the best is clearly not good enough.

3.3.3.2   An alternative analysis

Given the numerous problems encountered and engendered by these analyses, it is clear that there is no harm in attempting to find a more concrete solution. The first step in this direction is to consider again the status of the [j] glide in [jū]. In all the accounts discussed in the previous section, this glide was taken to be inserted by rule; however, this is by no means a self-evident assumption, and the [jū] sequence might also be considered a diphthong, at least underlyingly.

It certainly seems that at least one historical source for [jū] was diphthongal. Strang (1970) and Stockwell (1990) agree that Middle English <ewe>, <fewe>, <newe>, <triwe>/<truwe>, from Old English <eowu>, <fēawe>, <nēawe>, <trēowe>/<trīewe> suggest a shift of the /w/ from the onset of the second syllable into the nucleus of the first, giving [iu] or [ɛu]. Stockwell proposes that this resyllabification of /w/ caused the first part of the earlier diphthong to move in turn into the syllable onset; Strang (1970: 158) sees this 'syllabicity shift' as independent of the development of /w/, but accepts that <yeue>, <yowe>, <yoo> spellings, mainly from Northern dialects in the late thirteenth century, support a change from a falling to a rising diphthong. This diphthong subsequently merged with late Middle English /y:/ in French loans of the *issue*, *virtue*, *leisure* type, where Stockwell proposes a development of Cüu > Ciu > C^{i}iu > C^{i}u. In cases like *blue, shrew*, where Strang argues the /j/ was later lost, there is a further merger with /u:/ from Vowel Shift of earlier /o:/ in *doom, moon, boot*. More recent evidence suggests that the acceptability of /j/ in clusters has been progressively restricted. For instance, Gimson (1980) lists /lj-/ as acceptable in *lewd* [ljūd], *lure* [ljʊə], and *lucid* [ljūsɪd]. However, no [j] appears in *loom, loop, loose, lunar* and *lute*, and even in the forms Gimson lists, [lj] is now only common in conservative RP and with older speakers. However, /lj/ is permissible if /l/ can be resyllabified into the coda of the preceding syllable; thus, *postlude* and *interlude* have [ū] but *prelude* has [jū]. In most American English, [j] is also absent after coronals, unless the following vowel is unstressed, as in *venue* [vɛnjū], *virtue* [vɪrtjū] or [vɪrtʃū] and *issue* [ɪsjū] or [ɪʃū].

Two questions arise here: is there evidence for still regarding /jū/ as a rising diphthong in Modern English, and how do we account for the contexts in which /j/ was lost? To begin with the diphthong question, there are indeed analyses of /jū/ where an underlying diphthong is posited. For instance, Anderson's (1987) Dependency Phonology analysis treats [jū] as a diphthong [ɪu], derived either from long, tense /ɪu/, or from short, lax /ɪV/; the latter is an underlying combination of {i} plus the 'unspecified vowel'. I will not pursue Anderson's analysis in detail, partly because it relies on under- and un-specification, theoretical devices not employed here; what is more interesting is the speech error evidence, from Shattuck-Hufnagel (1986), which he uses to support it. This evidence, however, is not unambiguous. Shattuck-Hufnagel argues that speech error patterns are important in deciding whether [j] is nuclear or not, since earlier work has shown that 'polysegmental error units tend to respect the onset–rhyme boundary' (1986: 130) – in *clamp*, for instance, [l] may form an error unit with the preceding [k], since both are in the onset, but not with the following vowel. On the basis of seventy [jū] errors from the MIT error corpus, Shattuck-Hufnagel observes that, although the [jū] sequence may on occasion function as an error unit, as in *m*[jū]*sarpial* for *mars*[jū]*pial*, in a far larger number of cases, thirty-three in all, [j] constitutes an error unit in isolation from [ū], interacting with another C (see (3.33)).

(3.33)   rusing   *for*   using
          cues   *for*   crews
          [krūk-]   *for*   cucumbers
          [flūz-]   *for*   fuse blown
          writing rutensil *for* utensil

The fact that 'a /j/ before /ū/ interacts freely with other onset consonants in errors' (Shattuck-Hufnagel 1986: 132) might suggest that /j/ itself forms part of the onset. There are, however, no examples in the corpus of C/j/ acting as an error unit, as would be expected if /j/ is indeed an onset consonant, given that entire onsets composed of CC clusters do tend to function as error units in other cases.

Davis and Hammond (1995) identify various asymmetries between CyV and CwV sequences in American English, arguing that 'the onglide in a CwV sequence is treated as an onset while the onglide in a CyV sequence is treated as co-moraic with the following vowel' (1995: 160). Davis and Hammond (1995: 176) explicitly discount error evidence as inconclusive, but present evidence from two other sources. First, there are certain co-occurrence restrictions involving /j/: notably, it can appear after sonorant /m/ in *mute, music* (and likewise /n/ in British English), although this does not otherwise cluster as C_1; in American English again, clusters of coronal plus [j] are prohibited, which Davis and Hammond attribute to a homorganicity condition holding between onset and nucleus; and the vowel following [j] must be [u:]. Davis and Hammond also present data from two language games, Pig Latin and the Name Game, which seem to support a nuclear analysis of [j], although evidence is arguably stronger from the latter. In the Name Game, the initial consonant or consonant cluster of a name is replaced with [b], [f] and [m]. Although [Cw] clusters are replaced as a whole, in apparent [Cj] clusters, the C alone is replaced, with the [j] remaining (3.34).

(3.34) Claire   Gwen   Beula
        [kler]   [gwɛn]   [bjulə]
        [ber]   [bɛn]   [bjulə]
        [fer]   [fɛn]   [fjulə]
        [mer]   [mɛn]   [mjulə]

It would be interesting to test names like *Ruth*, where the initial consonant cannot cluster with [j]; if Name Game alternation produced [bjuθ], [fjuθ] and [mjuθ] rather than [buθ], [fuθ] and [muθ], this might instead suggest a productive process of j-Insertion. In the absence of such evidence, we must concur with Davis and Hammond (1995: 170) that 'Cw clusters pattern like true onset clusters and Cy clusters do not'.

Again, however, the situation is not clear-cut. Recall that evidence from speech errors potentially supports analyses of /j/ both as an onset consonant and as nuclear. Different data involving co-occurrence restrictions similarly seem to support different approaches: although Davis and

Hammond invoke homorganicity constraints in support of a nuclear account, strong evidence against a diphthongal analysis of [jū] comes from the relationship of phonotactics and syllable structure. Selkirk (1982b: 339) notes that one of the primary motivations for separating onset from rhyme and nucleus from coda, is the presence of phonotactic restrictions. For English at least,

> it is within the onset, peak and coda that the strongest collocational restrictions obtain, [since] the likelihood of the existence of phonotactic constraints between the position slots in the syllable ... is a reflection of the immediate constituent (IC) structure relation between the two slots: the more closely related structurally ... the more subject to phonotactic constraints two position slots are.

Selkirk alleges that English has *no* phonotactic restrictions between onset and nucleus. This claim would be refuted by the proposed diphthong /ɪu/, since the [j], or [ɪ] segment is permissible only after certain onset consonants: after /r/, /w/, /ʃ/ and /dʒ/, for instance, [ū] surfaces alone, without [j]. These distributional restrictions are easily explicable if [j] is an onset consonant, since phonotactic constraints within the onset are, Selkirk suggests, to be expected, and any rule inserting /j/ will simply not be permitted to contravene these phonotactic restrictions. But they are hard to account for if [j]/[ɪ] is nuclear, since we will then be faced with a situation where a single vowel is distributionally restricted on the basis of the preceding onset consonant(s).

Davis and Hammond address problems of this sort, as well as some difficulties with their Pig Latin data, by proposing, as Shattuck-Hufnagel (1986) and Borowsky (1990) also suggest, that /j/ 'moves' during the derivation from being closely bound to the /ū/ vowel to associating more regularly with other onset consonants: the underlying /ˈu/ diphthong is affected by an /ˈ/-to-[j] rule. Davis and Hammond argue that /ˈu/ can follow coronals underlyingly, as one would expect of a vowel; however, if a coronal ends up in the same onset as the resyllabified onglide, the onglide will be deleted by rule as the cluster contravenes the phonotactics.

I shall adopt Davis and Hammond's nuclear analysis of the onglide in [jū] in what follows, with some revisions which will be detailed below. Some further evidence from alternations like *reduce ~ reduction* and *study ~ studious*, which lack [j] in some American English, strongly supports a diphthongal analysis, at least underlyingly. Furthermore, given the constraints on my model of Lexical Phonology, I have no choice but to disallow a j-Insertion analysis in the majority of forms. Allowing j-Insertion in underived *cube, assume, reduce* and *venue* would mean exempting it from DEC and the Alternation Condition. Furthermore, having the same underlying vowel in *cute* and *cool*, or *dew* and *do*, requires either absolute neutralisation (as in Halle and Mohanan 1985), or an unacceptable level of exception-marking to stop *cool, do* and many others from undergoing j-Insertion (as in McMahon 1990). The exception rate will be high even if we account separately for restrictions on whole classes of preceding consonants, such as coronals in American English, using filters, and will be even higher in Scottish English, where there is no [ʊ], and *look, put, wood* have [u].

I will continue to transcribe the [jū] sequence as /jū/ underlyingly, to indicate that it is, exceptionally for English, a *rising* diphthong; and to highlight the fact that [j] does end up in the onset, as indicated by its palatalisation of preceding consonants in *duke* [dʒūk], *issue* [ɪʃū] and Scots *student* [ʃtʃudnʔ], *Hughie* [çui]. Indeed, since I assume that different speakers may have different underlying representations and derivations, it is likely that restructuring will have affected these forms in some grammars, shifting them from the diphthongal class to underlying /ū/ with a preceding palatal consonant. Davis and Hammond also regard their /ʹu/ diphthong as monomoraic; however, they require very widespread late lengthening, since so many of the reflexes of the vowel are long. It seems more appropriate to assume shortening under low stress than the reverse, to account for the fact that the final vowel in *venue* and *avenue* tends to be shorter or laxer than [jū] in *cube*, and similarly that *ambiguous* and *tabular* have shorter medial vowels than *ambiguity*. One might therefore adopt in essence Rubach's (1984: 49) proposal that a rule of u-Laxing operates whenever /ū/ is unstressed, although this process might be better formulated as shortening /ū/ while leaving it tense; on the other hand, this may be an automatic, low-level phonetic process, not requiring a specific phonological rule. The /jū/ diphthong then also accords with the usual tendency of English diphthongs to pattern with long vowels.

I assume, then, that non-alternating [ʊ] in *push, put*, etc., will be derived from /ʊ/; non-alternating [ʌ] in *pun, but* words, and the [ʌ] ~ [jū] alternation in *study* ~ *studious* and *sulphur* ~ *sulphuric* from /ʌ/; and *reduce* ~ *reduction, cube, venue*, and *ambiguous* from /jū/. I retain a rule of j-Insertion (3.35), applying in a very restricted set of alternating forms, including *studious* (~ *study*) and *tabular, angular* (~ *table, angle*). As we shall see, Vowel Shift also plays a part in the derivation of some of these alternations. This may seem an unacceptably mixed analysis, involving as it does both a novel underlying diphthong, and an inserted glide; however, I shall show that our Lexical Phonological constraints delimit derived from surface-true cases.

(3.35)   *j-Insertion*

$$\emptyset \;\rightarrow\; j \,/\, .(C) - \begin{bmatrix} + \text{high} \\ + \text{back} \\ + \text{round} \\ - \text{low} \\ + \text{tense} \end{bmatrix}$$

We need not dwell on *put, pull, pun, but, ambiguous, ambiguity, cube* and *venue* words further; where there is no alternation, the underlying vowel will simply be surface true. j-Insertion and Vowel Shift will be restricted to alternating forms, and I therefore turn to the three types of alternation involving [jū], namely *reduce ~ reduction*, where the derived form contains a laxing context; *study ~ studious*, where tensing occurs in the derived form; and *tabular, angular (~ table, angle)*.

Let us take the most straightforward case (though the one with most alternative derivations) first. Some speakers may not relate *table* and *tabular*, or *angle* and *angular*, productively; they will simply be listed independently, with underlying and lexical representations identical as befits non-alternating forms. For speakers who do derive *tabular* and *angular*, the inserted vowel might be /ū/: this vowel insertion will follow morphological derivation, and will in turn feed j-Insertion. Alternatively, the diphthong /jū/ might be the vowel inserted, with non-syllabic /j/ migrating later to the onset. Both options may be right, for different speakers. Furthermore, neither account is out of line with Davis and Hammond (1995) who, although in general discounting j-Insertion, do propose glide epenthesis for precisely these forms (1995: 179, fn.10). In the same footnote, they explicitly exclude *reduce ~ reduction* and *study ~ studious* from their investigation, given that these vowel alternations are post-coronal and [j] is therefore not involved for most American English.

We turn now to these *reduce ~ reduction* and *study ~ studious* alternations, which are slightly more complex, partly because English dialects fall into two sets here, those with /ʌ/ and those without it. In Northern and North Midland dialects of England, for instance, [ʊ] appears in all non-alternating words in which RP would have [ʊ] or [ʌ], and also replaces [ʌ] in alternating forms like those in the right-hand column of (3.36).

(3.36)   [ʊ]

     push   pun   study
     pull   but   reduction
     cushion   duck   profundity

In these varieties, underlying /jū/, which surfaces unchanged in *reduce*, will simply undergo -CC Laxing in *reduction* to give [ʊ]. Conversely, the underlying stem vowel for *study* ~ *studious* will be /ʊ/, the surface vowel of underived *study*, which will undergo CiV Tensing in *studious* to give [ū], with tensing feeding j-Insertion (3.35). In SPE and subsequent work (see especially Rubach 1984: 32, 40) the rule of CiV Tensing is restricted to non-high vowels; and /ʊ/ is, of course, [+ high]. However, it seems that high vowels are excluded in the literature solely on the basis of the front vowel: SPE gives examples only for /ɪ/, as shown in (3.37).

(3.37)   [ɪ], *not* [aɪ]
        SPE: punctilious, Darwinian, reptilian, vicious
        Rubach: artificial, prejudicial, avaricious

In all probability, /ʊ/ as well as /ɪ/ was excluded from the scope of CiV Tensing, by the addition of the specification [−high], simply on the grounds of economy; tensing of /ʊ/ was achieved in SPE by a special tensing and unrounding rule designed to produce [ɨ], so that applying CiV Tensing to /ʊ/ was never necessary. Since there is no empirical reason for excluding /ʊ/ from CiV Tensing, I propose that the rule should be applicable to all vowels save /ɪ/.

An analysis deriving *study* ~ *studious* from /ʊ/ and *reduce* ~ *reduction* from /jū/ can, then, account for dialects which lack /ʌ/. However, my analysis predicts that these Northern dialects represent the unmarked case, whereas in reality a relatively small proportion of English dialects lack /ʌ/; in RP, Scots/SSE and many (if not all) American English dialects, [ʌ] alternates with [(j)ū] while /ʊ/ never participates in morphophonemic alternations. Historically, of course, the Northern dialects with /ʊ/ but no /ʌ/ do represent the unmarked case, in that they are typical of the Middle English situation; orthoepical evidence for (probably allophonic) lowering and unrounding of /ʊ/ to [ʌ], with [ʊ] retained between a labial and another consonant, as in *pull*, *push*, *woman* and *wood*, first becomes available around 1640 (Dobson 1957: 93). Dobson attributes the retention of [ʊ] after labials to the lip position of /w p b f/ acting against the lip spreading required for [ʌ]; however, he notes that 'the rounding influence acted sporadically and produced inconsistent results, as is evident from the common words *put*, *but*, *butcher* and *butter*' (1957: 196). This eventually led to a phonemic split of /ʊ/ and /ʌ/, since 'the PresE distinction between words with [ʊ] and words with [ʌ] shows no regularity; [ʌ] occurs in positions that should favour [ʊ] in *wonder*, *pun*, *puff . . . but*, *bulk* and *bulb*' (Dobson 1957: 196).

Dialects with /ʌ/, such as RP, Scots/SSE (which, conversely, lack /ʊ/ – see chapter 4) and GenAm, are therefore historically more complex than the Northern English dialects, having undergone an additional sound change and innovated an extra phoneme, /ʌ/. The synchronic picture is concomitantly more complex in these innovating varieties.

Working on our assumptions up to now, we diagnose the underlying vowel in *study* and *studious* as lax /ʌ/, which surfaces unaltered in *study* but will undergo CiV Tensing in *studious*. In *reduce* ~ *reduction*, the underlier will be /jū/, with -CC Laxing in the derived form. However, tensing and laxing cannot be the whole story, since we also find differences in vowel height. In order for j-Insertion to operate in *studious*, we need raising as well as tensing to give the required [ū] (and this will be so even in American varieties where j-Insertion is not applicable); conversely, in *reduction*, we must account for the non-surfacing of /j/ and the vowel lowering.

The process which first comes to mind when considering a Modern English alternation involving tense and lax vowels of differing heights is, of course, Vowel Shift. As we saw in 3.3.2 above, Jaeger (1986: 86) argues that the derivation of alternations using the synchronic VSR no longer depends solely on which vowel pairings resulted from the Great Vowel Shift (and [(j)ū] ~ [ʌ] did not); instead, Modern English speakers are influenced by the frequency of alternations and their conformity with the English Spelling Rule. Consequently, certain alternations like [ū] ~ [ɒ] and [aʊ] ~ [ʌ], which were originally derived via Vowel Shift, are no longer perceived as part of the Vowel Shift set.

I contend that the opposite also holds: as the motivation for Vowel Shift changes, it not only comes to exclude alternations which were included earlier, but also to include alternations which did not involve the historical Great Vowel Shift. This is the case with [(j)ū] ~ [ʌ], which is historically an alternation of tense and lax vowels of the same height, complicated by the subsequent lowering of /ʊ/ in some dialects. As a relatively frequent alternation, with both elements commonly spelt

<u>, involving a tense and a lax vowel of different heights, [(j)ū] ~ [ʌ] could easily conform to an internalised Vowel Shift template. Indeed, psycholinguistic evidence (Jaeger 1986, Wang and Derwing 1986) suggests that this is the case: data from Jaeger's experiment in (3.14) above showed that speakers produced on average 75 per cent affirmative responses to this alternation, close to the 80–93 per cent for the four core alternations on which they had been trained, and well above the maximum 25 per cent affirmative response for vowel pairs to which they had been trained to respond negatively. It seems that synchronic phonological rules need not, and perhaps cannot be identical to their historical sources in a constrained lexical model. In dialects without /ʌ/, VSR will be irrelevant to the derivation of [jū] ~ [ʊ], presumably because an alternation must involve two surface vowels of different heights to be included in the Vowel Shift concept.

However, although VSR will produce a quality difference here, it will not alone produce quite the right quality difference; recall that the innovation of /ʌ/ has disrupted the system. In varieties with /ʌ/, the [(j)ū] ~ [ʌ] alternation will therefore involve VSR and two Level 1 Rounding Adjustment rules; tensed [ʌ̄] will round to [ō], which then shifts to [ū] via V̆SR in *studious*, while laxed [ʊ] will shift to [o] and subsequently unround to [ʌ] in *reduction, assumption*. In accents lacking /ʌ/, /ʊ/ will be exempted from V̆SR and the derivation of *reduce, reduction, study* and *studious* will be as shown in (3.38a), using only the tensing and laxing rules. In other varieties, /ʊ/ will be permitted to undergo V̆SR, and /ʌ/ need not be explicitly excluded either, since it will never appear in the correct context for shifting to occur, being itself derived via V̆SR in *reduction* and *assumption*. Derivations are shown in (3.38b).

(3.38)   a. *Varieties without /ʌ/*

		reduce	reduction	study	studious
	Underlying:	/jū/	/jū/	/ʊ/	/ʊ/
Level 1	Laxing:	–	ʊ	–	–
	Tensing:	–	–	–	u
Level 2	j-Insertion:	–	–	–	jū

b. *Varieties with /ʌ/*

		reduce	reduction	study	studious
	Underlying:	/ju/	/ju/	/ʌ/	/ʌ/
Level 1	Laxing:	–	ʊ	–	–
	Tensing:	–	–	–	ʌ̄
	ʌ̄-Rounding:	–	–	–	ō
	V̆SR:	–	o	–	–

	VSR:	−	−		−	ū
	o-Unrounding:	−	ʌ		−	−
Level 2	j-Insertion:	−	−		−	jū

So far, so good; but the puzzle still has one missing piece. j-Insertion, in its now severely limited role, will supply [j] in *studious* (and for some speakers, in *angular, tabular*). However, we are assuming underlying /jū/ in *reduce ~ reduction*, and here [j] fails to surface in the derived form. This is not a problem for American English, where the underlier will be monophthongal /ū/; but for other varieties, where [j] is permissible after coronals, we might require some filter or repair strategy, reflecting the absence of [j] before [ʌ]. In fact, this is not necessary, given the argument for underlying diphthongs in 3.3.1 above. Recall that the *divine ~ divinity* alternation was there derived from underlying /aɪ/. I argued that, as part of laxing, this diphthong lost its less prominent part, here the offglide, as shown in (3.11). If we extend this analysis to the diphthong /jū/, the onglide will drop and the remaining vowel lax, as shown in (3.39).

(3.39)   X   X   X   X   X
          | | →   ⫽ | → |
          j   ū   j   ū   ʊ

Not only does this analysis remove the requirement for specific deletion of /j/; it also indicates that /jū/, although its prominence pattern is uncharacteristic, patterns in terms of laxing with the other English diphthong involved in synchronic Vowel Shift alternations. This does seem to support Davis and Hammond's (1995) contention that /j/ in this sequence is initially nuclear.

In summary, I give sample derivations in (3.40) for [ʌ], [ʊ], [ū] and [jū] words, excluding the *reduce ~ reduction* and *study ~ studious* alternations which appear in (3.38) above, indicating the much reduced distance between underlying and surface forms as compared with any analysis discussed in the previous section.

(3.40)		ambiguous	ambiguity	cube/venue
	Underlying:	/jū/	/jū/	/jū/
	u-Laxing/shortening:	jū/jʊ	−	−
	Surface:	jū/jʊ	jū	jū
		pun	push	
	Underlying:	/ʌ/or /ʊ/	/ʊ/	
	= Surface:	ʌ or ʊ	ʊ	

	tabular				
Underlying:	Ø	*or*	Ø	*or*	jū
ū-Insertion:	ū		jū		–
j-Insertion:	jū		–		–
u-Laxing/Shortening:	jū/jʊ		jū/jʊ		jū/jʊ
Optional V reduction:	jə		jə		jə
Surface:	jū/jʊ/jə		jū/jʊ/jə		jū/jʊ/jə

3.4   Problems for Level 1 Vowel Shift Rule

Having established that problems for Vowel Shift of lax vowels are more apparent than real, we turn now to difficulties pertaining to any VSR operating on Level 1 of the lexicon. The first of these concerns other phonological rules which allegedly interact with Vowel Shift, while the second involves the Modern English strong verbs.

3.4.1   *Interacting rules*

If VSR applies on Level 1, so must any rules which are crucially ordered earlier. Halle and Mohanan (1985: 103–4) list various tensing and laxing rules, i-Lengthening, i-Rounding, Velar Softening and their ablaut rules for strong verbs, as necessarily preceding VSR. Since they order all but a subset of the tensing and laxing rules on Level 2, this poses an obvious problem for a model restricting VSR to Level 1.

Some of Halle and Mohanan's rules can immediately be discounted. Since [jū] and related vowels can be derived without recourse to /ɨ ɨ̄/, i-Lengthening and Rounding are not required. I shall also argue below that most strong verbs should be dealt with allomorphically rather than derived through a set of ostensibly regular phonological rules; I therefore reject Halle and Mohanan's ablaut rules. This leaves tensing, laxing, and Velar Softening.

It should be clear from 3.2 above that the interaction of tensing and laxing with VSR is even more crucial in this account than in Halle and Mohanan's. I assume that Trisyllabic, Suffix (before /-ɪk/, /-ɪd/ and /-ɪʃ/) and Pre-Cluster Laxing are all Level 1 processes, so that the interaction of V̆SR and laxing will be unproblematic. Not all tensing rules can be similarly ordered: Stem-Final Tensing must apparently operate on Level 2, since it affects underived *vary*, *city*. However, since Stem-Final Tensing does not feed V̄SR, this is irrelevant. CiV and Prevocalic Tensing, which do feed V̄SR (as in *comedian* and *algebraic* respectively), can both be regarded as Level 1 rules. Halle and Mohanan restrict Prevocalic Tensing to Level 2 on the basis of its alleged operation in underived *ammonia*, but since this never alternates with any form containing a lax vowel, I assume tense /ī/ underlyingly. Prevocalic Tensing will then be restricted to cases like *algebraic*, where tensed, shifted [ē] alternates with lax final [æ] in *algebra*.

We have now exhausted Halle and Mohanan's list of rules, with the exception of Velar Softening of /k g/ to [s dʒ], which must apparently be ordered on Level 2 since it applies in underived *reduce, oblige*; some further examples are given in (3.41).

(3.41)   critic ~ criticise   matrix ~ matrices
          medicate ~ medicine   reduction ~ reducent
          fungus ~ fungi   analogue ~ analogy

Velar Softening is often cited as part of the internal evidence for the synchronic status of VSR, on the grounds that Velar Softening is hard to formalise unless it precedes Vowel Shift. If VSR applies first, the context for Velar Softening will consist of a following front high tense [ī], the lax monophthongs [ɪ] or [ɛ], and the diphthong [aɪ]. However, if Velar Softening applies to pre-VSR representations, the context is the far more natural class of /ī ē ɪ ɛ/ – any non-low, non-back following vowel.

The facts of Velar Softening seem irreconcilable with a Level 1 Vowel Shift. However, Jaeger (1986: 76–7), reviewing the use of evidence from rule interaction in establishing the order and reality of rules, argues that '... before an internal claim of this sort can be convincing, the synchronic psychological reality and the phonetic accuracy of each rule must be substantiated'. Such substantiation seems unlikely for Velar Softening, which is not fully productive, and therefore applies to a lexically specified class of inputs, as shown by the contrasting softened and non-softened forms in (3.42).

(3.42)   Stoic ~ Stoicism   vs.   monarch ~ monarchism
          lyric ~ lyricist   vs.   anarchy ~ anarchist
          analog ~ analogise   vs.   diphthong ~ diphthongise
                                        (from Rubach 1984: 27)

In SPE, velar segments which are to undergo Velar Softening are lexically /k^d g^d/, where the superscript ^{d} corresponds to a diacritic [+ derived], to distinguish them from non-softening /k g/. Rubach (1984: 27) supports this lexical marking of the relevant 'subclass of Greek and Latin words'. If speakers learn the specific morphemes which undergo

Velar Softening, it is questionable whether achieving greater naturalness in the statement of the conditioning context of the rule, by ordering VSR after it, is of particular relevance or help (McCawley 1986: 30). It follows that the consequences which moving VSR to Level 1 will have for Velar Softening do not constitute a strong enough argument for revoking this step and retaining VSR on Level 2.

3.4.2   The strong verbs

The Modern English strong verbs which constitute the subject of this section will be defined for present purposes as all those verbs which do not simply add a dental suffix {D} (realised as [-t], [-d] or [-ɪd] depending on the preceding phonological context) to mark the past tense, but also, or instead, change the quality of the stem vowel. This set of strong verbs includes *keep ~ kept, sit ~ sat, hold ~ held, fight ~ fought, choose ~ chose, lie ~ lay, draw ~ drew* and perhaps 140 others (see Bloch 1947). The term 'strong' therefore designates not only historically strong verbs, but also historically weak verbs which now exhibit a vowel mutation in the past tense.

Halle (1977) and Halle and Mohanan (1985) both attempt to derive the past and present tense forms of these strong verbs using common underlying representations and semi-productive phonological rules, despite the fact that these verbs fall into very small sets of related forms, and can only be generated if a number of special rules and extremely remote underliers are adopted. Some of these special ablaut rules (as for *swim ~ swam*, for instance) will reflect the situation in Proto-Indo-European, where aspect seems to have been regularly expressed by ablaut. However, over the intervening 5,000 years or so, the language has evolved an entirely different tense-marking stratagem in the unmarked case. The derivation of the strong verbs is therefore highly relevant to one question of considerable theoretical importance: that is, is there a principled cut-off point between regular derivation and allomorphy or suppletion? Lass and Anderson (1975: xiii) identify various serious concerns for SGP, and argue that these

> seem to cluster around the basic problem of what we might call the 'determinacy' of phonological descriptions. To what extent, for instance, does the requirement that all non-suppletive allomorphy be referred to unique morphophonemic representations operated on by 'independently motivated' and 'phonetically natural' rules still hold? (And, for that matter, how can you tell, in cases less obvious than *go*:

went or *good: better*, whether you really have suppletion?) This issue seems to be at the bottom of the whole 'abstractness' controversy.

The Modern English strong verbs present a classic case of apparent phonological indeterminacy. However, I have argued above that a constrained model of Lexical Phonology will determine what aspects of phonology are derivable; and we shall see that the theory again makes a distinction between a small subclass of strong verbs whose surface alternations are derivable from a single underlier without recourse to special rules, and the great majority where a productive phonological account is ruled out for the present day language.

Let us first briefly review the treatments of the strong verbs in Halle (1977) and Halle and Mohanan (1985); for a much fuller and more detailed critique, see McMahon (1989, ch. 3). Halle (1977) deals with only a limited set of strong verbs (3.43).

(3.43)   a.   lie ~ lay   eat ~ ate   choose ~ chose
              drink ~ drank   sing ~ sang   begin ~ began   swim ~ swam
         b.   find ~ found   bind ~ bound   break ~ broke   wear ~ wore
              dig ~ dug   shrink ~ shrunk
         c.   write ~ wrote   rise ~ rose   speak ~ spoke   freeze ~ froze
              get ~ got   tread ~ trod

Halle argues that all these verb alternations can be captured by means of two allomorphy rules (see (3.44)), but that all the tense stem vowels must subsequently undergo Vowel Shift. Vowel Shift, in other words, obscures the fact that two comparatively simple processes are involved in deriving the past tense forms: past tense forms in (3.43a) become [+ low, − high], those in (3.43b) become [+ back], and those in (3.43c) undergo both changes.

(3.44)   Allomorphy (a) = V → [+ low, − high]
         Allomorphy (b) = V → [+ back]

Halle's analysis assumes that VSR will operate in both the past and the present tense forms of those verbs in (3.43) which have tense stem vowels. This is clearly incompatible with the view of VSR adopted here, where Vowel Shift is limited to cases of tense–lax vowel alternations, with the derived (i.e. tensed or laxed) vowel shifting. Even if we assume that Halle's allomorphy rules create a derived environment by changing some feature of the stem vowel, this will affect only past tense forms. Even if we reformulate the allomorphy rules, perhaps to rewrite the stem, unchanged but for the addition of outer brackets, in the present tense, this will not feed VSR, which requires a purely phonological derived environment, generally supplied by altering the value of [± tense]. Halle's Allomorphy (b) alters the value of the backness feature, which is not mentioned in the structural description of either VSR. Allomorphy (a) affects the height features, [± high] and [± low], which are included in the formulation of VSR; however, this will only allow us to derive the past tense forms of the verbs in (3.43a), since those in (3.43b) and (3.43c) involve the operation of Allomorphy (b), which may not feed VSR. Consequently, only a few forms of a few strong verbs from Halle's list can be handled using a Level 1 VSR, and these do not form a principled class distinct from the others in (3.43): their derivability is accidental.

Halle and Mohanan (1985) are rather more ambitious than Halle (1977), and claim to be able to handle all Modern English strong verbs but *go*, *make* and *stand*, the modals, and the auxiliaries *be*, *have* and *do*. They invoke not only VSR and the various tensing and laxing rules, but also ten special rules, each applicable to the stem vowels of a specially marked subset of strong verbs. These include Backing, Lowering and Shortening Ablaut (Halle and Mohanan 1985: rules 30–2), and rules forming and deleting /x/. Some derivations are shown in (3.45). A complete set of strong verb derivations can be found in McMahon (1989); note that Halle and Mohanan (1985) themselves provide no derivations.

(3.45)		*Present*		*Past*
			eat	
Underlying:			/ēt/	
Lowering Ablaut:		–		ǣt
VSR/Diphthongisation:		īyt		ēyt
			hold	
Underlying:			/hɛld/	
Backing Ablaut:		hold		–
o-Lengthening:		hōld		–
Diphthongisation:		hōwld		–
Surface:		[hōwld]		[hɛld]
			fight	
Underlying:			/fīxt/	
t-Suffixation:		–		fīxt]t
Cluster Shortening:		–		fɪxt]t
Degemination:		–		fɪxt
Lowering Ablaut:		–		fæxt
Backing Ablaut:		–		foxt

VSR/Diphthongisation:	fāyxt	–
x-Deletion:	fāyt	fot
o-Tensing:	–	fŏ$_t$t
o-Lowering:	–	fɔ$_t$t
Surface:	[fāyt]	[fɔ$_t$t]

	slay	
Underlying:	/slī/	
Lowering Ablaut:	slæ	–
Backing Ablaut:	–	slɨ̄
Shortening Ablaut:	–	slɨ
VSR/Diphthongisation:	slēy	–
i-Lengthening:	–	slɨ̄
i-Rounding:	–	slūw
Surface:	[slēy]	[slūw]

Halle and Mohanan order Backing, Lowering and Shortening Ablaut on Level 2, before VSR; they also derive a number of present tense forms like *bereave, eat, seek, choose, bind* and *bear*, which are clearly underived, via Vowel Shift. In general, Halle and Mohanan's attitude (1985: 106) is that the rules constitute the core of the phonology, while underliers are adjusted as necessary to fit in with these: 'Although any form can be made subject to any rule, provided only that the form satisfy the input conditions of the rule, it is by no means easy to assign to a form a representation such that a set of independently motivated rules will produce the prescribed output.'

As a result, their underlying representations are permitted to differ almost without limit from their surface counterparts: we find /bīx/ for *buy ~ bought*, /rɪn/ for *run ~ ran*, /kīm/ for *come ~ came*, /kɛtʃ/ for *catch ~ caught* and /drɪx/ for *draw ~ drew*. There are some segments which never surface, like /x/ (which may be inserted by rule or be present underlyingly, as in /bīx/ *buy*, /fīxt/ *fight*) and the back unrounded vowels /ʌ̄ i ɨ/; and we are faced with the usual problem of 'traditional' VSR, in that every verb with a tense stem vowel will have an underlying vowel distinct from surface. 'Duke of York' derivations are prevalent, since several verbs with tense stem vowels (including *eat ~ ate, choose ~ chose*, and *forsake ~ forsook*) undergo Lowering or Backing Ablaut simply to derive an appropriate input vowel for VSR, which then produces a surface vowel identical to the underlying one. Ablaut rules also apply in present tense forms – Backing Ablaut in *fall, hold, run, come, blow* and *draw*, Lowering Ablaut in *forsake, slay, catch, say, blow* and *draw*, and Shortening Ablaut in *give*. I contend that Halle and Mohanan's derivations are unrealistic and untenable, and that any problems their account of the strong verbs causes for the modified Level 1 VSR can surely be discounted.

A final possible argument for phonological generation of the past and present tense forms of strong verbs using Vowel Shift is that children may abstract a VSR on this basis: 'the vowel shift pattern ... is of course contained in quite basic vocabulary, notably in the inflectional morphology of verbs' (Kiparsky and Menn 1977: 65). If the strong verbs are the source of VSR, it is unacceptable to account for these verbs without such a rule. Evidence from Jaeger (1986), however, fails to support this claim. Jaeger's three-year-old informant understood and produced seventy-one strong verbs, but these involved twenty-seven different vowel alternations. Only 20 per cent involved VSR alternations; and these tended to be the least frequently occurring verbs. In short, it seems preferable to regard the strong verbs as learned, with their present and past tense forms lexically stored; VSR will then be irrelevant, and can remain on Level 1.

Our conclusion might seem to be that all Modern English strong verbs are irregular, and that all are equally irregular; hence Strang's (1970: 147) contention that 'the verbs that do not conform to the "regular" pattern of adding -*(e)d* in past and participle are so divergent that it is hardly worth trying to classify them'. However, Strang continues: 'One broad distinction that can be made is between verbs that have two stems, and an alveolar stop terminating the participle (*keep*, *kept*, *kept*), and the rest'; and indeed, it appears that this small subset of 'strong' verbs have their past tenses derivable via VSR, with the principles of LP predicting a clear cut-off point between the *keep* ~ *kept* class and those whose present and past tense forms are both lexically listed. The derivable strong verbs exhibit an alternation of tense vowel in the present tense and lax vowel in the past, and are listed in (3.46).

(3.46)

hear ~ heard	dream ~ dreamt	
creep ~ crept	deal ~ dealt	light ~ lit
feel ~ felt	keep ~ kept	hide ~ hid
kneel ~ knelt	mean ~ meant	slide ~ slid
leap ~ leapt	lean ~ leant	
sleep ~ slept	sweep ~ swept	
weep ~ wept	speed ~ sped	
feed ~ fed	lead ~ led	
plead ~ pled	bleed ~ bled	
breed ~ bred	meet ~ met	
read ~ read	bite ~ bit	

It is clear that these verbs exhibit two of the core surface Vowel Shift alternations, namely [ī] ~ [ɛ] and [aɪ] ~ [ɪ]. But can these be derived using a revised, Level 1 VSR?

Kiparsky (1982) suggests that past tense t/d-Suffixation operates twice in the English lexicon. Regular, weak verbs will receive their dental suffix on Level 2. However, a number of verbs, including those listed in (3.46), will be morphologically marked for a special Level 1 word-formation rule attaching the /t/ or /d/ suffix. For most of these Level 1 inflected verbs, the special *t/d* affixation rule is obligatory, and the later, regular Level 2 rule is blocked due to the EC (Kiparsky 1982); for a small number, however, the earlier rule is speaker-specific, so that the general rule may apply at Level 2 if the Level 1 rule is not selected, giving alternations of past tense forms like Level 1 inflected *dreamt* [drɛmt], *leapt* [lɛpt] or *knelt* [nɛlt] versus regular, weak Level 2 *dreamed* [drīmd], *leaped* [līpt] or *kneeled* [nīld].

This special morphological marking is all that is required to allow the past tense forms of the verbs in (3.46) to be derived from underliers equivalent to their present tense forms via VSR: the Level 1 affixation rule supplies the context for Pre-Cluster Laxing, which in turn feeds the lax-vowel V̌SR, as shown in (3.47). Verbs with /t/ or /d/ as final stem consonant, like *bite*, *meet* and *bleed* can be derived by V̌SR in the same way, but additionally show the operation of Degemination.

(3.47)		keep	bite
	Underlying:	/kīp/	/baɪt/
	t-Suffixation:	kīp]t	baɪt]t
	-CC Laxing:	kɪpt	bætt
	V̌SR:	kɛpt	bɪtt
	Degemination:	–	bɪt

The irregular verbs listed in (3.47) are the only ones which exhibit a surface Vowel Shift alternation, and which can be derived without either additional rules or special marking for VSR. Furthermore, these constitute a class distinct from all truly strong verbs, many of which have exhibited tense-based vowel alternations since Proto-Indo-European. In other cases, ablaut has arisen sporadically during the history of English (as in *sell* ~ *sold*, *tell* ~ *told*). However, the verbs in (3.47) were still weak as recently as early Middle English, and became 'strong' due to the innovation of two Middle English phonological processes, namely Pre-Cluster Shortening and the Great Vowel Shift. The diachronic development of /slip/ ~ /slɛpt/ is schematised in (3.48).

(3.48)

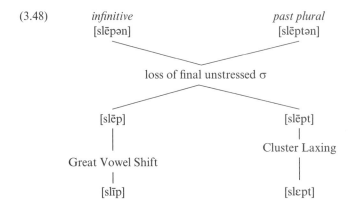

As (3.48) shows, early Middle English [slēpən], with past plural [slēptən], became [slēp] and [slɛpt] after the loss of final unstressed syllables and the general shortening of vowels before two tautosyllabic consonants. Finally, the Great Vowel Shift affected [slēp], giving [slīp].

It is possible, then, to derive certain 'strong' verbs through the regular phonological rules even in a well-constrained model. Modern English *sleep ~ slept* and so on are synchronically shown to be 'strong' by the special morphological marking causing dental suffixation on Level 1, and the derivation involves the synchronic reflexes of the two sound changes which initially created the alternation; although, as we have seen, the present tense form is synchronically underived in phonological terms, with the underlying, lexical and surface forms identical, while the past tense form undergoes laxing *and* V̆SR. This treatment of the verbs in (3.46) reflects the fact that these became irregular only relatively recently, and that they were propelled out of the weak class in a group, due to the advent of two sound changes. These derivable verbs also constitute the largest subclass of irregular verbs, and arguably preserve the most transparent relationship between present and past forms.

I propose to deal with the remaining strong verbs using allomorphy (although not in the sense of Halle (1977), where allomorphy rules were simply rules of the phonology which applied in a specified set of input forms). There is a good deal of support for this approach. For instance, Halle and Vergnaud (1987: 77) suggest that 'the different inflected forms of the English 'strong' verbs are determined by rules of the allomorphy component', although this idea is not developed further; while Wiese

(1996) proposes that, in German, umlaut is a lexical phonological rule, while the ablaut alternations in strong verbs are unpredictable, unproductive, and therefore allomorphic. Lieber (1982: 30) diagnoses allomorphy in cases where 'the relation between stem variants of a morpheme will not be predictable on any phonological or semantic grounds', and indeed uses the Modern English strong verbs as one example.

The question then is how we incorporate allomorphy into our grammar. There are various different approaches, although the common factor seems to be the assumption of more than one stored form per verb, with linking of these related entries on phonological, morphological, and/or semantic grounds (Lieber 1982, Spencer 1988, Wiese 1996). For instance, Lieber lists all allomorphs of each morpheme lexically, along with any information peculiar to each allomorph; thus, /profʌnd-/ is bound, while /swæm/ only occurs in the past tense. Semiregular forms with a common pattern will form an allomorphy class, and members of each class will be linked by morpholexical rules, which have the status of redundancy rules – an example is given in (3.49).

(3.49)   Morpholexical rule (i): $C_0 I N \sim C_0 æ N$
          or $C_0 V N \sim C_0 V[-high, +low]N$
          Morpholexical rule (ii): $C_0 I N \sim C_0 ʌ N$
          or $C_0 V N \sim C_0 V[+back]N$
          Allomorphy class (a), rule (i): members: sing ~ sang, swim ~ swam, ring ~ rang ...
          Allomorphy class (b), rule (ii): members: fling ~ flung, dig ~ dug, sting ~ stung ...

An advantage of this system of stored allomorphs and linking morpholexical rules is that, presumably, not all speakers need have any rule. Some speakers might learn individual verbs without abstracting any generalisations about specific verb classes; others might recognise similarities between verb pairs and innovate a linking rule.

Alternatively, we might adopt Spencer's (1988) interpretation of allomorphy rules as redundancy statements, which he argues can be seen as blank-filling applications of lexical rules. A morpholexical diacritic will trigger the appropriate structure-building rule, which 'constructs the phonological shapes of allomorphs, complete with morphosyntactic feature representation' (Spencer 1988: 625). The representation for a verb like *sing ~ sang* will then be as shown in (3.50).

For present purposes, it does not particularly matter which approach

(3.50)

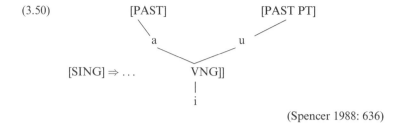

(Spencer 1988: 636)

we adopt to allomorphy in the strong verbs: the important issue is that there is support in the literature for handling these verbs using storage and linking rather than by adopting distant underliers and ill-motivated minor rules. The more interesting aspect of the strong verb story for us is the principled and orderly division which has emerged between verbs like *keep* ~ *kept* and *bite* ~ *bit*, which were weak until relatively recently and became 'strong' due to the operation of two sound changes whose synchronic reflexes are still involved in their derivation, and all the other strong verbs, which are of diverse origins and varying degrees of opacity, and which form only small subclasses at best. This well-motivated division is a direct result of the adoption of the bipartite tense and lax Vowel Shift Rule proposed above, and the anti-abstractness principles which can be imposed on a Lexical Phonology.

In (3.51), I have reduced a number of possible underlying systems for different varieties of Modern English to a single system for illustrative purposes; thus, /ɒ/ is bracketed since it may not appear in GenAm, while /æ/ and /ā/ are given as mutually exclusive options; see the discussion of the *father* vowel in section 3 above. Halle and Mohanan's (1985) vowel system is reproduced in (3.52) for comparison.

(3.51)

short		*long*		*diphthongs*
ɪ	ʊ	ī	ū	
ɛ	ʌ	ē	ō	aɪ aʊ ɔɪ
æ	(ɒ)	ǣ/ā	ɔ̄	

(3.52)

short	*long*	*diphthongs*
/ɪ/ bit	/ɨ/ ven*ue*	/ʊ/ put
/ɛ/ bet	/ʌ/ but	/o/ baud, shot
/æ/ bat	/a/ balm	/ɔ/ bomb

long		
/ī/ divine	/ɨ̄/ profound	/ō/ pool
/ē/ serene	/ʌ̄/ cube	/ɔ̄/ verbose
/ǣ/ sane		

The reanalysis of the synchronic VSR proposed above indicates three clear ways in which a constrained Lexical Phonology differs from SGP; these are relevant to the aims and objectives of lexicalist theory outlined in chapter 1.

(1) The strict imposition of constraints inevitably prohibits a maximally simple phonology, if simplicity means a minimal number of rules used maximally; thus, for instance, VSR becomes two rules instead of one, while the majority of lexical rules will apply only on Level 1, and free rides will therefore be eliminated. The evaluation metric will have to change for more concrete phonological models: the optimal phonology will no longer be the one with the most simple and elegant analyses, but the one which most closely adheres to the principles and constraints imposed on it, and which is consistent with both internal and external evidence.

(2) Synchronic phonological rules and the diachronic sound changes which are their source need not be identical, or indeed bear much resemblance to one another. This point has been exemplified by the Great Vowel Shift and its synchronic reflexes, the Vowel Shift Rules, which are formulated differently and have distinct inputs; for instance, the [aʊ] ~ [ʌ] alternation was historically a product of the Great Vowel Shift, but is not included in the synchronic Vowel Shift concept, while [jū] ~ [ʌ] is not historically a Vowel Shift alternation, but is now derivable via the VSR. Concrete lexicalist analyses reveal more enlightening, but less obvious connections between synchrony and diachrony, as shown by the treatment of the Modern English strong verbs, which revealed a principled division between those verbs like *keep ~ kept* which were most recently transferred from the weak to the strong class, and other verbs which have maintained their ablaut alternations for longer and which are arguably no longer synchronically derivable from a common underlying form.

(3) Different dialects may have different underlying forms for the same lexical items, and different underlying inventories of segments. Illustrations of such differences for varieties of English were given above from the low vowels, where some dialects will have an underlying and surface front vowel in *father* words, while others will have a back one. Similarly, the rejection of the catch-all Diphthongisation rule will mean that different varieties will have different underlying ratios of monophthongs to diphthongs.

I shall return to all of these issues in the chapters below, exploring in particular the relationship of sound changes and phonological rules, and the idea of underlying dialect differences versus pan-dialectal systems; these have taken second place so far to the development of the constraints of Lexical Phonology, and a comparison of a constrained model with that of Halle and Mohanan (1985). Although Halle and Mohanan restrict their attention to American English (and RP, to a limited extent), we have now reached a stage where we need no longer be restricted by a comparison with earlier models of Lexical Phonology. We can therefore range a little more widely in our consideration of English varieties, and will now introduce Scots and Scottish Standard English which have, as we shall see, certain interesting idiosyncracies in their vowel phonology.

4 Synchrony, diachrony and Lexical Phonology: the Scottish Vowel Length Rule

4.1 Introduction

> A typically English dialect is one which preserves a reflex of the West Germanic system of phonemic vowel length, having one set of lexically short and one of lexically long stressed vowel phonemes ... Scots dialects, on the other hand, are characterized by the disruption of this dichotomous pattern, resulting in the loss of phonemic length: vowel duration is to a large extent conditioned by the phonetic environment. (Harris 1985: 14)

The process generally credited with this disruption of 'normal' English quantity patterns, both diachronically and synchronically, is the Scottish Vowel Length Rule. SVLR was first formulated in 1962 by A.J. Aitken (after whom it is also known as Aitken's Law), although its effects had been noted much earlier in dialect studies such as Patterson (1860; Belfast), Murray (1873; Southern Scots), Grant (1912), Watson (1923; Roxburghshire), Dieth (1932; Buchan), Wettstein (1942; Berwickshire) and Zai (1942; Morebattle). In this chapter, we shall use the history and the synchronic status of SVLR and related processes as a test case of the way Lexical Phonology can model the development of a synchronic rule from its historical antecedent. This will essentially involve describing Scottish varieties in their own terms; in chapter 5, however, we shall compare the resulting system(s) with those developed above for RP and GenAm, raising the issues of dialect differentiation and variation. RP and GenAm have proved to be extremely closely related, and it is clear that these varieties have simply not diverged far enough, or for long enough, to provide us with conclusive evidence on the nature, extent and cause of underlying dialect divergence. First, however, we require an outline of the linguistic situation in Scotland, and of its origins.

4.2   A brief external history of Scots and Scottish Standard English

We know very little of the linguistic situation in early Scotland. There are traces of Pictish; Jackson (1955) argues that there were probably two Pictish languages, one Indo-European and the other of uncertain ancestry. However, evidence from the Pictish symbol-stones is limited and inconclusive, and the symbols may not be linguistic at all; as McClure (1995: 25) neatly puts it, 'the suggestion has been made that they are random jumbles caused by artisans who knew the *figurae* of the letters but not their *potestates*'.

Subsequently, a branch of Brythonic or *p*-Celtic was replaced by Gaelic, a Goidelic or *q*-Celtic language, following the invasion of the Scotti from Ireland in the fifth century AD. Gaelic spread rapidly across Scotland north of the Forth. Further south, the Anglo-Saxon conquest of Lothian in the seventh century introduced a Germanic competitor language in the form of the Old Northumbrian dialect of Old English: Scots is descended from Old Northumbrian, rather than from the Mercian, West Saxon and Kentish dialects which are the source of most Modern English in England. Synchronic differences between Scots and other varieties of English therefore at least partially reflect a dialect division in Old English, and *not* the influence of Gaelic. This common misconception merits comment immediately; there is remarkably little Gaelic influence on Scots, and indeed Gaelic has been progressively driven north and west by Scots since the introduction of Old Northumbrian to the Lothians (Ó Baoill 1997).

Lothian was ceded to the Scots in 973, but retained its Germanic language rather than adopting the majority language, Gaelic. Embryonic Scots was influenced successively by Norse, the language of the Viking invaders, and by Norman French, for although the Normans did not conquer Scotland, many were granted land by the Scottish Crown. Scots gradually gained in prestige, aided in this by the rise of the burghs which were founded by David I and his successors and settled largely by Scots speakers, and which rapidly became influential commercial centres. Divergence from English continued between the eleventh and fifteenth centuries, although during this period Scots is generally referred to as *Inglis*, with *Scotis* used for Gaelic. By the fourteenth century, French influence had begun to recede, and Gaelic was being gradually forced into the hills by expansionist Scots. Inglis appeared in literature with Barbour's *Brus* in 1375, and replaced Latin as the official language of the Scottish Parliament in 1424. By 1500, Scots was securely established as the official language of the court, judiciary and government, and it is at this point that *Scottis* is first used to describe 'the King of Scotland's Scots as opposed to the King of England's English' (Murison 1979: 8).

Middle Scots, under the Stewarts, enjoyed a notional Golden Age from around 1450 to 1560, as the official language of a reasonably successful independent kingdom, with a vibrant literary tradition exemplified by Henryson, Dunbar and Gavin Douglas. However, the linguistic balance in Scotland began to shift after the onset of the Reformation in 1560. Knox and his followers succeeded in establishing Presbyterianism, but in the absence of a Scots translation of the Bible, they used the Geneva English edition: 'from then on, God spoke English' (Kay 1988: 59). This distribution of the English Bible paved the way for the introduction of much more written English; English printers set up shop in Scotland, and English gradually became the standard literary language.

Scots truly began to decline after the Union of the Crowns in 1603, when James VI of Scotland became James I of England. The Scottish court moved to London, and the acquisition of spoken and written English became the key to successful self-aggrandisement. The linguistic impact is partially documented in Devitt (1989), where a sample of 121 Scottish texts written between 1520 and 1659 were scanned for five features which show distinctively different Scots and English forms; these included the relative clause marker (Scots *quh-* versus English *wh-*), and the present participle ending (Scots *-and* as opposed to English *-ing*). Devitt reports a gross, gradual increase from 18 per cent to 88 per cent English forms over this period; although the progression is slightly different for each feature, all follow broadly the same course. Finally, after the Union of Parliaments in 1707, English also became the language of law, education and administration in Scotland.

After the Jacobite uprising of 1745, Gaelic was also suppressed, but this did not benefit Scots. Gaelic had already by this period retreated behind the Highland Line, an imaginary frontier running roughly from Inverness to Oban. Scots was never spoken beyond the Highland Line: instead, English was widely taught here, so that speakers switched from Gaelic to English, uninfluenced by Scots. Inhabitants of the Gaelic and post-Gaelic areas today speak Highland English, which retains from Gaelic a distinctive intonation pattern, and some non-standard syntax, like the prevalent *It's Donald you'd be seeing/ It's to Skye you'll be going* construction. Scots features, however, are few.

Scots continued to lose ground in the Lowlands, while failing to gain a foothold in the Highlands. In the eighteenth century, it dropped out of use almost entirely as a written language; there have been various poetic revivals since, reflected in the verse of Robert Burns or the 'synthetic Scots' of Hugh Macdiarmid, but very little prose has appeared. Upwardly mobile middle-class Scots increasingly sought to replace their Scots with English, and in this trend we see the development of Scottish Standard English.

There seem to be three interacting sources for SSE. First, as many eighteenth century sources show (Jones 1995, 1997), Scots were made uncomfortably aware that their speech was not considered quite socially acceptable by their new English contacts; take as an example Buchanan's (1757 = 1968: xv) contention that:

> The people of North Britain seem, in general, to be almost at as great a loss for proper accent and just pronunciation as foreigners. And it would be surprising to find them writing English in the same manner, and some of them to as great perfection as any native of England, and yet pronouncing after a different, and for the most part unintelligible manner, did we not know, that they never had any proper guide or direction for that purpose.

Various bodies, including notably the Select Society of Edinburgh, took it upon themselves to rescue their Scottish fellows from this social affliction by providing just such a 'proper guide or direction', in the form of lectures and classes. Scots also assiduously read books which promised to weed out unwelcome Scotticisms. However, and here we find the second source for the particular shape assumed by SSE, these obviously concentrated on features of vocabulary, syntax and morphology, which could be set down easily in writing, while largely ignoring phonetics and phonology. One might appeal to the lectures and schools as a source of approved pronunciation; however, it seems that the journey to Edinburgh, particularly in winter, did not recommend itself to many London-based elocutionists, while the accents of those who did offer their services (famously including Sheridan) were such a mixed bag that this aspect of the instruction seems to have failed dismally. SSE, an amalgamation of Standard English grammar and lexicon with a Scots accent, came to be acceptable both within and outwith Scotland. As even Boswell admitted (see Kay 1988: 84), 'a small intermixture of provincial peculiarities may, perhaps, have an agreeable effect.' Indeed, the received wisdom by the end of the eighteenth century seems to be that Scottish accent features are incurable: 'The English accent can never be acquired; the attempt is hopeless ... Accent must then be abandoned as impossible, and English must, by all Scotsmen, be pronounced with the Scots accent' (Anon 1826: 224).

But which Scots accent? As we shall see in the next section, SSE shares phonological features with Scots, but the two are distinct systemically and distributionally, and these innovatory features cannot simply be seen as borrowings from RP – especially in view of the fact that, as McClure (1995: 79) tactfully puts it, 'the English accent known as RP is not a native form in Scotland, nor is it generally regarded as a social desideratum'. Jones (1993, 1995) argues convincingly that the phonological features of SSE are there, not by accident or default, but by design. Jones shows that Scottish writers of pronouncing dictionaries often based their norms, not on London English, but on a pre-existing Scottish professional variety characteristic of 'the college, the pulpit and the bar' (1993: 102). SSE may therefore be in origin a more organic and less artificial variety than is usually assumed.

Nonetheless, SSE is a standard variety, and the same concerns over its reality therefore arise as for RP and GenAm in 3.3.1 above. That is, as Giegerich (1992: 46) admits, 'the SSE accent is in a sense an analysts' artefact'. I use the term 'SSE' to mean the Scottish sociolinguistic equivalent of RP in England. Just as there are varieties within RP and GenAm, so SSE has slightly different characteristics in different areas of Scotland: the variety which I describe below as SSE is typical of middle-class Edinburgh and Glasgow speech – outlying areas like Aberdeen and the Border country share many but not all of its features. Like RP, SSE is now a native variety for many speakers; others maintain a Scots dialect as a home language, and use SSE in formal circumstances and in the education system, where Scots is typically discouraged. Code switching is therefore commonplace, and many Scots control a continuum from SSE to their local variety of 'braid Scots'. Scots dialects are particularly strongly maintained, as one might expect (Milroy and Milroy 1985), among working-class speakers in the cities, and in rural areas – and much of Scotland is rural. I shall now briefly consider some of the distinctive characteristics of Scots dialects and SSE.

4.3   The Scots dialects and Scottish Standard English: synchronic linguistic characteristics

Now that detailed information on Modern Scots dialects and their Older Scots antecedents is readily accessible in the *Edinburgh History of the Scots Language* (Jones 1997), the information on Scots below can be relatively brief. Johnston (1997b) provides a dialect map giving the conventional division into Mid or Central (including Ulster), Southern, Northern and Insular Scots, with the addition of a more modern sociolinguistic overlay reflecting the spread of innovations from the cities. A discussion and classification of dialect differences is beyond the scope of this work, and I shall generally concentrate on describing common Scots features rather than those which are specific to one dialect.

Scots speakers are likely to exhibit non-standard features in all areas of the grammar. In syntax, many Scots dialects have multiple negation, and there are also regional idiosyncracies like the role reversal of *bring* and *take* in Aberdeenshire, as seen in *I'm in the garden; could you take me out a drink?* In morphology, auxiliary plus negative sequences are contracted to give forms like *cannae, couldnae, dinnae, didnae*: these contractions have a limited distribution, however, and are replaced by *can ye no, do ye no*, etc., in tag questions. Scots is also peppered with non-standard lexical items, such as *fankle* for 'tangle', *skelf* for 'splinter', *glaur* for 'wet mud', *wabbit* for 'tired' and, in different parts of Scotland, *beagie, neap* or *tumshie* for 'turnip'. Some of these lexical and morphosyntactic features also make their way, often in a rather diluted form, into SSE (Miller 1993). However, it is the sound system of Scots and SSE and its development that form the topic for the remainder of this chapter.

4.3.1   Consonants
Varieties of English tend to be both conservative and markedly similar in their consonant systems. There are, however, some minor consonantal differences between Scots and SSE on one hand, and RP or GenAm on the other.

First, Scots and SSE retain the voiceless velar fricative /x/, which other English dialects have lost since Middle English. The distribution of /x/ is limited, and it tends to occur in distinctively Scots lexical items like *loch, dreich*; place and personal names such as *Auchtermuchty, Tulloch, Strachan*; and sometimes in words originally borrowed from Greek or Hebrew which have <ch>, like *epoch* [ipɔx] or *parochial* [parɔxiəl]. In Insular

Scots, it also commonly occurs in an initial cluster with /w/ in place of other Scots and SSE /kw/ – so *question* is [xwɛstʃən] and *queer* is [xwiːr].

Scots dialects and SSE also have the voiceless labio-velar fricative /ʍ/ (sometimes symbolised /hw/), which contrasts with /w/ in minimal pairs like *Wales* /w/ versus *whales* /ʍ/, or *witch* /w/ versus *which* /ʍ/. /ʍ/ is found in most words with <wh> spellings, although as Wells (1982: 409) observes, <w> spellings sometimes correspond to [ʍ] pronunciations, as in south-east Scots *weasel* [ʍiːzl], or <wh> to [w], as in *whelk* [wʌlk]. In Northern Scots, /ʍ/ has become a voiceless labial or labio-dental fricative, [ɸ] or [f], in all contexts, producing such characteristic Aberdeenshire pronunciations as [feːr] 'where' and [faː] 'who'.

A final difference concerns the distribution of /r/. Both RP and Scots/SSE have this phoneme, but because Scots and SSE are rhotic, its functional load here is far greater (see further chapter 6 below). As for realisation, very few Scots now consistently use trilled [r], although this is found occasionally in the north. The most common allophonic variants are the alveolar tap [ɾ] and the post-alveolar approximant [ɹ]; Wells (1982: 411) suggests that the tap often appears in the environments V–V and C–V, and the approximant V–C and V–#, with either initially.

4.3.2   *Vowels*

In (4.1), I reproduce the underlying vowel system for RP and GenAm which emerged from the emendations to Halle and Mohanan (1985) in chapters 2 and 3. An outline SSE/Scots system is listed in (4.2). Needless to say, each of these core systems contains a number of option points (often represented as bracketed vowels), and can be taken as temporary shorthand for a set of marginally different daughter systems; for a classification of Scots dialects using a similar system, see Catford (1958).

(4.1)   RP/GenAm

	short		*long*		*diphthongs*
	ɪ	ʊ	ī	ū	
	ɛ	ʌ	ē	ō	aɪ aʊ ɔɪ
	æ	(ɒ)	ǣ/ā	ɔ̄	

(4.2)   SSE/Scots

	short		*variable*		*diphthongs*
	ɪ		i	u	
	ɛ (ë)	ʌ	e (ø)	o	ai/ʌi ʌu ɔi
			a	ɔ	

The two vowels bracketed in (4.2), /ø/ and /ë/, are very frequently encountered in Scots and occasionally in SSE. /ø/, a mid front rounded vowel, appears dialect-specifically in words like *foot*, *floor*, *moon* and *spoon*; it is the result of fronting of /o:/ to /ø:/ in Scotland, Northumberland, Cumberland, Durham, North Lancashire and Yorkshire in the late thirteenth or early fourteenth century. Aitken (1977) distinguishes three Modern Scots dialect-specific patterns of realisation of earlier Scots /ø:/ (see (4.3)).

(4.3)   *floor*   *foot*
     A   [ø:]   [ø]
     B   [i:]   [ɪ]
     C   [e:]   [ø], [ɪ]

The length variation here results from the Scottish Vowel Length Rule, to be considered below. The quality differences seem to reflect variability in whether the /ø:/ vowel raised in the Great Vowel Shift, and the relative chronology of this raising, unrounding and SVLR.

/ë/ is more intriguing. Abercrombie (1979) notes that the first person to classify /ë/ as distinct from both /ɪ/ and /ɛ/ was A.J. Aitken, in whose honour it is sometimes called 'Aitken's vowel'. It is easy to see why /ë/ evaded notice for so long, for various aspects of its quality, origin and distribution (both areal and lexical) remain opaque.

/ë/ characteristically occurs in words like *bury*, *devil*, *earth*, *clever*, *jerk*, *eleven*, *heaven*, *next*, *shepherd*, *twenty*, *ever*, *every*, *never*, *seven*, *whether*; however, Winston (1970), who tested a number of subjects from Edinburgh University for the presence and use of /ë/, found that although all her informants had contrastive /ë/, there was not one word where they all consistently used it. In addition, /ë/ has a regionally defined distribution, occurring principally in dialects of the West, the Borders, Perthshire and at least some parts of Edinburgh.

As for the quality of /ë/, it is generally negatively defined (Wells 1982: 404):

> Where present, /ë/ is phonologically and phonetically distinct both from /ɪ/ and from /ɛ/, and in quality is typically somewhat less open than cardinal 3 and considerably centralised. The opposition can be tested by the triplet *river* vs. *never* vs. *sever*. If *never* rhymes neither with *river* (/ɪ/) nor with *sever* (/ɛ/), then it can be assumed to have /ë/.

Even less information can be gleaned on the origin of /ë/; perhaps the most plausible explanation is offered by Kohler (1964). Kohler notes that, in some Scots dialects, /ë/ is used in most of the words where SSE and RP have /ɪ/. He suggests that /ë/ was the original short vowel, but that /ɪ/ was later borrowed from English dialects and diffused variably through the same set of words. /ë/ tends to survive most consistently and widely in forms like *never, shepherd, seven*, where English dialects had /ɛ/ but Scots has /ë/ or native /ɪ/ – spellings like <niver> are relevant here.

There are a few other discrepancies between SSE and Scots dialects, some of which we shall return to below. For instance, whereas SSE has [u:] in *two*, Scots tends to have [e:], [a:] or [ɔ:], reflecting a pre-Great Vowel Shift monophthongisation of word-final /ai/ in frequently used lexical items; the resulting /a:/ was then either raised in the Vowel Shift giving modern [e:], or was retained after a labial consonant, which in some areas rounded the vowel. *Snow, blow* have Scots [ɔ:] rather than SSE [o:], ultimately as a result of twelfth century Long Low Vowel Raising; differential operation of the same sound change in the north and south also gives the characteristic Scots [e] of *stane, hame* as opposed to RP and SSE *stone, home*. Finally, the diphthong /au/ is marginal in Scots, since the Great Vowel Shift failed for /u:/ > /au/ in the North, so that /u/ is retained in Scots *house, out, cow*. /au/ is present only in a few place-names like *Cowdenbeath*, some specifically Scots lexical items like *howff* and *loup*, and words with earlier /ɔl/ > /ɔu/ > /au/ via l-Vocalisation, as in *gold* [gʌud] and *knoll* [nʌu]. For details of these and other Scots sound changes, see Johnston (1997a).

Our main concern here, however, lies in the different patterns of distribution between SSE (and Scots), RP and GenAm vowels shown in (4.4).

(4.4)		RP	GenAm	SSE
	beat/bee	i:	i:	i/i:
	bit	ɪ	ɪ	ɪ
	bait/bay	eɪ	eɪ	e/e:
	bet	ɛ	ɛ	ɛ
	bat	æ	æ	a
	balm/baa	ɑ:	ɑ:	a/a:
	bomb	ɒ	ɑ:	ɔ
	bought/law	ɔ:	ɔ:	ɔ/ɔ:
	foot	ʊ	ʊ	u
	food/who	u:	u:	u/u:
	but	ʌ	ʌ	ʌ
	boat/show	oʊ	oʊ	o/o:
	bite/buy	aɪ	aɪ	ʌɪ/a:i
	noise, boy	ɔɪ	ɔɪ	ɔi

bout, now	aʊ	aʊ	ʌu
beer	ɪə	iː	iː
bear	ɛə	eː	eː
pure	ʊə	uː	uː
bird	ɜː	ɜː	ɪ
word	ɜː	ɜː	ʌ
heard	ɜː	ɜː	ɛ
butt<u>er</u>	ə	ə	ə

There are several clear differences between the RP and GenAm systems on the one hand, and that of SSE on the other. Minor realisational discrepancies apart, these can be subsumed under one generalisation. In RP and GenAm, all those vowels which can appear in stressed open syllables (that is, all vowels except /ɪ ɛ æ ɒ ʊ ʌ ə/) surface consistently as long or diphthongal: Giegerich (1992) analyses these as alternative manifestations of underlying tenseness. A full discussion of the feature [± tense] must be deferred for the moment; let us accept for the moment that RP and GenAm are analysable in terms of six pairs of vowels, the members of which are qualitatively and quantitatively distinct but of roughly the same height (4.5).

(4.5)   /i/   /ɪ/   /u/   /ʊ/
        /e/   /ɛ/   /o/   /ʌ/
        /a/   /æ/   /ɔ/   /ɒ/ or /ɑ/

In SSE, this dual distinction of quantity and quality is not operative. Three of the oppositions are entirely lacking, with RP /ɑ/ ~ /æ/, /ɔ/ ~ /ɒ/ and /u/ ~ /ʊ/ each replaced by a single vowel in SSE, conventionally represented as /a/, /ɔ/ and /u/ respectively. There are consequently a number of minimal pairs in RP which become homophonous for Scottish speakers, although Abercrombie (1979: 75–6) points out that more anglicised speakers of SSE may import these oppositions from RP. Typically, the introduction of /u/ ~ /ʊ/ presupposes /ɔ/ ~ /ɒ/, which in turn presupposes /ɑ/ ~ /æ/: the low vowel contrasts are quite common in SSE, especially in Edinburgh, but the /u/ ~ /ʊ/ distinction is very rare and tends to be inconsistently maintained.

The three remaining vowel pairs, /i/ ~ /ɪ/, /e/ ~ /ɛ/ and /o/ ~ /ʌ/, are relevant for Scots and SSE; but the nature of the opposition is different from that in RP and GenAm. Diphthongisation in Scots dialects and in SSE is rare, even for the mid vowels /e/ and /o/, with the only surface diphthongs being realisations of the 'true' diphthongs /ʌɪ/ ~ /ai/, /au/ and /ɔi/. I have argued that these should be analysed as underlyingly diphthongal, and this goes for Scots/SSE as well as RP and GenAm, although the exact nature of their underlying representations for Scots/ SSE will be the subject of some discussion below. Nor does length consistently distinguish the members of these pairs, since quantity in Scots and SSE is largely non-contrastive and context-sensitive; as shown in (4.4), /i e o/ are therefore long only in certain circumstances. The Scottish Vowel Length Rule (Aitken 1981, McMahon 1991, Carr 1992) is the process responsible, and a preliminary version is given in (4.6).

(4.6)   SVLR: preliminary version

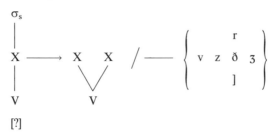

SVLR lengthens a certain set of vowels (to be defined later) when they precede /r/, any voiced fricative, or a bracket – the Lexical Phonological equivalent of a word or morpheme boundary. /i/ will consequently be long in *beer, breathe, key,* and *keyed,* but short in *keep, wreath, keen* and *need.* For the majority of vowels affected, SVLR simply controls an alternation of length, but for the diphthong /ai/, there is a concomitant change of quality with [ʌi] in short and [a:i] in long environments.

In the rest of this chapter, we shall focus on SVLR. Evidence from previous discussions and formulations of the process will be used to ascertain precisely what subset of vowels constitutes its input, and what feature specification might characterise that class. Experimental investigations of SVLR will be assessed; these include work by Agutter (1988a, b), who claims that 'the context-dependent vowel length encapsulated in SVLR is not, and perhaps never was Scots-specific' (Agutter 1988b: 20). The refutation of this assertion will involve a comparison of SVLR with a related lengthening process which operates in all dialects of English. However, before embarking on a detailed synchronic analysis, we must consider the historical source of SVLR: we shall see that a diachronic perspective is essential, here as in many other cases in this book, to a full understanding of the present day situation.

4.4   Internal history

We have already seen that RP is the descendant of the Mercian and West Saxon dialects of Old English, while Scots has Old Northumbrian as its ancestor. These southern and northern dialects of Old English developed into Southern and Northern Middle English. In the early Middle English of approximately 1250 AD, the Northern and Southern vowel inventories were markedly similar; a possible common early Middle English system is given in (4.7). Johnston (1997a: 64) gives a similar system for Older Scots, in terms of source vowels for particular lexical sets in the sense of Wells (1982).

(4.7)   i   u   iː   uː   iu   ui
         e   o   eː   oː
                        ɛː   ɔː   ɛi   ɛu   ɔi   ɔu
             a   æː   ɑː   ai   au

Between the thirteenth and the seventeenth century, a plethora of sound changes affected this common system. Some applied equally in the North and the South, while others affected the systems of the two areas differently, or were restricted to one area. Details of the changes for Scots can be found in Jones (1997b), Johnston (1997a) and McMahon (1989); I shall give details of only two changes, Middle English Open Syllable Lengthening and the Scottish Vowel Length Rule, with some discussion of the Great Vowel Shift where it is relevant to SVLR.

4.4.1   *Middle English Open Syllable Lengthening*

Middle English Open Syllable Lengthening (MEOSL) remains a controversial process, and one discussed in detail by Dobson (1962), Malsch and Fulcher (1975), Lieber (1979), Minkova (1982, 1985) and Ritt (1994); see also Hogg (1996), who argues that a regular but allophonic low-vowel Open Syllable Lengthening in Old English acted as 'the first harbinger' (1996: 70) of MEOSL. It is beyond contention that all short vowels lengthened in the North, and [−high] short vowels in the South, in certain environments around the early thirteenth century; some examples are given in (4.8).

(4.8)   OE   hara   æcer   mete   beofor   þrotu   wicu   sunu
         ME   hāre   ācre   mēte   bēver   þrōte   wēke   sōne

However, various aspects of MEOSL are still disputed, and Minkova (1982: 29) singles out three of the more problematic areas:

(1) The problem of the qualitative difference between the original short vowels and their lengthened reflexes.

(2) The behaviour of the high vowels /i/ and /u/ with respect to the change.

(3) The existence of a large number of exceptions to MEOSL.

Minkova herself deals with the third problem. She notes that, given the 'traditional' environment of /__ $C_1^2VC_0$# (which allows for medial /sp st sk/), a large number of exceptions to MEOSL become apparent. Authors of Middle English handbooks, like Jordan (1925) and Luick (1921), and also, more recently, Dobson (1962), have attempted to account for these exceptions by noting that many contain a liquid or nasal in the second syllable, or by grouping together items like *bodig, popig, penig, hefig* and postulating either secondary stress on *-ig* or long final /iː/. Sadly, these attempts at principled explanation are either non-explanatory (as in the first example above) or lack evidence (as in the second).

Minkova adopts a different approach, based on a complete list of words which are known to have been present in English at the time of MEOSL, meet the structural description of the process, and have survived to Present-Day English. She includes only items with original non-high vowels, since /i u/ lengthened inconsistently, and considers both native and Anglo-Norman material. Minkova splits the items on her word-list into two sets, one containing items which are still disyllabic in Modern English and the other composed of items which are now monosyllabic due to final schwa-loss, and calculates the percentage of the words in each set which have undergone MEOSL. She finds that only 16 per cent of the synchronically disyllabic words exhibit lengthening, while MEOSL has operated without exception in words which have also undergone schwa-loss. Minkova concludes that 'it is surprising that so much energy has been expended in trying to account for "exceptions" which make up over 80% of the entire material' (1982: 42), and recasts the environment for MEOSL (4.9).

(4.9)   / __ C_1^1e#, where e = /ə/

This reformulation indicates a definite link between MEOSL and schwa-loss, but does not determine their relative chronology: indeed, Minkova (1982: 46) argues that 'simultaneity is the only positive assumption we can make'. Jespersen (1922) also suggested that schwa-loss began in the North due to Norse influence, which was strongest in this area, and a concomitant loss of inflection. No case of this sort has been made for MEOSL, but the intimate connection of MEOSL and schwa-loss assumed by Minkova predicts that MEOSL too should have started in the North, since schwa-loss, a prerequisite for the lengthening, is first evidenced in this area; both processes subsequently spread south over a century or so.

Minkova (1985) develops her analysis of MEOSL in terms of foot structure, arguing that lengthening preserves perceptual isochrony of feet when these become defective as a result of schwa loss. This accounts for the predominant application of MEOSL in original disyllables, and the greater likelihood of lengthening in rhymes with non-branching peaks or codas. Ritt (1994), in turn, extends Minkova's work: using a parallel but larger corpus of Middle English items, he establishes that 94 per cent of items with unstable final syllables (that is, those subject to schwa loss) undergo lengthening. Ritt, however, includes MEOSL in a general schema of Middle English Quantity Adjustment, producing a composite statement of the probability of lengthening in any case based on a set of scalar features. For instance, Ritt shows that lengthening is more likely for low and back vowels; more likely before a single consonant than a cluster; and less likely in a syllable weighing two moras or less.

Neither of these environmental refinements, however, addresses the problem of 'the qualitative difference between the original short vowels and their lengthened reflexes' (Minkova 1982: 29). Two main sources of evidence indicate that MEOSL produced a qualitative as well as a quantitative change for non-low vowels. First, in twelfth and thirteenth century manuscripts, orthographic alternations are found between un-inflected and inflected forms of words (see (4.10)).

(4.10)	*wik* (nom. sg.)	*wekes* (pl.)	'week'
	sun (nom. sg.)	*sones* (pl.)	'son'
	iveles (gen. sg.)	*evel* (nom. sg.)	'evil'
	sumeres (pl.)	*somer* (nom. sg.)	'summer'

These spellings do not suggest simple lengthening; the fact that <i> alternates with <e> and <u> with <o> indicates that the Old English short vowels have both lengthened and lowered. Such evidence is available only for the high vowels, since the long high-mid vowels /e: o:/ and the long low-mid vowels /ɛ: ɔ:/ were not orthographically distinguished in Middle English, /e: ɛ:/ being written <e(e)> and /o: ɔ:/, <o(o)>. A second category of rhyme evidence is more relevant to the mid vowels. If MEOSL involved only a quantity change, one would expect the lengthened reflexes of Old English /i u e o/ to rhyme with

Middle English /i: u: e: o:/ respectively. Attested rhymes (4.11) do not show this pattern. Instead, they again indicate that MEOSL involved a quality change, whereby short high vowels in open syllables merged with long high-mid vowels, short high-mid vowels in the MEOSL environment merged with long low-mid vowels, and only /a/ merely lengthened.

(4.11)   (<OE *styrian* /i/) *stere*   – *were*   ME /e:/ (<OE /e:/) *Brus*
          (<OE *guma* /u/)   *gome*   – *dome*   ME /o:/ (<OE /o:/) *Cursor Mundi*
          (<OE /e/)   *beren*   – *leren*   ME /ɛ:/ (<OE /ɛ:/) Lieber 1979
          (<OE /o/)   *broken* – *stroken* ME /ɔ:/ (<OE /ɔ:/) Lieber 1979

Some additional evidence for this proposed quality change comes from the Great Vowel Shift. If our usual assumptions about this sound change are correct, the relevant non-low vowels must have lowered before shifting (Malsch and Fulcher 1975). *Week*, for instance, surfaces in Modern English with [i:]; this is consistent with its having had an /e:/ vowel in Middle English, but not /i:/, which would have produced modern /aɪ/. Similarly, *bear*, with Modern English [e:]/[ɛə], must have had /ɛ:/ at the time of operation of the Great Vowel Shift; if Old English /e/ had simply lengthened to /e:/ in Middle English, one would expect Modern English *[bi:r] or *[bɪə] 'bear'. The effects of MEOSL are schematised in (4.12).

(4.12)   Old English Middle English Old English Middle English

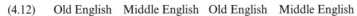

As Ritt (1994: 76) observes, 'one cannot avoid dealing with vowel quality as well, if a change in quantity causes, goes hand in hand with, or, generally speaking, is closely related to a quality change'. But there seems to be nothing inherent in a lengthening process like MEOSL that should lead to concomitant lowering; Pre-Cluster or Homorganic Lengthening, a tenth century vowel lengthening change, appears to have had no effect on quality (Ritt 1994: 82). One solution might be to identify some process affecting the set of short vowels, from which both Pre-Cluster Lengthening and MEOSL took their inputs, between the tenth and twelfth centuries. The obvious assumption would be that non-low short vowels lowered during this period; Dobson (1962) actually proposes that /i u/ had become high-mid and /e o/ low-mid before MEOSL, and quotes arguments by Trnka and Vachek to the effect that the resultant isolation of /i: u:/, which were left with no short congeners, caused them to move out of the monophthongal system altogether by diphthongising during the Great Vowel Shift. However, there is no direct evidence for this lowering.

An alternative explanation might be that the feature [± tense] became relevant in the English vowel system at around the time of MEOSL. Ritt (1994) proposes that Middle English long vowels were made tense; lengthened vowels would then merge with the long, tense vowel one degree of height lower. As Ritt (1994: 79) summarises: 'Although I lack positive evidence in much the same way as all other linguists who have dealt with the apparent lowering that accompanied Middle English vowel lengthening, it seems to me that this is by far the most economic explanation of the notorious mergers'.

There are two difficulties with such an analysis. The first involves the use and status of the feature [tense] itself, and particularly the question of its phonetic correlates. For the moment, let us simply note that lax vowels are characteristically produced with a lesser degree of constriction than their tense counterparts. X-ray evidence from Wood (1975: 110) indicates that the tongue height of a long, lax vowel will tend to be closer to that of a long, tense vowel of one degree less in height than to that of a long, tense vowel of the same height. Indeed, lax [ɪ:] was often produced with a lower tongue height than tense [e:] in Wood's experiments. Consequently, if we have short lax vowels, and long tense ones, then a lengthening of the lax ones might well involve automatic lowering. It seems worthwhile taking [tense] on trust briefly; however, a detailed justification follows in 4.5 below, since variability in the length–tenseness correlation will be central to the analysis of SVLR.

Secondly, we require evidence for some quality-based realignment of the Middle English vowel system, whatever feature(s) we choose to label this. Essentially, factors in the suprasegmental organisation of the language may account for the innovation of [tense] at just this period. During Middle English, the English stress system was undergoing a radical change, with the introduction of the phonologically determined Romance Stress Rule via French loans, alongside the earlier Germanic Stress Rule, which was morphologically determined and assigned main stress to the first syllable of each stem. Although syllable weight as a phonological variable appears to have existed in Old English, for instance as a factor determining the assignment of secondary stress, the introduction of the Romance Stress Rule initiated a more pervasive correlation between syllable weight and stress; the rule scans words right-to-left, and preferentially stresses heavy syllables (final in verbs, penultimate in nouns). If the first relevant syllable is not heavy, the stress is placed on the previous syllable, regardless of weight.

Hyman (1977: 47–9) notes that languages with a stress assignment system making reference to syllable weight always have a vowel length contrast (although length contrasts per se are not confined to languages with phonologically determined stress rules, as Old English and Polish demonstrate). And in languages where syllable weight is a phonological variable and there is a length contrast, there is almost always a quality distinction between long and short vowels of the 'same' height. When English, which already had a vowel-length contrast, borrowed the Romance Stress Rule, which refers to syllable weight, it might therefore be expected to acquire a tenseness, and thus a quality distinction between long and short vowels. Anderson (1984) further argues that languages will tend to implement a redundancy rule which correlates underlying length, or nuclear complexity, with phonological tenseness.

The question remains whether the innovation of [tense] preceded or followed MEOSL. There is some dialect and rhyme evidence for the persistence, at least initially, of two sets of long vowels, which one might see as lax and tense. For instance, in Yorkshire, Derbyshire, Lancashire, Staffordshire and other northern and north Midland areas of England, [ɛː] and [ɔː] from MEOSL have become Modern English [eɪ] and [oɪ], while older /ɛː/ (<OE /æː/) and /ɔː/ (<OE /ɑː/ and French loans) have developed to [iə] and [uə]. These facts suggest that 'the reflexes of short vowels in open syllables and of original OE long vowels were still kept distinct in the Middle English dialect from which the modern north Midland and northern dialects derive' (Lieber 1979: 16). In terms of rhyme evidence, Dobson (1962) quotes a stanza from *Troilus and Cryseyde*, with rhyme scheme ABABBCC, which exhibits the rhymes shown in (4.13).

(4.13)		A	*loore*	[ɔː] < OE /ɑː/
	MEOSL	B	*forlore*	[ɔː] < OE /o/
		A	*more*	[ɔː] < OE /ɑː/ (Comp. Adj.)
	MEOSL	B	*more*	[ɔː] < OE /o/ ('root')
	MEOSL	B	*bifore*	[ɔː] < OE /o/

According to Dobson, it is inconceivable, given Chaucer's rhyming practice, that he would have rhymed all five consecutive lines as A. This suggests that the A-line vowels and the B-line vowels must have been distinct at this time, perhaps as [ɔːᵢ] versus [ɔːᵢ]. One might then speculate that the correlation of short and lax was implemented earlier than that of long and tense, though little hangs on establishing a chronology. The main point here is that assuming a qualitative bisection of the Middle English vowel system, in addition to pre-existing distinctions of length, is helpful in accounting for the lowering associated with MEOSL of non-low vowels. I ascribe this qualitative difference to tenseness, and will justify this decision below in connection with SVLR.

4.4.2 The Great Vowel Shift
There is a very considerable literature on this change or series of related changes (see Lass 1989, 1992, Stockwell and Minkova 1990, Johnston 1992). However, the main point of this section is the identification of some discrepancies in the application of the Great Vowel Shift in the North and South, and the development of an input system for the SVLR. I therefore only list the stages of what is conventionally known as the GVS below in roughly chronological order, largely following Johnston (1980).

Stage 1 (c.1400–1450 North, 1450–1500 South)
In this earliest subshift, high-mid front (and, in the South, back) long monophthongs raised, while originally high long vowels diphthongised (4.14). The failure of /uː/ to diphthongise in the North, leading to Modern Scots /ku/ *cow* and /hus/ *house* versus RP /kaʊ/, /haʊs/, may be ascribed to earlier /oː/-Fronting; since there is no /oː/ to raise in the North, there is no pressure on /uː/ to diphthongise. SSE typically has diphthongal [kʌu] or [kaːu], the realisation varying speaker-specifically.

(4.14)

The high vowels are shown as shifting to some intermediate value, rather than directly to [ai] and [au], because an immediate full shift would counter-historically merge /iː/ with /ai/ and /uː/ with /au/ (Johnston 1997a). In other words, lexical items with original Middle English /iː uː/ and /ai au/ surface in Modern English with different vowels, so that /iː/

may not shift to /ai/, nor /u:/ to /au/, until /ai/ and /au/ have in turn moved away from these values; whether or not we regard avoidance of merger as a general linguistic tendency (see Lass 1976), it is clear empirically that no merger took place in this case. The precise identity of the intermediate values is much debated, and several options are given in (4.14). Although [əi əu] are frequently suggested, Lass (1989) argues against early centralisation on orthoepical grounds, pointing out that Hart's (1569) representations of *reid* 'ride' and *hound* 'hound' signal two unrounded front elements in the former, and two back rounded elements in the latter: indeed, 'no orthoepist before Hodges (1644) appears to report anything that could be construed as a central vowel in the relevant position' (Lass 1989: 91). Regardless of precise realisation, this intermediate stage of Vowel Shift for the original high vowels will be extremely important for the analysis of SVLR developed below.

Stage 2 (c.1450–1500 North, 1550–1620 South)
Whereas Stage 1 of the GVS affected the Northern and Southern vowel systems rather differently, Stage 2 produced the same results in both areas (4.15).

(4.15)   e: eu
          ↑   ↖
          ɛ: meat   u few   ɛi
          ↑   ↖
          a: name   ai rain

There is one discrepancy, resulting from the earlier monophthongisation of final /ai/ in Scots and the North in frequently occurring lexical items; this /a:/ raises regularly to /ɛ:/ in Stage 2 of the Vowel Shift (and subsequently to /e:/). However, in certain dialects of Scots, /a:/ failed to raise when preceded by a labial consonant. In this case, /a:/ might be retained, or, in other areas, the influence of the adjacent labial appears to have caused a post-GVS backing and rounding of /a:/ to /ɔ:/. These changes result in the various possible pronunciations of *two* in Scots discussed in 3.3.2 above.

Stage 3 (c.1490–1510 North, 1600–1630 South)
(4.16)   ɛi > ɛ: rain
                    ɔu > ɔ: grow (S only)
          au > ɒ: law

In Stage 3 of the GVS, the subshift of /au/ to /ɒ:/ again involves an intermediate, partial shift, since a direct movement of /au/ > /ɔ:/ would be ordered before the raising of /ɔ:/ > /o:/ in the final stage of the GVS, and the merger which would result is not attested: compare Modern Scots *law*, *cause*, *saw*, where /au/ > /ɔ/ (or /a/), with *throat*, *coal*, where the /ɔ:/ > /o:/ shift took place.

Two discrepancies between North and South are relevant to this stage of the GVS. First, whereas in the South all /ɛi/ (< /ai/) monophthongised to /ɛ:/, in the North this development took place only medially. Where /ɛi/ occurred word-finally in the North (and, it will be recalled, this will be the case only in relatively uncommon words, since final /ai/ in frequently occurring words had earlier monophthongised to /a:/), it remained diphthongal and developed to Modern Scots /ʌi/. This accounts for the differing pronunciations, in some varieties of Modern Scots, of *pail*, *pair*, *rain* with earlier medial /ɛi/ and thus modern /e/, and *pay*, *way*, with final /ɛi/ < /ai/, and modern /ʌi/. Again, this is of direct relevance to SVLR. Second, /ɔu/ monophthongised to /ɔ:/ only in the South, raising in the final stage of GVS to /o:/ and subsequently diphthongising to give RP /ou/. In the North, however, /ɔu/ is retained and later becomes /ʌu/, as in *grow*, [grʌu].

Stage 4 (c.1500–1550 North, 1690–1715 South)
In this final complex of shifts, the mid-front and low-mid back mono-phthongs raised, with /ɒ:/ becoming /ɔ:/, while the first element of the /eu/ diphthong also raised, giving /iu/ (see (4.17)).

(4.17)   e: >   i:
         ɛ: >   e:
         ɔ: >   o:
         ɒ: >   ɔ:
         eu   >   iu

After the completion of the GVS, /ʊ/ lowered to /ʌ/. This lowering was complete in Scots, partial in the South, and failed in the North of England, producing the present-day division of dialects with only /ʌ/, both /ʊ/ and /ʌ/, or only /ʊ/.

The Scots vowel system after the Great Vowel Shift is shown in (4.18).

(4.18)   *short*   *long*   *diphthongs*

         ɪ   ʌ   i: u: (iu)
         ɛ   ɒ   e: ø: o: ɔi ʌu ʌi
                 a   a: ɔ:

Note that /ɛ:/ has been lost completely through the operation of GVS, while /a:/ and /ɔ:/ are fairly marginal; /a:/ occurs only in certain dialects for earlier /a:/ (including /a:/ < /ai/) after a labial consonant, as in *two* [twa:], *away* [əwa:], while /ɔ:/ has the same origin in a different set of dialects, in which earlier /a:/ backed and rounded under the influence of a preceding labial – so [twɔ:], [əwɔ:]. The monophthongisation of earlier /au/ to either /ɔ:/ or /a:/ in words like *law*, *craw* 'crow' gives one additional source for these vowels. A system of the type shown in (4.18), with a few revisions to be discussed below, would have formed the input for SVLR.

4.4.3   The Scottish Vowel Length Rule

As we saw in 4.1, SVLR is generally held responsible for the neutralisation of vowel length in Scots and SSE, both synchronically and diachronically. Here, we shall concentrate on three aspects of the historical SVLR: its restriction to Scots and SSE; its approximate dating; and its effect on diphthongs.

4.4.3.1   Justifying the S in SVLR

If we are to establish SVLR as a Scots-specific phonological rule, we must first challenge Agutter's contention that 'the context-dependent vowel length encapsulated in SVLR is not and perhaps never was Scots-specific' (1988b: 20). I shall show in the next section that SVLR can be defended synchronically as a Scots-specific process; there is also evidence that SVLR was historically introduced only into Scots.

Harris (1985: ch.4) discusses the chequered history of Middle English /ɛ:/, the vowel of the MEAT class of lexical items. This class, although intact at the beginning of the early Modern English period, had merged in standard dialects by the eighteenth century with the MEET class. Controversy exists, however, over whether the MEAT class earlier merged with the MATE class (< ME /a:/) before splitting and re-merging with Middle English /e:/ at /i:/ (Dobson 1957, Luick 1921). Harris believes that a consideration of some Modern English dialects which retain a three-way contrast of MEET, MEAT and MATE words may shed further light on the dubious history of /ɛ:/; from our point of view, what is interesting is the strategies which dialects of different areas have implemented to keep these classes of words, with Middle English /ɛ: e: a:/, distinct.

MEET-MEAT-MATE contrasts persist in many varieties of

conservative Hiberno-English (Harris 1985: 232), various rural English dialects (Wells 1982), and some Scots dialects (Catford 1958). Harris discusses several strategies whereby dialects preserve the MEET-MEAT-MATE contrasts, including diphthongisation; the 'leapfrogging' of the reflex of Middle English /a:/ past that of /ɛ:/; and the use of length contrasts. However, these strategies are not evenly distributed across English and Scots dialects.

Harris considers five Modern Scots dialects which keep their reflexes of Middle English /ɛ: e: a:/ distinct – those of north-east Angus, Kirkcudbright, east Fife, Shetland northern Isles/Yell/Unst, and Shetland mainland/Skerries. One of these, Kirkcudbright, is a 'core', central Scots dialect with full implementation of SVLR, so that /i e ę/, the reflexes of Middle English /e: ɛ: a:/, are all positionally long or short. However, 'the other four dialect areas are typical of geographically peripheral areas of Scotland where Aitken's Law has not gone to completion' (Harris 1985: 254). Here, while the /i e/ reflexes of Middle English /e: ɛ:/ are subject to SVLR, the reflex of Middle English /a:/, which is /ɛ:/ in north-east Angus and Shetland northern Isles/Yell/Unst and /e:/ in east Fife and Shetland mainland/Skerries, is phonemically long. That is, in east Fife and Shetland mainland/Skerries, the reflexes of Middle English /ɛ:/ and /a:/ are qualitatively identical. However, SVLR affects one vowel, /e/ < /ɛ:/, while phonemic length remains in /e:/ < /a:/. The length difference is, of course, neutralised in SVLR long contexts, but is sufficient to maintain the contrast elsewhere, as can be seen from (4.19).

(4.19)   SVLR context   ME /ɛ:/   ME /a:/
          short   [met] 'meat'   [me:t] 'mate'
          long   ['e:ze] 'easy' ['le:ze] 'lazy'
          (from Buckhaven, east Fife: Harris 1985: 255)

The other three Scots dialects all differentiate Middle English /ɛ:/ from /a:/ qualitatively, as /e/ versus /ę/ in Kirkcudbright and /e/ versus /ɛ:/ in north-east Angus and Shetland northern Isles/Yell/Unst. The latter two dialects use conditioned versus phonemic length as an additional distinguishing strategy.

The significance of this dialect evidence for the status of SVLR becomes apparent from Harris's comparison with five English dialects which also maintain a three-way MEET-MEAT-MATE contrast. In all the English cases, the reflex of Middle English /ɛ:/ or /a:/ (or both) has diphthongised. In addition, some dialects preserve the original relative heights of these vowels, as in Westmorland, with /iə/ < ME /ɛ:/ and /ea/

< Middle English /a:/, while others reverse them; so, Devon and Cornwall has /ɛi/ < Middle English /ɛ:/ but /e:/ < Middle English /a:/. None of the English dialects uses vowel length differences to keep the MEAT-MATE distinction, since they all retain the reflexes of Middle English /e: ɛ: a:/ as phonemically long vowels or diphthongs and, in the absence of SVLR, there is no phonemic versus positionally determined length dichotomy. However, four out of the five Scottish dialects discussed by Harris maintain the MEAT-MATE distinction by exploiting the length difference created by the incomplete operation of SVLR, either as the sole distinguishing factor or along with the preservation of the relative vowel heights. The sole exception is Kirkcudbright, where SVLR has been implemented fully and no phonemically long vowels remain. No Scottish dialect uses the strategy of diphthongisation; this is in keeping with the tendency of Modern Scots and SSE long vowels to be realised as long steady-state monophthongs rather than sequences of vowel plus offglide. The geographical skewing of the different strategies employed in maintaining a MEET-MEAT-MATE distinction lends support to the hypothesis that SVLR was introduced diachronically only into Scots.

4.4.3.2   Dating the historical SVLR

Lass (1974: 320) sees the historical SVLR as bipartite, as shown in (4.20).

(4.20)   (a) All long vowels shortened everywhere except before /r v z ʒ ð #/
         (b) The nonhigh short vowels /ɛ a ɔ/ lengthened in the same
             environments.

The effect of SVLR is clear: before its operation, Scots, like other Middle English dialects, contrasted long and short vowels, whereas afterwards, Scots had innovated a system in which length is non-distinctive. Pullum (1974) argues that this reanalysis of the underlying Scots vowel system results directly from the introduction of SVLR, observing that: 'an immediate or even simultaneous consequence of the addition of a rule like Lass' formulation of Aitken's Law (a) to a grammar would be a restructuring by rule inversion: from underlying vowels *shortened* in all contexts *except* before /r v ð z ʒ #/, the language would shift to having underlying short vowels *lengthened* before /r v ð z ʒ #/'.

That is, the transition from historical to SVLR involves a classic case of rule inversion (Vennemann 1972), which is, as we shall see in 4.6 below, of great relevance to the application of Lexical Phonology to sound change. (4.21) shows the input and output systems for SVLR, to illustrate Pullum's proposed change.

(4.21)

Input

ɪ	ʌ	iː	uː		
ɛ	ɒ	eː øː	oː	ʌi ʌu ɔi	
	a	aː			

Output

ɪ	ʌ	i	u		
ɛ		e ø	o	ʌi ʌu ɔi	
		a	ɔ		

The output system in (4.21) also provides further support for the laxing and lowering of short vowels which was required above to account adequately for MEOSL. It is clear that the Modern Scots and SSE vowel system must include /ɛ a ɔ/, since each occurs in a fairly large set of lexical items (*men, bed, slept* for /ɛ/; *cot, caught, pot, law* for /ɔ/; and *back, trap, car* for /a/). In order to derive such a system historically, the short vowel system prior to the operation of SVLR cannot have been that of Old English, i.e. /i e a o u/, since the requisite length adjustments of SVLR would then have produced mergers of /i/ with /iː/, /u/ with /uː/, /e/ with /eː/, /o/ with /oː/ and /a/ with /aː/, and no source would be available for /ɛ/, while /ɔ/ would remain extremely marginal. We must rather assume a short lax vowel system /ɪ ɛ ʌ ɒ a/, with /ʌ/ having lowered from earlier /ʊ/ after GVS. Lass assumes that /a/ then merged with earlier /aː/ and /ɒ/ with earlier /ɔː/, while /ɛ/ lengthened in the appropriate SVLR long environments, fitting into the same system as the originally long vowels as a new underlyingly short vowel with contextually long realisations. In fact, as we shall see in the next section, the status of /ɛ/ vis-à-vis SVLR is unclear; we shall also consider reasons for the exceptionality of /ɪ ʌ/, which do not lengthen either synchronically or historically. As (4.21) shows, SVLR disrupted the correlation of length with [+ tense], and short with [− tense], which had held in English since around the time of MEOSL.

A fairly wide spread of dates for SVLR has been proposed: Lass (1976: 54) opts for the seventeenth century; McClure designates SVLR as 'a sixteenth-century sound change in Scots' (1977: 10); and Aitken half-commits himself to an earlier introduction '? in the fifteenth century' (1981: 137). Although it is not possible to be conclusive, evidence of several types suggests that SVLR was under way by the mid to late sixteenth century.

Johnston (1980: 380) opts for the period 1600–1640, stipulating that SVLR must follow GVS and precede lowering of /ʊ/; but neither of these claims is well supported. First, Johnston argues that /ʊ/ lowered to /ʌ/ before SVLR because he assumes that the descendants of Older Scots /i u/, which failed to lengthen by SVLR, are exempt on account of their height. However, the originally long high vowels /i: u:/ *were* affected by SVLR; and the date (from Dobson 1962) which Johnston accepts for lowering may also be rather late: the process may well have been sixteenth rather than seventeenth century in the North, since it is generally assumed to have operated immediately after the GVS, the last stage of which Johnston himself dates to c.1500–1550 in the North, although over a century later in the South. As far as interaction of SVLR with GVS is concerned, Harris also asserts that 'the shortening of historically long vowels ... post-dates the early stages of the Great Vowel Shift, since these vowels all appear in their shifted shapes' (1985: 23). Thus, *divine* has short [ʌi] in Modern Scots and SSE, shifted from earlier /i:/; similarly, *meat* has [i] from pre-GVS /e:/, and *coal*, [o] from /ɔ:/: if SVLR had preceded GVS, these vowels, in SVLR short contexts, would have been short and therefore ineligible for shifting. There is, however, persuasive evidence that SVLR and at least part of the GVS were contemporaneous. Recall that /i:/ is generally taken as having shifted initially to [ɛi], [ʌi] or [əi] by GVS, on the grounds that a direct shift to [ai] would predict an unwarranted merger with /ai/, which raised only later. This theoretical motivation for the intermediate shift is strongly supported by the orthoepical evidence, in which an open front first element is not attested until the 1740s (Lass 1989, in press). In Modern Scots and SSE, Older Scots /i:/ in SVLR long environments gives the long diphthong [a:i], whereas in short contexts we still find [ʌi]; McClure (1995: 51) interprets this as indicating that 'the diphthongisation of /i:/ by the Great Vowel Shift had begun before the operation of Aitken's Law, but was arrested in words where the Law resulted in shortening and carried to completion only in those where the vowel remained long.'

Some further evidence for a relatively early dating of SVLR comes from Harris (1985: 23). SVLR operates in Ulster Scots, at least for some vowels, and Harris argues that, since most Scottish settlers of Ulster migrated from the peripheral dialect areas of southwest Scotland during the Plantation of Ulster from 1601 onwards, 'the Aitken's Law changes must presumably have begun their diffusion outwards from the core dialects of central Scotland well before the seventeenth century if they were to be sufficiently advanced in southwest Scots before the Plantation of Ulster.'

Approaching the issue from the other end, it is clear that SVLR must have been well established by the eighteenth century. First, McClure (1995: 51) cites Shetland dialects where /d/ and /ð/ had merged by this time; however, vowels are long before [d̠] < /ð/, historically a lengthening environment, and short before [d̠] < /d/, as in [miːd̠] *meed* 'landmark' versus [nid̠] *need*. Primary sources from the eighteenth century, although rarely explicit, also testify to the general Scots neutralisation of length, in frequent comments to the effect that Scots cannot reproduce English vowel length distinctions. Thus, Buchanan (1770: 44) rather wearily tells us that 'I shall adduce but a few examples, out of a multitude, to shew how North-Britons destroy just quantity, by expressing the long sound for the short, and the short for the long'.

Similarly, Drummond (1767: 21) asserts that 'The sound of every vowel may be made long or short ... But to ascertain the time of pronouncing them is the greatest difficulty to the Scots, in the English Tongue.'

Jones (1997b: 294) extracts from various eighteenth century sources a series of characteristic Scots pronunciations, involving the alternations [i] ~ [ɛ], [e] ~ [a] and [o] ~ [ɒ], which 'appear to represent height contrasts, not unlike those characteristic of the Great Vowel Shift process itself, but in contexts where the affected vowels do not appear to meet the expected (and necessary) extended length criterion so intimately associated with it'.

This observation may provide further evidence of the interaction of SVLR with GVS: if the two overlapped chronologically, we might expect some extension of GVS to etymologically short vowels, at least in SVLR long environments. For instance, Elphinston (1787: 14) notes that Scots has *mak, tak, brak, mappel, apel, craddel, sadel*, as opposed to English *make, take, break, mapel, appel, cradle, saddel*, and *gairden, yaird, dazel, staig*, compared with English *garden, yard, dazzel, stag*. In the first set of forms, there seems to be raising in English but not in Scots, while the second set shows the opposite pattern; and in both cases, there is a very strong, though not exceptionless, correlation with SVLR short and long environments respectively.

Occasionally, an eighteenth century source is more explicit about vowel length in Scots. Two examples worthy of mention are Sylvester Douglas and Alexander Scot (see Jones 1991, 1993, 1995). We know rather little about Alexander Scot (or Aulaxaunder Scoat, as he signs himself), whose letter *The Contrast*, dated 1779, is the subject of Jones (1993). *The Contrast* is directed to a noble family, and describes the impressions of a Scot on returning to Scotland; in particular, Scot comments on changes, including linguistic ones, which he observes.

The important aspect of *The Contrast* for present purposes is Scot's use of five different orthographic representations for English [ai] (4.22).

(4.22)   1. <oy>   <oy>, <moy>, <oys>, <troyal> – stressed, syllable
                      final
          2. <oi>   <dasoir>, <foive>, <serproize> – pre-/r/, voiced
                      fricative
          3. <ey>   only <whey> 'why'
          4. <ei>   <daleited>, <steil>, <dazein>, <leik> – SVLR short
                      contexts
          5. <ai>   only <aither>, <naither>

Leaving aside the little-populated classes 3 and 5, Scot's system captures the environments of SVLR, with class 4 for short contexts, involving following voiceless consonants, voiced stops, /l/ and /n/, and classes 1 and 2 covering the long contexts. As we shall see below, experimental evidence demonstrates that final position produces longer vowels than following voiced fricatives and /r/.

The second source of explicit eighteenth century comment on Scots vowel length is Sylvester Douglas (Jones 1991), whose *Treatise on the Provincial Dialect of Scotland* (containing 'a table of words improperly pronounced by the Scotch, showing their true English pronouncing' (Jones 1991: 158)) was written in 1799. Douglas was born in 1744 near Aberdeen, and trained first in medicine, then in the law, becoming a barrister in 1776 and KC in 1793. Between 1795 and 1806 he was an MP for various constituencies, and in 1800, was elevated to the Irish peerage as Baron Glenbervie. He did not succeed in his ambition to rise to the English peerage, or to take up a cabinet post, although he did marry a daughter of Lord North (albeit, according to a commentator of the time, not a terribly attractive daughter). Douglas's *Treatise* contains various comments on vowel length in Scots. For instance (Jones 1991: 124), he mentions a Noun–Verb alternation of voicing which still carries with it an SVLR distinction of length for Modern Scots: 'In *thief* the *ie* has the first sound of the *e* shortened. Add the *e* at the end and as in *thieve* (where indeed the consonant is also altered) and the *ie* retains the same sound but protracted.'

Under EASE (Jones 1991: 190), Douglas gives more detail on the same vowel: 'The *ea* as in *appear* the *s* soft as in *please* ... pronounce in the same manner, *appease, disease, please, tease, lease* verb synonymous with *glean*. In the following words the *ea* has the same sound but shortened and the *s* is hard: *cease, decease, surcease, lease* verb and noun ... *release* ...'

Although Douglas's comments are enlightening, they are incomplete; the Treatise is not wholly systematic, and the alphabetically arranged pronouncing dictionary within it is extremely selective, so that the items which might be most informative often do not appear. In interpreting eighteenth century Scottish sources, we must also remember that the authors generally had at least one eye on the favoured English system. Jones (1991: 4) has 'no strong impression that Douglas is advocating the total abandonment of all Scottish vernacular features in favour of an undiluted London upper class norm'; but Douglas nonetheless subtitles his Treatise 'an attempt to assist persons of that country in discovering and correcting the defects of their pronounciation and expression'.

4.4.3.3 SVLR and diphthongs

The question of whether the historical SVLR affected diphthongs or only monophthongs is not one which is usually asked: the alternation of [ʌi] ~ [aːi] in *tide* ~ *tied*, featuring the only qualitative distinction in the SVLR set of vowels, has become a diagnostic of the modern process, and any attempt to exclude it from the historical version might seem perverse. I would, nonetheless, like to suggest that the historical SVLR was in fact restricted to monophthongs.

Part of the discussion here necessarily pre-empts aspects of 4.5 below, on the synchronic SVLR, without the fuller discussion which will follow there. It seems that, in SSE and Modern Scots dialects, two of the three true diphthongs, the vowels of *bout/now* and *noise/boy*, are unaffected by SVLR. The former, for some varieties, is consistently long /aːu/; for others, it is consistently short /ʌu/; and bear in mind that in Scots, this diphthong is marginal at best, given the failure of Middle English /uː/ to diphthongise in the GVS. The /ɔːi/ vowel would appear to be consistently long.

What, then, of the final true diphthong? Turning to Scots dialects first, recall that there is not in fact one diphthong in this general area: there are two, namely the [ʌi] of *way, pay* (< Middle English /ai/), and the [ʌi] ~ [aːi] of *tide* ~ *tied* (< Middle English /iː/). The former is uniformly short in Scots, and is not affected by synchronic SVLR; the latter indubitably is. To distinguish the two, I shall propose underlying /ʌi/ for the *pay, way* vowel, which does not vary in quality, and /ai/ for the *tide ~ tied* one, which does.

There are several reasons for thinking that none of these diphthongs was involved in the historical length neutralisation described by SVLR. None are conclusive, but together, they are indicative of a historical restriction of the process to monophthongs. First, there is the quality difference itself: why should the diphthong be the only vowel to do more than lengthen by SVLR? Without SVLR, we can still derive the [ʌi] ~ [aːi] alternation, since we have already seen that the GVS diphthongisation of /iː/ must be assumed to have undergone an initial, partial shift to [ʌi] before lowering later. I am here following an undeveloped suggestion from Johnston (1997a: 94), whereby 'A diphthong of this type would tend to have the longest V1 in the most sonorant environment: this would also favour a peripheral realisation. Now, the association with Aitken's Law might not be original.'

That is, lowering (giving greater peripherality) would be most likely where greatest lengthening was favoured; for Johnston, that means perhaps only in final position. He therefore proposes a phonemic split between the vowels of his lexical sets BITE and TRY, and there are indeed cases where such a split would seem to be justified: some Scots (and SSE) speakers have [ʌi] in words like *cider, spider, idle, pilot, title*, while others have long [aːi] (and not all words in the list need have the same vowel, for any one speaker). Milroy (1995) reports similar variant forms from his investigation of [ʌi]/[ei] versus [ai] in Newcastle: [ai] appeared in SVLR short environments such as *pride, wine, site, cycle*, predominantly in middle-class speakers, while working-class speakers tended to produce [ʌi]/[ei] in forms like *tied, higher, drive, sky, buy, my*. I shall return to this marginal contrast below. But equally, there are many cases where the SVLR generalisation holds robustly for this diphthong in Modern Scots and SSE; whatever the historical development of [ʌi] ~ [aːi] might have been, it has now been incorporated into the synchronic SVLR.

We shall see in 4.5 that no current version of SVLR, including the one presented here, can give a formal synchronic description of the input vowels and the effect of the process in a way which includes [ʌi] ~ [aːi], while also explaining why no other diphthong is involved. However, if the diphthong, like other diphthongs, was excluded from the process historically, but unlike other diphthongs, had its variant realisations reinterpreted as resulting from SVLR later, we should perhaps not be surprised by its apparent failure to fit the SVLR specifications in full.

There is one final aspect of the behaviour of [ʌi] ~ [aːi] which perhaps becomes clearer under this analysis. This is the similarity of the Scots/ SSE alternation with the North American process known as Canadian Raising (Chambers 1973, Gregg 1973), an alternation of [ʌi]/[əi] and [ʌu]/ [əu] before voiceless consonants, with [ai] and [au] elsewhere. Donegan (1993: 121), however, notes that this pattern 'is not limited to Canadian dialects, nor is it necessarily a raising': she shares with Gregg (1973) the view that the process is more likely to reflect lengthening and lowering before voiced consonants and boundaries than shortening and raising in voiceless contexts. In that case, lowering in Canadian varieties (and in Maryland, Minnesota, Virginia, Michigan, Georgia and the sundry other places it has been reported) could be seen as an extension of SVLR to an extra set of lengthening environments, namely voiced stops.

This, however, raises more questions than it solves. Why should only diphthongs be affected, when all Scottish versions of SVLR include at least some monophthongs? One might say that the diphthongal alternation, involving quality as well as quantity, was more easily perceptible; but that hardly counts for /au/, which is also affected in the North American cases, but which does not undergo SVLR in Scotland. On the other hand, if we see this as a separate change affecting Scots and the North American varieties, the differing inputs are unsurprising, since in Scots at the time of GVS the /au/ diphthong was extremely marginal and almost unattested in final position, where lengthening may have taken hold. The different environments of these lengthening processes also follow naturally: in Canadian and other North American varieties, as we shall see later, vowels already lengthen finally and before voiced consonants, and the diphthongal alternations are only perceived as different because quality as well as quantity is involved. But only in Scots, and in SSE as it developed, was there a further process with more radical phonological consequences, the Scottish Vowel Length Rule, for the diphthongal change to collapse with. I therefore assume in what follows that the historical SVLR was restricted to monophthongs. I also propose underlying /ʌi/ in Scots *pay, way,* versus lengthenable /ai/.

4.5   The Scottish Vowel Length Rule in Present-Day Scots and Scottish Standard English

Although there have been some dissenters (see Agutter 1988a, b), most commentators on Scots and SSE phonology, including Abercrombie (1979), McClure (1977), Aitken (1981), Lass (1974), Wells (1982) and Jones (1997b), assume SVLR to be operative in these varieties today. Lass (1974: 316), for instance, notes that 'It is well known that most modern Scots (i.e. Scottish English ...) dialects display a type of vocalic organisation radically different from that of non-Scots dialects', while for Wells (1982: 398), 'The Scottish vowel system is clearly distinct typologically from the vowel systems of all other accents of English (except the related Ulster) ....There are no long-short oppositions of the kind found in other accents.'

Although there may be general agreement that SVLR applies in Modern Scots, it is less clear how, where, and to what it applies. The purpose of this section is therefore to survey the experimental and theoretical literature on SVLR, and to provide as complete a statement as possible of its input, environment of operation, and interaction with other rules. In 4.6, we return to the history of SVLR, and the question of how it has come to be implemented as a lexical phonological rule in Modern Scots and SSE.

4.5.1   *The input to the Scottish Vowel Length Rule*

A working version of SVLR was given as (4.6) above, and is repeated as (4.23). Our main concern here is to replace the question mark in the input of the rule with an informative and motivated feature specification.

(4.23)   SVLR: preliminary version

$$\begin{matrix} \sigma_s \\ | \\ X \\ | \\ V \\ [?] \end{matrix} \longrightarrow \begin{matrix} X \quad X \\ \diagdown \diagup \\ V \end{matrix} \quad / \underline{\quad} \left\{ \begin{matrix} & & & r \\ v & z & \eth & 3 \\ & & &] \end{matrix} \right\}$$

All existing accounts of SVLR agree that it does not apply completely generally. Dialect studies like Dieth (1932), Watson (1923), Wettstein

(1942) and Zai (1942) propose monophthongal vowel systems including a set of 'vowels of variable quantity' (Zai 1942: 9), which are subject to lengthening before a voiced fricative, /r/ or a boundary, since SVLR lengthening occurs before inflectional suffixes, even when the consonant following the bracket does not itself constitute a lengthening environment; for instance, the stem vowel is long in *brewed* [bruːd] but short in *brood* [brud]. Some examples of affected vowels in long and short contexts are given in (4.24).

(4.24)	/i/	[i]	beat	wreath	leaf	bean	greed
		[iː]	beer	wreathe	leave	agree	agreed
	/ai/	[ʌi]	fight	life	lice	line	tide
		[aːi]	fire	live	lies	tie	tied

However, the dialect studies also include a subset of /ɪ ʌ ɛ ɛ̈/ as consistently short vowels, and sometimes a vowel which is always long, like /øː/ in Morebattle. I shall discuss the long set and the diphthongs first, and then the exceptional short vowels.

The set of 'lengthenable' monophthongs comprises /i u e o a ɔ/. Aitken (1981) notes that in some 'core' dialects, mainly in the Central Scots area, SVLR operates on all of these; elsewhere, there is a hierarchy of inputs to SVLR, whereby some varieties have only the high vowels /i u/ as lengthenable, others generalise SVLR to mid /e o/, and still others include low /a ɔ/ (Wells 1982, Johnston 1997b). When /a ɔ/ do not lengthen positionally, they tend to be consistently long, and consequently ineligible for SVLR, which as stated in (4.23), applies to vowels underlyingly associated with only a single X position. The question then is not why these are synchronically exempt from lengthening, but why they were resistant to historical shortening in SVLR short environments; and this is likely to reflect the greater phonetic correlation of length with low vowels (Fischer-Jørgensen 1990).

The diphthongs /ʌi/ and /ai/ were discussed in 4.4.3.2 above. The other diphthongs of Scots and SSE, /ɔi/ and /ʌu/, do not generally undergo SVLR. /ɔi/ is typically consistently long; information on /ʌu/ is more variable. Watson (1923) lists word-final lengthened [kʌuː] *cow*, [yʌuː] *ewe*, but asserts that the long diphthong is peculiar to Teviotdale, while Zai (1942: 14) observes long [æːu] 'only in the onomatopoeic word *mæːu* "to mew like a cat"'. Lass (1974) explicitly excludes his /au/ from the SVLR, on the grounds that it is extremely marginal in Scots; Johnston (1997b: 497) gives a complete list of /ʌu/ words, consisting of *coup, loup, howff, nowt, gold, dowse, roll, four, grow, knowe*. In many varieties, including Edinburgh Scots (Carr 1992), /ʌu/ is consistently short. This diphthong does occur more frequently in SSE, in items with unshifted /u/ in Scots; here /au/ is often consistently long, and may therefore constitute a borrowing from or an assimilation towards RP.

The Modern Scots/SSE descendants of Middle English short high /i u/ likewise fail to undergo the synchronic SVLR. In most Modern Scots dialects, these surface as consistently short [ɪ ʌ]; however, the reflexes of earlier /i u/ may vary in quality cross-dialectally – hence Lass's (1974: 336) assertion that 'quantity is now in effect neutralised in toto, but not segmentally neutralised for two (synchronically arbitrary but historically principled) vowels'. The 'Aitken vowel' /ë/, where it appears, is also consistently short.

We now come to the problem of /ɛ/. Lass (1974), Wells (1982), Aitken (1981), Harris (1985) and Johnston (1997b) all seem to assume that /ɛ/ forms part of the input for SVLR, but do not discuss it specifically. However, there is in fact little evidence for classifying /ɛ/ as lengthenable. In earlier dialect studies (Dieth 1932, Wettstein 1942), /ɛ/ is typically classified as non-lengthening: Grant (1912: §140) alone suggests that /ɛ/ may lengthen, but only under extremely limited circumstances, namely when it is used 'in words spelled *air*, *ere*, etc., instead of the old *e:*'. More recent experimental results are inconclusive: Agutter (1988a, b) did not test /ɛ/, and McClure (1977) and McKenna (1987), who did, were unable to include a full range of contexts. For instance, the absence of /ɛ/ from stressed open syllables means that no examples of this vowel word-finally or before inflectional [d] or [z] are available. /ɛ/ occurs relatively frequently before a consonant cluster with /r/ as the first element, as in *heard*, *herb* or *serve*, but SVLR is strongest before final /r/ (Aitken 1981), and perhaps operates only before final single consonants (although in the absence of conclusive experimental evidence, this must again remain a tentative and corrigible suggestion); and here /ɛ/ is rare. The pronoun *her* is unreliable because it is characteristically unstressed and produced with reduced schwa; other cases where /ɛ/ might be expected, like *their*, have [e] in Scots/SSE. Even in the few possible forms, like McClure's *Kerr* /kɛr/, a sequence of /ɛ/ plus an /r/ with any degree of retroflexion would prove almost impossible to segment accurately. Examples of /ɛ/ before a final voiced fricative (*Des* /dɛz/, *rev* /rɛv/) are only marginally easier to find; but McKenna (personal communication) reports that his subjects experienced some difficulty with *rev*, so that several of his data points were invalidated. The required contexts seem in some sense unnatural for

/ɛ/. McClure (1977) claims to have found results broadly in line with the length modification expected if SVLR ḍid affect /ɛ/; but only one informant, McClure himself, was tested, and his average vowel duration and range of durations were considerably higher than those of any speaker tested by Agutter (1988a, b). This makes McClure's findings unreliable, since it is at least possible that they reflect 'an exaggerated differentiation of vowel length in long and non-long contexts and extreme carefulness on the part of an informant who knew the purpose of the experiment' (Agutter 1988b: 15). Further experimental work is currently being undertaken, as outlined in Scobbie, Turk and Hewlett (1998), but no results are yet available.

If we accept that /ɛ/, along with /ɪ ʌ ë/, is an exception to SVLR, our next task is to ascertain whether these vowels constitute a natural class, and can be exempted from the rule in a principled way. I propose to use the feature [± tense]: short tense vowels will be eligible for SVLR, but non-lengthening /ɪ ʌ ɛ ë/ are [−tense].

This dichotomy can be substantiated on synchronic and diachronic grounds. Synchronically, the evidence is primarily distributional: for instance, tense vowels may characteristically occur in stressed open syllables, and this holds for the [+ tense] Scots/SSE vowels – *bee*, *blue*, *bay*, *bow*, *law*, *baa* have final /i u e o ɔ aɪ/. However, although *bit*, *but*, *bet* are possible, *[bɪ], *[bʌ], *[bɛ] are not. /ɛ/ shows other behavioural and distributional affinities with /ɪ ʌ ë/, as underlined by Dieth's (1932: 2) description of /ɪ ʌ ɛ ë/ as 'the phonetician's worry', since they are all interchangeable and hard to distinguish by ear. It is true that in careful speech, or when the items carry prominent or contrastive stress, many Scots speakers differentiate words like *fir* [fɪɹ], *fur* [fʌɹ] and *fern* [fɛɹn]; but in more casual registers or under low stress, /ɪ/ and /ʌ/ tend to fall together, and /ɛ/ often joins in too (see (4.25)).

(4.25)

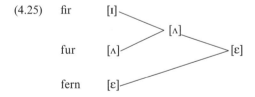

In diachronic terms, vowels which undergo SVLR, and those which are consistently and therefore underlyingly long, are precisely those which had some tense sources in Middle English. /i u e o/ have only long/

tense sources, namely post-Great Vowel Shift /i: u: e: o:/ respectively. Short low lax /æ ɒ/ lengthened by historical SVLR while /a: ɔ:/ (which were marginal in Scots after the GVS) shortened, producing mergers: Modern Scots/SSE /a ɔ/ consequently also have some tense sources. /ɪ ʌ ɛ̈/, however, are descended only from lax vowels, and here again /ɛ/ allies itself with the lax set, since all its possible long/tense sources were collapsed with other vowels during the Great Vowel Shift. Middle English /ɛ:/ raised to /e:/ and subsequently, in some cases, to /i:/, and although /a:/ in turn raised to /ɛ:/, it afterwards continued to /e:/, leaving the long half-open front slot empty. Middle English short lax /ɛ/ might be considered a suitable input to the lengthening subrule of the historical SVLR; but recall that the other short vowels which underwent contextual lengthening, /æ/ and /ɒ/, already had long counterparts in the system: /ɛ/ alone was isolated.

Giegerich (1992) points out one problem with the characterisation of SVLR input vowels as tense: why should the *tide, tied* vowels be [+ tense], but the other diphthongs [−tense], when in general English diphthongs ally themselves with the long or lengthenable tense mono-phthongs? There is no real issue here for /ɔi/, which will be tense, but underlyingly long; and the same is true for /au/ in SSE and those Scots varieties where it surfaces consistently long. In cases where it is consis-tently surface short, I propose the underlier /ʌu/, with a lax, unlength-enable first element. As for [ʌi]/[a:i], recall the proposal in 4.4.3.3 that the underlying form for the lengthenable diphthong should be /ai/, con-trasting with the *pay, way* vowel /ʌi/, which although restricted to final position, a long SVLR environment, is universally short.

This distinction is not necessary for SSE, where *pay, way* have /e/ [e:]; but arguably here too, the underlying vowel for the lengthenable diphthong should be /ai/. First, there is some evidence, as we shall see later, for a marginal contrast in SSE too, between short /ʌi/ and long /a:i/, since not all speakers maintain the expected SVLR pattern uni-formly; the existence of lexical exceptions to SVLR is of some relevance in determining where it applies in the phonology of Modern Scots and SSE. Second, SVLR interacts with the Modern English Vowel Shift Rules. I argued in chapter 3 above that the underlying diphthong which surfaces in *divine*, laxes trisyllabically in *divinity* and is then eligible for Lax Vowel Shift; the derivation is from /aɪ/ → /a/ → [ɪ]. The assumption that diphthong laxing involves loss of the less prominent element was supported by the *reduce ~ reduction* alternation, where Lax Vowel Shift was again involved, this time operating on the second element of the rising [ju] diphthong. If the underlying vowel of *divine* ~ *divinity* is /ai/ for Scots and SSE, the Vowel Shift derivation will produce the appropriate surface [ɪ]; but not if the underlier is /ʌi/.

I have assumed thus far that the underlying form in the case of alternation is the lexical representation of the underived form; and this would mean /ʌi/. There may, however, be one set of circumstances where we have to allow deviation from this general requirement, namely where there is a partial surface merger of two underlyingly distinct segments. In this case, proposing the surface form of the underived member as the underlier would suggest, counterfactually, that the merger was a full phonological one. The classic case here would be final devoicing in German, where the underived surface forms have voiceless stops, and the related but morphologically derived ones have voicing. But if we select voiceless stops as underlying, there is a conflict, since there are other, non-alternating morphemes which have invariant voiceless stops. There are then good phonological arguments for assigning underlying voiceless stops to the latter set, and voiced ones to the alternating forms. The Scots case is parallel to the German one, in that *pay*, *way* have unlengthenable [ʌi], which should surely preferentially be assigned underlying /ʌi/; if we are not to predict that the *tied* vowel is also quantitatively invariant, we must then prefer /ai/, the lexical representation of the derived alternant. This argument does not hold in precisely the same way for SSE, where as we have seen, *pay* and *way* are not diphthongal; but it will go through if there is an incipient split of underlying /ʌi/ (which is axiomatically unlengthenable) and /ai/, as I shall argue later. In that case, /ʌ/, whether monophthongal or part of a diphthong, is a good diagnostic of failure to lengthen; and SVLR can straightforwardly be stated as a lengthening rule. We still have the problem of deriving [ʌi] in SVLR short contexts which, as Carr (1992) points out, is a difficulty for all current analyses of SVLR. My proposal that SVLR initially affected only monophthongs, and that the [ʌi] ~ [aːi] alternation was later incorporated into it, complete with a pre-existing quality difference reflecting earlier and later GVS reflexes of original /iː/, at least puts the synchronic mismatch of diphthong and monophthongs into historical perspective.

The use of [+ tense] in the structural description of SVLR will, then, effect the appropriate exclusions, and is clearly synchronically and diachronically motivated, insofar as the feature [± tense] itself is motivated. However, as Halle (1977: 611) notes, 'the feature of tenseness has had a long and complicated career in phonetics', and its integrity and usefulness have been challenged. A short excursus to justify the use of [± tense] is therefore necessary; my contention that Lexical Phonology can capture necessary and relevant generalisations without undue abstractness will hardly benefit from avowed support for a 'pseudo-feature' (Lass 1976).

Lass (1976) bases his case for the abandonment of [± tense] largely on the fact that its measurable phonetic correlates are typically 'based on the presumed "effects" of tenseness. And all of these "effects" are independent variables, parameters that require independent notation in any case' (Lass 1976: 40). That is, when two vowels differ with respect to a cluster of phonetic factors such as relative height, backness and degree of rounding, each factor should be considered separately rather than ascribed as a set to 'an explanatory abstraction' (Lass 1976: 49) like tenseness. However, Halle (1977: 611), Giegerich (1992: 98) and Anderson (1984) all acknowledge the multiple correlations of tenseness with other features, but nonetheless maintain that [± tense] is necessary for classificatory reasons. As Anderson (1984: 95) puts it, 'there is a considerable amount of disagreement in the phonetic literature concerning the precise definition of this distinction. There is rather less disagreement, however, on the proposition that there is indeed something to be defined.'

In fact, Lass's arguments for the dismissal of [± tense] as a 'pseudo-feature' can be countered. First, [± tense] does, in fact, have verifiable phonetic correlates, as shown by Wood (1975). Wood used X-ray tracings of vowel articulations to demonstrate that tense and lax vowels differ consistently in degree of constriction and, less importantly, in pharyngeal volume. Furthermore, tense rounded vowels tended to show a greater degree of lip-rounding than the corresponding lax vowels. Wood's results from English, German, Egyptian Arabic, Southern Swedish and West Greenlandic Eskimo indicate that 'the articulatory gestures involved appear to be much the same irrespective of language, which points to a universal physiological and biological basis for the acoustical contrasts founded on [the tense–lax AMSM] difference' (1975: 111). Fischer-Jørgensen (1990) provides a critique of Wood's experimental method, which involved enlarging X-ray photographs from the phonetic literature and measuring tongue constriction and jaw opening from these; this is potentially problematic, in that the available material is somewhat restricted, and may not all be equally valid, or have been collected under sufficiently similar conditions. Nonetheless, Fischer-Jørgensen (1990: 106) concludes that Wood's sources are sound for American English and German at least, and that 'in spite of the restricted and somewhat uneven material the results seem to be pretty clear and reliable'. Moreover, Fischer-Jørgensen establishes that 'the tense-lax characteristic is supported by EMG measurements' (1990: 107), with tense vowels involving greater activity of the genioglossus muscle, and possibly also the inferior longitudinal muscle and the geniohyoid. Lax vowels in Fischer-Jørgensen's studies of American English and German also had higher F_1 (correlating with lower tongue height) and higher F_2 than their tense counterparts, as well as relatively high F_0, which Fischer-Jørgensen (1990: 131) establishes cannot be due purely to the shorter duration of the lax vowels.

Carr (1992: 96), considering Wood's results, counters that 'there is a difference between correlates and definitions. No-one doubts the phonetic reality of the properties we take to be the correlates which we associate with "tenseness". But clearly, demonstrating the reality of the correlates is not equivalent to defining the feature.'

I suspect I hear the grating of goalposts being moved here: but this phonological argument can also be answered. It is true that tenseness is intimately connected with tongue height, frontness/backness and degree of lip rounding, which can be individually described using independent features. However, the importance of these components for the tense–lax dichotomy lies not in their individual contributions, but in their conjunction; and the weighting of contributory features is not equivalent for different tense–lax pairs. So, although tense vowels tend uniformly to be more peripheral than their lax counterparts (Lindau 1978), the interpretation of 'peripherality' is fluid: a high front tense vowel will be higher and fronter than its lax counterpart, while a low back rounded tense vowel will be lower, more back, and more rounded. It is this variable clustering of features, which would be difficult to relate using only the contributory elements, that [± tense] is intended to encapsulate. This makes [± tense] extremely useful; as Giegerich (1992: 98) points out, 'the phonological classification of the English vowel system would without the use of this feature be an extremely difficult task'. It also, undeniably, makes [± tense] a *phonological* feature, and hence phonetically relatively abstract: Anderson (1981: 496) argues persuasively for the recognition of just such features, 'for which the evidence is sometimes (or perhaps always) indirect or inferential rather than observational'.

Having established that [± tense] does have measureable though variable phonetic markers, we must ascertain how the aggregation of these markers into a single grouping of tense versus lax is phonologically beneficial. It certainly appears that the use of [± tense] may make otherwise opaque natural processes explicable and characterisable; see the analysis of MEOSL in Lieber (1979) and 4.4.1 above. This is surely one of the major tasks of linguistics and a primary requirement of the formal and theoretical tools it employs. Lass also asserts that tenseness is definable only according to its effects (such as the presence of glides, in SPE terms), rather than 'on the basis of a prior (historically based) partitioning of the lexicon' (1976: 40): but we have already seen that a 'historically based' characterisation can readily be found for the four lax vowels /ɪ ʌ ɛ ɛ̆/ in Modern Scots/SSE, which form a historically motivated natural class as the only vowels in the inventory with no long (or tense) Middle English sources. These cannot be classified simply as short, since most, if not all Scots vowels are underlyingly short, but this group also fail to undergo SVLR.

Indicating the various ways in which 'tense' vowels differ from 'lax' ones individually, without subsuming these parameters under a unifying feature of tenseness, can therefore be shown to be intrinsically unsatisfactory for some languages. In particular, Wood rejects the possibility of deriving tenseness universally from length on the grounds that 'the relationship between *tenseness* and *quantity* can vary synchronically from language to language and diachronically from period to period in one and the same language' (Wood 1975: 110). Thus, while in at least some varieties of Modern English (see chapter 5) tenseness is predictable from length, both long and short vowels may be tense in Icelandic (Anderson 1984: 95–6). Recent work by Labov (1981) and Harris (1989), to be reviewed below, suggests that the æ-Tensing rule operative in varieties like Philadelphia, New York City and Belfast has led to underlying restructuring in some dialects, producing a distinction of short lax /æ/ and short tense /Æ/. This brings us to the frequent observation (Carr 1992, Giegerich 1992) that the tense–lax distinction is not so well motivated for low vowels as for higher ones. But [± tense] would hardly be the first feature to have a skewed distribution across different classes of segments: for instance, voicing is typically not contrastive for sonorants, while higher front rounded vowels are significantly more common than lower ones. What we may be seeing in the case of low vowels is the interference of two factors: the greater phonetic likelihood of lengthening in low vowels, and the fact that length is typically, though not universally, a sign of tenseness.

In diachronic terms, I have argued that in Middle English long vowels are consistently tense and *vice versa*; the advent of SVLR has disrupted this correlation for Scots/SSE, where tense vowels are now those which may become long, under certain phonetic circumstances (see 4.6 below). This position is not uncontroversial: for instance, Lass (1980) proposes, on the basis of evidence from John Hart's *Orthographie*, that laxing and lowering of Middle English /i e u o/ did not take place until the seventeenth century. Laxing of short vowels would then follow or overlap with the historical SVLR. However, Lass's dating can be questioned. His assumption is that, since Hart does not mention a qualitative distinction between long and short vowels, no such difference existed in the mid-sixteenth century: but as Lass also admits (1980: 85) that Hart 'does not discriminate tongue-height as an independent variable', Hart's failure to distinguish (lower) lax vowels from (higher) tense ones may reflect a failing of his descriptive system rather than providing evidence of late laxing.

Returning to the SVLR, there is one final 'how else?' argument for tenseness: if we do not classify the SVLR input vowels as [+ tense], what do we call them? Carr (1992: 109), in a Dependency Phonology analysis, makes three suggestions. First, vowels with the centrality component {ə}(namely /ɪ ʌ ɛ ʌu/) do not lengthen, although Carr himself notes that his assignment of {ə} is questionable, because of the [ʌi] ~ [aːi] alternation, and the pervasive Scots and SSE centralisation of /i/ and especially /u/. Secondly, invariably long vowels are exempt from SVLR, a point accepted above and independent of Carr's Dependency Phonology model. Finally, Carr (1992: 109) argues that 'the "colour" elements {i} and {u} seem crucial in determining participation in SVLR'; if /i u e o/ are the lengthenable vowels, then 'simple preponderance of these elements will suffice to characterise the input set'. Carr (1992: 111) contends that this use of the colour elements is preferable to [± tense] because SVLR in some varieties applies to only /i u/, 'and these cannot be picked out independently of /e/ and /o/ with the characterization [+ tense]'. But Carr's own account of the SVLR vowels as those where {i} and {u} are dominant will not pick out /i u/ alone either; he will have to specify that in the relevant varieties, lengthenable vowels are those composed solely of a colour element. In addition, for varieties where the low vowels undergo SVLR, since /a ɔ/ are in Dependency Phonology terms {a} and {a;u}, Carr cannot rely on the colour elements, and instead has to assume that single or dominant {a} also conditions lengthening.

There are two questions here: why is the use of the colour elements {i}, {u} and possibly {a} an improvement on a hierarchy of lengthenability depending on vowel height; and why should the colour elements in particular be involved? In fact, the two systems of notation seem equivalent, both expressing the greater likelihood of SVLR lengthening for higher vowels. However, there is a problem for Dependency Phonology here, since there is not generally a strong correlation of greater height with greater length: in fact, the reverse is the case (and note that, when the low vowels are exempt from SVLR, they are consistently long). The better correlation here, as Wood (1975) and Fischer-Jørgensen (1990) point out, is between height and tenseness, the latter in turn being signalled very frequently by greater length. Carr notes that Ewen and van der Hulst (1988) take {i} and {u} to constitute |Y|, a tongue-body constriction sub-feature, and concedes (1992: 111) that 'there may be some mapping between Ewen & van der Hulst's sub-feature and the feature [tense]'. The independence of these two accounts, and the rejection of tenseness, must surely be called into doubt. I therefore replace the question mark of (4.23) with the specification [+ tense] in (4.26); in different varieties, this may need to be supplemented with a height specification.

(4.26)   SVLR input: final version

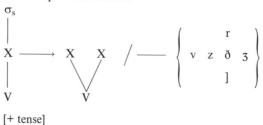

[+ tense]

4.5.2   *The Scottish Vowel Length Rule and Low-Level Lengthening*

4.5.2.1   Experimental evidence

As we have already seen, there are very few experimental investigations of vowel length in Scots and SSE. Leaving aside the limited and problematic study of McClure (1977), the only systematic experimental work on the supposed effects of SVLR is reported in two papers (Agutter

1988a, b) which embody an attack on the unity of SVLR and its restriction to Scots dialects and SSE. I shall briefly outline Agutter's investigation below, before proposing an alternative analysis of her data which corroborates the existence of SVLR as a productive but Scots-specific process.

Agutter obtained data from two male and two female SSE speakers, all middle class and from Edinburgh, and from two RP speakers, one male and one female, each from a different part of the UK. All were university students aged between eighteen and twenty-three. Each informant, recorded individually, produced a number of English monosyllables in an invariant frame sentence 'I say WORD sometimes.' The vowels tested were /ai i/, which Agutter assumes should undergo SVLR if there is such a process; /au/, which as noted earlier has an unclear status with respect to SVLR; /ɔ/, which Agutter asserts is consistently long; and /ɪ/, which is consistently short. These vowels appeared in the two sets of contexts in (4.27).

(4.27)   SVLR long contexts: -], -]d, -r, -v, -z, -ð
         SVLR short contexts: -t, -d, -n, -p, -b, -s, -f

Spectrograms of the monosyllables were produced, and vowel durations calculated by hand to the nearest centisecond. Weighted average values for each vowel for all speakers of each accent and for each context were then calculated, by multiplying average lengths per vowel per informant by the ratio 13.0/A, where 13.0 is an arbitrary average vowel length and A is the overall average vowel length for that informant. This weighting process is intended to allow a more meaningful comparison of the two accent groups by reducing the potentially distorting effect of idiolectal variation, which might be particularly severe given the small sample size. However, Agutter's weighting procedure may not be entirely valid for her results, since the technique used involves an assumption that any variation found will be normally distributed. Given that SVLR, as an accent-specific process affecting only certain vowels in certain contexts, would contravene this expectation and produce a skewed distribution, weighting might in fact mask exactly the variation Agutter is testing for.

There are other difficulties with Agutter's experiment. For instance, it is unclear how representative the informants were of their respective populations: in particular, SSE speakers are variably influenced by RP, and Agutter does not tell us whether her SSE informants had non-Scots characteristics like the /æ/ ~ /ɑ/, /ɒ/ ~ /ɔ/ and /ʊ/ ~ /u/ oppositions.

Furthermore, the distribution of informants across accent groups is unbalanced, with four SSE and two RP speakers, making further statistical testing difficult. Certain contexts were also unavailable for investigation due to accidental gaps in the English lexis; no monosyllables were found for /ɔ/ before /r ð s f/, /au/ before /v b p f/ or /i/ before /b/. The relative unfamiliarity of some of the words used, such as *mouthe*, *gawp* and *dowd*, is reflected in a number of gaps in the data, resulting from unusable tokens. The use of nonsense syllables would have solved the first problem, but whether it would have alleviated or exacerbated the second is debatable.

Agutter sees her results as inconsistent with a formulation of SVLR as Scots-specific, since they suggest that all vowels tested, for speakers of both groups, lengthened before all voiced consonants, albeit with consistently slightly greater duration in SVLR long environments. From these findings, Agutter concludes that 'SVLR is too restrictive in the set of contexts which it designates as long contexts in Scots' (1988b: 16); more radically, she argues that 'the context-dependent vowel length encapsulated in SVLR is not and perhaps never was Scots-specific' (1988b: 20).

We considered evidence in 4.4.3.1 above that SVLR was introduced historically only into Scots, and I shall show below that it is still restricted to Scots and SSE today. Agutter ascribes all the vowel length variation in her results to a single process; if this process is SVLR, then it must apply before all voiced consonants, and in RP. I believe that a more enlightening account of Agutter's data can be given if we assume that two overlapping processes are at work: SVLR in Scots and SSE, and a pan-dialectal low-level phonetic lengthening rule operating before all voiced consonants.

4.5.2.2   Low-Level Lengthening

There seems to be a consensus of opinion among phoneticians that vowels lengthen progressively according to the hierarchy of following consonants shown in (4.28), with even greater duration pre-pausally (House and Fairbanks 1953, Peterson and Lehiste 1960, House 1961, Delattre 1962, Chen 1970).

(4.28)	t	s	d,n,l	z,r
	voiceless stops	voiceless fricatives	voiced stops, nasals, /l/	/r/, voiced fricatives

increasing vowel duration →

This 'voicing effect' process certainly seems to apply in most varieties of English; it may not be characteristic of Northern English dialects (Roger Lass, personal communication), although again experimental evidence is lacking here. Peterson and Lehiste (1960) give measurements for American English which show that, while preceding consonants appear to have a negligible effect on the duration of following vowels, average vowel durations can more than double between the shortest context ([-p]) and the longest ([-z] for short vowels, [-ʒ] for long). Wiik (1965) gives similar results for RP. The most salient effect seems to be that of voicing: the vowel durations of Peterson and Lehiste's informants before voiced as opposed to voiceless consonants, in otherwise identical environments, formed a ratio of 3:2.

There are likely to be universal phonetic factors underlying the variable lengthening effect of following consonants (Zimmerman and Sapon 1958), perhaps reflecting the operation of a type of compensatory lengthening: if roughly the same time is allotted to each VC sequence in an utterance, and voiceless consonants are longer than voiced, vowels before voiced consonants may lengthen to maintain a quasi-constant duration for the VC sequence. Whatever the physiological or articulatory motivation for this lengthening process, evidence from Gandour, Weinberg and Rutkowski (1980) indicates that it operates as a language-specific phonological rule of English. Gandour *et al.* argue that, if the voicing effect is purely physiological and due to laryngeal adjustment of some kind, it would not be expected in oesophageal speech. They tested three normal adult males and three laryngectomised patients, all in their fifties. All had hearing in the normal range for their age-group, and none had speech impediments. The laryngectomees were recommended by speech pathologists as having fluent, highly intelligible oesophageal speech. Gandour *et al.* found that the duration of vowels before voiced consonants was significantly longer than before voiceless consonants for both groups, at the level of $p < 0.01$. There was no significant difference across speaker groups for duration before voiceless consonants, but vowels were significantly longer in voiced contexts for the oesophageal as opposed to the normal speakers. This extra length might be attributed to the slower average speaking speed for the laryngectomised patients, at 2.01 as opposed to 2.97 syllables per second; but if this were the only determining factor, we would expect the relative length difference to carry over to voiceless contexts. It would therefore appear that oesophageal speakers are signalling the voicing effect lengthening, and perhaps even exaggerating it, indicating that 'natural phonetic tendencies have apparently been expanded into a phonological rule of the grammar' (Gandour, Weinberg and Rutkowski 1980: 150). I shall call this lengthening process, which is dependent on the voicing effect, Low-Level Lengthening (LLL), and will argue below that it applies postlexically, while SVLR is a lexical phonological rule in Scots and SSE.

4.5.2.3   Evidence for the interaction of SVLR and LLL

If two interacting processes are indeed operating in Scots/SSE, but only one in non-Scots dialects of English, one would expect a number of predictions to be borne out by instrumental measurements such as those from Agutter's study.

(1) The same degree of lengthening should be apparent in RP and Scots/SSE for all vowels in environments which are long for LLL but short for SVLR, that is before voiced stops, nasals and /l/.

(2) A rather greater increase in length should be found for all RP vowels before voiced fricatives and /r/ (and pre-pausally), in accordance with the general scale of lengthening contexts in (4.28), and the degree of lengthening in these environments should be comparable for those Scots vowels which are exceptions to SVLR.

(3) For those Scots/SSE vowels which are subject to SVLR, in SVLR long contexts, an extra increase in duration due to the operation of both SVLR and LLL would be expected.

In fact, Agutter's data can be shown to be consistent with these predictions, and thus with the hypothesis that two distinct rules are operating in Scots/SSE. In my reanalysis of these data, I have used only simple numerical analyses, which are robust and give a general indication of trends in the results; since Agutter's data lack balance and contain a number of gaps, I do not believe they merit complex statistical treatment.

In my reanalysis, I grouped Agutter's contexts into three rather than her two groups, labelled short, long and SVLR environments in (4.29).

(4.29)   Short   = following /f s t p/
           Long   = following /b d n/
           SVLR   = following /v ð z r]d]/

The vowels /ai/ and /i/ were grouped together, as both are generally agreed to be subject to SVLR, and /ɔ/ and /ɪ/ were combined, since both are generally classed as exceptions to SVLR. /au/ was kept separate, to ascertain which pattern it might be following. Grouping vowels is advantageous in partially compensating for the small sample size by spreading and de-emphasising the effects of individual variation.

The values in (4.30) represent the mean durations in centiseconds for the three groups of vowels in each set of contexts and for each accent group, calculated from Agutter's measurements per vowel per speaker per context (Agutter 1988a: table 2). Where gaps occurred in Agutter's data due to mispronunciations or non-existence of lexical items, I excluded the context(s) with incomplete data for the subset of vowels concerned and for both accent groups. Standard errors were also calculated for each mean value, and are bracketed in (4.30).

(4.30)		*short*	*long*	*SVLR*
	/aɪ i/	12.9 (0.725)	18.3 (1.43)	21.6 (1.9)
RP	/aʊ/	16.5 (1.5)	22.0 (2.4)	25.3 (1.1)
	/ɔ ɪ/	13.1 (0.97)	15.5 (1.6)	17.7 (1.45)
	/ai i/	11.8 (0.65)	16.6 (1.55)	23.0 (0.79)
SSE	/au/	14.9 (0.86)	19.5 (2.12)	21.2 (1.06)
	/ɔ ɪ/	10.4 (1.01)	14.2 (1.35)	16.6 (1.13)

The values in (4.30) are graphed in (4.31), with error bars delimiting 95 per cent confidence intervals: these indicate that there is a probability of 95 per cent that the true population mean lies within this range.

In (4.31), RP vowels are universally longer than those of SSE speakers, except for the SVLR vowels /ai i/ in SVLR contexts, where this relationship is reversed. This trend is confirmed by a second set of calculations, again based on Agutter's data. Although, for reasons given above, I did not weight these results, the figures in (4.32) do represent a certain amount of standardisation. Here, the mean duration of each vowel group in short contexts is taken as the base, or 100 per cent, since no environmentally conditioned lengthening is assumed to be operating here. Vowel duration in long and SVLR environments is then expressed as a proportion of length in the short contexts. This assumption of a common base enables a comparison of like with like.

Although (4.30) and (4.31) make it clear that /au/ is behaving like /ɔ ɪ/ rather than /ai i/ in SSE, I have not combined the values for /au/ with those for /ɔ ɪ/, since these three vowels all exhibit gaps in the data in different contexts, and my policy on such gaps would involve unacceptably reducing the number of data points for a combined class.

(4.31)

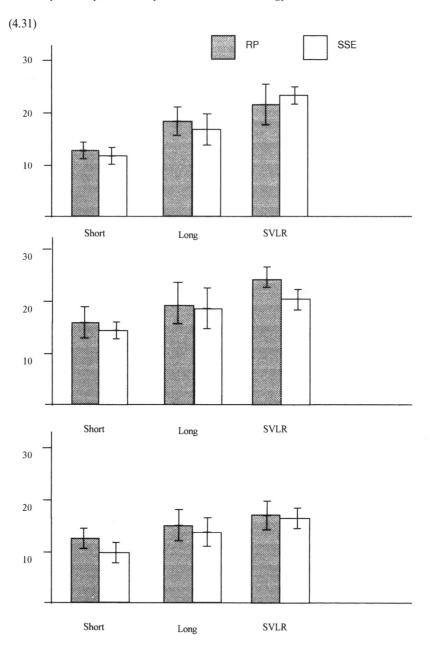

(4.32)		*Short* (%)	*Long* (%)	*SVLR* (%)
	/aɪ i/	100	141.9	168.9
RP	/aʊ/	100	133.3	153.3
	/ɔ ɪ/	100	118.3	134.8
	/ai i/	100	141.7	196.6
SSE	/au/	100	131.1	142.9
	/ɔ ɪ/	100	136.5	159.6

It is clear from the percentage figures in (4.32), and the histogram derived from these in (4.33), that all vowels in RP and all SSE vowels apart from /ai i/ in SVLR environments follow an equivalent pattern of lengthening, with 30–40% extra duration in long environments and a further 10–25% in the universally longer SVLR environments (the extreme contexts from the LLL schema). However, for only those vowels which are traditionally classed as subject to SVLR, and in SVLR long environments, a far greater degree of lengthening can be observed in SSE. /ai i/ lengthen by around 40% over short contexts in long environments in RP and SSE. If one process is responsible for all durational variation shown in (4.32), SSE /ai i/ should then show approximately 50–65% extra duration in SVLR contexts over short ones. However, the actual increase for /ai i/ is 96.6%, 27.7% greater than the percentage increase for the equivalent set of RP vowels.

My assertion that this extra duration is due to SVLR might be challenged in view of the fact that /ɔ ɪ/, the supposed exceptions to SVLR, lengthen by 59.6% in SVLR over short contexts in SSE, but by only 34.8% in RP, with a similar extra increase for SSE of 24.8%. However, as the histogram in (4.33) makes clear, this discrepancy is due to the failure of RP /ɔ ɪ/ to lengthen by the expected amount in long contexts, while SSE /ɔ ɪ/ do follow the general pattern here. In both cases the difference between long and SVLR contexts is approximately 20%. Thus, the apparent extra lengthening for SSE /ɔ ɪ/ is actually due to differences in the behaviour of the relevant vowels in long rather than in SVLR environments, and is probably an artefact of the experiment caused by the small number of informants in the RP class.

Around 25–30% of the durational change for /ai i/ alone, in SSE and in SVLR long environments, cannot be accounted for given Agutter's contention that one rule can explain all the attested length variation in both RP and SSE. On the other hand, these results are of exactly the type predicted if two processes, operating in partially overlapping environments, are involved; LLL, common to both accents, produces the shared

(4.33)

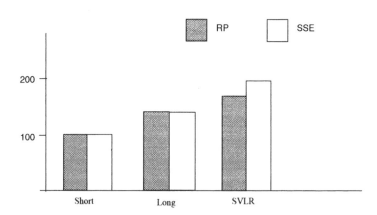

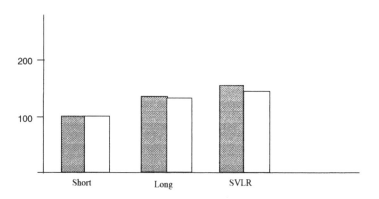

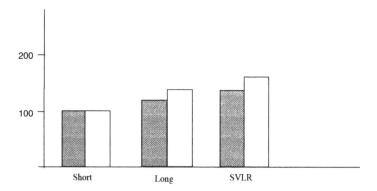

lengthening seen in (4.30)–(4.33), while SVLR accounts for the peculiarly Scottish additional lengthening which affects /ai i/ (and a variable set of other vowels not tested by Agutter) in the traditional SVLR environments.

4.5.2.4   The environment for SVLR

If LLL and SVLR do co-exist in SSE and Scots dialects, they must be individually characterised. In fact, each has a distinct input and environment: LLL applies to all vowels before all voiced consonants and word-finally (or, perhaps more accurately, pre-pausally), while SVLR is much less general, affecting only a subset of the vowel system, before voiced fricatives, /r/ and], the bracket used in Lexical Phonology to replace traditional word and morpheme boundary. We established and formulated the input conditions for SVLR in 4.5.1, and must now attempt to characterise the environment more satisfactorily. To do so, we must address the question of why vowel lengthening should occur preferentially in these particular SVLR contexts.

In universal terms, the relevant factors determining length seem to be voicing, and the different rates of transition between adjacent vowel and consonant closures: 'with stop consonants, the closure transition from a preceding vowel is shorter, since the achievement of a stricture of complete closure does not require the same degree of muscular control as that required for a fricative' (Harris 1985: 121). Harris therefore proposes a consonant scale from voiceless non-continuants at the extreme left, which do not lengthen vowels, to voiced continuants, which most affect the duration of preceding vowels, at the extreme right.

Ewen's (1977) Dependency Phonology formulation of the synchronic SVLR, and Vaiana Taylor's (1974) statement of the historical rule both rely on similar strength or sonority hierarchies. However, Harris (1985: 91) points out a number of problems with this interpretation of SVLR lengthening as 'preferential strengthening'. Most importantly, Vaiana Taylor's sonorance scale does not differentiate /l/ from /r/, and excludes nasals (which, according to similar sonority hierarchies proposed by Vennemann and Hooper, for instance, should be intermediate between voiced fricatives and liquids). On Ewen's syllabicity hierarchy, the elements involved in SVLR (i.e. vowels, liquid /r/ and voiced fricatives) similarly form a discontinuous sequence. The prediction of a typical sonority scale of the sort in (4.34) is therefore that lengthening should affect vowels in the context of nasals and liquids before it affects them in the environment of voiced fricatives, and this is certainly not the case for SVLR.

(4.34)   t s d z n l j i ii

———————————————————→

             sonority

However, Harris's voicing and continuance scale does seem to permit a positioning of nasals and /l/ which accounts for their status as long contexts for LLL but as short contexts for SVLR. Harris (1985: 122) classifies the nasals with the voiced stops on the grounds that 'the oral gesture required for nasal stops is the same as that required for oral stops, i.e. an abrupt, ballistic movement appropriate for a stricture of complete closure. This manner of articulation ... favours a shorter duration of preceding vowels. Hence nasals are Aitken's Law "short" environments.'

Harris separates the liquids by analysing /l/ as [−continuant] and /r/ as [+ continuant], citing cross-linguistic evidence that /l/ typically patterns with non-continuant segments. Although Chomsky and Halle (1968) initially classify all liquids as continuants, they recognise this as problematic. As Harris (1985: 123) points out, the difficulty disappears if the articulation of non-continuants is taken to involve a blockage of the airflow along the sagittal plane of the oral tract. This redefinition is now fairly standard, giving a combined voicing and continuancy scale as shown in (4.28) above, repeated as (4.35).

(4.35)   t   s   d,n,l   z,r
          voiceless   voiceless   voiced stops,   /r/, voiced
          stops   fricatives   nasals, /l/   fricatives

———→

                increasing vowel duration

The environments for SVLR and LLL are readily statable in relation to this scale. In RP and GenAm, the one relevant lengthening rule applies progressively before all voiced consonants, both continuants and non-continuants; that is, everywhere to the right of the vertical line in (4.36), and with even greater length pre-pausally, although the scale has been restricted at present to consonantal environments.

(4.36)   RP, General American: Low-Level Lengthening

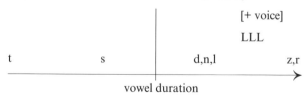

In Scots, this rule also applies, in the same environments, but SVLR also operates before voiced continuants, thus on the right of the right-most vertical line in (4.37).

(4.37)   Scots/SSE: LLL and SVLR

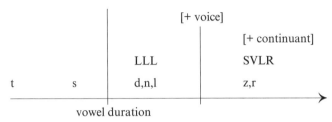

It is interesting to note (Nigel Vincent, personal communication) that a similar generalisation of allophonic vowel lengthening, but in the opposite direction, is taking place in Modern French, where older speakers have long vowels before the voiced continuants /v z ʒ ʁ /, giving long-short alternations in pairs like *vif* (m.) ~ *vive* (f.) 'lively', but younger speakers also have long vowels before voiced stops, as in *vague* 'wave', *robe* 'dress'.

We can now formulate the SVLR environment in feature terms as in (4.38).

(4.38)   SVLR input and environment

$$\begin{matrix} \sigma_s \\ | \\ X \\ | \\ V \end{matrix} \longrightarrow \begin{matrix} X \quad X \\ \diagdown\diagup \\ V \end{matrix} \Big/ \underline{\quad\quad} \left\{ \begin{bmatrix} + \text{ voice} \\ + \text{ continuant} \\ ] \end{bmatrix} \right\}$$

[+ tense]

4.5.2.5   The ordering of SVLR and LLL in a Lexical Phonology

Various criteria for distinguishing lexical from postlexical rule applications are suggested by, for instance, Kiparsky (1982) and Mohanan (1982, 1986); a subset is given in (4.39).

(4.39)

Lexical	*Postlexical*
Speakers aware of operation	Speakers unaware
Binary output	Scalar
Sensitive to morphology	Purely phonetically conditioned

Although, as we saw in chapter 2, there is reason to believe that the divide between lexical and postlexical rule applications is more of a cline than a rigid and unbridgeable division, there is some support for these criteria. For instance, although some postlexical rule applications, such as glottalling in English, are markers or even stereotypes, most are automatic phonetic processes, like aspiration of voiceless stops in English, and native speakers fail to observe their effects. It seems that LLL meets this criterion; according to Delattre (1962: 1142) 'Some speakers will make a distinctive difference of length between *bomb* and *balm*, but they will make a larger difference of length – though non-distinctive – between *leap* and *leave*. And the naive subject will easily be made conscious of the first difference of length but not the second.'

However, Scots/SSE speakers do seem to be generally aware of the differences produced by SVLR (or can easily be made aware of them). SVLR thus appears to control a binary, categorisable distinction of length; LLL, on the other hand, increases the duration of long and short vowels by a variable amount, depending on the nature of the following consonant: its output is therefore essentially non-binary.

Mohanan's major criterion for distinguishing between lexical and postlexical rules involves sensitivity to the morphology: 'A rule application requiring morphological information must take place in the lexicon' (1986: 9). LLL might initially seem to be lexical by this criterion, since sensitivity to morphological information would include sensitivity to the presence of boundaries, and vowels are lengthened word-finally. However, it seems that LLL affects vowels utterance-finally, or pre-pausally, rather than word-finally; if pauses are inserted after syntactic concatenation (Mohanan 1982), any rule referring to the position of pauses is necessarily postlexical. SVLR, on the other hand, is clearly sensitive to morphological information, and indeed a boundary is included in its structural description. SVLR lengthens vowels word-finally, but also before regular inflections, even when the consonant following the boundary is not itself a lengthening context; the vowel is therefore lengthened in *sees* [si:z] and *keyed* [ki:d], and in *brewed* and *tied* but not *brood* and *tide*.

LLL can therefore be classified as clearly postlexical, and SVLR as tenuously lexical. SVLR operates when the affected vowel is stem-final and in a Class II derived or regularly inflected form, or in the first stem of a compound, but not in morphologically underived forms with similar phonological contexts; relevant data (from Harris 1989) are shown in

(4.40). In chapter 2, I argued that Class II derivation, regular inflection and compounding all take place on Level 2; so must SVLR.

(4.40)

[i]	[i:]	[u]	[u:]
feed	key]ed	brood	brew]ed
Healey	free]ly	Souness	blue]ness
feline	bee]line	stupid	stew]pot

[o]	[o:]	[ʌi]	[a:i]
road	row]ed	tide	tie]d
bonus	slow]ness	Reilly	dry]ly
Snowdon	snow]drop	typ]ing	tie]pin

Carr (1992) presents three types of evidence which may indicate that SVLR also applies on Level 1. First, in Scots and SSE the vowel in ablaut past tense forms like *rode, strode* (as opposed to *road*) is long: Carr argues that Level 1 ablaut rules, in the style of Halle and Mohanan (1985) provide a derived environment for lengthening in these cases. Secondly, Noun Plural Fricative Voicing is said to feed SVLR on Level 1, in *life ~ lives, leaf ~ leaves* and *hoof ~ hooves*. Finally, Carr cites the cases in (4.41), from Allan (1985).

(4.41)

[straːiv]	'strive' (V)	[strʌif]	'strife'
[juːz]	'use' (V)	[jus]	'use' (N)
[ədvaːiz]	'advise'	[ədvʌis]	'advice'
[ëkskjuːz]	'excuse' (V)	[ëkskjus]	'excuse' (N)

The ablaut and Noun Plural Fricative Voicing examples are variable, and a pattern of length attributable to SVLR is only observable for some speakers; this, however, is what one might expect of Level 1 rules, which seem to control alternations mid-way between the fully productive and the fully lexicalised.

Carr (1992) argues that, although SVLR applies at Level 1 in ablaut past tenses and Noun Plural Fricative Voicing cases; in general lengthening takes place precyclically on Level 2, before affixation. Thus, in *row, rowed*, SVLR applies at Level 2 in open syllables: Carr (1992) prefers this context to the following boundary] assumed above since his version will include cases like *spider, pylon*, where McMahon (1991) has to assume reanalysis with a 'false' morpheme boundary for those speakers with lengthened vowels.

However, very little of Carr's evidence allows clear conclusions to be drawn on the level ordering of SVLR. First, I have argued above that ablaut past tenses in Modern English should not be derived by rule, even on Level 1; instead, all those outside the *keep ~ kept* class should be treated as having two lexical entries. In that case, forms like *rode, strode* do not constitute Level 1 derived environments for SVLR, and must be stored with a long vowel underlyingly. In historical terms, their long vowel is the result of analogy with regular past tense forms like *rowed, snowed*, which are eligible for SVLR on Level 2. I shall argue in the next section that this operation of analogy was partly responsible for the extension of SVLR from Level 2 to Level 1; and indeed, this account predicts that for some time, when ablaut was still a semi-productive process, it would have fed SVLR in these forms on Level 1. Now, however, we have fossilised and stored alternations, and part of that storage involves the vowel length historically attributable to SVLR. Carr (1992: 104–5) claims that invoking analogy in this way is non-explanatory, and tantamount to accepting that SVLR does apply in these forms. I disagree: it is tantamount to accepting that SVLR *did* apply in these forms, when its conditions were met by the application of a preceding process on Level 1. The demise of that process for Modern English speakers means that although the effects of historical SVLR are still discernible in cases like *rode*, they are now part of a learned alternation. Anderson (1993: 425) also points out that ablaut *per se* cannot be responsible for feeding SVLR in these cases, as Carr claims, since lengthening takes place only before the past tense marker -*d* (and not in *wrote*, therefore). Since SVLR in regular past tenses always involves a vowel-final stem, which in the normal course of events will attract a following past marker -*d*, this supports my proposal of analogy between *rowed* and *rode*, rather than a (semi-) productive connection with ablaut.

Secondly, and perhaps surprisingly, Carr does not use Allan's (1985) evidence in (4.41) above to support his proposal of Level 1 SVLR. Allan argues that the *advise* ~ *advice* cases represent Verb to Noun zero-derivation, which according to Kiparsky (1982) is a Level 1 process. However, if this is so, Carr's precyclic SVLR would counterfactually lengthen both forms. Carr is therefore forced to analyse these as denominal zero derivations, which Kiparsky (1982) assigns to Level 2; but his only grounds for so doing are that *half* ~ *halve* and *mouth* ~ *mouthe* 'look more plausibly like cases of N → V zero derivation', and that this can automatically be extended to the *advise* ~ *advice* alternations. Even so, Carr must then allow SVLR to apply on Level 2 in open syllables, and on Levels 1 and 2 before voiced continuants, the only apparent advantage being the lack of reference to]. But again, there are two objections. Carr's assumption of open-syllable SVLR does not seem well motivated: there are speakers who lengthen the vowel in *pylon*, *spider*, but equally there are others who do not, and yet another group who lengthen one but not the other. The evidence in 4.4.3.2 above from Milroy (1995) on SVLR in Newcastle and Donegan (1993) on Canadian Raising also suggest that exceptionally long and short diphthongs occur fairly frequently, and that perhaps a split of /ʌi/ from /ai/ is in progress. Furthermore, the use of] in phonological rules reflects the interaction of morphology and phonology which is central to LP: of course it is important to allow for purely phonological conditioning, but it is equally vital to recognise cases where morphological factors are paramount, and allow the phonology to refer to these. I shall argue in 4.6 that the historical reanalysis of SVLR from LLL necessarily involves both analogy and reference to], and that the incipient contrast of /ʌi/ and /ai/ is also central to the continued development of SVLR. I therefore maintain the formulation of SVLR suggested in (4.38): SVLR will apply on Levels 1 and 2; but in the former case, will be restricted by the Derived Environment Condition.

4.6 From sound change to phonological rule

4.6.1 Standard Generative Phonology and Lexical Phonology

We have now built up a picture of the present-day SVLR, detailing its input, environment and ordering, and justifying its separation from postlexical LLL. However appropriate this separate characterisation may be, it misses the intuition that the two rules are in some sense related, as evidenced by the inclusion of SVLR inputs and environments in the set of operational contexts for LLL. I shall argue that this relationship can be accounted for in diachronic terms, and that SVLR has been 'derived' historically from LLL, and become a lexical rule fairly recently.

This development of SVLR will be shown to exemplify a probably rather common 'life cycle' of sound changes, which may begin as low-level rules, then move into the lexicon, and eventually become opaque and promote restructuring at the underlying level, producing dialect and ultimately language variation. We shall see that LP reveals connections of synchrony and diachrony which were impossible to capture in SGP.

To recap, the Standard Generative approach to historical linguistics assumed that each sound change, once implemented, is incorporated directly into the adult speaker's phonological rule system as the final rule, moving gradually up into the grammar as subsequent changes are introduced (King 1969). Restructuring of the underlying representations during acquisition by later generations of speakers is theoretically permitted, but infrequently invoked, so that the historical phonology of a language will be almost directly mirrored in the order of its synchronic phonological rules. The only extractable generalisations are that the 'highest' rules will correspond to the oldest changes, and that a sound change and the phonological rule into which it is converted will be identical or markedly similar – although we have already encountered several rules, including the Vowel Shift Rules and SVLR itself, which differ significantly in their optimal synchronic statement from their historical source.

The SGP appoach casts no light whatsoever on the implementation of sound change in a speech community, on which there are two, apparently diametrically opposed, views. The Neogrammarian position holds that sound change is phonetically gradual but lexically abrupt, while the lexical diffusionists (Wang 1969, 1977; Chen and Wang 1975) argue that many sound changes are, conversely, phonetically abrupt and lexically gradual. Labov (1981) aims to resolve this controversy by considering evidence from language change in progress; but the data include cases of Neogrammarian *and* diffusing changes, leading to an apparent *impasse* where we are 'faced with the massive opposition of two bodies of evidence: both are right, but both cannot be right' (Labov 1981: 269). Labov's solution is to recognise two distinct types of sound change, differentiated by the characteristics in (4.42).

(4.42)	*Lexical diffusion*	*'Neogrammarian' change*
Discrete	yes	no
Phonetic conditioning	rough	fine
Lexical exceptions	yes	no
Grammatical conditioning	yes	no
Social affect	no	yes
Predictable	no	yes
Learnable	no	yes
Categorised	yes	no
Dictionary entries	2	1
Lexical diffusion	yes	no

Labov adds that Neogrammarian changes involve modifications to low-level output rules, while lexical diffusion causes a redistribution of some abstract class into other classes. Finally, he tentatively proposes that certain features are associated with certain types of change: for vowels, low-level, Neogrammarian sound changes will manipulate features of fronting, backing, raising, rounding and so on, while the more abstract diffusing changes will involve tensing and laxing, lengthening and shortening, and monophthongisation and diphthongisation.

In SGP, Labov's two types of sound change have no clear analogues. However, Kiparsky (1988) points out that the sets of properties characteristic of diffusing and Neogrammarian changes overlap to a considerable extent with the properties of lexical and postlexical rules shown in (4.43).

(4.43)	*Lexical*	*Postlexical*
	Apply within words	Also apply between words
	Have lexical exceptions	Apply across the board
	May be cyclic	Non-cyclic
	Binary/discrete output	Gradient/scalar
	Observable/categorisable	Speakers unaware
	Sensitive to morphology	Phonetically conditioned
	Structure Preserving	May introduce novel segments or features

Some of the criteria in the relevant columns of (4.42) and (4.43) match exactly: for instance, both lexical rules and diffusing changes have discrete, categorisable effects observable by speakers, may have lexical exceptions, and are sensitive to morphological information. Kiparsky argues that a number of less obviously connected properties are also related: for instance, a diffusing change may extend beyond its original conditioning context, producing lexical selectivity and therefore lexical exceptions; an incomplete diffusing change will also retain a residue of lexical exceptions. Kiparsky also relates the necessity for two dictionary entries, which Labov cites as a property of diffusing changes, to Structure Preservation, which states that no lexical rule may introduce or operate on a feature which is not underlyingly distinctive.

However, a complete identification of diffusing and Neogrammarian changes with lexical and postlexical rules respectively may be too inflexible, as not all lexical rules necessarily start out as diffusing changes; they may begin as low-level, automatic and phonetically motivated Neogrammarian changes, but subsequently percolate into the more abstract regions of the grammar, becoming synchronically lexical rules. Harris (1989) discusses one such example, the rule of æ-Tensing.

æ-Tensing applies in a number of varieties of Modern English, including the New York City, Philadelphia and Belfast dialects, producing tense [Æ] (which is typically realised as long, diphthongised and relatively centralised) before a variable class of tautosyllabic consonants.

In Philadelphia, tensing occurs only before anterior nasals and anterior voiceless fricatives; in New York, it applies additionally before voiced stops; and in Belfast, tense [Æ] also surfaces before /l/ and voiced fricatives. The examples in (4.44) would hold for all three dialects.

(4.44)   Lax: tap, bath, match, manner, ladder, wagon ...
         Tense: pass, path, laugh, man, manning, man hours ...

Harris (1989: 48) proposes that æ-Tensing was historically an automatic, phonetically motivated change, operating in the hierarchy of environments in (4.45).

(4.45)   voiceless   voiced oral   nasals   voiceless
         stops   non-continuants   fricatives
         _____→
         increasing likelihood of tensing

However, in the varieties mentioned above, æ-Tensing is now a lexical rule: it may be lexically selective, as in Philadelphia, where *mad, bad, glad* have tensed [Æ] although /d/ is not generally a tensing context in this dialect; and Labov (1981) reports that lax [æ] and tense [Æ] are subject to categorial discrimination by New York and Philadelphia speakers. æ-Tensing is also sensitive to morphological information, since it applies before heterosyllabic consonants followed by], as in *manning*.

The only factor which might argue against the characterisation of æ-Tensing as lexical is its contravention of Structure Preservation, since Harris follows Halle and Mohanan (1985) in assuming that [± tense] is not part of the underlying feature inventory for English. However, Harris tentatively suggests that newly lexicalised rules may violate Structure Preservation temporarily, with the reassertion of Structure Preservation perhaps determining the direction of future change, although he produces no clear evidence of this determinative role of Structure Preservation.

Harris's discussion of æ-Tensing suggests that sound changes may be incorporated into the synchronic grammar by passing through a number of stages. Changes may be phonologised as postlexical rules, but may subsequently acquire properties from the lexical syndrome, notably sensitivity to morphological structure, and become lexical phonological rules; these may initially violate Structure Preservation, but might be predicted to attain conformity with this principle over time. Newly lexical rules may also begin to diffuse, as is the case with æ-Tensing in Philadelphia, where the tense reflex is now appearing before /d/ in certain lexical items. Ultimately, a lexical rule may cease to be transparent and productive: for instance, the number of lexical exceptions may increase to a point where the rule is no longer readily learnable. The rule itself will then be lost, but its effects will be incorporated into the underlying representations, as is the case for æ-Tensing in RP. Here, the historical short /æ/ class has split, with the tense reflex merging with /ɑ/ from other sources in *path* and *laugh*.

If these suggestions are substantiable, LP gains considerably in a number of domains. Labov's two types of sound change can be matched with credible synchronic counterparts, and his notion of more and less abstract changes linked with the lexical–postlexical division (although, as Harris notes, æ-Tensing shows that Labov's correlation of particular features with only one type of change or rule cannot be maintained). The lexicalisation of rules and their eventual loss also provides a mechanism for altering underlying representations and for the introduction of surface and underlying variation between dialects, as we shall see in chapter 5. In the next section, I shall show that SVLR provides further evidence for these proposals, and constitutes an arguably even clearer illustration of the life-cycle suggested above, albeit with some interesting differences from æ-Tensing.

4.6.2 The life-cycle of the Scottish Vowel Length Rule

The historical SVLR, as characterised in Lass (1974) and Pullum (1974) and summarised in 4.4.3.2 above, was a bipartite lengthening and shortening change, which was probably introduced in the sixteenth century. A slightly modified version of Lass's formulation is given in (4.46). Recall that in some varieties, low or non-high vowels were exempt from a., and are therefore consistently long synchronically.

(4.46) a. All long vowels shortened everywhere except before /r v z ð ʒ/ or].
   b. Short vowels with tense sources (i.e. *not* /ɪ ʌ ɛ/) lengthened in the same contexts.

Lass's SVLR clearly makes vowel length predictable. Pullum (1974) therefore argues that the implementation of the historical SVLR would inevitably have led to rule inversion (Vennemann 1972), restructuring the underlying Scots vowel system. In other words, speakers would no longer learn a vowel system with an underlying length contrast, plus a complex neutralising rule; instead, they would abduce that all vowels are underlyingly short, and lengthen a subset before /r/, voiced fricatives and boundaries. In a theory incorporating underspecification, one might alternatively propose (see Anderson 1993) that most or all Scots vowels are unspecified for length, with SVLR operating in a blank-filling capacity. Carr (1992) rejects this approach, partly on the grounds that the application of underspecification theory to metrical properties like length is unclear. Carr also points out, as I argued in chapter 1, that radical underspecification makes the operation of the central constraints of LP almost impossible to ascertain. I shall show in chapter 5 that underspecification also brings other disadvantages; for the moment, I assume that the majority of Scots and SSE vowels became underlyingly short following the historical SVLR.

However plausible this account may be, it treats SVLR very much as an isolated phenomenon. I assume instead that LLL and SVLR constitute two stages in the life cycle of sound changes illustrated above with æ-Tensing. We can see the 'voicing effect' lengthening as an English-specific phonologisation of a universal tendency, as discussed in 4.5.2.2. This automatic phonetic process has been phonologised in most varieties of Modern English as the postlexical rule of Low-Level Lengthening, which affects all vowels before voiced consonants. However, in Scots dialects and SSE, a further stage of phonologisation has taken place: the extreme lengthening environments of the LLL schema were phonologised in Scots/SSE as a separate rule, which has acquired certain properties characteristic of lexical rule applications, and hence been relocated in the lexical phonology. The overlapping contexts of LLL, which operates before voiced consonants and pauses, and SVLR, which applies in these varieties only before voiced continuants and boundaries, are shown in (4.47).

(4.47)   Scots/SSE: LLL and SVLR

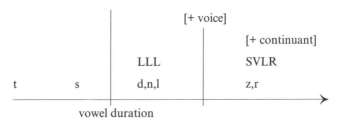

This separation of the two processes, and the eventual lexicalisation of SVLR, seems likely to have begun with a modified version of Lass's (1974) historical SVLR, whereby tense vowels underwent some additional lengthening in Middle Scots before voiced continuants and pre-pausally. Since these are the contexts which are in any case most conducive to vowel lengthening, and since one general characteristic of tense vowels is their greater length relative to lax vowels, this extra increase in duration might have been sufficient to cross the perceptual threshold for durational differences, making this lengthening labellable, as previous lengthening controlled by LLL had not been (and arguably, still is not). If speakers could auditorily distinguish tense vowels in these extreme lengthening contexts from all other vowels, we might propose a perceptual recategorisation, whereby just these vowels in these SVLR long contexts were reinterpreted as long, and all others as short. This account is in line with an analysis of phonologisation proposed by Harris (1986), who observes that phonetic variation may have either intrinsic or extrinsic sources. Intrinsic factors include universal phonetic constraints, while extrinsic factors are language-specific and might include control by a phonological rule. The intrinsic factors governing the voicing effect lengthening summed up in LLL are principally voicing, and the rate of closure transition. According to Harris (1986), phonologisation involves the systematisation of intrinsic differences; specifically, variation resulting from intrinsic causes is reinterpreted as having some external source. In the case of SVLR, lengthening in the extreme environments of the voicing effect schema is attributed to a Scots/SSE-specific lengthening rule. Harris further suggests that such reinterpretation may be due to system-specific exaggeration of a variant 'to the extent that it can only be subsequently interpreted in extrinsic terms' (1986: 123). This suggestion is relevant to SVLR in two ways. First, the separation of SVLR from the intrinsically determined voicing effect lengthening may be due to this system-specific exaggeration. Secondly, the putative exaggeration might be understood to involve, not only additional lengthening in long contexts, but also an opposing reaction of shortening in other environments – hence the tendency of Scots vowels to be shorter in SVLR short contexts than comparable vowels in RP (Agutter 1988a, b). Harris further assumes that previously intrinsic contrasts, once extrinsically determined, may percolate deeper into linguistic structure, as we can see from the subsequent history of SVLR.

By affecting only tense vowels with tense sources, the historical SVLR also disrupted the previously perfect correlation of tenseness with length. After the introduction of SVLR, tense vowels could no longer be defined as those vowels which are always long, but rather as those which are *sometimes* long; that is, those vowels with audibly long realisations in some contexts. From this point, it is a very small step to assume that [+ tense] became the crucial feature specification defining the input to the synchronic SVLR, which would then have separated from LLL. Scots speakers would no longer operate with an underlying vowel system contrasting long and short vowels; instead, length would be predictable on the basis of the pre-existing feature [± tense] and the new SVLR. However, LLL was also retained, continuing to produce minor and arguably inaudible alterations in the length of all vowels.

The next question is how the nascent SVLR came to apply lexically; and the most feasible course involves analogy. We can assume that the final vowel in infinitival forms like *die, row* would have lengthened by LLL and the new SVLR. However, there is no lengthening context for SVLR in the past tense forms *died, rowed* or present *dies, rows* which would surface with a short vowel in post-SVLR Scots. A tendency towards restoring iconicity might have caused the lengthening to be generalised into this originally inappropriate environment. This innovation would have led to the reformulation of the rule to include a bracket or boundary, making SVLR sensitive to morphological information and therefore lexical. This analogical extension would then also extend to ostensibly similar past tense forms like *rode, strode*, where SVLR would have applied productively until the ablaut past tenses became fossilised.

Once a rule has acquired some characteristic of lexical application in this way, and consequently been propelled into the lexicon, we might expect it to begin to exhibit further properties of lexical rules. This is the case for SVLR; for instance, lexical rules generally produce results which are observable or categorisable by native speakers, and many Scots/SSE speakers can in fact distinguish long vowels in SVLR contexts from short ones elsewhere. This observability does not entail that the length contrast must be present at the underlying level, since it is generally assumed within LP that speaker judgements on distinctness of sounds are based on the lexical rather than the underlying level (Mohanan 1986): vowel length in Scots/SSE will then be a 'derived contrast' (Harris 1989), which is produced during the lexical derivation.

This assumption that vowel length is no longer underlyingly distinctive in Scots/SSE is important from the point of view of Structure Preservation, which permits lexical rules to operate on or introduce only underlyingly distinctive features. If SVLR neutralised the long–short contrast early in its life-cycle, it synchronically manipulates a non-contrastive feature, and therefore contravenes Structure Preservation, at least in those varieties of Scots in which long vowels do not form part of the inventory of basic prosodic templates. Adopting Borowsky's (1990) restriction of Structure Preservation to Level 1 will not help, since SVLR applies on both Level 2 and Level 1. Furthermore, Kiparsky (1988) asserts that, once rules become lexical, they are free to undergo lexical diffusion. However, I have given no indication that SVLR is undergoing or has undergone such diffusion.

In fact, there are signs of incipient lexical diffusion of SVLR, although this is at present limited to the diphthong /ai/. As we have seen, the long realisation, [aːi], is now being generalised into lexical items lacking long contexts, giving [paːilɔn] *pylon*, [spaːidər] *spider* (compare [wʌidər] *wider*), and [vaːipər] *viper* (compare [wʌipər] *wiper*). This extension of long [aːi] is still sporadic, speaker-specific and highly variable, but appears to be spreading; indeed, Aitken (1981), Abercrombie (1979) and Wells (1982: 399ff.) consider the evidence sufficient to posit a phonemic split of /ʌi/ ~ /aːi/, a point echoed by Donegan (1993) for Canadian Raising. It is possible, as Carr (1992) suggests, that SVLR has simply been extended to apply in open syllables, at least for some speakers; but why would this affect only one vowel, and why should it be so inconsistent across speakers and lexical items?

We may then propose that /ʌi/ and /aːi/ are now both part of the underlying vowel system for Scots/SSE; this /ʌi/ will merge with /ʌi/ found word-finally in Scots, in *pay, way* words. The establishment of this marginal contrast is of some theoretical importance, since it both testifies to the lexical diffusion of SVLR, and marks a tenuous re-establishment of the length contrast in Scots/SSE. In varieties without consistently long low vowels, the introduction of underlying /aːi/ will provide the only evidence of a length contrast above the lexical level (with the possible exception of a few irregular past tense forms), and will therefore go some way towards guaranteeing that SVLR obeys Structure Preservation. It remains to be seen whether SVLR will continue its diffusion through the other pairs of vowels; given that a quality difference is only apparent for the diphthong, this may be unlikely.

The account of the development of the SVLR given above can be seen to support Kiparsky's (1988) association of diffusing changes with lexical rules, and Neogrammarian changes with postlexical rules, given Harris's (1989) proviso that Neogrammarian/postlexical processes may develop diachronically into lexical rules. SVLR also, to some extent, supports the notion of a life-cycle of changes and rules, suggested by Harris's (1989: 55) view that implementation as a postlexical rule; lexicalisation; and fossilisation, loss, and integration into the underlying representations reflect 'different stages in the ageing process of sound change ... whereby individual changes ... percolate deeper and deeper into the linguistic system'.

However, there are three differences between SVLR and Harris's example of æ-Tensing. First, æ-Tensing has become lexical *in toto* in the varieties where it remains productive, whereas SVLR represents only a partial lexicalisation of LLL, which remains postlexically even in the varieties which have innovated SVLR. Secondly, Harris (1989: 54) proposes that, although a newly lexicalised rule may not be structure preserving, 'the reassertion of Structure Preservation would then be predicted to dictate the direction of any subsequent change'. The diffusion of SVLR, with the generalisation and incipient contrastivity of long [a:i], may represent a case of precisely this reassertion, since the reintroduction of an underlying length contrast will produce renewed conformity of SVLR with Structure Preservation. The principles and constraints of LP seem in some sense both synchronically and diachronically 'real', since they not only control the structure of the synchronic phonology, but are also reasserted when disrupted by ongoing change.

Finally, and perhaps more strikingly, SVLR does not seem to be following exactly the same life cycle as æ-Tensing. æ-Tensing has caused a change at the underlying level in some dialects, but only at the end of a period of increased opacity and fossilisation as a lexical rule, which is ultimately lost. However, SVLR neutralised the vowel length distinction in Scots before becoming, or while becoming, a lexical rule. We may then be dealing with two variants of the pathway from sound change to rule to underlying restructuring. One, outlined by Harris, would be characteristic of processes like æ-Tensing, which simply alter some feature value. The other would involve processes like SVLR, which neutralise some pre-existing feature contrast at the sound change stage (and may go on to cause underlying changes later too, as for the first type). This development might be characteristic only of processes which, like SVLR, are analysed in SGP as involving rule inversion. We return to this issue in chapter 6, in connection with the deletion and insertion of /r/ in non-rhotic varieties of English, which involves another case of rule inversion.

5 Dialect differentiation in Lexical Phonology: the unwelcome effects of underspecification

5.1 Introduction

The investigation of the Scottish Vowel Length Rule in the last chapter raises important issues for the modelling of sound change in Lexical Phonology, a topic to which we shall return in chapter 6. However, it also relates very directly to a synchronic question we have touched on several times already, namely the degree to which different dialects of the same language can vary. Of course, SVLR is a process specific to Scottish varieties; this kind of variation in the form, order and inventory of phonological rules is already familiar from Standard Generative Phonology. But we have departed from the SGP line in also allowing dialectal divergence in the underlying representations: for instance, various vowel oppositions (such as the RP and GenAm *Sam ~ psalm* and *pull ~ pool* pairs) are simply neutralised *in toto* in Scots and SSE; and we saw in chapter 3 that the *father* vowel should be analysed as underlyingly front in some varieties of English, and back in others.

We might regard these minor, scattered examples as still compatible with a generally panlectal approach to phonology; in 5.5.2 below, however, I shall propose a far more general and more radical underlying dialectal difference, involving the dichotomising feature(s) which establish the structure of the whole vowel system. I shall argue that in some varieties of English only [± tense] is underlyingly relevant; in others, only length; and in still others, both. This approach is clearly incompatible with a panlectal analysis; but as we shall see in 5.5.3, rejecting panlectal phonology is no great loss. Less obviously, this analysis is relevant to underspecification theory, which I ruled out, though essentially without argument, in chapter 2. In 5.5.4 below, I shall show that arguments against underspecification are accumulating in many phonological models, and that its effects are particularly serious and unwelcome in Lexical Phonology. Most notably, whereas a constrained LP will enforce an analysis of each variety in its own terms, implying quite far-reaching underlying divergence, the use of underspecification means that abstractness can be readily reintroduced, and that shared underliers can be permitted in cases where they are not warranted.

5.2   Length, tenseness and English vowel systems

Let us begin with RP and Scots/SSE. In RP, as we have already established, there are six pairs of vowels, as listed in (5.1), the members of which are distinguished partly by length (with the vowels on the left consistently longer), and partly by quality, or tenseness (with long vowels more peripheral and frequently also diphthongised).

(5.1)	/i:/	/ɪ/	/u:/	/ʊ/
	/e:/	/ɛ/	/o:/	/ʌ/
	/ɑ:/	/æ/	/ɔ:/	/ɒ/

In SSE and Scots dialects, this dual distinction of quality and quantity is not operative. The /ɑ:/ ~ /æ/, /ɔ:/ ~ /ɒ/ and /u:/ ~ /ʊ/ oppositions are entirely lacking, and members of the remaining pairs, /i/ ~ /ɪ/, /e/ ~ /ɛ/ and /o/ ~ /ʌ/, are distinguished primarily by quality, quantity being predictable by the Scottish Vowel Length Rule. If we accept that [+ tense] is the crucial specification for SVLR input vowels, it follows that Scots and SSE vowels are underlyingly, contrastively [+ tense] or [− tense]. In a full-entry theory of the lexicon, all vowels will also be short (or singly attached, in autosegmental terms); and in varieties where SVLR affects only vowels of a certain height, there will also be underlyingly long vowels in the system. Nonetheless, the crucial dichotomising feature for the Scots and SSE vowel system is tenseness.

We have already noted that RP vowels fall into two classes, long tense and short lax: the question is how these are to be analysed at the underlying level. Three approaches have been adopted in the literature: in SPE, [± tense] is the underlyingly relevant feature, and a late redundancy rule links [+ tense] with [+ long] and [− tense] with [− long]; Halle and Mohanan (1985) take the opposite point of view, with length bisecting the underlying system and tenseness introduced subsequently; and Halle (1977) proposes that both length and tenseness are specified underlyingly.

There are arguments against at least the first two analyses. If only [± tense] is underlyingly contrastive, the stress rules will have to be sensitive to tenseness rather than length, going against the tendency to make prosodic processes responsive to prosodic features. There is also the historical problem that, assuming [± tense] was introduced into the vowel system in Middle English, as I argued on the basis of Open Syllable Lengthening in the last chapter, we know of a process which might allow this feature to supplant length as underlyingly relevant in SSE, namely the SVLR, but have no equivalent in the history of RP. We might then prefer to assume underlying length only; however, Halle and Mohanan (1985) require various additional lexical tensing rules (they propose, for instance, independent but mysteriously nearly identical pairs of rules like Stem-Final Lengthening and Stem-Final Tensing, or Prevocalic Tensing and Prevocalic Lengthening), and encounter certain derivational problems unless [± tense] is introduced extremely early in the derivation by redundancy rule. In that case, it might just as well be specified underlyingly, which is Halle's (1977) position. His assumption that [± tense] and length are independently specified underlyingly largely follows from his adoption of long-tense and long-lax low vowels for American English; but even without such vowels, we might wish to consider tenseness and length as independent because they are so frequently manipulated separately across dialects and across time: see Giegerich (1992: 3.7), for instance, who argues that length distinctions in Australian English do not correlate straightforwardly with tenseness.

Our conclusion, then, is either that length alone is underlyingly distinctive in RP, or that both length and [± tense] are. This situation differs clearly from that of Scots and SSE, at least in varieties where SVLR has been fully implemented: here, only [± tense] is distinctive and length, which was contrastive historically, has been neutralised by the SVLR. Length will have only one underlying value, whereas both length and tenseness have both feature specifications available at the underlying level in RP. If each variety is analysed on its own terms, we therefore produce an underlying dialect difference.

Our next question is whether, in a Lexical Phonology, this analysis *could* be revised to derive the two dialects from the same underlying system. The usual course of action in the SGP tradition would involve reanalysing SSE, which has innovated in this case, in accordance with RP, and the crucial step would therefore be to make length underlyingly contrastive in SSE. The simplest way to achieve this is to assume that no rule inversion took place in the history of SVLR, making the synchronic process, like its antecedent sound change, a bipartite length neutralising process as in (5.2).

(5.2)   Pseudo-synchronic SVLR
a. Long vowels shorten everywhere except before /r v z ʒ ð/ or]
b. Short vowels (except /ɪ ɛ ʌ/) lengthen before /r v z ʒ ð/ and].

If we decide that [± tense] should be underlyingly distinctive in RP and SSE, subrule (5.2b) can be modified to refer to short tense vowels; if not, some other way must be found of excluding /ɪ ɛ ʌ/.

Of course, the only motivation for this analysis is the desire to derive RP and SSE from a common set of underlying features: it would not be preferred if each dialect were considered in its own right, from either a synchronic or a diachronic point of view. Furthermore, the proposal of a system with length underlyingly distinctive, but neutralised on the surface, creates obvious problems of learnability: a child acquiring SSE will be required to divide her vocabulary along synchronically opaque lines by reversing the historical SVLR in order to internalise vowels of the appropriate length in lexical items at the underlying level. For instance, the learner will hear words like [fat] *fat* and [het] *hate*, with surface short vowels, and have to decide whether these have underlyingly long vowels which shorten by SVLR or short vowels which remain short in this short context, and conversely words like [faːr] and [heːr] with surface long vowels, which might reflect underlyingly long vowels with length retained, or lengthened short vowels. The learner clearly cannot obtain the necessary information from observation. Furthermore, if SVLR operates on Level 1, then the Derived Environment Condition will not permit it to lengthen or shorten vowels in underived environments; and the vast majority of forms involved (including *fat*, *hate*, *far* and *hair*) will be underived. Even if SVLR applies on Level 1 only in environments specifically derived on that stratum, underived applications on Level 2 are generally disfavoured from a learnability point of view by the Alternation Condition.

A Lexical Phonology without underspecification therefore performs relatively realistically with respect to the analysis of dialect variation, permitting and perhaps even requiring limited differentiation at the underlying level. The distinctions established here will also extend in various ways to other varieties of English. Even within Scots there is a difference between the core, central Scots dialects where SVLR applies throughout the tense vowel system, and where only [tense] is relevant underlyingly, and those where some vowels are consistently long on the surface, and therefore at the underlying level too. Similarly, Lindsey (1990) argues for an underlying distinction between RP and GenAm, based on the treatment of loanwords. He points out that GenAm speakers typically assign to the stressed syllables of loanwords the vowels of *hod* (= *balm*), *hayed, heed, hoed* and *who'd*, corresponding to ortho-graphic <a e i o u> respectively, while RP speakers typically interpret the same orthographic representations as the *had, head, hid, hod, hood* vowels, albeit with more exceptions and a variable additional process of lengthening in open syllables. Lindsey argues that the motivation for these different strategies, 'given cross-dialectal uniformity of spelling, must be sought in differing phonological representations' (1990: 108). He proposes that, universally, languages will prefer to assign unmarked or default feature values to loans. Following SPE markedness conventions, this would predict that languages with their underlying vowel systems structured as tense versus lax will assign [+ tense] values, which is what we find in GenAm. On the other hand, since shortness is unmarked relative to length, vowel systems dichotomised according to length will have short vowels assigned to loans, as is the tendency in RP. Lindsey speculates that the inconsistencies in RP may in fact indicate that both [± tense] and length are underlyingly relevant: since both tenseness and shortness are unmarked, there is scope for a markedness clash, which might account for the more variable behaviour of RP speakers. Lindsey also provides further evidence for the more central role of length in RP: for instance, 'the difference between the duration of long-tense vowels and short-lax vowels is greater in RP than in American dialects' (1990: 113), while a comparison of the inherent vowel duration specifications for American and British speech synthesis systems reveals an increased long/short ratio for RP. Again, collapsing this underlying distinction simply to unify the system for the two varieties would lose Lindsey's explanation for the different treatment of loans.

5.3   For and against the identity hypothesis

It seems clear that the constrained model of Lexical Phonology assumed here will be unable to generate all surface differences between related dialects from a common underlying inventory and set of representations, or at least that such composite analyses will be strongly dispreferred for reasons of learnability and coherence with external evidence. In terms of the abstractness of the synchronic system proposed for individual varieties, this has obvious advantages. However, before accepting this conclusion unconditionally, we should ask what independent evidence there might be for or against panlectal phonology (see also McMahon 1992).

Variation studies were certainly not central to the early generative enterprise, where dialects of a single language were derived from the same set of underlying representations in phonology (Thomas 1967, Newton 1972, Brown 1972) or deep structures in syntax (Klima 1964); surface divergences followed from differences in the form, ordering and inventory of rules. The only controversy involved the character of the basal, underlying forms themselves, which were sometimes argued to be drawn uniquely from one dialect (Brown 1972), and sometimes to be neutral between dialects (Thomas 1967). In short, although distinct languages were permitted to differ at the underlying level, related dialects were not. Early synchronic generative linguistics thus adopted the diachronic methodology of internal and comparative reconstruction, whose practitioners aim to reduce variation to earlier invariance (Hock 1986).

Every assumption in the previous paragraph can be, and has been, challenged. First, the derivation of dialect differences from a single set of underlying forms follows from the assumption that grammars should be maximally simple and economical, and that differences in the rule system 'cost' less than differences in the underlying representations. Evaluation according to simplicity, however, is based solely on internal evidence from distribution and alternation, and often conflicts with external evidence involving language change, dialect variation, speech errors and speaker judgements, for instance. The issue of simplicity relates directly to the claim that 'long-term memory constraints prompt speakers to limit storage to idiosyncratic information and to maximize the computing of predictable information' (Harris and Lindsey 1995: 48) – a view which, as Harris and Lindsey continue, 'has never been seriously defended in the psycholinguistic literature'. Even more interestingly for present purposes, Harris and Lindsey raise this point in a critique of underspecification theory, which is similarly predicated on the alleged need for maximal simplicity at the underlying level. As we shall see in the next section, underspecification is open to many of the same objections as the identity hypothesis; we should not therefore be tempted to retain these assumptions of simplicity purely because they allow underspecification. Indeed, Goldsmith (1995b: 17) argues that underspecification is by no means the only, or indeed the most obvious solution even if simplicity is seen as a general desideratum.

The identity hypothesis also logically includes the problematic premise that synchronic dialect differences result from changes in a language which was formerly without variation. This attitude is sometimes made explicit, as in Newton's (1972: 1) description of the dialects of Modern Greek as 'the outcome of historical changes acting on an originally uniform language'. Of course, no known extant or attested language is without variation (as dialect atlases of e.g. Middle English show), and not even reconstructed languages like Proto-Indo-European are entirely homogeneous (pace Pulgram 1959, 1961); as Hock (1986: 569) observes, 'isoglosses for ... different changes intersect in such a criss-crossing fashion as to suggest a single, dialectally highly diversified proto-language'.

We might shrug this objection off as wilful misinterpretation of professional shorthand (on the principle that everybody knows we don't mean the predicted invariance really existed, even if some early generativists seem to get a bit carried away sometimes). It is less easy to evade the fact that defining related dialects as sharing the same underlying forms, but different languages as differing at the underlying level, prevents us from seeing dialect and language variation as the continuum that geographical and sociolinguistic investigation has shown it to be. Even the traditional family tree model of historical linguistics is based on the assumption that dialects may diverge across time and become distinct languages; but this pattern is obscured if related dialects cannot differ underlyingly, while related languages characteristically do. It follows also that the status of the basal forms of generative dialectology is unclear, especially if they are neutral between dialects. Brown (1972), in a study of Lumasaaba which involves the derivation of southern forms from northern ones, produces two highly significant disclaimers. First, she notes that 'it is not suggested here that the model of Common Lumasaaba phonology outlined here bears any relation to the process of language acquisition or production for any speaker of any dialect of Lumasaaba' (1972: 147). A little later, she adds that 'I do not suggest that the southern dialects derive historically from any existing northern dialects, nor that the presentation [here] provides a reasonable framework for a synchronic description of any one of the southern dialects. My intention is simply to demonstrate that the dialects can be shown to be related to each other by a small number of quite general rules' (1972: 171). The power of SGP means that this aim can easily be achieved; however, the validity of a basal level which is avowedly synchronically, diachronically and psycholinguistically inadequate or even irrelevant must surely be called into question.

Instead, LP encourages a view whereby even different speakers may have different underlying representations and rule systems, a case made convincingly by Giegerich (in press). This in turn allows potential incorporation of insights from sociolinguistics (Labov 1972, Milroy and Milroy 1985, Milroy 1992), where cumulative innovations by individual speakers are recognised as the key to understanding language variation and change. Without a way of according theoretical status to such innovations, and of modelling the shift from individual to dialect to language variation, we lose these valuable connections. Since most of the historical work in SGP preceded these sociolinguistic insights, it is perhaps not surprising that SGP lacked a coherent diachronic side. But there is no excuse now.

There seems no compelling reason to retain the identity hypothesis. Chambers and Trudgill (1980: 50), although accepting this conclusion in principle, worry that 'unless differences in lexical entries are constrained in some way, it does mean that it would in theory be possible ... to incorporate totally unrelated varieties such as English and Chinese into the same system'. Of course, if different dialects are to become different languages across time, there should be a continuum between dialect and language variation, and distantly related, though not unrelated, languages may therefore show residual similarities in their grammars. The loss of a linguistic definition of dialect may also be a minor problem, since *language* and *dialect* may more fruitfully be regarded as sociopolitical rather than purely linguistic notions. Nonetheless, one important goal for future research might be an assessment of how much variation is compatible with subsumption under a common underlying system. Although I suspect that finding a general answer to that question is a forlorn hope, the development of constrained models of phonology like the one presented here may be a step in the right direction in supplying a limit to the variation which can be included in any specific case.

Nonetheless, before concluding that underlying dialectal identity is unwarranted, we should consider inter-dialectal communication. In SGP, the identity hypothesis automatically accounted for comprehension between speakers of varieties of the same language. Adaptive accommodations of non-standard towards standard forms simply involved manipulations of low-level rules: as Harris (1985: 341) documents, non-standard speakers were assumed to invoke 'footstep-following' (the adoption of a rule from the target standard variety) or 'step-retracing' (the loss or suppression of a rule usually implemented in the non-standard dialect but not in the target). If underlying unity is essential to allow for cross-dialectal communication and adaptive change, then a Lexical Phonology which cannot incorporate common underlying forms and derive all necessary surface differences by rule must, after all, be inadequate.

However, varieties of English may differ to an extent irreconcilable with inclusion in a common underlying system; in these cases, adaptive changes cannot be analysed simply as manipulations of rules. Harris (1984) provides a particularly compelling syntactic case of this kind from Hiberno-English, which incorporates a four-way present-tense distinction of simple *he goes*, progressive *he's going*, iterative perfective *he does go*, and iterative imperfective *he be's going*. Harris argues that these are not borrowings from Irish, but retentions from Early Modern English, some shared with other varieties of English. He also contends that the degree of divergence from the standard is incompatible with derivation by rule from a shared source. Instead, he extends the familiar picture of the creole continuum, where 'shifting between basilectal and acrolectal poles proceeds via the radical restructuring of underlying representations, not merely through the manipulation of low-level rules' (1984: 314), to the interface between standard and non-creole vernacular constructions.

Furthermore, 'If we are attempting to establish a theory of language which claims to explain how native speakers understand each other, we must also investigate how it is they often misunderstand each other' (Lodge 1984a: 15). That is, communicative breakdowns do occur among speakers of different, but related varieties: the SGP assumption of common underlying forms should presumably rule out this possibility (although this is not made explicit in the SGP literature, given that communicative breakdown is a matter of performance). Harris (1984) reports mismatches and misunderstandings between even superficially similar syntactic constructions; and Lodge (1984a: 15) raises the interesting question of how speakers can understand another variety without necessarily being able to produce it, when both abilities should follow from a common underlying system. For instance, northern English speakers lacking the [ʊ] ~ [ʌ] distinction can understand these vowels in RP, but may not be able to mimic them. Along similar lines, Lodge (1984b) presented eighty-eight undergraduates with spoken forms like [peʔɹəɫ] *petrol*, [mɑs] *mass*, [bʌɫ] *bull* and [stɹeː] *straw*, asking them whether they used these forms themselves; had heard them but would not use them; guessed that there might be English speakers who did use them; or felt they were not possible English forms. Quite a number of his informants, including some from the areas where the focus forms are attested, judged them as non-English; one Belfast student felt not even a foreigner would use [bʌɫ], a Belfast form. Lodge argues that 'if forms are not accepted as being English by native speakers, then this is an indication that a panlectal approach to phonology ... is inappropriate ...' (1984b: 21).

Harris concludes that 'in general it is fair to say that cross-dialectal understanding succeeds *in spite of* structural differences rather than because of complete structural identity' (1985: 346). To understand related varieties, speakers will, when necessary, invoke *ad hoc*, idiosyncratic comprehension or pattern-matching strategies. As for adaptive change, we might invoke 'shifts in the selection of alternative lexical representations rather than the manipulation of synchronic process rules' (Harris 1985: 341). In other words, altering output to conform to some target standard variety involves lexeme-by-lexeme phonemic redistribution. This assumption shows affinities with Andersen's (1973) important hypotheses on abductive change, whereby learners who *have* restructured their underlying inventories may nonetheless innovate one-off pattern-matching rules to forestall correction by older speakers retaining underlying and hence surface forms appropriate to an earlier stage of the language. These intermediate speakers may be crucial to the progress of a change, since their restructured underliers, though conflicting with their own corrected production, may make them more likely to accept novel pronunciations by the next generation.

It seems, then, that we are justified in renouncing the identity hypothesis, and in favouring phonological models which, unlike SGP, do not or, even better, *cannot* derive all surface dialect forms from a single underlying level. It follows that a language, in Lexical Phonological terms, must be seen as a collection of related varieties, but with no underlying identity or unity. As Lass (1987: 4) puts it:

> To say that 'Scots is a dialect of English' does not imply the (real) existence of an 'English' of which it's a dialect. Rather that 'English' is the name given to a cluster of (relatively) mutually comprehensible speech forms (the dialects) that share more features with each other than they do with any other conventionally named dialect clusters ('Dutch', 'German', etc.).

If we are not tied to a notion of language as common underlying system, then we can also account for the gradual divergence of dialects becoming the gradual divergence of languages; on this analysis, dialect and language variation are only quantitatively, not qualitatively distinct. Of course, core systems (like the one Lass (1987: 5) calls 'a semi-fictitious idealised "core" English') can be useful expository shorthand; I used just such a composite system for Scots dialects and SSE in chapter 4. But such core systems cover a multitude of real dialect-specific and indeed speaker-specific systems, and the extent to which they are themselves 'real' in any sense will depend on what is allowed in the phonological model we are using.

5.4   Underspecification

It seems scarcely credible that we can begin to trust a phonological model – and a rule-based one, at that – to draw meaningful boundaries between what is derivable and what is not. Such possibilities have been explored before, but the ingenuity of phonologists has typically subverted them, as with the tendency of Lexical Phonologists (like Halle and Mohanan (1985)) to order rules on Level 2, specifically to evade DEC. We encounter a precisely parallel problem in this case, if we allow the disruptive influence of underspecification.

5.4.1   An outline
Before assessing the numerous challenges to underspecification posed in a diverse range of phonological models, and examining why its effects are particularly pernicious in LP, we must explore the alleged advantages which have led to its becoming an expected ingredient of phonological theory in the first place.

Underspecification theory (Archangeli 1984, 1988; Kiparsky 1982, 1985) is based squarely on the Standard Generative evaluation metric, which values grammars highly if they mark only idiosyncratic properties at the underlying level, filling in predictable features using rules and conventions. It therefore rests, like the identity hypothesis, on the assumptions that grammars in general, and underlying representations in particular, should be maximally economical, and that computation is favoured over storage. Underspecification presupposes neutralisation, markedness and the elimination of redundancy; and the main application of the theory so far has been in the domain of autosegmental analyses of harmony processes and feature spreading. For instance, Steriade (1979) discusses Khalkha Mongolian vowel harmony (see (5.3)).

(5.3)   a. (i) Harmonise [back] on all vowels
             (ii) Harmonise [round] from non-high vowel to non-high vowel

      b. ɑx-ɑɑs   'from elder brother'
         düüg-ees 'from younger brother'
         ex-ees   'from mother'
         ör-òòs   'from debt'
         xot-oos   'from city'
         morin-oos 'from horse'

The high round vowels [u] and [ü] are opaque to rounding; they are not themselves affected, and do not allow the feature to spread to their right. However, high unrounded [i], although not subject to rounding harmony, is transparent to the spreading rule, as shown by *morinoos*. Steriade proposes that only initial vowels should be specified for the features [back] and [round]; these values will spread throughout the word. However, [u] and [ü] will also be marked as [+ round], to show their status as opaque vowels; the spreading process will be blocked by this existing specification. A default rule will later assign [− round] to those underspecified vowels unaffected by rounding harmony, including [i] and any vowel following [u] or [ü].

This sort of argument represents a persuasive way of handling feature spreading. However, underspecification has been extended to other domains in two main ways, leading to the subtheories of contrastive specification and radical underspecification: although I shall present these individually here, it should be noted that the line between them is not always obvious (Goldsmith 1990: 243).

Contrastive specification, the less extreme application of underspecification theory, follows from the earlier notion of redundancy and deals uniquely with non-distinctive features, which are hypothesised to have the single underlying specification [0F]. For example, sonorants in English are all voiced, making voicing non-distinctive for this class of sounds; the underlying representations of sonorants would therefore contain the underspecified value [0 voice], with [+ voice] filled in subsequently by a redundancy rule. Radical underspecification, on the other hand, extends also to distinctive features: its focus is not contrastivity, but predictability. Radical underspecification is more strongly directed towards the achievement of simplicity than contrastive specification, and is motivated by the Feature Minimisation Principle (5.4).

(5.4)   Feature Minimisation Principle (Archangeli 1984: 50):
          'A grammar is most highly valued when underlying representations
          include the minimal number of features necessary to make different the
          phonemes of the language.'

For instance, while English sonorants are uniquely voiced, obstruents
surface as contrastively voiced or voiceless. However, radical underspecification requires us to mark *either* [+ voice] or [−voice] underlyingly; let us select [+ voice]. Obstruents which surface as voiceless will
be underlyingly [0 voice], with a default rule filling in the appropriate
specification during the derivation.

In this case, the default rule is arguably universal, since obstruents are
cross-linguistically more frequently voiceless than voiced. However,
values can also be supplied by ordinary language specific phonological
rules. For instance, Trisyllabic Laxing changes the long, tense initial
vowel of *divine* to short and lax in *divinity*; but it could also operate in a
structure-building rather than a structure-changing way to supply the
specifications [−tense] and [−long] (or single-attachment) for the first
vowel of words like *sycamore*, which could then be left unspecified for
these features at the underlying level. Since the rule manipulates contrastive features, it does not violate Structure Preservation; and since the
DEC affects only structure-changing applications, it will not affect TSL
here, although it will block laxing of vowels with an underlying [+ tense]
specification in an underived environment, removing one of the major
objections to earlier blank-filling analyses raised by Stanley (1967).
Stanley also asserted that the option of having [0F] as well as [+F] and
[−F] at the underlying level really converts binary features into ternary
ones; but Kiparsky (1982) argues that this does not apply in a lexicalist
model of underspecification, where in any environment, only the marked
specification /+F/ *or* /−F/, and the unmarked specification /0F/, will be
allowed. The picture is further complicated by the existence of two
different versions of radical underspecification (Mohanan 1991): the
context-sensitive variety, as adopted by Kiparsky, holds that both values
of a feature cannot be specified in the same environment, while Archangeli's context-free radical underspecification makes the prediction that
only one value may be marked underlyingly in any environment.

5.4.2   Problems for underspecification

Underspecification – and the more radical the better – seemed an
indispensable part of 1980s derivational phonology. There has been a

typical 1990s backlash against it. Several phonological frameworks have ruled it out altogether: for instance, Prince and Smolensky (1993: 188) note that the unmarkedness of coronals and their diversity and frequency in segment inventories are irreconcilable within underspecification, and conclude that Optimality Theory should 'abandon underspecification in favor of markedness theory'. Similarly, underspecification is rejected in Government Phonology because it conflicts with the autonomous interpretation hypothesis (Harris and Lindsey 1995), which holds that phonological elements should be directly interpretable at all levels. Even within rule-based derivational phonology, underspecification is increasingly challenged (Mohanan 1991, Steriade 1995), for reasons of unlearnability, psychological implausibility, and theory-internal contradiction.

We have already seen that underspecification is predicated on simplicity, and on an alleged though rarely defended preference for computation over storage. Harris and Lindsey (1995: 48) argue, however, that this implies an inefficient model of lexical access: 'Just as an archived computer text file has to be de-archived before it can be accessed, so would a speaker-hearer have first to "unpack" the condensed, underspecified form of a lexical entry before submitting it to articulation or recognition.'

This problem also cuts the other way, in terms of learnability. Archangeli (1988: 192) notes that the learnability of a contrastively specified system depends on the learner's knowledge of both distinctive and non-distinctive features; thus, the child must initially internalise a fully specified representation, then strip out non-contrastive specifications algorithmically. This assumption guarantees the existence of a single contrastively specified underlying representation for any system, but we must ask what would motivate a child, having internalised the fully specified representation which is necessarily prior to a contrastively specified level, to identify and remove the redundant information, only to reintroduce it in time for the phonetics.

Radical underspecification is not so learner-friendly. In particular, there is considerable indeterminacy over which feature value should be marked at the underlying level, and indeed which feature is to be selected in the case of 'balanced mutual dependencies' (Harris and Lindsey 1995: 47, and see further below). While contrastive specification guarantees a single set of underlying forms per system, radical underspecification thus permits a variable, theoretically unlimited number of underlying systems for any set of surface forms. Archangeli (1988: 193) admits that 'the learnability of [such] a system becomes quite a challenge', and argues that, although decisions may sometimes be made on language-specific grounds, frequently guidance from Universal Grammar will be needed. Radical underspecification therefore requires a directive theory of Universal Grammar: underlying forms are decided on universal grounds, and universal principles constrain the ordering of redundancy rules. It is interesting in this context that Optimality Theory, with its particularly strong conception of UG, nonetheless rejects underspecification.

There have been attempts to justify underspecification in psycholinguistic terms: for instance, Stemberger (1992) argues that radical underspecification is supported by speech error evidence, claiming that in tasks involving pairs of phonemes, 'if one of the phonemes is underspecified relative to the other, there are more errors on the underspecified phoneme' (1992: 496). However, Stemberger's argument relies on his characterisation of /ε/ as the maximally underspecified vowel phoneme of English: since [ε] appears rather late in child language, this conflicts with the usual hypothesis that underspecified vowels are acquired early. Similarly, Lahiri and Marslen-Wilson (1991) propose underspecified entries in the mental lexicon as a solution to the notorious problem of matching highly variable perceived forms to the appropriate underliers in speech recognition systems. The Cohort Model is a parallel information processing system, which assumes activation of all words in the mental lexicon beginning with the same sound sequence as the sensory input. As more input is heard, this cohort of eligible forms is continuously assessed, and mismatches trigger a fall in activation level for the affected candidates, until the best candidate is recognised. However, this model rules out late entry of candidates into the cohort; yet since onsets vary considerably in connected speech, the right candidate might be excluded initially, and only recognised relatively late in the procedure. Lahiri and Marslen-Wilson's Underspecified Cohort Model attempts a resolution by invoking underspecification, which would allow initial matching over a wider range of forms.

Lahiri and Marslen-Wilson (1991) hypothesise that a value specified underlyingly will match only the same value in the input; the opposite value will be a mismatch. An underspecified value will provide a better match for the unmarked surface value, but will also be a partial match for the marked surface value. Lahiri and Marslen-Wilson report a series of gating experiments, where subjects were asked to give word choices for heard stimuli, based on Bengali, where vowel nasalisation is contrastive, with [+ nasal] the marked value, and English, where vowel nasalisation is redundant. In both languages, oral vowels become nasalised by assimilation to a following nasal consonant. The results seem to support the underspecification hypothesis. In Bengali, almost no words with underlyingly nasal vowels were given in response to stimuli containing oral vowels. Responses with nasal vowels were initially given to inputs with surface nasal vowels, regardless of the presence or absence of a nasal consonant; however, subjects progressively became aware of the nasal consonant condition, and began matching only oral vowel responses in cases of assimilation. However, in English, subjects consistently interpreted vowel nasalisation as signalling a following nasal consonant.

Ehala (1992) provides a detailed critique of the Underspecified Cohort Model, focusing on three main problems. First, he argues that the degree of underspecification will either be incompatible with the spread of phonologically possible variants for each lexical item, or will not allow underlying forms to be kept distinct. For instance, Lahiri and Marslen-Wilson (1991) consider English *hand* in *hand you* [ndʒ], *hand me* [mm] and *hand care* [ŋk]. Since both /h/ and /d/ are potentially deletable, they should be totally unspecified; and in view of its assimilatory behaviour, /n/ also cannot be specified for place. The resulting underlier /æN/ will not be unique; but with a less radical version of underspecification, the underlying form will not be compatible with its full range of attested surface realisations. Secondly, Lahiri and Marslen-Wilson argue that marked information cannot be altered by phonological rule, since this would produce surface forms not matching their underliers. However, Ehala (1992) notes that neutralisation processes potentially delink and hence effectively erase marked feature values, which are then substituted by later redundancy rules axiomatically supplying unmarked values. Thus, Lahiri and Marslen-Wilson predict that English *disbar, disguise* should not be recoverable since the underlyingly voiced consonant after [s] surfaces as voiceless; but listeners can understand these forms. This might be resolved by disregarding mismatches of only a single feature value; but since Lahiri and Marslen-Wilson introduce their Underspecified Cohort Model to deal with precisely such mismatches, underspecification would then lose its value. Finally, Lahiri and Marslen-Wilson's model predicts that speakers should not use predictable information in speech recognition; however, Ehala (1992) argues that English speakers use lack of aspiration as a cue for underlying stop voicing. In general, then, the incorporation of underspecification into word recognition is not particularly successful.

Perhaps most importantly, some of the main phonological predictions of underspecification theory seem difficult to maintain. For instance, Hualde (1991) notes that in radical underspecification, unmarked vowels, defined as those behaving asymmetrically, will be unspecified under-lyingly, with the proposed empty vowel slot being filled by default feature values. However, Hualde argues that in the Arbizu dialect of Basque, suffixes beginning with an empty vowel slot, subsequently specified as [e], must be distinguished from those beginning with underlying /e/. Radical underspecification will enforce identity between these two classes, both starting out with an empty vowel, and will therefore lose this distinction. Similarly, McCarthy and Taub (1992) contend that even coronal under-specification, surely the best-known and apparently most robust example, is contentious: although many papers have claimed that coronal underspecification in English extends throughout the phonology, 'It is ... remarkable that there is also a considerable body of evidence that coronals, even plain alveolars like *t* or *n*, must actually be *specified* for [coronal] in English phonology' (1992: 364). McCarthy and Taub provide nine such cases, many of which involve the conflict that plain alveolars must be seen as unspecified for [coronal] to explain their special phonological behaviour, but also form a natural class with marked coronals like [ʃ θ], which can be unified only using [+ coronal]. For instance, American English prohibits initial coronal plus [ju], while the diphthong [au] can only be followed by a coronal, as in *mouth(e)*, *mouse*, *lout*, *gouge*: but both restrictions hold regardless of whether the coronal is marked or unmarked. In short, 'although [coronal] underspecification explains much about English phonology, it also encounters significant difficulties' (McCarthy and Taub 1992: 366).

Moving away from the language-specific, although radical underspeci-fication is avowedly based on cross-linguistic considerations, notably relating to markedness and Universal Grammar, it may inhibit cross-system comparison. One of the major problems of early structuralist linguistics was the theoretical impossibility of equating or even com-paring a given phoneme in one language with the 'equivalent' phoneme in another: since members of a system are definable only in terms of the elements with which they contrast, and since two languages will have different systems of phonological oppositions, comparison between systems is strictly invalid. It seems likely that the adoption of radical underspecification will reintroduce or even exacerbate this difficulty, as the same surface segments will be underspecified in potentially very different ways according to the other elements in the system. Even within a single system, it is often unclear exactly what shape underspecified forms should take. Very frequently, issues of mutual dependency arise (Harris and Lindsey 1995, Mohanan 1991, Steriade 1995): for instance, if segment structure depends on syllable structure and vice versa, which should we regard as derived? Why is there general agreement that sonorants should be underlyingly unspecified for [voice], but not that voiceless segments should be unspecified for [sonorant]? And how do we decide the best way of distinguishing an underlyingly placeless vowel from no segment at all? As Steriade (1995: 135) notes, 'the choice between marking an underlying null segment by using a stricture feature like [+ sonorant] or ... a place feature like [+ high] remains arbitrary. No credible principle will lead us to the desired conclusion'.

It is all too easy to bandy about apparent justifications like naturalness, simplicity and predictability without exploring them in depth. As Mohanan (1991: 300) comments, 'For more than three decades, the assumption that underlying representations may not contain predictable information ... has been accepted as an unquestioned dogma in generative phonology'; but if we follow Mohanan and address this dogma directly, we find two perhaps surprising facts. First, 'underspecification does not directly follow from predictability. It follows only if we subscribe to some further principle such as Lexical Minimality' (Steriade 1995: 121). As Goldsmith (1995b: 17) remarks, underspecification is not the only, or even the obvious way of encoding simplicity either. And secondly, the definition of predictability underlying underspecification theory is not the one usually found in other sciences, where it straightforwardly means the opposite of unpredictable (Mohanan 1991: 288):

> When one tosses a coin, the result is random or unpredictable because we cannot tell whether the outcome will be heads or tails. Suppose we use the following convention: if it is heads, we write [+ head], and if it is tails, we write nothing. Since there is now a 'rule' that interprets the absence of any specification as tails, Archangeli's notion of predictability would imply that tails is predictable, but heads is not! Clearly, we must not confuse rules that interpret linguistic notation with rules that predict what can be observed in linguistic phenomena.

We might hesitate over adopting a further principle like Lexical Minimality in view of the fact that many 'predictable' features are in fact required in the phonology, as pointed out by McCarthy and Taub (1992) for [coronal] in English. Others, which would be supplied routinely by phonological or redundancy rules in underspecification theory, seem not to need specification at all: Keating (1988: 275) argues that 'under-specification may persist into phonetic representations' in cases of phonetic transparency, for instance, where a segment like /h/ may incorporate purely transitional values for certain features, and may also allow neighbouring segments to interact freely, notably in vowel-to-vowel coarticulation. Harris and Lindsey (1995) argue that these cases are compatible with their element theory, which assumes monovalent features and purely privative oppositions: indeed, a privative system will be significantly less powerful than an equipollent one, but will nonetheless predict strong asymmetries of the type originally used to motivate underspecification. For example, if [round] is a single-valued feature, we would expect roundness to participate in phonological operations like spreading, but 'there is no way of expressing a complementary system in which "absence-of-round" is harmonically active' (Harris 1994: 93). Underspecification here is 'trivial and permanent' (Steriade 1995: 157).

Of course, if underspecification is inherent and monovalent, many redundancy rules and structure-building operations will simply disappear. Mohanan (1991: 301) sees this as the right approach in any case: since he regards underspecification and default rules; structure changing linking rules; and constraints and structure changing rules as three implementational variants, and argues that we require constraints and structure changing processes independently in any case, it follows that 'structure building rules should be eliminated from segmental phonology'. This proposal is seconded by Steriade (1995). One might argue that structure building rules are still necessary for prosodic purposes, and Mohanan's statement leaves the door open for this; but recent developments in LP may make the situation clearer here. Most notably, Giegerich's (in press) model of base-driven stratification rules out the pre-morphology cycle, on which structure building applications of stress and syllabification have hitherto been located. In that case, underspecification might provide the only motivation for maintaining such structure-building operations, making the whole argument irreducibly circular.

5.4.3 *Underspecification in Lexical Phonology*
If underspecification is increasingly recognised as problematic regardless of phonological model, it is several degrees of magnitude worse in Lexical Phonology. As we have seen, many of the strategies encouraging abstract analyses in SGP, typically involving free rides and distant

underliers, are disfavoured or prohibited in LP, meaning that underlying representations have generally been approximated to surface forms. It is hard to resist the temptation to see underspecification as an alternative strategy for reintroducing abstractness.

For instance, different degrees of underspecification involve different degrees of departure from the optimal lexicalist analysis of dialect distinctions. As we saw in 5.2 above, an analysis of RP and Scots/SSE on their own terms reveals substantial underlying differences: while RP vowels are variably short or long and lax or tense, tenseness alone is relevant at least for core varieties of Scots, with all vowels underlyingly short and tense vowels lengthened during the derivation by SVLR.

If we introduce contrastive specification, the situation does not change dramatically, and the underlying differences remain. In RP, only tense-ness or length need be distinctive: I select length as underlyingly contrastive, for the reasons given in 5.2 (see also Lindsey 1990). If all RP vowels are specified as either long or short and as [0 tense] underlyingly, some redundancy rule must subsequently fill in the appropriate values. Archangeli (1988) holds that such redundancy rules should operate as late as possible in the derivation, and this is reinforced in LP by Structure Preservation, which restricts rules mentioning non-distinctive features to the postlexical component. This may be problematic in the present case, since although tenseness is non-contrastive, a number of severe deriva-tional difficulties arise if it cannot be referred to in the lexicon; Halle and Mohanan (1985), for instance, claim that [± tense] is not underlyingly distinctive but that various tensing rules must nonetheless apply lexically. There might be two ways around this: Borowsky (1990) assumes that Structure Preservation is operational only on Level 1; and Kiparsky's (1985: 93) version of Structure Preservation implies that, if a rule introduces only *unmarked* specifications, it may operate lexically. If in the unmarked case for English, [+ tense] is associated with long and [− tense] with short vowels, a redundancy rule making this correlation may indeed be lexical, allowing length alone to be specified at the underlying level for RP, with [± tense] introduced early in the lexicon.

As far as Scots/SSE is concerned, contrastive specification will leave all (or at least most) vowels marked [0 long] underlyingly. They will, however, still be specified as [+ tense] or [− tense]. Length will be filled in by the SVLR for tense vowels before /r/, voiced fricatives and boundaries, while shortness will be supplied by a subsequent redundancy rule affecting tense vowels in non-lengthening contexts and lax vowels everywhere. Crucially, however, the feature bisecting the underlying vowel system of RP will still be length, while in SSE it will be tenseness.

If radical underspecification is introduced, this underlying difference can be made to vanish. In RP, underspecification will be extended to length. Vowels will either be specified underlyingly as [+ long] and [0 long], or as [−long] and [0 long] (or the autosegmentalised equivalents), with the missing value supplied partly by the lexical lengthening/tensing or shortening/laxing rules applying in a structure-building capacity, and partly by universal default rules. As far as tenseness is concerned, we can either retain the underlying specification of all vowels as [0 tense], or choose also to mark either [+ tense] or [−tense] at the underlying level, and assign the other by default rule.

In Scots/SSE, we shall have to choose one value for length at the underlying level. If we assume that vowels are [−long] and [0 long] (ignoring those which surface as consistently long), we neatly characterise those vowels not subject to the SVLR, the former set. Those vowels specified [−long] will surface as consistently short, while those which begin as [0 long] will be marked as long before /r/, voiced fricatives and boundaries, and as short in other contexts. There are two ways of achieving this. First (see 5.5a), we could allow SVLR to specify vowels as [+ long] in lengthening contexts, then formulate a default rule to supply the value [−long] elsewhere.

(5.5)   Scots / SSE

a.	i (SVLR long)	i (SVLR short)	ɪ
Underlying:	0 long	0 long	−long
SVLR:	+ long		
Default:		−long	
b.	i (SVLR long)	i (SVLR short)	ɪ
Underlying:	0 long	0 long	−long
Neutralising SVLR:	+ long	−long	

However, there is absolutely nothing to stop us from following another route, returning to a version of SVLR far closer to its historical formulation. On this analysis (5.5b), SVLR would be bipartite, assigning [+ long] before /r/, voiced fricatives and boundaries, and [−long] elsewhere. As a structure-building rule, SVLR could apply on Level 1 of the lexicon, despite the DEC. There might ostensibly be a problem with Structure Preservation, which is intended to stop lexical rules from referring to non-distinctive features; but since the definition of 'non-distinctive' adopted in the literature on underspecification involves lack of specification at the underlying level, and since this analysis assumes that vowels are underlyingly [−long] or [0 long], which is quite as specified as any underlying feature can be, I fail to see how Structure Preservation or anything else can rule this out. As for tenseness, this can be treated in either of the ways suggested above for RP: vowels could be specified as [0 tense] and either [+ tense] or [−tense], with a default rule supplying the missing value, or all vowels could begin as [0 tense], with some combination of universal principles and language-specific rules conspiring to assign [−tense] by redundancy rule to /ɪ ɛ ʌ/ and [+ tense] to everything else. If we pursue the option of introducing [± tense] by redundancy rule very early in the lexicon, before the operation of SVLR, [+ tense] might be correlated with [0 long] vowels and [−tense] with [−long] ones. (5.6) gives a possible derivation along these lines for RP and SSE.

(5.6)	RP	i (SVLR long)	i (SVLR short)	ɪ
	Underlying:	0 long, 0 tense	0 long, 0 tense	−long, 0 tense
	Default:			
	[−long] → [−tense]			−tense
	[0 long] → [+ tense]	+ tense	+ tense	
	[0 long] → [+ long]	+ long	+ long	
	SSE	i (SVLR long)	i (SVLR short)	ɪ
	Underlying:	0 long, 0 tense	0 long, 0 tense	−long, 0 tense
	Default:			
	[−long] → [−tense]			−tense
	[0 long] → [+ tense]	+ tense	+ tense	
	Neutralising SVLR:	+ long	−long	
	OR SVLR:	+ long		
	Default:		−long	

Nor are these the only options in a radically underspecified Lexical Phonology. For instance, we could also analyse SSE as having [+ tense] and [0 tense] but only [0 long] underlyingly, with a lengthening-only version of SVLR affecting tense vowels in lengthening environments and default rules supplying [−tense] and [−long] later. This would keep the synchronic SVLR more strictly distinct from its historical predecessor. However, it would not necessarily maintain the difference between RP and SSE at the underlying level, since we can easily approximate RP to SSE, with [+ tense], [0 tense] and [0 long] and two default rules, one supplying [−tense] and the other correlating length with [+ tense] and shortness with [−tense] (see (5.7)): this equally may not be the best account, but it is certainly a possible one, and may demonstrate that whatever analysis we select for one of the dialects, we can apply to the other.

(5.7)	RP	i (SVLR long)	i (SVLR short)	ɪ
	Underlying:	0 long, + tense	0 long, + tense	0 long, 0 tense
	Default:			
	[0 tense] → [−tense]			−tense
	[α tense] → [α long]	+ long	+ long	−long
	SSE	i (SVLR long)	i (SVLR short)	ɪ
	Underlying:	0 long, + tense	0 long, + tense	0 long, 0 tense
	SVLR:	+ long		
	Default:			
	[0 long] → [−long]		−long	−long
	[−long] → [−tense]			−tense

It follows that, in a Lexical Phonology with radical underspecification, we can maintain the dialect identity hypothesis of SGP; and although the bipartite synchronic SVLR of the underspecification analysis does not strictly mirror its historical counterpart, this is purely by virtue of its structure-building rather than structure-changing function. The general motivation for structure-building rules was questioned in the previous section. At the very least, the bipartite SVLR is far closer than the lengthening-only version to its historical antecedent; and this again may represent a step backwards, retarding the reflection of historical developments in the synchronic grammar. A neutralising SVLR was also rejected earlier on the grounds of learnability: it is not at all clear that the child would be better able to acquire the underspecified system, especially given the doubts raised by practitioners of underspecification over the learnability of *any* radically underspecified representation (Archangeli 1988: 193).

In short, there may be machinery in linguistic theory that leaves doors open for us which are better off closed. Radical underspecification may be one such piece of apparatus; and if so, it is not compatible with a highly constrained model of LP in which we wish to explore not only synchronic system design, but also dialect divergence and language change, and their impact on the rules *and* the underlying representations. Contrastive specification might be permitted to remain, perhaps limited to features which behave autosegmentally in a particular language, since it does not conflict so clearly with the constraints of LP, or with its relatively concrete assumptions on language acquisition (Mohanan 1986, and chapter 2 above).

However, we might want to go further than this and rule out under-specification altogether (particularly if non-binary features were introduced into LP, an option I shall consider in the next chapter), because it bleeds the constraints of LP, making their application opaque and their enforcement impossible. This is particularly noticeable from Borowsky (1990), who adopts Kiparsky's context-sensitive version of radical under-specification. First, underspecification affects Structure Preservation. Borowsky (1990: 116) assumes that different partially specified underliers may merge on the surface once all features have been filled in. She also argues that Structure Preservation means no segment which is not a phoneme of the language can be derived on Level 1, where 'if the segment /x/ is not a phoneme of English there is no occurrence of it, or a partially specified form of it, anywhere in the lexicon' (1990: 30). However, underspecification means this is hard to check: we would have to take all potentially eligible underlying segments, put them through all phonological and default rules, and see if /x/ is in fact derived (and if so, given Borowsky's contention that Structure Preservation switches off after Level 1, at what level).

Borowsky also uses underspecification to derive free ride effects. For instance, the Sanskrit *ruki* rule retroflexes /s/ after /r u k i/. In SGP, retroflexes in underived environments would have been derived from /s/ via a free ride through the *ruki* rule. In LP, the DEC would block such derivations; but if retroflexes are underlyingly unspecified for [retroflex], the *ruki* rule can apply in a structure-building capacity, evading the DEC and favouring what is essentially a diacritic analysis. In cases of Velar Softening, Borowsky marks non-softening velars as underlyingly [+ back] and softening ones as [0 back], allowing Velar Softening to supply [−back] in underived *accident* as well as derived *criticism*; this again is a clear notational variant of the SPE use of $/k^d g^d/$ for softening velars. Similarly, Borowsky reanalyses those rules which Halle and Mohanan (1985) restricted by fiat to Level 2, as blank-filling operations on Level 1.

Borowsky (1990: 73) notes that we can stop rules from applying in underived environments; but 'This is simply to miss a generalization from my point of view.' She also argues that an analysis using two rules instead of one (which would be the case for the Vowel Shift Rules advocated in chapter 3 above) 'is not quite in the spirit of our enterprise' (1990: 94). But these are not arguments: they are restatements of the assumptions of SGP, which do not sit easily with the constraints and limitations of LP. In a constrained model, the constraints effectively choose our analyses for us, as we have seen in the last two chapters: but if we allow underspecification, it almost always allows these constraints to be circumvented. Borowsky's conclusion from this is that we should abandon the Strict Cyclicity Condition (our Derived Environment Condition), since 'the use of underspecification removes many classic cases which motivated the SCC' (1990: 28). Logically, this can be interpreted as an argument against either the SCC or underspecification: although underspecification is now frequently associated with LP, it 'can in principle be accepted or rejected independently of the other ideas of lexical phonology' (Goldsmith 1990: 243). The arguments presented here and in the previous chapters lead me to favour a version of LP which retains the DEC and rejects underspecification. Since underspecification permits analyses which would otherwise be ruled out, and is incompatible with the reduction of abstractness and coherence with external evidence characteristic of a lexicalist model, I conclude, to misquote Borowsky (1990: 94), that it 'is not quite in the spirit of our enterprise'.

6   *English /r/*

6.1   Introduction

In chapter 1, I quoted Labov (1978) in defence of my intention to reintegrate synchronic and diachronic evidence. Labov's (1978: 281) view is that, provided we adopt the uniformitarian principle, and therefore accept that 'the forces which operated to produce the historical record are the same as those which can be seen operating today', we can use the linguistic present to explain the linguistic past. However, if we are serious about the reintegration of synchrony and diachrony, the connection should work both ways: that is, the linguistic past should ideally also help us understand and model the present.

The first part of the equation has already been proved: in chapter 4, I showed that a possible life-cycle for sound changes and phonological rules can be formulated in Lexical Phonology. The default case was represented by æ-Tensing; and a variant pathway, involving two cycles of alteration of the underlying representations, was required for processes like the Scottish Vowel Length Rule, which involve historical rule inversion. A model designed primarily for synchronic phonological description therefore provides insights into change. In this chapter, I hope to show that we can indeed also use the past to explain the phonological present, with special reference to English /r/, which is of particular relevance because it has been discussed in a variety of phonological frameworks (see Broadbent 1991, McCarthy 1991, 1993, Scobbie 1992, Donegan 1993, Harris 1994, Giegerich in press); is characterised by interesting interactions between /r/ itself and preceding vowels; and arguably again involves rule inversion. We shall see that the ostensibly arbitrary synchronic process of [r]-Insertion in varieties with both linking and intrusive [r] is in fact historically principled, and that the synchronic situation has been produced by a series of historical steps, each conditioning the next. Moreover, each of these steps seems still to be preserved in some variety of Present-Day English. This further notion of the interaction of historical change and synchronic variation is familiar from creolistics: Bickerton, for instance, in describing the creole continuum in Guyana, claims that 'a synchronic cut across the Guyanese community is indistinguishable from a diachronic cut across a century and a half of linguistic development' (quoted by Romaine 1988: 165). We shall see that this also holds, *mutatis mutandis*, for the English speech community in its widest sense.

However, it is not enough to explain synchronic patterns with reference to the changes which have created them: we must also account for the contributory changes themselves. To do so, I suggest we require further reference to phonetic parameters, and indeed a wholesale revision of the feature system: to this end, I shall tentatively propose the incorporation of the gestural system of representation used in Articulatory Phonology (Browman and Goldstein 1986, 1989, 1991, 1992; McMahon, Foulkes and Tollfree 1994, McMahon and Foulkes 1995, McMahon 1996) into Lexical Phonology.

But this reliance on historical and phonetic evidence does not mean the analysis arrived at is phonology-free: on the contrary, a highly constrained phonological model will again force us to draw certain conclusions, not only about the current status of /r/, but also about its history. Thus, as in previous chapters, some arguments below will be historical, but others will be theory-internal, depending on particular properties of the model assumed here. The emphasis on formal models distances this approach a little from Labov (1978): while he defines the linguistic present largely in terms of social influences on speakers, and the quantitative analysis of inter- and intra-personal variation, I believe that part of a synchronic phonological analysis must also involve idealisation from these data and consequent model building and evaluation. Where such models cast light on the interaction between synchronic phonology, dialect variation and sound change, this may in itself be evidence for that view.

6.2   English /r/: a brief outline

Accents of English fall into two broad groupings (with some further refinements, as we shall see) with respect to /r/. The actual phonetic realisation of /r/ is not constant across all varieties: it is very frequently an alveolar or post-alveolar approximant, but may be a tap, especially initially or intervocalically, in Scottish varieties, or an r-coloured schwa in some contexts in General American. There are also pockets of uvular fricatives [ʁ] in Aberdeen, and among older speakers in Northumberland and Durham (Wells 1982, Lass 1987: 94); and the labio-dental approximant [ʋ] is increasingly common in urban areas (Foulkes 1997). Although issues of phonetic realisation will be of some concern below, when we turn to the history of /r/, synchronically they are not of central importance; for convenience, I shall therefore generally use [r] notation, not to indicate an alveolar trill, but as shorthand for the various realisations of /r/ found across the accents of English.

In rhotic accents, [r] is pronounced in all possible phonological contexts: word-initially, as in *red*; intervocalically, as in *very*; finally, as in *letter*; and in clusters, as in *bread* or *herd*. As a rule of thumb, [r] surfaces wherever there is an <r> in the spelling. Furthermore, in rhotic accents, the set of vowels which can occur before /r/ tends to be identical, or near identical, to that found before other consonants or word-finally: thus, in Scottish Standard English (SSE), the vowels in *bee* and *beer* are phonologically the same (although see 6.5 below), giving /bi/ and /bir/. Likewise, SSE speakers have /e/ in *hay* and /er/ in *hair*; /a/ in *spa* and /ar/ in *spar*; /ɔ/ in *law* and /ɔr/ in *north*; /o/ in *foe* and /or/ in *four*; and /u/ in *queue* and /ur/ in *cure*. Irish, Scottish and Canadian English, as well as General American, some English English accents, and some Caribbean varieties, are rhotic (Wells 1982); but the vowel inventories found before /r/ vary considerably across dialects, and limited mergers, such as the American *merry = marry = Mary*, do occur. [r]-loss is also still in progress in some areas: Romaine (1978) reports a final zero variant for some working class Edinburgh schoolchildren, most commonly in her male informants, while Sullivan (1992) documents rapidly decreasing rhoticity for younger urban speakers in Exeter.

Non-rhotic accents are found in England, Wales, the Eastern and Southern states of the USA, Australia, New Zealand and South Africa. Here, [r] does not surface synchronically in all phonological contexts, or in all forms with orthographic <r>. Historical [r] is retained word-initially and intervocalically, but has been lost pre-consonantally and pre-pausally, so that [r] appears in *red*, *very* and *bread*, but not in *herd* or *letter*. Furthermore, in non-rhotic accents, the inventory of non-low vowels before historical [r] tends to differ from those found elsewhere: *beer*, *hair*, *four* and *cure* will typically have centring diphthongs, with a schwa offglide, while *bee*, *hay*, *foe* and *queue* have /i:/, /eɪ/, /oʊ/ and /u:/.

There is also a merger of short /ɪ ɛ ʌ/ before historical /r/, typically as [ɜ:], so that Scots *bird, herd, word* [bɪrd], [hɛrd], [wʌrd] correspond to RP (and other non-rhotic) [bɜ:d], [hɜ:d], [wɜ:d].

In many non-rhotic varieties, alternations of [r] and Ø in simple and derived forms within the same paradigm have arisen because of the retention of historical [r] pre-vocalically but its loss finally and preconsonantally; examples are given in (6.1).

(6.1)   [r] retained initially: *red, robe, rate . . .*
         [r] retained intervocalically: *very, hurry, soaring . . .*
         [r] lost: *beard, sword, heart . . .*

         Alternations of [r] ~ Ø:
         soar[Ø] ~ *soa*[r]*ing* ~ *soa*[r] *in the sky*
         fear[Ø] ~ *fear*[Ø]*ful* ~ *fea*[r]*ing* ~ *fea*[r] *of flying*
         for[Ø] ~ *fo*[r] *Anna*
         star[Ø] ~ *sta*[r]*y*; *sugar*[Ø] ~ *suga*[r]*y*
         letter[Ø] ~ *put the lette*[r] *in here*
         Peter[Ø] ~ *Pete*[r] *isn't my favourite person*

This alternating, etymological [r], in derived intervocalic contexts either word-internally or across word-boundaries, is known as linking [r]. It is present in most non-rhotic accents, but rather infrequent in South Africa and the Southern States of the USA, a fact to which we shall return below. In the Southern USA, /r/ may also optionally be elided intervocalically, giving *Carolina* [kæˈlanə] and *very* [vɛ:ɪ].

A further development in non-rhotic accents other than those of the Southern USA and South Africa involves so-called intrusive [r]. This unetymological [r] appears intervocalically, again word-internally and across word-boundaries, in the same environments as linking [r] (see (6.2)).

(6.2)   Intrusive [r]:
         saw[Ø] ~ *saw*[r]*ing*; *withdraw*[Ø] ~ *withdraw*[r]*al*
         banana[Ø] ~ *banana*[r]*y*; *magenta*[Ø] ~ *magenta*[r]*ish*
         Kafka[Ø] ~ *Kafka*[r]*esque*; *Shaw*[Ø] ~ *Shaw*[r]*ism*
         law[Ø] ~ *law*[r] *and order*
         comma[Ø] ~ *put the comma*[r] *in there*
         idea[Ø] ~ *the idea*[r] *is*
         Anna[Ø] ~ *Anna*[r] *isn't my favourite person*

Let us turn now to the question of how these non-rhotic varieties arose, and how they are best accounted for in synchronic terms.

6.3   Non-rhotic /r/: an insertion analysis

6.3.1   An orthoepical interlude

It is generally assumed that non-rhotic accents of English became non-rhotic via three sound changes, which are traditionally listed separately and sequentially (Wells 1982): these are Pre-/r/ Breaking, Pre-Schwa Laxing/Shortening and /r/-Deletion, and are shown in (6.3). In brief, a schwa is inserted between any vowel and [r]; the pre-existing long vowels shorten and lax before this new schwa; and finally the [r] drops.

(6.3)   Pre-/r/ Breaking: Ø > /ə/ / /i: e: o: u: ai au/ __ /r/

[bi:r]	>	[bi:ər]	*beer*
[tʃe:r]	>	[tʃe:ər]	*chair*
[mo:r]	>	[mo:ər]	*more*
[ʃu:r]	>	[ʃu:ər]	*sure*
[fair]	>	[faiər]	*fire*
[taur]	>	[tauər]	*tower*

Pre-schwa Laxing/Shortening: /i: e: o: u:/ > [ɪ ɛ ɒ ʊ] / __ /ə/

[bi:ər]	>	[bɪər]	*beer*	
[tʃe:ər]	>	[tʃɛər]	*chair*	(> [tʃɛ:])
[mo:ər]	>	[mɒər]	*more*	(> [mɔ:])
[ʃu:ər]	>	[ʃʊər]	*sure*	(> [ʃɔ:])
[faiər]	>	[faɪər]	*fire*	(> [faɪə] or [fɑ:])
[tauər]	>	[tauər]	*tower*	(> [tauə] or [tɑ:])

r/-Deletion: r > Ø / __ {C, pause}

Wells (1982: 210ff.) assumes that these changes took place after about 1750, since their results can be observed in RP and other south-eastern English varieties; in the southern hemisphere extraterritorial Englishes of Australia, New Zealand and South Africa, where English was introduced after this period; and in the non-rhotic accents of the earliest North American settlements, but not in rhotic General American. Wells also notes that the relative chronology implied by (6.3) may not be appropriate: while Breaking must have preceded /r/-Deletion, Laxing could equally well have followed it. However, Wells's absolute chronology must also be cast into doubt, since there is evidence for at least Breaking from well before 1700, and precisely *because* the first American colonies are non-rhotic, and seem likely to have been at least partially so at the time of settlement. Breaking and /r/-Deletion were probably gradual changes which were under way, producing variants in the speech community, before 1700.

There is a considerable amount of orthoepical and other evidence to support this hypothesis. For instance, John Hart (1569) gives phonetic transcriptions of [feiër] 'fire', [meier] 'mire', [o'er] 'oar', [piuër] 'pure', [diër] 'dear' and [hier] 'here'; assuming that [ë] and [e] indicate something close to schwa, we can conclude that Breaking was at least an option by the late sixteenth century. Jespersen (1909: 318) notes parallel sixteenth century spellings like <fiery, fierie, fyeri> for earlier <fyry, firy>; and similar spellings like <shower> (< OE <scūr>), <tower> (< French <tour>) and <briar> (< ME <brere>) have been maintained, indicating that Pre-/r/ Breaking must have been well-established before the fixing of the modern spelling system. By the eighteenth century, evidence for Breaking is much more explicit and commonplace. For instance, Abraham Tucker (1773) provides a special symbol *v* and notes that 'it is commonly inserted between "ē, ī, ō, ū" and "r", as in "there, beer, fire, more, poor, pure, our," which we pronounce "thevr, bivr, fvivr, movr, puvr, vuvr"' (1773: 14). It is quite clear that Tucker's *v* is intended to correspond to schwa: he recognises the vowel as a ubiquitous casual speech marker, noting that 'there are none of the vowels but what are often changed into "*v*" in common talk' (1773: 15); and he also identifies it with the schwa used in hesitations, observing that 'we can draw it out to a great length upon particular occasions, as when the watchman calls "past ten *v-v-v* clock," or when a man hesitates till he hits upon some hard name, as "This account was sent by Mr. *v-v-v* Schlotzikoff, a Russian"' (Tucker 1773: 14). Tucker's observation that 'This short "*v*" is easiest pronounced of all the vowels ... and therefore is a great favourite with my country men, who tho not lazy are very averse to trouble, wishing to do as much work with as little pains as possible' (ibid.), also seems highly appropriate for schwa.

While the long high and mid monophthongs were developing into centring diphthongs before /r/, low /ɑ ɔ/ seem to have lengthened in the same context. The earliest evidence for this lengthening is probably from Cooper (1687), who observes that *a* is short before word-final /r/, as in *bar, car, tar*, but long before /rC/, as in *barge, carp, tart*, while *o* is long before certain specific final clusters including /rn/ *horn* and /rt/ *retort*. This lengthening seems subsequently to have spread, as evidenced by Mather Flint (Kökeritz 1944). James Mather Flint is a fascinating character; born in the early years of the eighteenth century and brought up by his uncle in Newcastle, he spent most of his life in Paris after his fanatically Jacobite family fled to France in 1717. Mather Flint became a

Catholic priest, but also published (in 1740) a guide to English pronunciation for French speakers, in which he observes that /r/ 'rend un peu longue la voyelle qui le précède' (Kökeritz 1944: 41), giving examples like *barb, guard, arm, yarn.* Similarly, *o* is said to lengthen before *rd, rk, rm, rn* (Kökeritz 1944: 20). Mather Flint also notes the difference between words like *name* and those like *care, chair, bear,* where he observes that the vowel is 'un peu ouvert' on account of the following /r/, thus providing an early description of modern [eɪ] versus the centring diphthong [ɛə]. The three pronouncing dictionaries from the 1760s and 1770s surveyed by Beal (1993) reveal that long [ɑː] was primarily found before /rC/ clusters, but might also appear before final /r/ in certain lexical items, such as *far, mar* and *tar.* Finally, Walker (1791) indicates that /ɑ ɔ/ are categorically long before final /r/, pointing out in connection with *a* that 'we seldom find the long sound of this letter in our language, except in monosyllables ending with r̠, as fa̠r, ta̠r, ma̠r, &c. and in the word fa̠ther' (1791: 10). More generally, Walker notes that when *a* and *o* 'come before double r̠, or single r̠, followed by a vowel, as in ar̠able, ca̠rry, ma̠rry, or̠ator, ho̠rrid, fo̠rage, &c. they are considerably shorter than when the r̠ is the final letter of the word, or when it is succeeded by another consonant, as in ar̠bour, ca̠r, ma̠r, o̠r, no̠r, fo̠r' (Walker 1791: 15). Walker equates this variant of *o*, 'the long sound produced by r̠ final, or followed by another consonant, as fo̠r – fo̠rmer' (1791: 22) with the vowel written <au>, as in *laud.*

The merger of earlier /ɪr/, /ʌr/ and /ɛr/ as /ɜːr/ in *bird, word, herd* words also seems to have been under way by the eighteenth century; indeed, Jespersen (1909: 319) argues that /ɪr/ and /ʌr/ had begun to coalesce by around 1600. Mather Flint (Kökeritz 1944: 72) again provides relevant evidence, including *fir* and *fur* in a list of pairs of words which sound identical but are spelt differently, and noting (Kökeritz 1944: 70) that the same vowel appears in *herd, search, dirge, girl, earn, learn, disperse, rehearse, earth* and *birth.* Although he does not explicitly discuss the quality of this vowel, he observes that the *earn, learn* vowel is long: this presumably generalises to the other words in the class, and indicates that the merged reflex of Middle English /ɪr ʌr ɛr/ had lengthened by the mid-eighteenth century. Sheridan (1786: 28–9) also reports this merger as ongoing: he blames the actor-manager Garrick, 'who, according to the Staffordshire custom, ... called gird gurd, birth burth, firm furm. Nay he did the same when the vowel e̠ preceded the r̠, heard was hurd, earth urth, interr'd inturr'd, &c.' Sheridan notes with disapproval that 'His example was followed by many of his imitators on the stage' (1786: 29). Finally, discussing i̱, Walker (1791: 15) notes that:

> The letter ṟ ... seems to have the same influence on this vowel, as it evidently had on a̱ and o̱ ... the i̱, coming before either double ṟ, or single ṟ, followed by a vowel, preserves its pure, short sound, as in irritate, conspiracy, &c. but when ṟ is followed by another consonant, or is a final letter of a word with the accent upon it, the i̱ goes into a deeper and broader sound .... So fiṟ, a tree, is perfectly similar to the first syllable of ferment, though often corruptly pronounced like fuṟ, a skin. Siṟ and stiṟ are exactly pronounced as if written suṟ and stuṟ.

This merger, along with the processes of lengthening, Pre-/r/ Breaking and Pre-Schwa Laxing, produced a restricted inventory of vowels before /r/; distributional restrictions of this sort are found in rhotic varieties, as witness the General American homophony of *Mary, merry, marry,* but are typically more extensive in non-rhotic dialects. The particular inventory of vowels preceding historical /r/ in RP and similar southern British English varieties is shown in (6.4); other dialects will be discussed briefly in 6.5 below. As (6.4) shows, historical /r/ in the ancestor of RP, following the vowel changes outlined above, came to stand after only five vowels: these are long low [ɑː ɔː]; [ɛː], when optionally smoothed from [ɛə]; [ɜː], which we might regard as long schwa; and schwa itself, which may be the offglide of a centring diphthong. Further smoothing of [ʊə], [ɔə], [aɪə] and [aʊə], which is variable but spreading in all but the most conservative current RP, does not increase this inventory.

(6.4)	[ɔː]	*oar, floor, for, lore, shore ...*
	[ɑː]	*star, bazaar, far ...*
	[ɪə]	*beer, fear, near, here ...*
	[ɛə] ~ [ɛː]	*care, there, air, square ...*
	[ʊə] ~ [ɔː]	*assure, pure, cure, gourd ...*
	[ɔə] ~ [ɔː]	*more, lore, four, force ...*
	[ɜː]	*stir, fir, fur, word, err, heard ...*
	[aɪə] ~ [ɑː]	*choir, fire ...*
	[aʊə] ~ [ɑː]	*flower, tower ...*
	[ə]	*letter, better, father, sugar, figure ...*

If Pre-/r/ Breaking were indeed under way in the late sixteenth century, /r/-Deletion could have been in progress from the same period, accounting for the non-rhotic nature of the first, eastern American colonies. In fact, /r/-Deletion is arguably a misnomer: the [r] seems to have undergone a gradual, dialectally variable weakening change, which resulted in eventual loss in non-onset positions. Indeed, Lass (1993) argues that /r/-loss was implemented over around 500 years, and was manifested in two phases. The earliest was sporadic and restricted to particular lexical items, such as *bass* 'fish' < OE <bærs>, ME <bars>, and *worsted* from <Worthstead>, which is recorded as <wosted> in 1450; in <worsted>, an etymological spelling has been reintroduced. We find occasional rhymes and spellings indicating this item-specific loss from the fifteenth to the seventeenth centuries: thus, the fifteenth century Cely Papers have <monyng> 'morning', <passel> 'parcel' and the inverse spelling <marster> 'master', while in 1642, Lady Sussex writes <passons> 'persons' (Lass 1993). Seventeenth century loans also indicate some loss of [r]: Spanish *salva* is borrowed as <salver>, but Dutch *genever* 'gin' as <geneva>.

However, we are more concerned with the second phase of /r/-Deletion, a general weakening and loss of [r] in non-onset positions. Jespersen (1909: 318) argues that Old English and Middle English /r/ was probably a trill in all positions: this seems to have weakened to a tap, then an approximant, and is finally subject to conditioned loss in non-rhotic varieties. The tap remains intervocalically, and occasionally initially, for many Scots and Irish speakers; but approximants are fairly consistent finally and pre-consonantally. As we have seen, the weakened approximant reflex is similarly retained intervocalically and initially in non-rhotic accents, while the zero alternant has been innovated before consonants and pauses. In other words, across all varieties of English, weaker realisations of historical /r/ are found in coda positions (the translation of the C/pause disjunct from (6.3) in syllabic terms), while stronger reflexes are maintained in onsets. Since pre-consonantal and pre-pausal positions have been shown to be prime lenition sites cross-linguistically, and specifically in other studies of consonantal weakening in English (Leslie 1989, Harris and Kaye 1990, Harris 1994, Tollfree 1995), this distribution is exactly what we would expect.

Again, orthoepical evidence suggests that weakening of /r/ can be traced back to the mid-seventeenth century, given Ben Jonson's (1640: 47) comment that 'R ... is sounded firme in the beginning of the words, and more <u>liquid</u> in the middle, and ends.' The actual loss of /r/, like pre-/r/ vowel lengthening, seems to have begun pre-consonantally, and spread to word-final position in cases where no vowel-initial word or suffix follows to sanction resyllabification of /r/ into an onset. Harris (1994: ch.5) claims that Walker (1791) provides the first evidence of loss, with his observation that London /r/ 'is sometimes entirely sunk' (1791: 50). However, a range of earlier and more specific observations can also be found. Viëtor (1904) claims that Theodor Arnold in 1718 is the first to note /r/ loss, giving examples of pre-consonantal contexts such as *mart*, *parlour* and *scarce* in which /r/ is 'mute'. Similarly, Jespersen (1909: 360) cites König, who in 1748 diagnosed mute /r/ in *horse, parlour, partridge* and *thirsty*, among others. As we have seen, Mather Flint in 1740 testifies to vowel lengthening before /r/; but he also tells his French readers that 'dans plusieurs mots, l'*r* devant une consonne est fort adouci, presque muet' (Kökeritz 1944: 41). In fact, he italicises *r* before consonants, explaining that 'vous verrez souvent aussi l'*r* en Italique, les Anglois l'adoucissant beaucoup plus que les François & ne le prononçant que très foiblement, sur tout lorsqu'il est suivi d'une autre consonne' (Kökeritz 1944: 3).

Mather Flint italicises final *r* only very sporadically: this may indicate that /r/ had not yet been lost in this position, although we can probably conclude that it was already very weak. On the other hand, the presence of a final schwa offglide or extra vowel length alone, or the variable retention of [r] prevocalically, may have interfered, so that Mather Flint may be transcribing a final /r/ which is only variably pronounced. The same goes for Tucker (1773), who, as we have seen, describes Pre-/r/ Breaking, using the special symbol *v* for schwa. Tucker (1773: 35) claims that *v* is easy to pronounce and consequently ubiquitous, but that the same cannot be said for /r/: 'Upon rendering the end of the tongue limber, so that it will shake like a rag with the bellows, it will rattle out "r", but this requiring a strong stream of breath to perform, makes it the most laborious letter of all, and consequently as much out of our good graces as I said "*v*" was in them.'

Tucker goes on to report that 'you shall find people drop the "r" in "fuz, patial, savants, wost … backwad," and many other words, and whenever retained we speak it so gently that you scarce hear a single reverberation of the tongue' (1773: 35–6). Again, the fact that the example words all have preconsonantal /r/, and Tucker's representation of *there* as 'the*v*r', might indicate that [r] had not been lost word-finally at this period. Alternatively, Tucker may have used 'the*v*r' to indicate that [r] was variably pronounced (whether contextually, when a vowel followed, or depending on speech rate or other sociolinguistic factors).

Sheridan's assertion that 'R … has always the same sound, and is never silent' (1781: 34), along with Walker's (1791: 50) similar claim that

/r/ 'is never silent', may initially seem to constitute counter-evidence; Walker's statement in particular seems inconsistent with his description, on the same page, of London /r/ as 'sometimes entirely sunk'. However, we must recall the tendency towards prescriptivism in many grammarians of the time, which means that ongoing changes are often denied, and supposedly 'ideal', archaic pronunciations encouraged. In the Preface to his Dictionary (1780: 4), Sheridan admits that the spelling and pronunciation he records 'scarce deviates from that used ... in Queen Anne's reign' (1702–14); he therefore seems unreliable as a reporter of actual contemporary usage, and indeed, his assertion that /r/ never deletes may tell us quite the opposite. Similarly, Kökeritz, in his commentary on Mather Flint's work (Kökeritz 1944: 155), interprets Walker's statement as indicating that 'in the contemporary London dialect r̲ had been silent for a long time, although elocutionists probably endeavoured to pronounce it'. Indeed, Walker himself seems to acknowledge the extreme weakness or loss of final and preconsonantal /r/ by suggesting that speakers aiming at 'polite' usage may produce initial [r] in *Rome*, *river*, *rage* as forcibly as they wish 'without producing any harshness to the ear'; 'but b̲a̲r̲, b̲a̲r̲d̲, c̲a̲r̲d̲, h̲a̲r̲d̲ &c. must have it nearly as soft as in London' (1791: 50). For Walker to recommend such a pronunciation, it must have been socially acceptable and therefore well established in the (developing) standard.

It seems, then, that /r/ in coda positions was weakening by the seventeenth century; this weakening went substantially further in some dialects than in others, and [r] dropped, having first conditioned certain diphthongisations, lengthenings and mergers in preceding vowels, from the eighteenth century onwards. The loss of [r] seems to have begun preconsonantally, and proceeded to word-final position, and Lass (1993) assumes it was again a gradual process, being completed during the nineteenth century. In some present-day varieties, this historical development has in a sense been arrested part-way, since in certain parts of Yorkshire and Lincolnshire (Wells 1982), /r/ has been lost medially when preconsonantal, but not finally. /r/-Deletion also increased the phonemic vowel inventory in non-rhotic dialects by removing the conditioning context for the centring diphthongs. These began as contextually determined allophones of /i: e: u: o:/, but became contrastive, although still defective in distribution, after the loss of postvocalic /r/. In 6.5, we shall return to these historical developments, and argue that they need not be seen as individual changes, but can instead be modelled as an integrated complex. For the moment, however, let us turn to the present-day non-rhotic varieties they have created.

6.3.2   Rule inversion and [r]-Insertion

Rhotic varieties of English, of course, preserve the historical situation before /r/-Deletion and most or all of the associated vowel changes. The next closest to this historical period would be an accent which maintained /r/-Deletion as a synchronic phonological rule. Such varieties are rare. For instance, some accents of the Southern USA (Harris 1994) have neither linking nor intrusive [r], so that no [r] is pronounced in *soaring*, *soar in, sawing* or *saw in*; they also lack [r] in forms with historical clusters like *beard, harp*. But in such cases, [r]-Deletion is not a synchronic process: the absence of [r] has simply led subsequent generations of speakers to set up underlying forms lacking /r/, except word-initially in *red, bright*. In certain Southern US accents (Wells 1982), [r]-Deletion has also operated intervocalically, giving forms like [vɛɪ] 'very'. If such pronunciations occur categorically for a speaker or group, we might propose /r/-less underliers here, too; if they are optional, we might suggest underlying /r/ and an intervocalic deletion rule controlled by formality or speed of speech. Alternatively, we might assume no underlying /r/, and spelling pronunciations in formal styles (as discussed below for RP). However, other speakers of Southern US English (Kenyon and Knott 1953, Wells 1982, Lass 1987) do have linking [r], but not intrusive [r]. In these cases, although there can be no justification for proposing underlying /r/ in non-alternating forms like *beard, harp*, we might argue for /r/ in *soar, letter, spar* (but not *saw, comma, spa*), with a synchronic analogue of /r/-Deletion pre-pausally and pre-consonantally. This might seem to be at odds with my usual mechanism for determining underlying representations, since /r/ will appear underlyingly in underived *soar, letter*, where it will not surface: however, an argument can be made for this on the grounds of partial surface merger outlined for Scots /ʌi/ versus /ai/ in chapter 4, since there are parallel morphemes like *saw, comma* which do not attract [r] in any circumstances, and the most appropriate underlying distinction would then be /r/ in the *soar* class versus final vowel in *saw*. A similar analysis might be fitting for those speakers of South African English (Wells 1982, Lass 1987), who have linking without intrusive [r]; most, however, seem to replace both with a glottal stop. This might best be accounted for by assuming underlying /r/ only in *red* and *bright* words. In *soar, saw, letter, comma, spar* and *spa*, there would be no underlying /r/; resulting vowel hiatuses would be broken by [ʔ], with occasional linking [r] reflecting orthographic influence, and again there would be no synchronic /r/-Deletion. We return below to the interaction of /r/ with other synchronic hiatus-breakers.

The great majority of non-rhotic varieties of English, however, have both linking and intrusive [r]. I assume that such varieties arose historically by way of rule inversion (Vennemann 1972) of the earlier /r/-Deletion change, producing a synchronic rule of [r]-Insertion. This hypothesis is by no means new (Johansson 1973, Pullum 1974, Wells 1982), but it has fallen rather into disrepute lately, as many recent discussions of /r/ have adopted alternative solutions. I shall survey some of these in 6.4, but first outline the inversion hypothesis briefly.

Recall that [r] had dropped finally and pre-consonantally, for some speakers at least, by the mid to late eighteenth century. These speakers would still have underlying /r/ in *red, bright, very, harp, soar* and, *beer* words, but would delete it in the appropriate environments in the last three, producing linking [r] alternations in words like *soar, beer*. I assume that succeeding generations of speakers would fail to learn underlying /r/ except word-initially and intervocalically, in *red, bright, very* words; linking [r] would then be derived by a synchronic rule of [r]-Insertion, as informally shown in (6.5).

(6.5)   [r]-Insertion: $\emptyset \rightarrow [r] \ / \ /ɑ: \ ɔ: \ ə/ \ \_\_ \ V$

We shall return to the formulation of [r]-Insertion, and the question of whether it is an exact complementary or inverse of /r/-Deletion, in 6.5 below. However, it is important to note here that rule inversion is a phonologist's construct: the two rules under discussion are independent, although diachronically related. In other words, a deletion rule is proposed for the earlier stage, and an insertion rule for the present-day situation, because in each case this represents the best analysis of the varieties involved. The relationship between the two is parallel to that obtaining between the historical Great Vowel Shift and the synchronic Vowel Shift Rule, as discussed in chapter 3 (although in that case rule inversion was not involved): the processes are independently postulated on evidence from the relevant periods, but given a broad diachronic perspective, the present-day rule is the descendant of the earlier one.

Rule inversion in this case reflects problems of learnability, and the reasonable expectation of speakers that forms which sound the same should behave the same. After [r]-Deletion, speakers would be unable to distinguish *spar* from *spa*, or *soar* from *saw*, or to tell which was the form which should appear with [r] in intervocalic contexts. It is hardly surprising that they should regularise their system, by introducing [r] intervocalically, regardless of whether the underlying form in question was [r]-final or vowel-final. Since this in turn would lead to surface convergence of underlyingly distinct forms, we would expect a further regularisation at the underlying level, with final /r/ lost altogether (in line, incidentally, with the assumptions of my model of Lexical Phonology on the formation of underlying representations), and [r] supplied between schwa or a long low vowel, and any following vowel. This leads automatically to the innovation of [r]-Insertion, and to intrusive [r].

Intrusive [r], like linking [r], appears both word-internally (*banana*[r]*y*, *withdraw*[r]*al*) and across word boundaries (*law*[r] *and order*, *India*[r] *and Africa*). For many speakers, it is extraordinarily productive, operating in foreign words, acronyms, and when speaking (or singing, in the case of Latin) foreign languages: some examples are given in (6.6) (and see Jespersen 1909).

(6.6) Intrusive [r] in foreign words:
      the social milieu [miːljɜːr] *of Alexander Pope*
      the junta [xʊntər] *in Chile*
      the Stella Artois event [stɛləɹɑːtwɑːɹəvɛnt]

      Acronyms:
      as far as BUPA[r] *is concerned*

      English speakers' pronunciations of foreign languages:
      German: *ich habe*[r] *einen Hund*
      Latin: *hosanna*[r] *in excelsis,*
             dona[r] *eis requiem*
(data partly from Wells 1982: 226)

Intrusive [r] is clearly contextually restricted, in that it appears only after /ɑː ɔː ə/: however, when any other vowel is reduced to schwa, it does attract intrusive [r]; data from a number of non-rhotic varieties appear in (6.7).

(6.7) Intrusive [r] and vowel reduction:
            tomato[ər] *and cucumber production*
            the window[ər] *isn't clean*
      Cockney: *I'll tell you how* [jəræː]
               to it [tərɪʔ]
      Norwich: *run over by a* [bərə] *bus*
               out to[ər] *eat, quarter to*[ər] *eight*
(data partly from Wells 1982, Trudgill 1974)

[r] also interacts productively with other phonological processes and with other hiatus breakers. We have already considered its complementarity with [ʔ] in South African English; the contexts of insertion for [r] are also precisely those not available for [j], which appears after high- and mid-front vowels, and [w], the preferred hiatus breaker after high- and mid-back vowels. An example of such interaction is given in (6.8). In *potato and*, a speaker with a final long-mid monophthong in *potato* will introduce [w], but reduction to schwa will trigger [r]-insertion. In *potato hot*, [h] may be pronounced, and if so no hiatus arises; but if it is elided, then either [w] or [r] will again be introduced, depending on the quality of the preceding vowel.

(6.8)   Interaction of [r]-Insertion with glide-formation and /h/-dropping:
          potato and onion: *potat*[owən] or *potat*[ərən]
          Is the potato hot?   *potat*[ohɒt], or *potat*[owɒt], or *potat*[ərɒt]

These connections of /r w j h/ in Modern English are especially interesting given Lutz's (1994) suggestion that these relatively weak consonants have all undergone parallel weakening during the history of English, both positionally and structurally. Whereas in Old English they could appear in onset or coda position, they have undergone gradual attrition in codas, vocalising and fusing in various ways with preceding vowels. One might add that /l/, the other English liquid, is undergoing vocalisation in various English dialects (Tollfree 1995, Harris 1994); there is also an intrusive [l], reported in Bristol forms like *America*[l], *Anna*[l] (and historically, the name *Bristol* itself) – hence the old joke about the Bristollian with three daughters called Idle, Evil and Normal. Intrusive [l] is also fairly productive in some American English varieties, including South Central Pennsylvania, Newark and Delaware (Gick 1997), where earlier patterns of word-final vocalisation with intervocalic linking [l] have been reanalysed for some speakers as productive [l]-intrusion in overlapping but not identical environments to those triggering [r]-Insertion elsewhere: thus, we find *draw*[l]*ing*, *Sau*[l] *is*, *saw*[l] *is*, *Ha*[l] *is*, *how*[l] *is*.

Despite the general productivity of [r]-insertion, some speakers of, for instance, RP (Gimson 1980, Wells 1982) seem to suspend it, particularly word-internally. This suspension depends in part on the phonological context, since linking and intrusive [r] are disfavoured by another [r] in the immediate environment, as in *the emperor of Japan*, *a roar of laughter* (Jones 1956: 197, Wells 1982). Johansson (1973) and Pullum (1974) argue that this is best analysed as a restriction on the [r]-epenthesis rule, whereby [r] fails to appear in dissimilatory contexts; /r/s, and indeed liquids in general, are very commonly involved in dissimilation. However, the suspension of intrusive [r] in particular appears to depend primarily on the sociolinguistic context, and particularly on formality. Most straightforwardly, we might assume that [r]-Insertion can be blocked by reference to the spelling: an RP speaker saying *withdrawal* may be, or become aware that there is no orthographic <r> and therefore not supply phonetic [r]. This hypothesis is consistent with the fact that suspension of intrusive [r] seems most common in more formal speech, where spelling consciousness may be greater. It is also in accord with recent work by Giegerich (1992, in press), who argues on the basis of alternations between schwa and full vowels that spelling may inform or even drive phonological rule applications. Orthographic <r> is certainly used differently by non-rhotic and rhotic speakers: for rhotic speakers, it means essentially 'say [r] here', whereas for non-rhotic speakers it can signal a property of the preceding vowel, and can therefore be used for disambiguation, as in (6.9).

(6.9) 'This cook, too, couldn't pronounce the word. It's not pah-eller; it's pie-ey-yar.'
(Michael Bateman, *The Independent on Sunday Review*, 6/9/92)

Conversely, the spelling of historical vowel plus [r] sequences is breaking down in some respects for non-rhotic speakers. We find variant spellings, like <caterwaul> versus <cat-a-waul>, and confusion as to whether [pælɑːvə] should be spelled with final <er>, <a> (like *pavlova*) or <ah> (like *howdah*) (6.10). If speakers are suspending [r]-Insertion by referring to the orthography, no wonder they are only partially successful.

(6.10) *palaver ~ palava ~ palavah*
'Midnight cats cat-a-wauling'
(Shirley Hughes (1997) *The Nursery Collection*; Walker: 55)

Additionally, we might account for variable lack of intrusive [r] with reference to adaptive rules (Andersen 1973, Disterheft 1990), which were also discussed briefly in connection with inter-dialectal communication in 5.3 above. Disterheft is particularly concerned with the question of how linguistic change can take place without prejudicing inter-generational communication, and concludes that the mechanism responsible involves adaptive rules, 'ad hoc rules used by learners to disguise output which, because of improper rule formulation, does not match that of their models. They adapt forms/structures to correspond to what community norms dictate' (1990: 182). These rules smooth the transition between generations, so that even catastrophic changes do not jeopardise communication. They do not stop or reverse a change, but temporarily obscure the effects of some abductive innovation: in other words (Disterheft 1990: 184), adaptive rules are the diachronic correlate of accommodation. In the speech community, the adaptive rules will gradually become optional, used only in formal situations or when talking to older people; and ultimately, they are lost as the novel form becomes the norm. In addition, speakers with the change and the adaptive rule in their grammars are assumed to correct children producing the innovatory forms less frequently. All this means that the change will become apparent only very gradually.

Let us apply this hypothesis to the case of [r]. At the point when younger speakers were innovating [r]-Insertion, older speakers with the deletion rule would still be producing linking but not intrusive [r]. Younger speakers with intrusion might be corrected, and respond by setting up an adaptive rule, so that intrusive [r], although the result of a new rule, and subsequent rule inversion and change at the underlying level, would seem to creep very gradually into the language. Intrusive [r] has been stigmatised from its earliest stages (see Mugglestone 1995): Hullah (1870: 53–4) considers it 'a characteristic of cockney breeding, as *Maidarill* (for Maida Hill – not unpardonable in an omnibus conductor), and *Victoriarour Queen* – quite unpardonable in an educated gentleman'. It is still generally frowned upon by present-day Standard British English speakers at least, and modern RP speakers might therefore still use some sort of adaptive rule, in formal situations or with older interlocutors. This seems even more likely given Campbell and Ringen's (1981) hypothesis that sound changes or phonological processes may be suspended as part of assimilation to a prestige model, and that this tendency may also be spelling-based. Note, however, that being sensitive to public opinion about a particular feature, and indeed disapproving of it oneself, does not guard against producing it, as Sweet's quotation in (6.11) makes admirably clear.

(6.11)   I have for some years been in search of a 'correct speaker'. It is very like going after the great sea-serpent … I am inclined to the conclusion that the animal known as a 'correct speaker' is not only extraordinarily shy and difficult of capture, but that he may be put in the same category as the 'rigid moralist' and 'every schoolboy' – that he is an abstraction, a figment of the brain (Sweet 1881: 5–6)

6.4 Alternative analyses

The alternative to [r]-insertion is, logically, some form of deletion. Although the analyses I consider here do not typically interpret this deletion as the direct loss of a segment, they are unified in considering the underlying forms of *soar*, *spar* and *letter*, as well as *saw*, *spa* and *comma*, as having final /r/, in whatever shape their model assumes it to take. I will briefly outline four such analyses below, from declarative phonology (Scobbie 1992), natural phonology (Donegan 1993), Government Phonology (Harris 1994) and a constraint-based lexicalist model (McCarthy 1991). There is an account of English /r/ within Optimality Theory (McCarthy 1993), which I do not include here because it overlaps significantly with McCarthy (1991); the latter, however, considers a wider and more interesting set of data; and the novel aspects, involving OT itself, have been criticised elsewhere already (Blevins 1997, Halle and Idsardi 1997, McMahon 1998a, b). Some of the problems which arise in these analyses are common to all, and I shall raise these at the end of 6.4.1.

6.4.1 *Scobbie (1992), Donegan (1993)*

Scobbie (1992) claims that forms with intrusive [r] have been assimilated over time from an /r/-less to an /r/-ful class. That is, the underlying representations for *idea*, *saw*, *baa* and *Canada* are now /aɪdiər/, /sɔːr/, /baːr/ and /kænədər/ for speakers with both linking and intrusive [r], while etymological /r/ remains in *clear*, *soar*, *spar*, *letter*. Speakers then select a 'weak (less occlusive, strident, consonantal or long) phonetic interpretation of coda /r/' (1992: 9).

Similarly, Donegan assumes that 'r in a syllable-fall (before consonant or pause) loses its r-colouring, becoming ə' (1993: 117). Because this lenition is exceptionless in non-rhotic varieties, speakers hearing final schwa (or /ɑː ɔː/) will 'undo' the weakening to arrive at underlying final /r/. However, they may also, inappropriately, hypothesise lenition in *comma*, *spa*, *saw* words, and therefore assume underlying /r/ here, too. In Donegan's opinion, 'The "intrusive r" does not, then, intrude because the speaker makes up an r-insertion rule. Instead, the r appears by analysis, when speakers assume that, because some final schwas represent /r/'s, other final schwas do so as well' (1993: 119). That is, the change is purely perceptual: 'speakers with intrusive r's perceive final [ə]'s as /r/'s ... Speakers without intrusive r's can perceive final schwas as /ə/'s (or they can ignore them)' (ibid.).

Both Scobbie and Donegan assume that intrusive [r]s arise from underlying /r/s innovated either by analogical extension, or by perceptual recategorisation. In Present-Day English, /r/ is then weakened in codas. Invoking weakening rather than deletion is in itself problematic, since /r/ cannot be assumed to become schwa in every instance: many speakers lack a schwa offglide after /ɑː ɔː/, while both schwa and [r] surface in linking and intrusive contexts in *the idea is*, or *farther away*: [r] and [ə] are clearly not in complementary distribution. Donegan's perceptual interpretation raises further questions. Since Donegan assumes that linking [r] preceded intrusion historically, it seems reasonable to claim that speakers might learn underlying /r/ in alternating *letter*, where [r] would surface only prevocalically. However, we must then accept that subsequent generations could acquire underlying /r/ in *comma*, by perceptual reanalysis of the final [ə], despite its lack of alternation and hence of surface [r]. That is, the deletion accounts assume acquisition of underlying /r/ in non-alternating forms, which thereby become alternating. In such a phonology, it seems hard to see how we are to rule out underlying /r/, which would then delete categorically, in final clusters like *harp*, *beard*. Donegan's account of the diachronic development of the non-rhotic system also seems incomplete: she argues that some speakers perceive [ə] as /r/, while others perceive it as /ə/ (or, indeed, ignore it). However, there is no insight into why this discrepancy should arise; and surely, if we are to ascribe present-day features to historical developments, we should make some attempt to understand the history.

However, there are also more general difficulties, which are shared by Harris (1994) and McCarthy (1991). All these accounts assume a piecemeal, analogical extension of underlying /r/ to words with final /ɑː ɔː ə/. Of course, this is highly likely to represent the starting point of the generalisation of [r], and is consistent with my hypothesis of subsequent rule inversion; but that rule inversion, or some parallel regularising force, is necessary to account for the great regularity and productivity of linking and intrusion for many non-rhotic speakers now. The underlying /r/ analyses put intrusive [r] for non-rhotic speakers on a par with the fact that some rhotic speakers, Scots for instance, happen to have categorical [aɪdɪər] for *idea*, or with West Country hyperrhoticity (Wells 1982), where rhotic speakers again may pronounce [r] medially in *kha*[r]*ki*, or finally in *comma*[r], *Anna*[r], regardless of the following context. But this is truly a sporadic, speaker-specific phenomenon, affecting individual lexical items or lexical sets; in all probability, it simply reflects the exposure of British rhotic speakers to quantities of non-rhotic speech, for instance via the spoken media. When rhotic speakers hear [r], they are likely to assume underlying and hence categorically pronounced /r/, and some confusion is inevitable. Intrusive and linking [r] for non-rhotic speakers do not share these characteristics: even when intrusion is suspended, the deciding factors seem to be socio-linguistic rather than lexical.

It is true that a change which proceeded analogically might conceivably result in a regular system; but analogy usually leaves tell-tale gaps. Even more damaging, however, is the question of where intrusive [r] does appear, rather than where it does not. Underliers like /rɔ:r/ 'raw', /kæfkər/ 'Kafka', /ʃɑ:r/ 'Shah' may simply be unfamiliar, but others are downright improbable. We would have to assume, for instance, that a speaker hearing *Stella Artois*, or *BUPA*, or *dona* (in Latin *dona eis requiem*), or even seeing them on the printed page, would immediately set up underlying forms with final /r/. Any phonologist wishing to derive past tense forms of strong verbs from present tense bases would also have to posit /r/ in the underlying representation of *see*, because of intrusive [r] in *saw*[r]*it* (Johansson 1973). In this case, we would have to assume that there was no underlying /r/ historically, because of the absence of a centring diphthong in *see* (as opposed to *seer*), but that /r/ was innovated here, in an entirely inappropriate phonological context, in order to allow [r] to surface prevocalically in the past tense form. Forms with optional reduction, like *tomato, potato*, raise parallel problems: presumably, these would require alternative lexical entries with either a final rounded vowel, or final schwa plus /r/, rather than two productive and interacting processes of vowel reduction and [r]-insertion. Children's errors, like [əˈræpl] 'an apple' (Johansson 1973: 61), *the*[r] *animals*, *a*[r]*aeroplane* (Foulkes 1997: 76) can also be explained most easily given an insertion rule: the child may not yet have learned the prevocalic allomorph of the indefinite article, and the schwa-final article creates a hiatus which provides an appropriate context for [r]. In a deletion account, we must assume that the child has set up an allomorph of the article with final /r/: since such forms are reasonably frequent for children, but exceptionally rare for adults, why does this allomorph not persist? Finally, slower speech seems to produce fewer [r]s; insertion rules are typically constrained by pauses, presumably in this case because the hiatus is less likely to be perceived under these conditions. However, a deletion or weakening rule would have to operate more frequently in slower speech, contradicting the normal association of deletion with fast and casual registers. These shared problems should be borne in mind as we turn to two further analyses assuming underlying /r/ in unetymological contexts.

6.4.2   McCarthy (1991)

McCarthy argues that Eastern Massachusetts linking and intrusive [r], which appear intervocalically, following /ɑː ɔː ə/, are unanalysable in a model assuming only deletion or insertion. Instead, McCarthy claims that non-rhotic dialects of English are characterised by the non-directional statement r ~ Ø, which states that [r] alternates with zero. The contexts in which each term appears will be determined by various constraints in the phonology.

First, McCarthy cites Level 1 alternations such as those in (6.12), where some derived forms surface with [r], and others without.

(6.12)   Homer [Ø] ~ Home[r]ic   danger [Ø] ~ dange[r]ous
            doctor [Ø] ~ docto[r]al
    BUT   algebra ~ algebraic   aroma ~ aromatic
            idea ~ ideal

McCarthy proposes distinct underlying forms, such as /howmər/ versus /æveldʒəbrə/ to account for the surface patterns. /r/-Deletion then removes /r/ preconsonantally or prepausally in *Homer*, while [r]-Insertion adds [r] in *algebra* before a vowel-initial word, as in *Algebra*[r] *is my favourite subject*. There is an implied ordering argument here, such that insertion and deletion both operate postlexically, or at least after Level 1. Working on this assumption, we cannot assume either deletion or insertion in both sets of forms, given the presence of [r] in *Homeric* but its absence from *algebraic*.

Secondly, McCarthy argues that the behaviour of schwa provides evidence for underlying /r/ in certain forms but not others. McCarthy contends that *fire, pare, fear, sure, four, flour* cannot have underlying final centring diphthongs or triphthongs, because, in Eastern Massachusetts, the schwa frequently deletes when a vowel-initial suffix or word follows: thus *fear of, paring, firing* are typically, in McCarthy's transcription, [fiyrəv], [peyrɪŋ], [fɑyrɪŋ], although 'a trisyllabic pronunciation of words like *firing* is possible in more monitored speech' (1991: 8). This variable loss of schwa would not in itself present a problem; the difficulty arises because, in a parallel set of words like *power, layer, rumba, Nashua, Maria*, the final schwa is consistently preserved prevocalically, in contexts like *powering* [pɑwərɪŋ], *layer of* [leyərəv], *Maria is* [məriyərɪz]. To deal with the discrepancies between these two sets of forms, McCarthy argues that we must assume underlying /r/ in cases where schwa need not surface, giving /fiyr/ *fear*, /fayr/ *fire*; these undergo schwa-epenthesis if /r/ deletes, and presumably also optionally in more formal speech styles, in contexts like *fearing, fire it*, thus making the centring diphthongs derived segments. On the other hand, *power, layer, Maria* and so on, where schwa is allegedly always present, must have final underlying schwa and [r]-Insertion prevocalically.

McCarthy's third piece of evidence for the necessity of both insertion and deletion involves function words. He claims that, although linking [r] appears regularly after *for, our, they're, their, are, were, neither* and so on, intrusive [r] exceptionally fails to surface intervocalically after reduced forms like *shoulda, coulda, gonna, gotta, wanna*; after *did you, should you*, as in *Did you answer him?*; after low-stress *to, by, so*, as in *Quick to add to any problem*; after *do*, as in *Why do Albert and you ... ?*; or after the definite article, as in *the apples*. McCarthy therefore claims that underlying /r/ must be present in those function words with orthographic <r>, where it will be deleted in codas; however, function words lacking orthographic <r> have no final /r/.

McCarthy further argues (1991: 11) that rule inversion 'does not characterize any real mechanism of historical change', on the grounds that the resulting synchronic rule is almost always morphologised: this would not be the case for [r]-Insertion, but if /r/-Deletion is maintained synchronically, as McCarthy claims it is for Eastern Massachusetts in the shape of the non-directional statement of alternation r ~ Ø, there can have been no inversion. The distribution of [r] and zero is determined by the two well-formedness conditions in (6.13).

(6.13) a. Coda Condition: *VrX]
        b. Word Structure Constraint: *V]$_{wd}$

(6.13a) tells us that the output of r ~ Ø in codas must be zero, since [r] is banned from this position by the Coda Condition. However, r ~ Ø in onsets results in [r], because the Word Structure Constraint in (6.13b) prohibits word-final vowels: it will therefore come into operation at the end of Level 1, when the category Word becomes available. It will only operate after /ɑː ɔː ə/ because McCarthy analyses diphthongs and non-low long vowels as glide-final; and will not apply to function words, which are not of the category Word, and hence cannot attract intrusive

[r]. Postlexically, underlying /r/ and derived [r] will either be resyllabified into an onset, or deleted.

McCarthy therefore claims to have demonstrated that both insertion and deletion processes, or at least a symmetrical statement subsuming both, are necessary in present-day non-rhotic varieties to account for the facts of linking and intrusive [r]. However, his analysis is not conclusive. First, his argument that no historical rule inversion has taken place is not entirely supported by the facts. Notably, McCarthy explicitly proposes underlying /r/ only in forms which surface with non-prevocalic schwa: the Level 1 cases like *Homer, danger, doctor* have final schwa; so, naturally, do the examples illustrating supposed schwa-epenthesis, such as *fire, rear, pare*; and so do the reduced function words, including *gonna, wanna, to, the*. We must assume that historical /r/-Deletion caused conclusive loss of underlying /r/ for later generations of speakers in clusters like *harp, beard*. However, when first proposing the synchronic co-existence of insertion and deletion, McCarthy (1991: 4) notes that 'It is still unreasonable to set up distinct underlying representations for *spa* and *spar*, so of course there has been some reanalysis, but both rules are required in any case.' McCarthy does not specify what this reanalysis is, although the answer can probably be gleaned from the rest of the paper: since linking [r] in *spa*[r]*is* is derived via [r]-Insertion (1991: 12), and since McCarthy is quite clear that 'No internal evidence of the kind available to language learners would justify an underlying distinction between *spa* and *spar*, which are homophones in all contexts' (1991: 13), we must conclude that *spar* has lost its underlying /r/ over time, rather than that *spa* has gained one. Consequently, for final [ɑː ɔː] words, the equivalent of rule inversion has indeed taken place: earlier deletion has become present-day insertion. Note, however, that *spa* begins as surface-true /spɑː/, has final [r] inserted at the end of Level 1, and, if no following onset is available for resyllabification, then has the [r] deleted postlexically. Such Duke of York derivations are incompatible with a concrete phonology.

If underlying final /r/, and co-existing deletion and insertion, are relevant only to words with schwa, then McCarthy's case against historical rule inversion is not entirely solid. Moreover, his objection to this alleged change on the grounds that the resulting rule is morphologised does not hold for certain examples not included in Vennemann (1972), including the Scottish Vowel Length Rule, to which we shall return in 6.6. SVLR began as a neutralising change lengthening short vowels before /r/, voiced fricatives and boundaries, and shortening long ones in all other contexts, but now lengthens tense vowels before /r/, voiced fricatives and boundaries, having done away with the earlier underlying vowel length distinction. It is only 'morphologised' in the sense that] is included in its structural description; this is hardly surprising given that rule inversion seems generally to correspond in Lexical Phonological terms to a progression from postlexical to lexical rule application, and one characteristic of lexical rules is their reference to morphological information. It is understandable that linguists should be sceptical of Standard Generative notions like rule inversion: but this seems to be a case where a Standard Generative suggestion deserves sympathetic attention.

A second difficulty concerns the change of directional r → Ø to symmetrical r ~ Ø in non-rhotic varieties. McCarthy treats this as a straightforward generalisation, and claims that it accounts for the innovation of intrusive [r]. But if some schwa-words retained final underlying /r/ while others lost it, what commonality might learners perceive in order to motivate [r]-intrusion? Alternatively, do the underliers change in all schwa cases except the Level 1 derived forms, the *fire, pare* set and function words like *for, or, neither*, where there is explicit evidence (according to McCarthy) for the retention of underlying historical /r/? Even here, it is not clear that the evidence is strong enough: would a (statistically calculable, but not categorical) difference in the absence of schwa be sufficient for speakers to set up underlying /r/ in *pare* but schwa in *power*? It looks suspiciously as if McCarthy's account of the history goes through only on the assumption of rule inversion – which he rejects.

Let us return now to the three types of evidence adduced by McCarthy for the maintenance of both insertion and deletion. Recall first that McCarthy posits underlying /r/ in *Homer, danger, doctor*: this is then deleted prepausally and preconsonantally, but surfaces before vowels, including vowel-initial suffixes, giving Level 1 derived *Home*[r]*ic, dange*[r]*ous, docto*[r]*al*. On the other hand, *algebra, aroma, idea* must lack underlying /r/, since no [r] surfaces in Level 1 derived *algebraic, aromatic, ideal*. Clearly, this suggests that neither deletion nor insertion alone can account for these data.

However, these data fit neatly into the [r]-Insertion account developed above, which would predict linking [r] intervocalically in *doctoral, dangerous*, but not in underived *doctor, danger* (unless a vowel-initial word follows). There is one apparent difficulty, which involves Vowel

Shift: Pullum (1974: 90) argues that *severe ~ severity* could not be generated from a common underlier via an [r]-Insertion rule. In fact, a common underlier can be assumed: following my usual assumptions on constructing underlying forms, it must be /səviə/. The context for [r]-Insertion will then be satisfied by the addition of the *-ity* suffix on Level 1, which creates a /ə/–V hiatus. Obviously, Pullum is worried by the derivation of [ɛr] from /iə/ in *severity*; but this is also manageable in my version of Vowel Shift. Thus, for instance, *divine* has the underlier /dəvaɪn/; in *divinity*, the addition of *-ity* triggers Trisyllabic Laxing. For diphthongs, this process is assumed to remove the second element and lax and/or shorten the first, giving [æ], which undergoes the Lax Vowel Shift Rule to [ɪ] (a parallel analysis applies for the *reduce ~ reduction* alternation). Since the centring diphthongs are also falling diphthongs, the foregoing analysis can be extended to them: so, when *-ity* is added to *severe* /səviə/, Trisyllabic Laxing will produce [ɪ], which will then regularly undergo Lax Vowel Shift to [ɛ], the appropriate surface form. Clearly, [r]-Insertion must precede Trisyllabic Laxing in such cases, and must therefore apply on Level 1, so that all its effects cannot be derived from McCarthy's Word Structure Constraint, which becomes relevant only at the output of Level 1.

Level 1 linking [r] in *doctoral, dangerous, severity* can therefore be derived quite straightforwardly using only [r]-Insertion. Of course, McCarthy proposes underlying /r/ in these cases to distinguish them from the *algebra, aroma, idea* class; so the real challenge is to account for the latter. McCarthy suggests one way of achieving this: in his view, these latter forms lack underlying /r/, but have final [r] added by [r]-Insertion, acting on the instructions of the Word Structure Constraint, at the end of Level 1. It will then be deleted non-prevocalically at the postlexical level, creating another Duke of York derivation. In *algebraic*, the tensing rules will have produced /eyɪr/), not an environment for [r]-Insertion. Likewise, if all Level 1 morphology has operated before the Word Structure Constraint comes into play, forms like *ideal* and *aromatic* will not be receptive to [r]-Insertion, since in *ideal* the [r] would have to appear in the inappropriate context V __ C, while in *aromatic*, a [t] is present in the '[r] slot'.

Although [r]-Insertion must precede Trisyllabic Laxing on Level 1 to derive *severity*, it could equally follow the various tensing rules on the same Level. However, there is another, potentially more satisfactory approach, which also accounts for the apparently unprovoked appearance of [t] in *operatic, aromatic, Asiatic, dramatic*, and the shortened shape of *ideal*. McCarthy does not discuss these irregular affixes, and we must conclude that he regards them as variants of the Level 1 *-ic, -al* suffixes. However, the conditions on these variants are hard to grasp: how do we state a restriction which effectively only allows the *-tic* allomorph when intrusive [r] would otherwise surface? Some examples are given in (6.14); the hypothetical [r] forms which 'should' surface are on the left, and the actually occurring derived forms on the right.

(6.14) *phobia[r]ic   *phobic*
        *saliva[r]ary   *salivary / salivatory*
        *opera[r]ic, drama[r]ic *operatic, dramatic*
        *stigma[r]ise   *stigmatise*
        *idea[r]al   *ideal*

While the *doctoral, dangerous, severity* forms are regularly derived and relatively productive, the forms in (6.14) show variable clipping or other extraneous consonants, and are unproductive and isolated. It may well be, then, that these are not synchronically derived, but are instead learned, stored forms: the blocking of [r]-Insertion here then ceases to be a synchronic issue, and becomes a diachronic one. Datings in the OED reveal that the first attestations of the forms in (6.14) are invariably early, and almost all precede our first evidence for intrusive [r] in the late eighteenth century; hence, these forms date from a period when intrusive [r] was not yet available as a hiatus breaker. For instance, *dramatic* is attested in 1589; *operatic*, which the OED assumes to be formed analogically on the basis of *dramatic*, in 1749; *salivatory* from 1699 and *salivary* from 1709; and *stigmatise* from 1585. More recent or more regular and productive formations, like those in (6.15), can indeed appear with [r], supporting the hypothesis that its absence from the cases in (6.14) reflects historical pre-emption by forms derived by varying strategies and now stored.

(6.15) *withdraw[r]al*   *saw[r]ing*
        baa[r]ing   *Shah[r]ist*
        banana[r]y   *saw[r]able, draw[r]able*
        Shah[r]ify   *quota[r]ise, quota[r]isation*

McCarthy's second problematic set of data, involving variable absence of schwa, is equally tractable. Recall that McCarthy posits underlying /r/ in forms like *fear, pare, fire*, but not in *layer, power, rumba, Nashua, Maria*, to account for the fact that schwa always surfaces before [r] in the second set (in *layering, Maria[r]is*), but very infrequently in the first (in *firing, fear of*). However, the fact that *firing, fear of* can be trisyllabic in more formal speech surely argues for underlying schwa, which would then be deleted in fast or casual speech, rather than schwa epenthesis in formal styles. One might then propose underlying schwa and no underlying /r/ in all of *fear, fire, pare, layer, power, Maria* and the rest; the now-familiar rule of [r]-Insertion; and a late, optional process of schwa deletion. Of course, we must still explain why schwa deletes so much more frequently in *pare* than in *power*. For one thing, *pare* and *power*, even when both are pronounced with schwa, are structurally distinct: in *pare*, schwa forms the offglide of a diphthong and is therefore tautosyllabic with the preceding vowel, while in *power*, schwa and /aʊ/ are heterosyllabic. Interestingly, in RP, smoothing of the centring diphthongs /ɛə/, /ɔə/, /ʊə/ to [ɛː], [ɔː] is common, but the reduction of more complex triphthongal /aɪə/, /aʊə/ to [aə] or [ɑː] (as in *fire, flour*) occurs even more frequently, supporting the idea that a simplification of complex rhymes may be the main motivation. Similarly, in RP schwa also does not delete in *rumba, Nashua* or *Maria*, but very frequently does in [pɑːrɪŋ] *powering*, [lɛːrɪŋ], *layering*, where the stem containing the erstwhile schwa is still unambiguous without it: *Marie* and *Maria*, however, may be quite different people, and goodness knows what a *rumb* is (apart from a form violating English phonotactics on account of its final cluster).

Finally, we return to the function words, which seem to attract linking but not intrusive [r], so that McCarthy posits underlying /r/ in *for, our, were, neither*, but not in *wanna, to, do, the*. In an [r]-Insertion account, the first set will lack underlying /r/, and have linking [r] regularly inserted, while the remaining function words might be marked as exceptional to [r]-Insertion (since, as McCarthy notes, function words are frequently exceptional to generalisations and rules affecting 'real' words). Alternatively, Carr (1991: 51) suggests that [r]-Insertion across word boundaries is blocked by postlexically formed foot structures, and cannot cross the foot boundary in cases like *wanna eat*. However, none of these solutions is required in another set of non-rhotic dialects, such as many non-RP varieties in England, where *wanna eat, gonna ask* do attract intrusive [r]; similarly, the examples in (6.7) showed that reduced *to, by, you* can attract [r] in Norwich and Cockney, for instance. Even in these dialects, *do* tends not to have following [r], probably because the vowel does not fully reduce to schwa, but retains some of its height and rounding, making a [w] glide more likely. Although the definite article also appears in McCarthy's set of function words, it is not clear that it fits into the category of potential [r] contexts: in *the apples*, the prevocalic allomorph [ði:] should be selected, and the resulting hiatus will then be broken by [j]. Only if the preconsonantal [ðə] allomorph were chosen would an appropriate context for [r]-Insertion arise: and we have already seen that exactly this pattern is found in speech errors and child language. In short, McCarthy's three sets of data, which he claims necessitate both synchronic deletion and insertion of [r], are in fact quite consistent with an insertion-only account, while McCarthy's own analysis is flawed in several respects. There is nothing here to make us abandon [r]-Insertion; on the contrary, we may have found some extra arguments for it.

6.4.3   Harris (1994)

Harris considers four dialects: system A is rhotic; B has linking but not intrusive [r]; C is the typical non-rhotic type with both linking and intrusive [r]; and D is the Southern US variety with [r] in *red*, *bread* and variably in *very*, but generally in neither linking nor intrusive contexts. We shall focus on his treatment of systems B and C.

Harris (1994) presents an element-based phonology, within a principles-and-parameters framework grounded on ideas of phonological licensing. Harris assumes that approximant [ɹ] is composed of two elements, coronal R and neutral vocalic @ (the latter corresponding to the 'cold vowel' v° of Kaye, Lowenstamm and Vergnaud 1985, 1990); a tap would contain only R.

In non-rhotic varieties, Harris assumes that no underlying /r/ remains in non-alternating forms like *party*, *harp*, but that alternating *fear*, *soar* contain a final floating /r/ (6.16). These varieties have also innovated the Non-Rhoticity Condition, which licenses R only in onsets.

(6.16)   'Floating' /r/. Harris (1994):

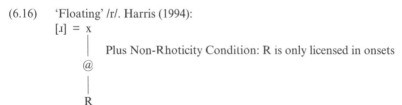

The two elements of the constellation are not realised together: instead, @ is incorporated into a preceding nucleus, lengthening and lowering the pre-existing vowel, or appearing as a schwa offglide: the centring diphthongs are therefore derived segments for Harris (which, incidentally, rules his approach out immediately for my version of Lexical Phonology: since centring diphthongs appear in underived environments like *fear, hair, poor*, they must be present underlyingly). This absorption of @ also accounts for the restricted set of vowels, /ɑː ɔː ə/, which can precede linking and intrusive [ɹ] synchronically. As for the R element, if a vowel follows floating /r/, it brings with it an empty onset, onto which R docks: it is then licensed and can be pronounced. If no vowel follows, R stays floating. Whereas McCarthy (1991) proposed effectively both insertion and deletion processes, Harris therefore combines deletion with a variety of underspecification, and argues that this account holds for dialects with linking [r] only, or both linking and intrusive [r]; the latter simply have floating R in more forms, in *spa* as well as *spar*, for example. The difference between his dialects B and C 'is thus purely a matter of lexical incidence' (1994: 250).

In representational terms, Harris's analysis of [r] as R versus [ɹ] as @ plus R means the change from trill to tap to approximant in the history of English, which is generally described as weakening, translates into elemental complication. Furthermore, since the @ will realign regardless of the fate of R, cases where R is licensed by a following empty onset should produce taps, while most realisations are in fact approximants (see Foulkes (1997) for data from Newcastle and Derby): in that case, another source of @ must presumably be found to add to the relocated R. More conceptually, it is not obvious why a constraint like the Non-Rhoticity Condition should suddenly appear in the grammar of a particular variety (see also Broadbent 1991). One might argue that such an analysis is simpler than one invoking an [r]-Insertion rule in some varieties and an /r/-Deletion process in others; but notions of simplicity are notoriously subjective, and issues of the universality of constraints and their motivation would have to be addressed in detail before a valid comparison could be made, as I suggested in chapter 1. Finally, as with Scobbie's and Donegan's work, there is the familiar question of how a gradual, sporadic, analogical extension of final [r] could lead to the extremely consistent appearance of intrusive [r], even in novel or foreign words, documented earlier in this chapter.

What, then, of the restricted set of vowels which precede /r/ in non-rhotic varieties? As we have seen, Harris proposes that the @ element influences the quality and quantity of preceding vowels, and argues that this is preferable to an arbitrary statement that [r] happens to surface only after /ɑ: ɔ: ə/. I shall return to the general issue of arbitrariness in the next section, but note for the moment that the insertion analysis is not unidirectional either. That is, it accepts both that /r/ affects the vowels, and that /ɑ: ɔ: ə/ determine the presence of [r], but regards the first conditioning factor as diachronic and the second as synchronic. In historical terms, /r/, and specifically its weakening and eventual deletion in codas, did affect the preceding vowels; synchronically, because of the intervening rule inversion, this translates into the conditioning of [r] by a particular set of vowels.

Harris (1994: 252–3) provides one interesting historical argument, noting that his analysis and mine make different predictions about relative chronology:

> Rule inversion firmly implies that the intrusive C-system pattern is an off-shoot of an older non-intrusive B. By contrast, the floating-*r* account is entirely neutral on the question of historical precedence. It would be entirely consistent with the latter analysis if intrusive *r* arose independently of etymological linking *r*. In fact ... it would not be surprising to discover cases of intrusive *r* in **rhotic** dialects.

To take the orthoepical evidence first, Harris claims that Walker (1791) provides the first indication of deletion of coda /r/, and of linking [r], but that 'A generation before John Walker's description of smooth versus rough *r*, Thomas Sheridan was castigating Londoners for inserting *r* after the final < -a >-vowel of words such as < Belinda > and < Dorlinda > (sic).' This suggestion that intrusive [r] may predate the linking type clearly goes against all predictions made by the rule inversion account. However, let us examine Sheridan's comment more closely. It occurs in his *Lectures on Elocution*, and is part of a passage dealing with 'vice[s] in the cockney pronunciation' (Sheridan 1762: 34). His main objection is to 'the changing the sound of the last syllable of words ending in ow, whereever it is not sounded like a dipthong, but like a simple o, (which is always the case when the last syllable is unaccented) into er – as feller for fellow – beller, holler, foller, winder, – for bellow, hollow, follow, window. As also adding the letter r to all proper names ending in *a* unaccented, as Belindar, Dorindar, for Belinda, Dorinda' (ibid.). We can draw several conclusions from this, and as it turns out, none are detrimental to [r]-Insertion. First, it might seem chronologically significant that Sheridan mentions only intrusive, and not linking [r]; however, we have already seen (6.3.1 above) that, in his Dictionary and Grammars (see, for instance, Sheridan 1780, 1781), Sheridan's intentions are prescriptivist rather than descriptivist, and he deliberately archaises the pronunciations he recommends: his claims that <r> is never silent must be interpreted in this light. It is also notable that, although he does not allude to linking [r] in the Dictionary or Grammars, intrusive [r] does not figure in these works either. On the other hand, in the *Lectures on Elocution*, Sheridan is anecdotally selecting certain features of 'vulgar speech' and warning his audience against them. He may simply have hit upon intrusive rather than linking [r] first – perhaps as an Irishman himself, and therefore presumably originally a rhotic speaker, the sin of commission impressed itself on him more forcibly than the sin of omission whereby etymological [r] was dropped before pauses and consonants. Rhotic speakers today still seem particularly sensitive to intrusive [r]. Alternatively, he may mention intrusive [r] because it is a relatively recent innovation, just gaining ground in the speech community, as opposed to linking [r] which may already have been fairly well-embedded. This is not pure speculation: the orthoepical works surveyed in 6.3.1 above indicated that clear evidence for /r/-Deletion, and for linking [r], dates from the early eighteenth century – a generation before Sheridan, in fact.

We might, then, taking Harris's part, object that Sheridan's evidence indicates a broader distribution of intrusive [r] than in current non-rhotic varieties, supporting its independence from linking [r]. That is, when Sheridan writes 'winder, Dorinder', how are we to know that these were restricted to prevocalic position? The answer is that, although Sheridan may not make this plain, others do: Ellis (1849: 37), for instance, comments that 'An r̠ is very often inserted by Londoners after a̠ [= [ə] AMSM], a', ɔ., when a vowel follows; thus "the law̠r̠ of the land, Jemima̠r̠ Ann, Sarah̠r̠ Evans." This has given rise to the idea, that the Londoners pronounced law, Sarah as law̠r̠, Sarah̠r̠, which is not the case.' Sheridan's contemporary Elphinston (1787; quoted by Jespersen 1909: 370) also explicitly connects linking with intrusive [r]: after discussing [r]-loss, he comments that 'Dhe same cauz (febel vocallity in dhe end) haz made Grocenes [i.e. vulgarity] assume r̠ in (dhe colloquial) idear and windowr, for idea and window.' Furthermore, the hypothesis that intrusive [r] was innovated independently of and earlier than linking [r] is not borne out by the present-day distribution of vowels. If intrusive [r] were earlier, and if /r/ is floating R plus nuclear @, with the latter affecting the quality of all preceding vowels, why is there a centring diphthong and prevocalic [r] in *beer is*, *purist*, but not in *seeing* or *viewing*? This contextual restriction means intrusive [r] must be connected with, and even be an offshoot of a prior linking type.

Of course, the weaker form of Harris's argument, which holds that evidence for linking and intrusive [r] begins to appear roughly contemporaneously, is not problematic: rule inversion, and therefore intrusion, would be predicted to be a rapid, if not immediate response to deletion for some speakers – and recall that weakening and sporadic deletion had been going on since the mid-seventeenth century. There is also a theory-internal argument from Lexical Phonology here. My assumption that underlying representations for underived forms are typically identical to their lexical representations will be violated in varieties with linking [r] only. I have also argued that the constraints of LP, if applied rigorously, might be of diachronic rather than synchronic relevance: that is, their violation might motivate some historical restitution; and this might be precisely such a case. If some historical development, like the loss of coda [r], means underlying representations conflict with the usual conditions on them, they might not persist for long – such a stage might be predicted to be transient. It is interesting in this connection that varieties with linking [r] only are rare today, and that evidence for intrusion comes hot on the heels of evidence for [r]-loss.

Harris also argues that intrusive [r] is not restricted to non-rhotic dialects, as conventionally assumed, but that it appears also in 'some present-day conservative rhotic dialects ... [as] demonstrated by spellings such as <yeller, feller, swaller> for <yellow, fellow, swallow>' (1994: 253), and presumably also hyperrhotic pronunciations like *china*[ɹ], *banana*[ɹ], [kɑːɹki] *khaki*. Again, Harris (1994, fn. 40) assumes that rhotic speakers have innovated underlying /r/ in the relevant forms. As for the motivation for this sort of development, Harris argues for a progressive disfavouring of final schwa in English; this disfavouring began with the widespread loss of final schwa in Middle English, but different strategies have had to come into play in more modern times, following the relatively recent borrowing of a fairly extensive set of words including *sofa, comma, Laura, Sheena, banana, china, vanilla, America*. In both non-rhotic and rhotic varieties, in Harris's view, the principal strategy is the internalisation of underlying /r/, floating or not.

However, we can maintain rule inversion in non-rhotic dialects, and still account for the rather different phenomenon of hyperrhoticity in rhotic dialects in a variety of ways. For instance, final [ɑː ɔː ə] may attract [r] in rhotic British accents because the majority of British English speakers are non-rhotic, and therefore such vowels will frequently be heard with intrusive [r]. That is, rhotic speakers may mislearn words by assuming underlying /r/ because they hear alternating [r] ~ Ø from non-rhotic speakers: this sporadic, analogical extension corresponds to the analysis Harris, Scobbie, Donegan and others have proposed for non-rhotic varieties. But the characterisation of extraneous [r] for rhotic speakers as a purely lexical development need not extend to non-rhotic dialects. First, as noted above, [r]-Intrusion in non-rhotic varieties is typically much more regular and systematic, and seems best suited to a rule-governed account. Second, some evidence for our mislearning hypothesis comes from America, where, conversely, the majority of speakers and the principal standard variety, General American, are rhotic, and where this has had parallel but opposite effects on the non-rhotic minority, including the well-known re-rhoticisation of New York City (see Labov (1972) and 6.6 below). Finally, clear evidence for regarding intrusive [r] and hyperrhoticity as separate phenomena comes from their distribution: intrusive [r], as we know, occurs only intervocalically, and after a restricted set of vowels. Hyperrhotic [r] follows the same set of vowels, reflecting its possible origin in imitation of non-rhotic speakers, but is not restricted to intervocalic position: Wells (1982) cites *khaki, camouflage* with [r] between [ɑ:] and C, while rhotic speakers may have categorical final [r] in schwa words like *comma, idea, Anna, Laura*.

An alternative, dialect-internal explanation for words with final schwa is outlined in Hughes and Trudgill (1979: 32). This hypothesis relies on the fact that a number of words with final schwa were borrowed into English either while [r] was being lost non-prevocalically, or thereafter. These words are generally assimilated to other phonological classes, perhaps because of disfavouring of final schwas of the type suggested by Harris, with different options being exercised in different dialects. In non-rhotic varieties, schwa-final forms were treated in the same way as those with historical /ər/, and therefore, after rule inversion, developed an [r] ~ Ø alternation controlled by [r]-Insertion. In rhotic dialects, where the retention of final [r] meant there were no schwa-final words, strategies varied. For instance, in Southampton, *comma, banana, vanilla* words adopted the pattern of *butter, letter*, with categorical final [r], giving [bəna:nər], [vənɪlər]; this accounts for West Country hyperrhoticity. In Bristol, on the other hand, *comma, banana, vanilla* seem to have been assimilated to the pattern of *apple, bottle*, with the other English liquid, giving intrusive [l].

In short, neither Harris's historical evidence nor his dialectal data support his contention that linking and intrusive [r], in varieties with both, are independent. It is worth noting finally Harris's (1994: 254) criticism of

> the notion that intrusive-*r* dialects are the direct descendants of a non-rhotic B-type system which lacks the phenomenon. The germ of this idea seems to be buried in a prescriptive myth, according to which non-standard dialects are deviant outgrowths from a central standard stem whose phonology somehow faithfully mirrors the orthography.

This is an extraordinary statement, and seems to reduce to the assertion that it is prescriptivist to hypothesise for present-day varieties with both linking and intrusive [r] a historical ancestor with linking [r] only. My [r]-insertion account does make this assumption, but purely diachronically: I have presented contemporary evidence showing that a linking-only stage existed, albeit relatively briefly. Even this was only an intermediate stage: all non-rhotic dialects are, on a longer historical view, derived from some rhotic ancestor. Indeed, in rhotic dialects, the phonology of [r] 'faithfully ... mirrors the orthography'. But surely this is not a prescriptivist statement, partly because it simply reflects a historical fact, and partly because, by a typical quirk of linguistic fate, rhotic varieties of English, at least in Britain, are now typically non-standard – as is the appearance of intrusive [r], which is now becoming the non-rhotic norm and impressing itself successfully on RP.

Perhaps the best gloss we can put on Harris's statement is that different varieties should not necessarily be derived synchronically from a common core, a point I have been arguing throughout this book. It is precisely because I do hold to this view, and because of the conditions on my model of Lexical Phonology, that I must of necessity propose [r]-Insertion in varieties with linking and intrusive [r], and [r]-Deletion in dialects with linking only (thus, ironically, Harris analyses these two types of variety as much more similar than I do). The arguments against underspecification in chapter 5 above rested on similar grounds, namely that underspecification permits common underlying systems for different varieties where they are not warranted. But ruling out underspecification is one good reason why I could not in any case incorporate Harris's floating /r/ analysis into my Lexical Phonology. This is not underspecification in its usual sense: in the normal case, features are absent and filled in during the derivation, whereas here, the floating elements are present from the start, but are attached (optionally for R, obligatorily for @)

later. Nonetheless, there is absence of attachment in the early stages; and more worryingly, if R is not adjacent to an empty onset, it is left floating, and not realised on the surface; yet it is not deleted. This is perhaps a mirror image of underspecification (present but unwanted material, rather than absent and required material), but the problems it gives rise to are likely to be the same. Similarly, Giegerich's (in press) analysis of [ɹ] and schwa as arising in different contexts from the same empty underlying melody will not be pursued here, as my prohibition on underspecification equally rules it out.

6.5   Synchronic arbitrariness and diachronic transparency

6.5.1   The problem

There is one last apparent problem for [r]-Insertion, which I have not addressed so far, but which is frequently cited as the knock-down argument against it by proponents of alternative analyses: this involves apparent arbitrariness. Harris (1994: 246–7) succinctly expresses the issue in his claim that [r]-Insertion

> is potentially arbitrary in two respects. First, the process itself must be considered arbitrary, unless grounds can be provided for assuming that it must be *r* that is inserted rather than any other randomly selectable sound ... There is no obvious local source in the surrounding vowels ... There is another respect in which R-Epenthesis is in need of justification. Why should it take place in the context it does, between vowels as long as the first is non-high? Would we have been surprised if it had applied in any other environment?

There have been attempts to establish a non-arbitrary conditioning context for [r]. Broadbent (1991) presents an element-based account of [r] in non-rhotic varieties, concentrating mainly on data from West Yorkshire, where intrusive [r] is not stigmatised, and is therefore freely and productively produced, without the variable suppression found in RP. Broadbent observes that [r] is used as a hiatus breaker, compares it with the appearance of [j] and [w] in similar intervocalic contexts, and analyses all three as instantiations of a general process of glide formation. This is not strictly an insertion rule, but involves the spreading of some property of the preceding vowel to an adjacent empty onset to produce a surface glide: this gives [j] after high and mid long front vowels, [w] after high and mid long back vowels, and [r] after those other non-high vowels which can occur word-finally, namely [aː ɒ ə ɛ ɜː ɒ] (6.17).

(6.17)   [j] glide: *see it*   [siːjɪt]
                         pay as   [peːjəz]
         [w] glide: *do it*   [duːwɪt]
                         going   [goːwɪn]
         [r] glide: *idea of*   [aɪdiəɹəv]
                         Shah of Persia [ʃaːɹəfpɜːʒə]
                         law and order [lɒːɹənɒːdə]
                         was it   [wɒɹɪt]
                         yes it is   [jeɹɪtɪz]

Because Broadbent's approach involves spreading rather than insertion, it can be incorporated into a declarative model. It also formalises an insight a number of phonologists have used in accounting for the restricted distribution of intrusive [r], by invoking the characteristics of the preceding vowel. For instance, Johansson (1973) argues that /ɑː ɔː/ are schwa-final, and that schwa is the common factor which triggers [r]-Insertion (although this would not help with the rather different set of West Yorkshire trigger vowels), while McCarthy (1991) analyses all non-low long vowels as glide final, and claims that this glide blocks [r]-Insertion (although again this may not generalise to other varieties). Certainly, glide insertion and [r] must be related; we have already seen that [r] interacts with [j w] and [ʔ] formation, and also with other phonological processes such as [h]-dropping and vowel reduction.

Nonetheless, it seems that Broadbent's approach must be rejected. First, it makes wrong predictions; Broadbent (1991: 296) claims that 'systems can have either linking and intrusive r or neither, but linking without intrusive r is not possible.' The data presented above speak against this, since we have seen that some varieties of Southern States USA and South African English do seem to have linking [r] only. It is also hard to see how Broadbent would account for the history of non-rhotic [r] if she predicts that no prior linking stage could have existed.

Secondly, Broadbent's account of spreading is incomplete: it is easy to establish what elements must be spreading to form [j] and [w] (I and U respectively, when these are the heads of preceding vowels), but much less straightforward for [r]. Broadbent attempts to isolate a common factor from the vowels after which [r] surfaces, and identifies the element A; but this is not the head of all relevant vowels. Consequently, although 'the simplest assumption to make is that r-formation occurs when A is the head of a relevant segment', this 'raises questions regarding the elemental composition of all non-high vowels, and clearly this requires further work' (Broadbent 1991: 299). In other words, Broadbent's account of [r] requires a wholesale reanalysis of the element structure of vowels, which she does not carry out. Finally, Broadbent (1991) gives no further details on how [r] results from A; if A spreads to an empty onset as an operator, as Broadbent assumes, this will produce schwa. In later work (Broadbent 1992), she argues that the correct output will arise if A can 'pick up coronality' at some stage of the derivation; but there is no clear source for the coronal element.

Indeed, attempts to connect the features of /r/ to those of preceding, conditioning vowels may be doomed to failure, insofar as English /r/ itself covers so many variant realisations. Despite the best efforts of phoneticians (Lindau 1985) to identify an articulatory or auditory property unifying the class of rhotics, what makes an /r/ an /r/ also remains unclear cross-linguistically. Ladefoged and Maddieson (1996: 245) are forced to conclude that 'Although there are several well-defined subsets of sounds (trills, flaps, etc.) that are included in the rhotic class, the overall unity of the group seems to rest mostly on the historical connections between these subgroups, and on the choice of the letter "r" to represent them all.'

It is hardly surprising that attempts to establish the affinities of /r/ with preceding vowels have proved fruitless, when we cannot even establish satisfactorily why /r/s form a natural class with themselves. This returns us to the accusation of arbitrariness with which we began this section. If anything, Broadbent's work makes matters even worse for [r]-Insertion, since her data from West Yorkshire indicate that the conditioning context may vary from dialect to dialect, and a random and variable set of vowels seems even harder to deal with than a random and fixed one. It is true that some of the West Yorkshire vowels are only realisational variants of the RP set, and that others are included because of the different phonotactic conditions operative in the different dialects; but nonetheless, the sets are distinct. How, then, are we to defend [r]-Insertion by demonstrating why [r] should be the segment inserted, and in these particular environments? Of course, this relates, as Harris points out, to the question of whether vowels affect the following /r/, or whether /r/ affects the preceding vowels. In fact, there is a single, historical solution to this composite problem of why and where [r] should be inserted.

6.5.2   Using the past to explain the present

We must begin by accepting, in the face of the evidence presented above, that there is no way of making the vowels conditioning [r]-Insertion synchronically principled; they do not share any feature, with [r] or with each other, which would make context and output a natural class. In short, [r]-Insertion is indeed synchronically arbitrary, as its critics allege. However, if we consider [r]-Insertion diachronically, and accept that insertion is a result of prior deletion, there is nothing arbitrary about it at all. From the historical point of view, the structural description of [r]-Insertion makes perfect sense.

Recall that the eighteenth century sound changes of Pre-/r/ Breaking and Pre-Schwa Laxing (shown in (6.3) above) meant that /r/, at the time of /r/-Deletion, could only appear, in the incipiently non-rhotic dialects, following a limited set of vowels. For the ancestor of RP, this set consisted of [ɑː ɔː], schwa, which may be the second element of a centring diphthong, and [ɜː], which we may think of as long schwa. Further optional smoothing adds [ɛː] to the set, although this does not greatly affect later developments, since there are no English words with final [ɛː] which do not also have etymological following /r/. These vowels, and some example words, were listed in (6.4). Since [r] could occur only after these vowels, and since it was the consonant deleted in these environments (there being no parallel or alternative process of [k]- or [m]-loss, say), it follows that [r] should be inserted after the same vowels, as a function of rule inversion. In cases where vowels from this set appear finally in words lacking historical /r/, the new process of [r]-Insertion will then regularly provide [r] when any vowel follows, leading automatically to intrusive [r]. This historical connection seems to have been obscured by the fact that the rules of /r/-Deletion and [r]-Insertion do not look like exact inverses when written, as shown in (6.18).

(6.18) /r/-Deletion: r > Ø /   ___ {C, pause}
        [r]-Insertion: Ø → r / /ɑː ɔː ə/ ___ V

Obviously, the input and the structural change are inverses: [r] and zero change places. However, the problem lies with the rest of the structural description; whereas V and the disjunction of C and pause clearly are opposites (if something happens before vowels, it precisely does not happen before consonants and pauses, and vice versa), the absent left context in the deletion rule has been replaced for [r]-Insertion by a particular group of vowels which, as we know, will be different for different varieties. It is, of course, nonsense to argue that /ɑː ɔː ə/, or any other subset of vowels, is the inverse of zero, and phonologists have therefore tended to assume that the left-hand environment for insertion has appeared either by accident or by sleight of hand on the part of fans of insertion rules. In fact, the solution is deceptively simple: the left-hand context for deletion does not have to be written. It is the succeeding consonant or boundary which conditions deletion, and the preceding context would simply consist of the entire set of vowels after which [r] could, at that time, appear. The issue of cross-dialectal variation in the set of conditioning vowels is also easily resolvable: in West Yorkshire, the inventory of vowels and the quality of low vowels is rather different from that of RP; thus, the vowels after which [r] deleted, and after which it is now inserted, are likely to vary to some extent. Finally, the introduction of this historical viewpoint resolves the quarrel over what conditions what in modern non-rhotic varieties: does /r/ have some effect on preceding vowels, or are the vowels responsible for the presence or absence of [r]? Well, both: that is, although /r/, or more precisely a complex of sound changes associated with it, did historically alter the quality and quantity of preceding vowels in ways we shall explore further below, it is now that resulting set of residual vowels which governs the realisation of [r]. All this means that the set of vowels conditioning [r]-Insertion is precisely predictable in historical terms – the present-day reflexes of the vowels after which [r] could appear at the time of deletion, are those which will trigger insertion in any given dialect. Nonetheless, this set of vowels remains arbitrary synchronically, depending as it does on the course of particular sound changes in particular varieties of English.

6.5.3   Modelling the past

This is not, however, the end of the story. It is all very well to explain the present with reference to the past, but this only pushes the explaining back one step unless we have a clear idea of what happened historically, as well as why: to reverse Labov's (1978) desideratum, we can only hope to understand the present-day situation if and when we feel fully at ease with the past. If we are to account for [r]-Insertion in terms of historical /r/-Deletion, we must understand what the rationale for this change was, and why it happened only in certain varieties of English. As we have seen, some phonologists propose that certain constraints or conditions were innovated in particular dialects, although such accounts are typically incomplete and do not fully explain why the constraints should be dialect-specific. We therefore return to the history of /r/-Deletion.

We saw in 6.3.1 above that there is good orthoepical evidence for a gradual weakening of /r/ in all varieties of English, from a trill to a tap, and thence to an approximant. In some rhotic accents, like Scots and SSE, for instance, the stronger tap realisation is maintained in onsets, although an approximant is now more common in coda position. This weakening, along with a number of changes affecting vowels before [r], led eventually to the loss of [r] except before vowels in those varieties in which it had weakened fastest and farthest; there are sporadic cases of /r/-loss from the fifteenth century onwards (Lass 1993), but weakening seems to have got under way on a grand scale in the seventeenth century, with wholesale deletion from the early eighteenth century onwards.

In (6.3) I stated the changes leading up to the present-day non-rhotic situation in standard handbook fashion, as the three sequential developments of Pre-/r/ Breaking, Pre-Schwa Laxing, and /r/-Deletion. This sort of statement, whether in terms of segments or of binary features, is not particularly illuminating; and nor is the separate listing of the three developments, which do not seem to have much in common except that the first feeds the second and the third must logically have followed the first. I repeat these changes in (6.19) for convenience.

(6.19) Pre-/r/ Breaking: Ø > /ə/ / /i: e: o: u: ai au/ __ /r/

[bi:r]	>	[bi:ər]	*beer*
[tʃe:r]	>	[tʃe:ər]	*chair*
[mo:r]	>	[mo:ər]	*more*
[ʃu:r]	>	[ʃu:ər]	*sure*
[fair]	>	[faiər]	*fire*
[taur]	>	[tauər]	*tower*

Pre-schwa Laxing/Shortening: /i: e: o: u:/ > [ɪ ɛ ɒ ʊ] / – /ə/

[bi:ər]	>	[bɪər]	*beer*	
[tʃe:ər]	>	[tʃɛər]	*chair*	(> [tʃɛ:])
[mo:ər]	>	[mɒər]	*more*	(> [mɔ:])
[ʃu:ər]	>	[ʃʊər]	*sure*	(> [ʃɔ:])
[faiər]	>	[faɪər]	*fire*	(> [faɪə] or [fɑ:])
[tauər]	>	[tauər]	*tower*	(> [tauə] or [tɑ:])

r/-Deletion: r > Ø / __ {C, pause}

The question is whether we can model the relationship among these changes in a more perspicuous way. Recall that /r/ seems to have been progressively weakening through the Early Modern period in English generally, with the greatest weakening in coda positions, and with certain dialects, which would become non-rhotic, furthest advanced in this weakening. It seems unlikely that we can isolate the social, linguistic and demographic factors which placed certain varieties in the vanguard of the change, although it might be possible to reconstruct some such contributory factors from our knowledge of sound change in progress (Labov 1978). Contemporary evidence reviewed above suggests that Pre-/r/ Breaking took place alongside this weakening; but it need not necessarily have been an independent change, or restricted to those dialects which would become non-rhotic. Even in rhotic varieties like Scots (see (6.20); from Mather and Speitel 1986), a minimal schwa offglide frequently appears between non-low /i e u o/ and a following /r/; this may also be accompanied by lengthening, since /r/ is a long context for SVLR.

(6.20)   *Linguistic Atlas of Scotland, Scots Section, Vol. III, Phonology.*
          Dounby, Orkney
          /i³/   *beer, hear*
          /e³/   *bear, chair, more*
          /o³/   *before, boar*
          /u³/   *flower*
          /a:/   *barn, war, work*
          /ɔ:/   *born, north, worn*

          Beith, Ayrshire
          /i:³/   *beer, hear*
          /e:³/   *bairn, bear, more*
          /o:³/   *before, bore, north*
          /ü:³/   *flower, our, pour*
          /ä:/   *barn, work, hard*
          /ɔ:/   *dark, where, war*

This partial schwa is rarely perceived by speakers, perhaps because of the acoustic and articulatory similarity of [ə] and approximant [ɹ], to which we shall return below, or the general vowel lengthening which takes place before [r] in any case. Thus, the schwa in rhotic varieties can be ascribed to the realised [r]; in non-rhotic dialects, the present-day absence of [r] means that the resulting centring diphthongs have phonemicised: as Wells (1982: 214) notes, schwa before [r] is 'a very natural kind of phonetic development', and 'it is perhaps possible to regard it as allophonic in rhotic accents, although in non-rhotic accents (including RP) it is clearly phonemic' (Wells 1982: 216). The increased prominence of schwa in centring diphthongs is therefore clearly bound up with the loss of non-prevocalic [r] in non-rhotic varieties; the question is exactly how this can be modelled.

This line of enquiry may not seem very promising, given the difficulties encountered earlier in discovering any phonological feature unifying /r/ and the relevant vowels. Such insights are certainly not going to be forthcoming in LP as it stands at present, with its old-fashioned and problematic binary feature system, which has been retained as a result of the concentration on organisation within the lexicalist model at the expense of work on representation. It may be that we can model these changes, and assess the connections among them, more adequately with a more innovatory feature system, and I propose the gestural framework provided by Articulatory Phonology (Browman and Goldstein 1989, 1991, 1992; McMahon, Foulkes and Tollfree 1994), at least as an interesting possibility. Gestures could be incorporated into even the most restricted version of LP, since their unary nature means they would be subject only to inherent monovalent, rather than radical underspecification.

In Articulatory Phonology, the primitive unit is the gesture, an abstract unit which generates some vocal tract constriction. Underlying representations consist of 'scores' of overlapping gestures, which signal contrast and distinctiveness; but these same gestures can, by the application of dynamical equations, be transformed into characterisations of temporally continuous physical movements. The gestural model is very limited, in that no deletion or insertion of gestures is permitted, but has nonetheless been particularly successful in accounting for fast and casual speech processes, and the sound changes to which these give rise. This is achieved by invoking two alterations which gestural scores may undergo: fast speech renditions may differ from canonical forms in the magnitude of gestures, or in the degree of overlap of gestures, and these two modifications are claimed to account for apparent weakenings, insertions, deletions and assimilations.

Let us consider two examples, involving gestural reduction and overlap, and hence weakening and loss of a consonant; a far wider range of possible changes is considered in McMahon, Foulkes and Tollfree (1994) and McMahon and Foulkes (1995).

(6.21) shows a case of lenition, encoded as reduction in the magnitude of a gesture. Here, a stop becomes a fricative because the closed labial gesture is not fully formed, and the resulting critical labial gesture produces a percept of close approximation. In (6.22), the speaker in both cases makes the appropriate gesture for the [ktm] cluster, but changes in timing in the fast speech rendition mean that the closed alveolar gesture for [t] is wholly overlapped and hidden by the velar and labial gestures for the adjacent consonants, so that the [t] is not heard. Cross-generationally, these weakenings and deletions may become absolute, so that the fricative, or the form without /t/, may be learned and hence become canonical.

(6.21)   Consonant lenition in Articulatory Phonology: Tuscan /kapo/

Section of canonical gestural score for /kapo/

Tongue Body	a	o
Lips	closed labial	
Glottal	wide	
	[a p o]	

Section of gestural score for [kaɸo], showing diminished labial gesture

Tongue Body	a	o
Lips	critical labial	
Glottal	wide	
	[a ɸ o]	

(6.22)   Consonant loss in Articulatory Phonology

Gestures for section of canonical form of *perfect memory*

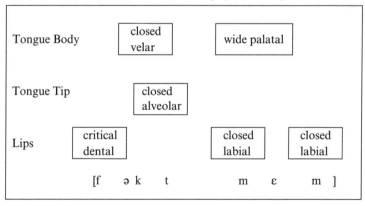

Gestures realigned temporally for section of *perfect memory* in casual speech

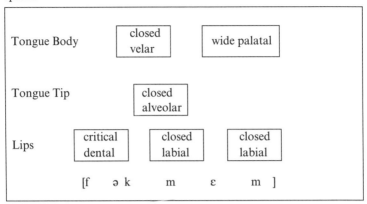

In the case of /r/-Deletion, we see both weakening and apparent loss of a segment. In gestural terms, we might regard the progressive lenition as a gradual reduction in the magnitude of the /r/ gestures. Furthermore, these gestures, although still present in the speakers' underlying gestural score, may have been overlapped and hidden an increasing proportion of the time by the gestures appropriate to a following consonant; as we saw in 6.3.1 above, orthoepical evidence suggests that [r]-loss began pre-consonantally, spreading later to pre-pausal position. Occurrence in, or resyllabification into an onset would protect /r/ from the gestural hiding, although not from all the weakening. However, I suggest that the gestures for /r/ were not entirely hidden but rather, in their weakened state, misparsed by hearers and attributed to the pre-existing, partial schwa which preceded /r/; and here, we must make reference to acoustic phonetics. Spectrograms for approximant [ɹ] and [ə] show marked similarities (McMahon 1996), except that F3 for [ɹ] is typically lower. The articulatory strategies speakers use to maintain this low F3 seem to be both variable and vulnerable, in that any relaxation of articulatory effort will allow F3 to raise, increasing its perceptual similarity to schwa. As we have seen (6.20), even in rhotic varieties a minor schwa offglide on preceding vowels may be part of the characteristic signature of an approximant [ɹ] in any case; this is phonetically very natural, since the tongue will tend to pass through the appropriate articulatory configuration for schwa on its way from most vowels to [ɹ]. It seems that the more the /r/ is weakened, the greater the propensity for hearers to perceive a full schwa vowel in its stead: Jetchev (1993) provides a similar account for apparent vowel insertion changes in Slavic. It is important to note that, in Articulatory Phonology, the stage of gestural hiding is taken to be transitory, and the next generation of speakers will be predicted to learn a form with no underlying /r/, in accord with the rule inversion analysis. This proposal therefore differs critically from Harris's (1994) assumption that floating /r/ can continue to float cross-generationally.

Pre-Schwa Laxing/Shortening would follow, again not as a separate, independently motivated change, but as an automatic consequence, this time phonological. That is, since English has no long diphthongs, with a long first and short second element, the incorporation of schwa into the nucleus would necessitate changes in the pre-existing vowel, which would reduce in length, and concomitantly modify in quality, to give the familiar centring diphthongs. This development is required to maintain the single syllable conformation of words like *beer, chair, sure, more.* However, although this outline is appropriate for the non-low vowels, /ɑː ɔː/ do not always follow the same pattern. Some older speakers of RP, for instance, may maintain schwa after /ɔː/ in *oar, floor* and /ɑː/ in *spar, star*; but younger RP speakers, and all speakers of many other non-rhotic varieties, lack schwa in these contexts. The weakening /r/ seems to have been perceived after low vowels, not as schwa, but as additional vowel length. Browman and Goldstein (1991: 331) propose that compensatory lengthening does not involve an increase in the duration of vowel gestures: however, part of the vowel gestures are typically hidden by those of an adjacent consonant, and if the consonantal gestures are deleted, those of the vowel are uncovered and perceived as extra length. The question is why this discrepancy of length for low vowels and schwa for the others should have arisen.

A solution might be sought in the gestural composition of /r/ and the vowels concerned, but the gestural analysis of vowels is still too tentative and incomplete to make this a fruitful area for investigation at present (Ladefoged 1990, Foulkes 1993). However, there may be a more straightforward historical answer. As Strang (1970: 112–13) points out, /iː eː uː oː/ were already long at the time of Breaking and /r/-Deletion, while the low vowels were short, and lengthened only as a function of /r/-Deletion. That is, /ar/ and /ɒr/ in *card, horse* underwent compensatory lengthening to /ɑː ɔː/, while the non-low vowels, being already long, could not lengthen further. This may combine with a more general phonetic explanation: the extent of jaw opening for the low vowels, and the fact that [r] and [ɹ] seem crucially to be produced with a non-high tongue body (Francis Nolan, personal communication), may mean that the articulators are less likely to pass through a schwa stage in transit from a low vowel to [ɹ] than when a higher vowel is involved. Interestingly, it is not only the low vowels which lengthen without attracting schwa; this also happens with 'the (probably) mixed vowel resulting from the confusion of *i, u,* and *e* … as in *first, turn,* and *earl*' (Jespersen 1909: 359). This vowel was historically short, but is now long /ɜː/, and Jespersen explicitly ascribes this lengthening to the effects of /r/-loss. But /ɜː/ is not a low vowel, and nor were any of its ancestors /ɪ ɛ ʌ/. We cannot therefore claim that only low vowels before /r/ fail to attract schwa; but again, considering historical vowel length can help, since all the ancestors of /ɜː/ were short.

We also know that low vowels lengthened in contexts other than before /r/, giving [ɑː] for many speakers in *calm, palm, bath, laugh, grass.* We cannot be sure in which dialects this lengthening began, but from its present-day results, we can conclude that it must have been under way relatively promptly in the ancestor of RP, given the underlying distinction which now obtains between /æ/ *Sam* and /ɑː/ *psalm,* as well as between /ɒ/ and /ɔː/ (see also Harris 1989). We might then speculate that schwa will follow low vowels in those dialects where the low vowels had already lengthened before /r/-Deletion, but that in varieties where /a ɒ/ were still short, /r/-Deletion was accompanied by compensatory lengthening. When the schwa is then lost, as for many younger RP speakers, this can be ascribed to the optional and encroaching operation of smoothing, which applies to all centring diphthongs except /ɪə/ (and even this is affected in some varieties of Australian English – see Wells 1982). All of this supports our contention that the explanation for the pervasive absence of schwa after low vowels is perhaps partly articulatory, but primarily historical, and based on the length of vowels at the time of /r/-Deletion.

I conclude, then, that short vowels at the time of /r/-loss underwent compensatory lengthening as a function of the disappearance of /r/, while for long vowels, the residual /r/ gestures were perceived as schwa, leading to laxing and shortening of the long preceding vowel to preserve syllable structure. This sort of pattern, with schwa and length in complementary distribution, is not entirely unfamiliar, especially to historical linguists. For instance, Saussure was led to postulate the Proto-Indo-European laryngeals because of the mutually exclusive appearance of unexpected length and unexpected schwa; and again, both testified to the earlier existence of a single, presumably consonantal sound (Lindeman 1987).

Pre-/r/ Breaking, Pre-Schwa Laxing/Shortening and /r/-Deletion now emerge, not as three unrelated developments, but as an integrated complex of changes. We can also account for the apparently asymmetrical behaviour of low and non-low vowels in particular non-rhotic dialects. However, we are faced with a final, and potentially even more serious question: if these developments are so natural, and follow so obviously from the weakening of /r/, why did only some English dialects become non-rhotic?

This is, of course, an impossibly big question, relating as it does to the issue, central in much current work on linguistic variation and change (Milroy 1992), of why low-level phonetic processes are only sometimes phonologised, or why only certain variants develop into changes. Nonetheless, we can offer two partial answers. One involves the speed of change: those dialects in which /r/-weakening was farthest advanced seem to be those which progressed to /r/-Deletion, whereas rhotic varieties preserve an earlier stage with less extreme weakening. The question of why weakening began earlier or progressed faster in some dialects than in others may be beyond recovery, given the time depth involved. The second partial explanation relates to general systemic tendencies. If the loss of /r/ is closely connected with the perception of weakened /r/ gestures as schwa, we might rather tangentially seek an account of retention of /r/ in terms of non-perceptibility of schwa. Certain dialects of English seem to have a general tendency towards diphthongisation, while others are fundamentally monophthongal, and the former are typically non-rhotic, the latter rhotic. For instance, non-rhotic dialects characteristically have the 'true' diphthongs /aɪ aʊ ɔɪ/, the centring diphthongs, and diphthongal reflexes of post-Great Vowel Shift long high-mid /e: o:/. Jespersen (1909: 325) argues that diphthongal [eɪ] was established by around 1750, around the time of the formation of the centring diphthongs, and [oʊ] not much later. On the other hand, Scots, SSE and Hiberno-English lack all but the three 'true' diphthongs (and even /aʊ/ is marginal in Scots). Perhaps in dialects where most long vowels are diphthongised, the partial schwa preceding /r/ would have been more readily perceived as the offglide of a diphthong. Again, of course, we may seem to be pushing the explanation one stage further back: why should some dialects be more prone to diphthongisation than others? Aitchison (1989) argues that languages (or dialects) may be caught in a spiral of changes leading in the same direction, giving the effect of a diachronic conspiracy: once a change has taken place, it may provide a template or otherwise channel subsequent changes along a similar route. So a relatively minor change of diphthongisation in certain early English dialects may have started the 'snowball' that effectively leads to the present-day distribution of [r] in non-rhotic varieties. However, the diphthongisation changes must have built up over a considerable period of time, making it rather unlikely that the initial step can be identified: we are then in a sadly common situation for historical linguists, able to see the effects but only hypothesise about the ultimate cause. What is clear, however, is that the synchronic formulation of [r]-Insertion, in terms of the segment involved and the vowels which condition it, becomes completely non-arbitrary from a historical perspective.

6.6   Lexical Phonology and English /r/

Our next task is to assess where [r]-Insertion applies synchronically, in my model of Lexical Phonology. As we have seen in earlier chapters, lexical and postlexical rule applications are characterised by discrete sets of properties, which although not as decisively distinct as assumed in the early days of LP, when the division of lexical from postlexical rules was seen as absolute, nonetheless provide useful diagnostics for the level of application of rules, and for the historical movement into the lexicon characteristic of many low-level sound changes: recall from chapter 4 the typical pathway represented by æ-Tensing (Harris 1989), schematised in (6.23).

(6.23)   Neogrammarian sound change

↓

Postlexical rule (Detroit, Chicago)
↓

Lexical rule (Philadelphia, New York, Belfast)

↓

Lexical diffusion: *alters underlying forms* (RP *pat ~ pass*)

Historically, æ-Tensing began as a Neogrammarian sound change, being purely phonetically conditioned; it then became a postlexical rule in some varieties of English, and a lexical rule in others. Ultimately, in some accents like RP, the rule itself is lost, although its effects are retained, being integrated into the underlying representations to encode a new distinction, in this case between /æ/ and /ɑː/. If we were focusing on

RP particularly, the diagram in (6.23) would show all the steps through which the variety had passed on its way to the present-day situation. Each step is also preserved in some variety of English.

However, not all sound changes seem to be incorporated into the grammar in the same way, and in chapter 4 I identified an alternative pathway, this time involving the Scottish Vowel Length Rule. Historically, SVLR also began as a low-level process which lengthened vowels before voiced consonants. This sound change became the postlexical phonological rule of Low-Level Lengthening. However, in Scots and SSE, a rule inversion has occurred, such that an earlier, neutralising process which shortened long vowels and lengthened short ones in opposing sets of contexts, became a lengthening process. This altered the underlying status of length in the affected varieties: vowels begin as contrastively long or short, but after the rule inversion, all are underlyingly short, with length supplied by rule in particular environments. Scots and SSE are now the only accents of English where vowel length is essentially predictable and non-contrastive, although more recent lexical diffusion of long [aːi] to forms like *spider, viper, pylon* may indicate the beginnings of a second change to the underlying representations, whereby /ʌɪ/ and /aːi/ become distinctive. This means that contrastive length seems gradually to be being reintroduced, although SVLR is not simply reversing itself, since long and short vowels are not being restored to their earlier, historical distribution (6.24).

(6.24)   Neogrammarian sound change

$\downarrow$

Postlexical lengthening rule (very general)

$\downarrow$

Lexical lengthening plus shortening rule (Scots/SSE)
Rule inversion to lengthening rule: *alters underlying forms*

$\downarrow$

Lexical diffusion for /ʌɪ/; /aːi/ becomes distinctive
Alters underlying forms: still very variable.

Since [r]-Insertion is also the result of a rule inversion, it might be expected to follow the same pathway as SVLR. We have established that /r/-Deletion was not a sudden change, but began as a low-level, general weakening, which ultimately resulted in loss of [r] in coda positions. The resulting phonological rule of /r/-Deletion was later converted, via rule inversion, into [r]-Insertion; and there is a concomitant change at the underlying level, as forms like *spar, war, letter,* which had underlying /r/ at the time of /r/-Deletion, lose it. Thus far, the progression from gradual sound change, to phonological rule, to a present-day, inverted version of this rule accompanied by an alteration in the underlying forms, mirrors the pathway followed by the SVLR. However, if [r]-Insertion does belong to the same class of processes as the SVLR, we should also be able to find some evidence of a second change at the underlying level during its history.

Such evidence may indeed exist, although, as for SVLR, it is fragmentary and highly variable. This involves the situation in New York City (Labov 1972), a previously non-rhotic area which has this century been progressively re-rhoticising, presumably because of influence from rhotic General American. Labov's work indicates that many speakers, as well as producing categorical [r] in linking [r] forms, giving a revised paradigm of *war, warring, war is* all with [r], have extended [r] to non-prepausal environments for intrusive [r] forms. Similarly, [r] is also found in preconsonantal environments with historical [r]; the combined influence of orthographic < r > and rhotic General American speakers has reintroduced [r] in *guard, heard, harp;* but again, hypercorrection extends this into words with the same structure but without etymological [r], like *god,* which has [ɑ:] in New York speech. This might be interpreted as the provision of a new context for intrusive [r], but could equally indicate the acquisition of underlying /r/ in new forms. For instance, newly rhotic New York speakers may have *guard* and *god,* and *law* and *lore,* as homophones rather than minimal pairs; and if these have surface [r] in all contexts, we must assume underlying /r/. This sort of data is precisely parallel to our findings for the SLVR, where a second alteration in the underlying representations again gave new, unhistorical or counterhistorical forms, and again seemed to operate by gradual lexical diffusion. The steps in the history of [r] suggested by these examples is set out in (6.25).

(6.25)   Deletion sound change

   ↓

   Postlexical and lexical/or postlexical deletion rule

   ↓

   Postlexical and lexical insertion rule

Rule inversion: *alters underlying forms*

↓

[r]-Insertion applies to forms without historical /r/

↓

[r] appears before pauses and consonants.
Highly variable. *Alters underlying forms.*

As (6.25) shows, we begin, for non-rhotic varieties, with a deletion sound change, which becomes a phonological deletion rule, and is then inverted into an insertion rule; at this point, the underlying representations are altered as underlying non-prevocalic /r/ is lost, whereupon the inserted [r] is generalised to forms without historical /r/. The final step, which is by no means settled, involves the inclusion of underlying /r/ in forms which did not have it historically, and where it would not be inserted by the rule. As we have seen, this parallels the ongoing development of /aːi/ in Scots. Furthermore, as with æ-Tensing and the SVLR, each step after the first in (6.25) is preserved in some varieties of English: dialects with linking [r] only would maintain the deletion process; those with linking and intrusive [r] have insertion; and it may be that re-rhoticising varieties exemplify the last stage.

Synchronically, for a variety with linking and intrusive [r], it seems that [r]-Insertion must apply postlexically, since it operates across word boundaries in *fear of flying* or *severe attack*, but also on both Levels 1 and 2. It operates regularly in Level 2 derived forms like *soaring*, *saw*[r]*ing*, *banana*[r]*y*. As for Level 1, we saw in 6.4.2 above that [r]-Insertion applies in *doctoral, dangerous* and *severity*, and that in the last case it must be ordered before Level 1 Trisyllabic Laxing. In apparent counterexamples like *algebraic, ideal, dramatic*, [r]-Insertion is either blocked by tensing rules, or by pre-existing, alternative derived forms. [r]-Insertion therefore applies throughout the derivation, at Levels 1 and 2 as well as postlexically.

However, the earlier stage of /r/-Deletion may not have applied lexically. Certainly on Level 1, the Derived Environment Condition would have ruled it out: recall that [r] is not deleted in derived environments – rather, the derived environment is required for the retention of [r], by resyllabification into an adjacent onset. Consequently, /r/-Deletion may indeed have been a solely postlexical process, bringing the historical pathway followed by [r]-Insertion and associated processes even closer to that of the SVLR and its postlexical lengthening source. Both differ from the standard pathway of sound change – postlexical rule – lexical rule – incorporation into the underlying forms, as represented by æ-Tensing, by incorporating an extra step: they cause two changes in the underlying representations, not one. The first takes place at the time of the rule inversion; the second is later, and involves a gradual generalisation of the inserted or derived sound into new underived environments, where it would not appear according to the rule. Thus, a series of regular steps leads to apparently odd irregularities. The case of /r/ therefore also supports my earlier suggestion that the processes falling into this second class, which alter the underliers twice in their life-cycle, may be those which would have been analysed in Standard Generative Phonology as involving a rule inversion.

There remains, however, a disparity in the analysis here. I have argued for a gestural, Articulatory Phonology analysis of [r]-Deletion, but have only stated present-day [r]-Insertion as segment-based (Ø → r / /ɑː ɔː ə/ __ V). How far is the commitment to gestures intended to go? In fact, dealing with this sort of insertion process using Articulatory Phonology is not straightforward, and requires revision of the model in various possible ways, precisely because there is no synchronic source in the immediate context for the gestures comprising [r], and Articulatory Phonology as currently formulated does not permit direct insertion or deletion of gestures.

There is strong evidence that 'real' phonological processes exist, which nonetheless are unanalysable in Articulatory Phonology in its currently constrained state. That is, although Articulatory Phonology can deal enlighteningly with fast and casual speech processes and the sound changes to which these give rise, the very limited gestural manipulations permitted by Browman and Goldstein are not sufficient to deal with the subsequent phonological rule stage in all cases. For instance, Nolan (1993) and Holst and Nolan (1995) consider assimilatory behaviour of /s/ before [ʃ] in contexts like *restocks shelves*, based on visual reading of spectrograms. They report four categories of results: type A involved [s], with no assimilation; B and C had intermediate degrees of assimilation, with or without an initial partial [s]; but for type D, there was full assimilation, and the output of [ʃ] showed no trace of [s]. Holst and Nolan (1995) argue that types B and C can be dealt with under the Articulatory Phonology assumptions of gestural blending, but that type D must be seen as a higher-level, cognitive process replacing /s/ with /ʃ/ pre-production. This argument is supported by the electropalatographic results reported in Nolan, Holst and Kühnert (1996), who claim that Articulatory Phonology requires some supplementary mechanism to model 'arbitrary facts about the sound patterns of a language – by name, the phonological rule' (1996: 127).

The question is what form this supplement should take. Zsiga (1993, 1997), working on the basis of parallel gradient versus categorical processes in English and Igbo, argues that the difference lies in the units: gestures are needed at the postlexical level, but feature geometries have to be assumed lexically. Because gestures involve specification of actual extent in time, they can be used to model gradient phenomena, whereas features encode only simultaneity and precedence. At the output of the lexicon, a mapping of autosegmental features onto gestures takes place, partly on universal and partly on language-specific grounds. Conversely, McMahon, Foulkes and Tollfree (1994) contend that gestures should be adopted as the primary phonological unit at all levels, lexical and postlexical, and that the gradient versus categorical distinction resides in different constraints on rule application at different levels. Browman and Goldstein (1991: 334) already accept that 'some phonological alternations are so complex as to not permit an adequate description using gestural principles', and specifically note that cases of rule inversion are likely to represent one case where 'other principles or sources of constraint are ... required to completely explicate patterns in phonology'. These 'other principles' could be promoted on an *ad hoc* basis, but McMahon, Foulkes and Tollfree (1994) argue that it is less arbitrary, as well as not requiring a complete withdrawal of the accepted conditions on gestural manipulations, to exploit the existing lexical–postlexical division and the well-known limitations on lexical rule applications, notably the Derived Environment Condition. A good deal of further work will be required to determine which approach is the right one, or whether aspects of both need to be integrated into the eventual composite lexical–articulatory model: we need to know more about the gestural configuration of vowels and of the different realisations of English /r/, the latter badly requiring experimental work; and it is also not clear that the boundary between the two types of constraints on gestural processes should be at the output of the lexicon, given that [r]-Insertion itself applies across word-boundaries and in view of the affinities Carr (1991) notes between lexical and early postlexical rules. But all this is work for the future.

6.7   Retrospect and p[r]ospect

Natural Phonology and Morphology, in Wurzel's (1989: 196–7) words,

> investigate the language systems or the components of language systems that are the result of processes of change and that are themselves in the process of changing. To neglect change and changeability in language is equivalent to idealizing away a property that determines its very essence, something constitutive of human language as a whole. Thus, it is not surprising that, given a purely synchronic approach, many grammatical facts defy explanation which, from a historical point of view, are quite explainable.

In this book, I have tried to show how Lexical Phonology helps us understand the connections between the phonological past and the phonological present. The dependency between the two is necessarily bidirectional. A constrained, rule-based, derivational model makes testable predictions on the course sound changes follow, as they develop from low-level variation into postlexical and then lexical rules. This is not the same as the recapitulation of history found in SGP, where sound changes and phonological rules were essentially identical: instead, variant pathways into the grammar are determined by issues of learnability and by the constraints on the model. The consequence is that present-day rules, like the Vowel Shift Rules and [r]-Insertion, have altered considerably with respect to their predecessors, the Great Vowel Shift and [r]-Deletion (the latter being, as I showed above, a label for a number of interrelated phonetically and phonologically motivated changes which together set the scene for Modern English linking and intrusive [r]). In all these cases, an appropriately constrained Lexical Phonology helps determine the analysis we select in interesting ways, blocking particular options and enforcing others. Apparently arbitrary present-day processes can equally be shown to be explicable in diachronic perspective.

The constraints on Lexical Phonology, namely the Derived Environment Condition, the Alternation Condition, construed as a condition on learnability, and Structure Preservation, are also both synchronically and diachronically relevant and active. The DEC limits the application of Level 1 rules, and determines the point at which alternations must be regarded as fossilised, and hence incorporated into the underlying representations: recall from chapter 3 the ex-Vowel Shift alternations, such as *food ~ fodder, profound ~ profundity*, which the model rules out for Present-Day English, and the related fact that irregular verb past tenses could be derived productively only for the relatively recently developed *keep ~ kept* type. The Alternation Condition makes a phonology with a rule on Level 1, controlled by DEC, more highly valued from the point of view of learnability than a less constrained model with the same rule on Level 2: this implies (Giegerich in press) that Level 2 phonology will be rather limited or in some languages may not exist at all. This has a further consequence for Structure Preservation, which itself appears to play a diachronic role in encouraging the further lexical diffusion of alternations derived via a Level 1 rule, leading to incipient underlying contrast for SSE /ʌi/ ~ /aːi/. Violations of Structure Preservation tend to occur with Level 2 rules, which in this model are low-valued in any case, although they may represent a temporary, new lexicalisation of a rule on its way to Level 1. If there are so few truly Level 2 rules (as opposed to actual Level 1 rules which have been ordered on Level 2 in the past to defuse the operation of the DEC), it is no wonder that phonologists have been unable to decide on the role of SP on Level 2.

Representational decisions in this model also have strong derivational consequences. The lack of underspecification means a theory of possible underlying representations is required, and the application of both DEC and the Alternation Condition encourages a restrictive approach: hence the rather concrete underliers adopted here, which typically correspond to the lexical representation of non-alternating forms or the underived member of alternating sets. Rejecting underspecification also reveals the operation of the constraints of Lexical Phonology, making them harder to bypass; and leads to a more realistic approach to dialect variation by allowing historical changes to accumulate at the underlying level, not only in the rules. Historical analyses, based on contemporary evidence, also provide us with maps of variation in English dialects for processes like SVLR and [r]-Insertion; diachronically, each step determines the next, while synchronically, each step is maintained in some variety. Finally, if we incorporate a version of Articulatory Phonology into the model, as argued tentatively in connection with English [r], low-level variation can be modelled using limited gestural manipulations; but when these are interpreted cross-generationally as segment insertion or deletion, the resulting synchronic rule may have to become lexical. Here we find another new perspective on Structure Preservation: it seems on this view that late postlexical, low-level processes really can create new information, but not randomly: new information can arise only if it is motivated in its context. When that context changes, or the insertion or deletion is learned as categorical, truly new gestures may be introduced, contravening Structure Preservation, which is therefore a useful diagnostic of a rule that is lexicalising, but has not yet penetrated into the underlying representations.

In short, the phonological model presented here attempts to connect synchrony, diachrony, variation and phonological theory in a non-fortuitous way, and to show that all are mutually informing. In developing phonological theory, we must consider issues beyond synchronic, variety-specific alternation and distribution on the one hand, and universal constraints on the other. Given a summary as apt as Johansson's (1973: 67), I am happy to relinquish my authorial right to the last word:

> It is the object of linguistics to determine how abstract phonology should be and, ultimately, the psychological reality of phonological descriptions. If this problem is to be solved, more evidence of the kind provided by linking and intrusive /r/ must be found. The search for such evidence, which is available in historical change ... first language acquisition, interference in second language learning ... etc., would seem to be a more relevant task than constructing elegant but untestable phonological descriptions.

Bibliography

Abercrombie, David (1979). 'The accents of Standard English in Scotland'. In Aitken, A.J. and T. McArthur (eds.). *Languages of Scotland*. Edinburgh, Chambers: 69–84.

Agutter, Alex (1988a). 'The dangers of dialect parochialism: the Scottish Vowel Length Rule'. In Fisiak, J. (ed.). *Historical Dialectology*. Berlin, Mouton de Gruyter: 1–22.

(1988b). 'The not-so-Scottish Vowel Length Rule'. In Anderson, John M. and Norman Macleod (eds.). *Edinburgh Studies in the English Language*. Edinburgh, John Donald: 120–32.

Aitchison, Jean (1989). 'Spaghetti junctions and recurrent routes: some preferred pathways in language evolution'. *Lingua* 77: 151–71.

Aitken, A.J. (1977). 'How to pronounce Older Scots'. In Aitken, A.J., M.P. McDiarmid and D.S. Thomson (eds.). *Bards and Makars: Scots Language and Literature, Mediaeval and Renaissance*. Glasgow University Press: 1–21.

(1981). 'The Scottish Vowel Length Rule'. In Benskin, M. and M.L. Samuels (eds.). *So Meny People, Longages and Tonges*. Edinburgh, Middle English Dialect Project: 131–57.

Allan, Scott (1985). 'A note on AYE distribution'. *Journal of Linguistics* 21: 191–4.

Allen, Margaret (1978). *Morphological Investigations*. Unpublished PhD Dissertation, University of Connecticut, Storrs, Conn.

(1980). 'Semantic and phonological consequences of boundaries: a morphological analysis of compounds'. In Aronoff, Mark and Mary-Louise Kean (eds.). *Juncture*. Saratoga, Calif., Anma Libri: 9–28.

Andersen, Henning (1973). 'Abductive and deductive change'. *Language* 49: 765–93.

Anderson, John M. (1987). 'Contrastivity and non-specification in Dependency Phonology'. Manuscript, University of Edinburgh.

(1993). 'Morphology, phonology and the Scottish Vowel-Length Rule'. *Journal of Linguistics* 29: 419–30.

Anderson, Stephen R. (1981). 'Why phonology isn't "natural"'. *Linguistic Inquiry* 12: 493–539.

(1982). 'Where's morphology?' *Linguistic Inquiry* 13: 571–611.

(1984). 'A metrical reinterpretation of some traditional claims about quantity and stress'. In Aronoff, Mark and R. Oehrle (eds.). *Language Sound Structure*. Cambridge, Mass., MIT Press: 83–106.

(1992). *A-Morphous Morphology*. Cambridge University Press.

Anon (1826). *The Vulgarities of Speech Corrected, With Elegant Expressions for Provincial and Vulgar English, Scots and Irish*. London, Bulcock.

Archangeli, Diana (1984). *Underspecification in Yawelmani Phonology and Morphology*. Unpublished PhD Dissertation, MIT.

(1988). 'Aspects of underspecification theory'. *Phonology* 5: 183–207.

Aronoff, Mark (1976). *Word Formation in Generative Grammar*. Cambridge, Mass., MIT Press.

Aronoff, Mark and S. Sridhar (1983). 'Morphological levels in English and Kannada, or Atarizing Reagan'. In Chicago Linguistics Society, *Papers from the Parasession on the Interplay of Phonology, Morphology and Syntax*: 3–16.

Badecker, W. (1991). 'Affix raising and the level ordering hypothesis'. *Lingua* 83: 103–32.

Bailey, Charles-James N. (1982). 'The garden path that historical linguistics went astray on'. *Language and Communication* 2: 151–60.

(1996). *Essays on Time-Based Linguistic Analysis*. Oxford, Clarendon Press.

Bauer, Laurie (1990). 'Beheading the word'. *Journal of Linguistics* 26: 1–31.

Beal, Joan (1993). 'Lengthening of *a* in eighteenth-century English: a consideration of evidence from Thomas Spence's *Grand Repository of the English Language* and other contemporary pronouncing dictionaries'. *Newcastle and Durham Working Papers in Linguistics* 1: 2–17.

Bladon, R. and A. Al-Bamerni (1975). 'Coarticulation resistance in English /l/'. *Journal of Phonetics* 4: 137–50.

Blevins, Juliette (1997). 'Rules in Optimality Theory: two case studies'. In Roca, Iggy (ed.) *Derivations and Constraints in Phonology*. Oxford, Clarendon Press: 227–60.

Bloch, B. (1947). 'English verb inflection'. *Language* 23: 399–418.

Booij, Geert and Jerzy Rubach (1987). 'Postcyclic versus postlexical rules in Lexical Phonology'. *Linguistic Inquiry* 18: 1–44.

Borowsky, Toni J. (1989). 'Structure Preservation and the syllable coda in English'. *Natural Language and Linguistic Theory* 7: 145–66.

(1990). *Topics in the Lexical Phonology of English*. New York, Garland.

Bresnan, Joan (1982). *The Mental Representation of Grammatical Relations*. Cambridge, Mass., MIT Press.

Broadbent, Judith (1991). 'Linking and intrusive r in English'. *University College London Working Papers in Linguistics* 3: 281–302.

(1992). Paper presented at the Manchester Phonology Workshop.

Brockhaus, Wiebke (1990). 'Colourful leagues: a government phonology approach to final obstruent devoicing in German'. *University College London Working Papers in Linguistics* 2: 270–95.

Bromberger, Sylvain and Morris Halle (1989). 'Why phonology is different'. *Linguistic Inquiry* 20: 51–70.

Browman, Catherine P. and Louis Goldstein (1986). 'Towards an articulatory phonology'. *Phonology Yearbook* 3: 219–52.

(1989). 'Articulatory gestures as phonological units'. *Phonology* 6: 201–51.

(1991). 'Gestural structures: distinctiveness, phonological processes, and historical change'. In Mattingly, I.G. and M. Studdert-Kennedy (eds.). *Modularity and the Motor Theory of Speech Perception*. Hillsdale, N.J., Lawrence Erlbaum: 313–38.

(1992). 'Articulatory Phonology: an overview'. *Phonetica* 49: 155–80.

Brown, Gillian (1972). *Phonological Rules and Dialect Variation*. Cambridge University Press.

Buchanan, J. (1757). *Linguae Britannicae Vera Pronunciatio*. Facsimile R.C. Alston (ed.) (1968), *English Linguistics 1500–1800*, Volume 39. Menston, Scolar Press.

(1770). *A Plan for an English Grammar-School Education*. London.

Campbell, Lyle and Jon Ringen (1981). 'Teleology and the explanation of sound change'. In Dressler, Wolfgang U., Oskar E. Pfeiffer and John R. Rennison (eds.). *Phonologica*. Innsbruck, Innsbrucker Beitrage zur Sprachwissenschaft: 57–68.

Carr, Philip (1991). 'Lexical properties of postlexical rules: postlexical derived environment and the Elsewhere Condition'. *Lingua* 85: 41–54.

(1992). 'Strict cyclicity, structure preservation and the Scottish Vowel-Length Rule'. *Journal of Linguistics* 28: 91–114.

(1993). *Phonology*. London, Macmillan.

Catford, J.C. (1958). 'Vowel-systems of Scots dialects'. *Transactions of the Philological Society*: 107–17.

Chambers, J.K. (1973). 'Canadian raising'. *Canadian Journal of Linguistics* 18: 113–35.

Chambers, J.K. and Peter Trudgill (1980). *Dialectology*. Cambridge University Press.

Charette, Monik (1990). 'Licence to govern'. *Phonology* 7: 233–53.

(1991). *Conditions on Phonological Government*. Cambridge University Press.

Chen, Matthew (1970). 'Vowel length variation as a function of the voicing of the consonant environment'. *Phonetics* 22: 129–59.

Chen, Matthew and William S-Y. Wang (1975). 'Sound change: actuation and implementation'. *Language* 51: 255–81.

Chomsky, Noam (1965). *Aspects of the Theory of Syntax*. Cambridge, Mass., MIT Press.

(1970). 'Remarks on nominalization'. In Jacobs, R., and P. Rosenbaum (eds.). *Readings in English Transformational Grammar*. Waltham, Mass., Blaisdell: 184–221.

(1981). *Lectures on Government and Binding*. Cambridge, Mass., MIT Press.

Chomsky, Noam and Morris Halle (1968). *The Sound Pattern of English*. New York, Harper & Row.

Churma, Donald G. (1985). *Arguments from External Evidence in Phonology*. New York, Garland.

Cole, Jennifer (1995). 'The cycle in phonology'. In Goldsmith, John (ed.). *The Handbook of Phonological Theory*. Oxford, Blackwell: 70–113.

Coleman, John (1995). 'Declarative lexical phonology'. In Durand, Jacques and Francis Katamba (eds.). *Frontiers of Phonology: Atoms, Structures, Derivations*. London, Longman: 333–82.

Cooper, Christopher (1687). *The English Teacher*. London.

Corbett, G., N. Fraser and S. McGlashan (eds.). (1993). *Heads*. Cambridge University Press.

Crothers, J. (1971). *On the Abstractness Controversy*. Project on Linguistic Analysis, second series. Berkeley, Calif., Phonology Laboratory, Department of Linguistics, University of California.

Davis, Stuart and Michael Hammond (1995). 'On the status of onglides in American English'. *Phonology* 12(2): 159–82.

Delattre, P. (1962). 'Some factors of vowel duration and their cross-linguistic validity'. *Journal of the Acoustical Society of America* 34: 1141–2.

Devitt, Amy J. (1989). *Standardizing Written English: Diffusion in the Case of Scotland, 1520–1659*. Cambridge University Press.

Dieth, E. (1932). *A Grammar of the Buchan Dialect*. Cambridge, Heffer.

Disterheft, Dorothy (1990). 'The role of adaptive rules in language change'. *Diachronica* 7: 181–98.

Dobson, E.J. (1957). *English Pronunciation 1500–1700*. Oxford, Clarendon Press.

(1962). 'Middle English lengthening in open syllables'. *Transactions of the Philological Society*: 124–48.

Donegan, Patricia (1993). 'On the phonetic basis of phonological change'. In Jones, Charles (ed.). *Historical Linguistics: Problems and Perspectives*. London, Longman: 98–130.

Dorian, Nancy (1993). 'Internally and externally motivated change in language contact settings: doubts about dichotomy'. In Jones, Charles (ed.). *Historical Linguistics: Problems and Perspectives*. London, Longman: 131–55.

Drummond, James (1767). *A Grammatical Introduction to the Modern Pronunciation and Spelling of the English Tongue, for Private Perusal and for Public Schools*. Edinburgh.

Durand, Jacques (1990). *Generative and Non-Linear Phonology*. London, Longman.

(1995). 'Universalism in phonology: atoms, structures and derivations'. In Durand, Jacques and Francis Katamba (eds.). *Frontiers of Phonology: Atoms, Structures, Derivations*. London, Longman: 267–88.

Durand, Jacques and Francis Katamba (eds.) (1995a). *Frontiers of Phonology: Atoms, Structures, Derivations*. London, Longman.

(1995b). 'Introduction'. In Durand, Jacques and Francis Katamba (eds.). *Frontiers of Phonology: Atoms, Structures, Derivations*. London, Longman: xiii–xviii.

Ehala, Martin (1992). *On the Psychological Reality of Underspecification: Evidence from Spoken Word Recognition*. Unpublished MPhil Essay, Department of Linguistics, University of Cambridge.

Ellis, A.J. (1849). *The Teacher's Guide to Phonetic Reading*. London, Pitman.

Elphinston, J. (1787). *Propriety Ascertained in her Picture, or Inglish Speech and Spelling Rendered Mutual Guides, Secure Alike from Distant, and from Domestic, Error*, Volume 2. London.

Ewen, Colin (1977). 'Aitken's Law and the phonatory gesture in Dependency Phonology'. *Lingua* 41: 307–29.

Ewen, Colin and Harry van der Hulst (1988). '[high], [low] and [back], or [I], [A] and [U]'. In Coopman, P., and A. Hulk (eds.). *Linguistics in the Netherlands 1988*. Dordrecht, Foris.

Farrar, Kimberley J. (1996). *The Role of Contact in the Explanation of Syntactic Change*. Unpublished PhD Dissertation, Department of Linguistics, University of Cambridge.

Fischer-Jørgensen, Eli (1990). 'Intrinsic F0 in tense and lax vowels with special reference to German'. *Phonetica* 47: 99–140.

Foulkes, Paul (1993). *Theoretical Implications of the /p/ > /f/ > /h/ Change*. Unpublished PhD Dissertation, Department of Linguistics, University of Cambridge.

(1997). 'English [r]-sandhi: a sociolinguistic perspective'. *Histoire Epistémologie Langage* 19: 73–96.

Gandour, J., B. Weinberg and D. Rutkowsky (1980). 'Influence of postvocalic consonants on vowel duration in esophageal speech'. *Language and Speech* 23: 149–58.

Gick, Bryan (1997). 'The intrusive L'. Paper presented to the American Dialect Society, Chicago, January 1997.

Giegerich, Heinz J. (1986). 'Relating to metrical structure'. In Durand, Jacques (ed.). *Dependency and Non-Linear Phonology*. London, Croom Helm.

(1988). 'Strict Cyclicity and Elsewhere'. *Lingua* 75: 125–34.

(1992). *English Phonology: An Introduction*. Cambridge University Press.

(1994). 'Confronting reality: phonology and the literate speaker'. In Stamirowska, K., Z. Mazur and A. Walczuk (eds.). *Literature and Language in the Cultural Context: Proceedings of the Inaugural Conference of the Polish Association for the Study of English*. Krakow, Universitas: 157–73.

(in press). *Lexical Strata in English: Morphological Causes, Phonological Effects*. Cambridge University Press.

Gimson, A.C. (1962 1st edn.; 1980 4th edn.). *An Introduction to the Pronunciation of English*. London, Arnold.

(1973). 'Phonology and the lexicographer'. *Annals of the New York Academy of Sciences* 211: 115–21.

Goldsmith, John (1990). *Autosegmental and Metrical Phonology*. Oxford, Blackwell.

Goldsmith, John (ed.). (1993a). *The Last Phonological Rule: Reflections on Constraints and Derivations*. University of Chicago Press.

(1993b). 'Introduction'. In Goldsmith, John (ed.). *The Last Phonological Rule: Reflections on Constraints and Derivations*. University of Chicago Press: 1–20.

(ed.). (1995a). *The Handbook of Phonological Theory*. Oxford, Blackwell.

(1995b). 'Phonological theory'. In Goldsmith, John (ed.). *The Handbook of Phonological Theory*. Oxford, Blackwell: 1–23.

Goyvaerts, D.L., and G. Pullum (eds.). (1975). *Essays on the Sound Pattern of English*. Ghent, Story-Scientia.

Grant, W. (1912). *The Pronunciation of English in Scotland*. Md., McGrath.

Gregg, R.J. (1973). 'The diphthongs ʌi and aɪ in Scottish, Scotch-Irish and Canadian English'. *Canadian Journal of Linguistics* 18: 136–45.

Guthrie, M. (1967–71). *Comparative Bantu: An Introduction to the Comparative Linguistics and Prehistory of the Bantu Languages*. Farnborough, Gregg International Publishers.

Halle, Morris (1962). 'Phonology in generative grammar'. *Word* 18: 54–72.

(1973). 'Prolegomena to a theory of word formation'. *Linguistic Inquiry* 4: 3–16.

(1977). 'Tenseness, vowel shift and the phonology of the back vowels in Modern English'. *Linguistic Inquiry* 8: 611–25.

Halle, Morris and William J. Idsardi (1997). '*r*, hypercorrection, and the Elsewhere Condition'. In Roca, Iggy (ed.). *Derivations and Constraints in Phonology*. Oxford, Clarendon Press: 331–48.

Halle, Morris and K.P. Mohanan (1985). 'Segmental phonology of modern English'. *Linguistic Inquiry* 16: 57–116.

Halle, Morris and Jean-Roger Vergnaud (1987). *An Essay on Stress*. Cambridge, Mass., MIT Press.

Hargus, Sharon (1993). 'Modelling the phonology–morphology interface'. In Hargus, Sharon and Ellen M. Kaisse (eds.). *Studies in Lexical Phonology*. New York, Academic Press: 45–74.

Hargus, Sharon and Ellen M. Kaisse (eds.). (1993). *Studies in Lexical Phonology*. New York, Academic Press.

Harris, John (1984). 'Syntactic variation and dialect divergence'. *Journal of Linguistics* 20: 303–27.

(1985). *Phonological Variation and Change: Studies in Hiberno-English*. Cambridge University Press.

(1986). 'Phonetic constraints on sociolinguistic variation'. *Sheffield Working Papers in Language and Linguistics* 3: 120–43.

(1987). 'Non-Structure Preserving rules in Lexical Phonology: Southeastern Bantu harmony'. *Lingua* 73: 255–92.

(1989). 'Towards a lexical analysis of sound change in progress'. *Journal of Linguistics* 25: 35–56.

(1990). 'Segmental complexity and phonological government'. *Phonology* 7: 255–300.

(1992). 'Licensing inheritance'. *University College London Working Papers in Linguistics* 4: 1–44.

(1994). *English Sound Structure*. Oxford, Blackwell.

Harris, John and Jonathan Kaye (1990). 'A tale of two cities: London glottalling and New York tapping'. *The Linguistic Review* 7: 251–74.

Harris, John and Geoff Lindsey (1995). 'The elements of phonological representation'. In Durand, Jacques and Francis Katamba (eds.). *Frontiers of Phonology: Atoms, Structures, Derivations*. London, Longman: 34–79.

Hart, John (1569). *An Orthographie*. London.

Hock, Hans Henrich (1986). *Principles of Historical Linguistics*. The Hague, Mouton de Gruyter.

Hockett, C. (1954). 'Two models of grammatical description'. *Word* 10: 210–31.

Hoekstra, Teun, Harry van der Hulst and Michael Moortgat (1981). *Lexical Grammar*. Dordrecht, Reidel.

Hogg, Richard (1996). 'Old English Open Syllable Lengthening'. *Transactions of the Philological Society* 94(1): 57–72.

Holst, Tara and Francis Nolan (1995). 'The influence of syntactic structure on [s] to [ʃ] assimilation'. In Connell, Bruce and Amalia Arvaniti (eds.). *Phonology and Phonetic Evidence: Papers in Laboratory Phonology IV.* Cambridge University Press: 315–33.

Hooper, Joan Bybee (1976). *An Introduction to Natural Generative Phonology.* New York, Academic Press.

House, A.S. (1961). 'On vowel duration in English'. *Journal of the Acoustical Society of America* 33: 1174–8.

House, A.S. and G. Fairbanks (1953). 'The influence of consonant environment upon the secondary acoustical characteristics of vowels'. *Journal of the Acoustical Society of America* 25: 105–13.

Hualde, Jose (1991). 'Unspecified and unmarked vowels'. *Linguistic Inquiry* 22: 205–9.

Hughes, Arthur and Peter Trudgill (1979). *English Accents and Dialects.* London, Arnold.

Hullah, J. (1870). *The Cultivation of the Speaking Voice.* Oxford.

Hyman, Larry M. (1977). 'On the nature of linguistic stress'. In Hyman, Larry M. (ed.). *Studies in Stress and Accent.* Los Angeles, Department of Linguistics, University of Southern California.

  (1993). 'Problems for rule ordering in phonology: two Bantu test cases'. In Goldsmith, John (ed.). *The Last Phonological Rule: Reflections on Constraints and Derivations.* University of Chicago Press: 195–222.

Jackson, K. (1955). 'The Pictish language'. In Wainwright, F.T. (ed.). *The Problem of the Picts.* Edinburgh, Nelson: 129–66.

Jaeger, Jeri J. (1986). 'On the acquisition of abstract representations for English vowels'. *Phonology Yearbook* 3: 71–97.

Janson, Tore (1991/2). 'Southern Bantu and Makua'. *Sprache und Geschichte in Afrika* 12/13: 63–106.

Jensen, J. and M. Stong-Jensen (1984). 'Morphology is in the lexicon!' *Linguistic Inquiry* 15: 474–98.

Jespersen, O. (1909). *A Modern English Grammar on Historical Principles.* London.

  (1922). *Language, its Nature, Development and Origin.* George Allen & Unwin, London.

Jetchev, G. (1993). '/r/ misperception and Slavic historical phonetics'. Poster presented at the Fourth Conference on Laboratory Phonology, Oxford.

Johansson, Stig (1973). 'Linking and intrusive /r/ in English: a case for a more concrete phonology'. *Studia Linguistica* 27: 53–68.

Johnston, Paul (1980). *A Synchronic and Historical View of Border Area Bimoraic Vowel Systems.* Unpublished PhD Dissertation, Department of English Language, University of Edinburgh.

  (1992). 'English vowel shifting: one great vowel shift or two small shifts?' *Diachronica* 9: 189–226.

  (1997a). 'Older Scots phonology and its regional variation'. In Jones, Charles (ed.). *The Edinburgh History of the Scots Language*. Edinburgh University Press: 47–111.

(1997b). 'Regional variation'. In Jones, Charles (ed.). *The Edinburgh History of the Scots Language*. Edinburgh University Press: 433–513.

Jones, Charles (ed.). (1991). Sylvester Douglas: *A Treatise on the Provincial Dialect of Scotland*, Edinburgh University Press.

(1993). 'Scottish Standard English in the late eighteenth century'. *Transactions of the Philological Society* 91(1): 95–131.

(1995). *A Language Suppressed: The Pronunciation of the Scots Language in the Eighteenth Century*. Edinburgh, John Donald.

(ed.). (1997a). *The Edinburgh History of the Scots Language*. Edinburgh University Press.

(1997b). 'Phonology'. In Jones, Charles (ed.). *The Edinburgh History of the Scots Language*. Edinburgh University Press: 267–334.

Jones, Daniel (1956). *The Pronunciation of English*. Cambridge.

Jonson, Ben (1640). *The English Grammar*. Facsimile (1972) Alston, R.C. (ed.). *English Linguistics 1500–1800*, Volume 349. Menston, Scolar Press.

Jordan, R. (1925). *Handbuch der mittel-englischen Grammatik*. Heidelberg.

Kaisse, Ellen M. (1990). 'Towards a typology of postlexical rules'. In Inkelas, Sharon and Draga Zec (eds.). *The Phonology–Syntax Connection*. CSLI Publishers and University of Chicago Press: 127–43.

Kaisse, Ellen and Sharon Hargus (1993). 'Introduction'. In Hargus, Sharon and Ellen Kaisse (eds.). *Studies in Lexical Phonology*. New York, Academic Press.

(1994). 'When do linked structures evade Structure Preservation?'. In Wiese, Richard (ed.). *Recent Developments in Lexical Phonology*. Düsseldorf, Heinrich Heine Universität: 185–204.

Kaisse, Ellen and Patricia Shaw (1985). 'On the theory of Lexical Phonology'. *Phonology Yearbook* 2: 1–30.

Kay, Billy (1988). *Scots: The Mither Tongue*. London, Grafton Books.

Kaye, Jonathan (1989). *Phonology: A Cognitive View*. Hillsdale, N.J., Lawrence Erlbaum Associates.

(1995). 'Derivations and interfaces'. In Durand, Jacques and Francis Katamba (eds.). *Frontiers of Phonology: Atoms, Structures, Derivations*. London, Longman: 289–332.

Kaye, Jonathan, Jean Lowenstamm and Jean-Roger Vergnaud (1985). 'The internal structure of phonological elements: a theory of charm and government'. *Phonology Yearbook* 2: 305–28.

(1990). 'Constituent structure and government in phonology'. *Phonology* 7: 193–232.

Kean, Mary-Louise (1974). 'The strict cycle in phonology'. *Linguistic Inquiry* 5: 179–203.

Keating, Patricia (1988). 'Underspecification in phonetics'. *Phonology* 5: 275–92.

Kenyon, J.S. and T.A. Knott (1953). *A Pronouncing Dictionary of American English*. Springfield, Mass., Merriam.

King, Robert D. (1969). *Historical Linguistics and Generative Grammar*. N.J., Prentice-Hall.

Kiparsky, Paul (1973 (= 1968)). 'How abstract is phonology?' In Fujimura, O. (ed.). *Three Dimensions of Linguistic Theory.* Tokyo, Taikusha.

(1982). 'Lexical phonology and morphology'. In Yang, I.-S. (ed.). *Linguistics in the Morning Calm.* Seoul, Hanshin: 3–91.

(1985). 'Some consequences of Lexical Phonology'. *Phonology Yearbook* 2: 85–138.

(1988). 'Phonological change'. In Newmeyer, F.J. (ed.). *Linguistics: The Cambridge Survey. I: Linguistic Theory – Foundations.* Cambridge University Press: 363–415.

Kiparsky, Paul and Lise Menn (1977). 'On the acquisition of phonology'. In Macnamara, J. (ed.). *Language Learning and Thought.* New York, Academic Press: 47–78.

Klima, E.S. (1964). 'Relatedness between grammatical systems'. *Language* 40: 1–20.

Kohler, Klaus (1964). *Aspects of the History of English Pronunciation in Scotland.* Unpublished PhD Dissertation, Department of English Language, University of Edinburgh.

Kökeritz, Helge (1944). *Mather Flint on Early Eighteenth Century English Pronunciation.* Uppsala, Skrifter utgivna av Kungl.

Kuno, S. (1974). 'The position of relative clauses and conjunctions'. *Linguistic Inquiry* 5: 117–36.

Kurath, Hans and Raven I. McDavid (1961). *The Pronunciation of English in the Atlantic States.* Ann Arbor, University of Michigan Press.

Labov, William (1972). *Sociolinguistic Patterns.* Philadelphia, University of Pennsylvania Press.

(1978). 'On the use of the present to explain the past'. In Baldi, Philip and Ronald N. Werth (eds.). *Readings in Historical Phonology.* University Park, Pennsylvania State University Press: 275–312.

(1981). 'Resolving the Neogrammarian controversy'. *Language* 57: 267–308.

Ladefoged, Peter (1990). 'On dividing phonetics and phonology'. In Kingston, J. and Mary Beckman (eds.). *Papers in Laboratory Phonology I: Between the Grammar and Physics of Speech.* Cambridge University Press: 398–405.

Ladefoged, Peter and Ian Maddieson (1996). *The Sounds of the World's Languages.* Oxford, Blackwell.

Lahiri, Aditi and William Marslen-Wilson (1991). 'The mental representation of lexical form: a phonological approach to the recognition lexicon'. *Cognition* 38: 245–94.

Lakoff, George (1993). 'Cognitive phonology'. In Goldsmith, John (ed.). *The Last Phonological Rule: Reflections on Constraints and Derivations.* University of Chicago Press: 117–45.

Lass, Roger (1974). 'Linguistic orthogenesis? Scots vowel quantity and the English length conspiracy'. In Anderson, John M. and Charles Jones (eds.). *Historical Linguistics. II: Theory and Description in Phonology.* Amsterdam, North Holland: 311–52.

Lass, Roger (1976). *English Phonology and Phonological Theory.* Cambridge University Press.

(1980). 'John Hart vindicatus? A study in the interpretation of early phoneticians'. *Folia Linguistica Historica* I: 75–96.

(1987). *The Shape of English*. London, Dent.

(1989). 'How early does English get 'modern'? Or, what happens when you listen to orthoepists and not to historians'. *Diachronica* 6: 75–110.

(1992). 'The Early Modern English vowels noch einmal again: a reply to Minkova and Stockwell'. *Diachronica* 9: 1–13.

(1993). 'How real(ist) are reconstructions?' In Jones, Charles (ed.). *Historical Linguistics: Problems and Perspectives*. London, Longman: 156–89.

(1997). *Historical Linguistics and Language Change*. Cambridge University Press.

(in press). 'Phonology and morphology'. In Lass, Roger (ed.). *The Cambridge History of the English Language, Volume III: 1476–1776*. Cambridge University Press.

Lass, Roger and John M. Anderson (1975). *Old English Phonology*. Cambridge University Press.

Lehmann, Winfred P. (1973). 'A structural principle of language and its implications'. *Language* 49: 47–66.

Leslie, David (1989). 'Consonant reduction in English'. Paper presented at the London Phonology Seminar.

Lieber, Rochelle (1979). 'On Middle English lengthening in open syllables'. *Linguistic Analysis* 5: 1–27.

(1981). *On the Organization of the Lexicon*. Bloomington, Ind., Indiana University Linguistics Club.

(1982). 'Allomorphy'. *Linguistic Analysis* 10: 27–52.

Lightfoot, David (1991). *How to Set Parameters: Arguments from Language Change*. Cambridge, Mass., MIT Press.

Lightner, T (1971). 'Generative phonology'. In Dingwall, W.O. (ed.). *A Survey of Linguistic Science*. University of Maryland Press: 498–574.

Lindau, Mona (1978). 'Vowel features'. *Language* 54: 541–63.

(1985). 'The story of r'. In Fromkin, V.A. (ed.). *Phonetic Linguistics*. Orlando, Fla., Academic Press: 157–68.

Lindeman, Fredrik O. (1987). *Introduction to the 'Laryngeal Theory'*. Oslo, Norwegian University Press.

Lindsey, Geoff (1990). 'Quantity and quality in British and American English vowel systems'. In Ramsaran, Susan (ed.). *Studies in the Pronunciation of English: A Commemorative Volume in Honour of A.C. Gimson*. London, Routledge: 106–18.

Lodge, K.R. (1984a). *Studies in the Phonology of Colloquial English*. London, Croom Helm.

(1984b). 'Testing native speaker predictions of variant forms of English'. *University of East Anglia Papers in Linguistics* 20: 21–7.

Luick, Karl (1921). *Historische Grammatik der englischen Sprache*. Leipzig.

Lutz, Angelika (1994). 'Vocalisation of 'post-vocalic r' – an Early Modern English sound change?' In Kastovsky, Dieter (ed.). *Studies in Early Modern English*. Berlin, Mouton de Gruyter: 167–85.

Malsch, Derry and Roseanne Fulcher (1975). 'Tensing and syllabification in Middle English'. *Language* 51(2): 303–14.

Mascaró, Joan (1976). *Catalan Phonology and the Phonological Cycle*. Unpublished PhD Dissertation, Department of Linguistics, MIT.

Mather, J.Y., and H.H. Speitel (1986). *The Linguistic Atlas of Scotland: Scots Section*. Volume III. London, Croom Helm.

Matthews, P.H. (1974). *Morphology*. Cambridge University Press.

(1981). *Do Languages Obey General Laws?* Inaugural lecture of the University of Cambridge. Cambridge University Press.

McCarthy, John (1991). 'Synchronic rule inversion'. In Sutton, L.A., C. Johnson and R. Shields (eds.). *Proceedings of the 17th Annual Meeting of the Berkeley Linguistics Society*. Berkeley, Calif., Berkeley Linguistics Society: 192–207.

(1993). 'A case of surface constraint violation'. *Canadian Journal of Linguistics* 38: 169–95.

McCarthy, John and Alison Taub (1992). Review of Paradis, Carole and Jean-François Prunet (eds.). *The Special Status of Coronals: Internal and External Evidence. Phonology* 9: 363–70.

McCawley, James D. (1986). 'Today the world, tomorrow phonology'. *Phonology Yearbook* 3: 27–44.

McClure, J. Derrick (1977). 'Vowel duration in a Scottish dialect'. *Journal of the International Phonetics Association* 7: 10–16.

(1995). 'English in Scotland'. In Burchfield, Robert (ed.). *English in Britain and Overseas: Origins and Developments. The Cambridge History of the English Language*, Volume V. Cambridge University Press.

McKenna, Gordon (1987). 'Wha's like us? Aitken's Law and the voicing effect revisited'. *Edinburgh University Department of Linguistics Work in Progress* 20: 156–63.

McMahon, April (1989). *Constraining Lexical Phonology: Evidence from English Vowels*. Unpublished PhD Dissertation, Department of English Language, University of Edinburgh.

(1990). 'Vowel shift, free rides and strict cyclicity'. *Lingua* 80: 197–225.

(1991). 'Lexical Phonology and sound change: the case of the Scottish Vowel Length Rule'. *Journal of Linguistics* 27: 29–53.

(1992). 'Underspecification theory and the analysis of dialect differences in Lexical Phonology'. *Transactions of the Philological Society*: 81–119.

(1996). 'On the use of the past to explain the present: the history of /r/ in English and Scots'. In Britton, Derek (ed.). *English Historical Linguistics 1994*. Amsterdam, Benjamins: 73–89.

(1998a). 'Evolution and phonological constraints'. Paper presented at the 2nd International Conference on the Evolution of Language, London.

(1998b). 'Optimality Theory and the challenge of the language-specific'. Paper presented at the 10th International Conference on English Historical Linguistics, Manchester.

McMahon, April and Paul Foulkes (1995). 'Sound change, phonological rules and Articulatory Phonology'. *Belgian Journal of Linguistics* 9: 1–20.

McMahon, April, Paul Foulkes and Laura Tollfree (1994). 'Gestural representation and Lexical Phonology'. *Phonology* 11: 277–316.

Miller, J. (1985). *Semantics and Syntax: Parallels and Connections.* Cambridge University Press.

(1993). 'The grammar of Scottish English'. In Milroy, James and Lesley Milroy (eds.). *Real English: The Grammar of English Dialects in the British Isles.* London, Longman: 99–138.

Milroy, James (1992). *Linguistic Variation and Change.* London, Blackwell.

(1995). 'Investigating the Scottish Vowel Length Rule in a Northumbrian dialect'. *Newcastle and Durham Working Papers in Linguistics* 3: 187–196.

Milroy, James and Lesley Milroy (1985). 'Linguistic change, social network and speaker innovation'. *Journal of Linguistics* 21: 339–84.

Minkova, Donka (1982). 'The environment for Open Syllable Lengthening in Middle English'. *Folia Linguistica Historica* III: 29–58.

(1985). 'Of rhyme and reason: some foot-governed quantity changes in English'. In Eaton, Roger, Olga Fischer, Willem Koopman and Frederike van der Leek (eds.). *Papers from the 4th International Conference on English Historical Linguistics.* Amsterdam, Benjamins: 163–78.

Mohanan, K.P. (1982). *Lexical Phonology.* Unpublished PhD Dissertation, Department of Linguistics, MIT.

(1986). *The Theory of Lexical Phonology.* Dordrecht, Reidel.

(1991). 'On the bases of radical underspecification'. *Natural Language and Linguistic Theory* 9: 285–325.

Mohanan, K.P. and Tara Mohanan (1984). 'Lexical Phonology of the consonant system of Malayalam'. *Linguistic Inquiry* 15: 575–602.

Mugglestone, Lynda (1995). *Talking Proper: The Rise of Accent as Social Symbol.* Oxford, Clarendon Press.

Murison, D. (1979). 'The historical background'. In Aitken, A.J. and T. McArthur (eds.). *Languages of Scotland.* Edinburgh, Chambers.

Murray, J. (1873). *The Dialect of the Southern Counties of Scotland.* London, Asher & Co.

Newton, B. (1972). *The Generative Interpretation of Dialect.* Cambridge University Press.

Nolan, Francis (1993). 'Phonetic and phonological assimilation'. Paper presented at the Workshop on Cognitive Phonology, Manchester.

Nolan, Francis and Paul Kerswill (1990). 'The description of connected speech processes'. In Ramsaran, Susan (ed.). *Studies in the Pronunciation of English.* London, Routledge: 295–316.

Nolan, Francis, Tara Holst and Barbara Kühnert (1996). 'Modelling [s] to [ʃ] accommodation in English'. *Journal of Phonetics* 24: 113–37.

Ó Baoill, Colm (1997). 'The Scots-Gaelic interface'. In Jones, Charles (ed.). *The Edinburgh History of the Scots Language.* Edinburgh University Press: 551–68.

Ohala, Manjari (1974). 'The abstractness controversy: experimental input from Hindi'. *Language* 50(2): 225–35.

Padgett, Jaye (1995). Review of Goldsmith (ed.). 1993. *Phonology* 12: 147–55.

Pandey, P.K. (1997). 'Optionality, lexicality and sound change'. *Journal of Linguistics* 33: 91–130.

Patterson, D. (1860). *The Provincialisms of Belfast and the Surrounding Districts Pointed Out and Corrected*. Belfast, Mayne.

Peterson, G. and Ilse Lehiste (1960). 'Duration of syllable nuclei in English'. *Journal of the Acoustical Society of America* 32: 693–703.

Postal, Paul (1968). *Aspects of Phonological Theory*. New York, Harper & Row.

Prince, Alan and Paul Smolensky (1993). *Optimality Theory: Constraint Interaction in Generative Grammar*. Manuscript, Rutgers University/University of Colorado at Boulder.

Pulgram, Ernst (1959). 'Proto-Indo-European reality and reconstruction'. *Language* 35: 421–6.

(1961). 'The nature and use of proto-languages'. *Lingua* 10: 18–37.

Pulleyblank, Douglas (1986). *Tone in Lexical Phonology*. Dordrecht, Reidel.

Pullum, Geoffrey (1974). 'Sheltering environments and negative contexts: a case against making phonological rules state things that don't happen'. *Edinburgh Working Papers in Linguistics* 4: 31–41.

Ramsaran, Susan (ed.). (1990a). *Studies in the Pronunciation of English*. London, Routledge.

(1990b). 'RP: fact and fiction'. In Ramsaran, Susan (ed.). *Studies in the Pronunciation of English*. London, Routledge: 178–190.

Ritt, Nikolaus (1994). *Quantity Adjustment*. Cambridge University Press.

Roca, Iggy (ed.). (1997a). *Derivations and Constraints in Phonology*. Oxford, Clarendon Press.

(1997b). 'Derivations or constraints, or derivations and constraints?'. In Roca, Iggy (ed.). *Derivations and Constraints in Phonology*. Oxford, Clarendon Press: 3–41.

Romaine, Suzanne (1978). 'Postvocalic /r/ in Scottish English: sound change in progress?' In Trudgill, Peter (ed.). *Sociolinguistic Patterns in British English*. London, Edward Arnold: 144–57.

(1988). *Pidgin and Creole Languages*. London, Longman.

Rubach, Jerzy (1984). 'Segmental rules of English and cyclic phonology'. *Language* 60: 21–54.

Scobbie, James (1992). 'Against rule inversion: the development of English [r]-sandhi'. Poster presented at the 7th International Phonology Meeting, Krems, Austria.

Scobbie, James, Alice Turk and Nigel Hewlett (1998). 'The articulation of Scottish vowels'. Paper presented at the Sixth Conference on Laboratory Phonology, University of York.

Selkirk, E. (1982a). *The Syntax of Words*. Cambridge, Mass., MIT Press.

(1982b). 'The syllable'. In van der Hulst, Harry and Norval Smith (eds.). *The Structure of Phonological Representations*, Volume 2. Dordrecht, Foris: 337–78.

Shattuck-Hufnagel, Stephanie (1986). 'The representation of phonological information during speech production planning: evidence from vowel errors in spontaneous speech'. *Phonology Yearbook* 3: 117–50.

Sheridan, T. (1762). *A Course of Lectures on Elocution*. London.

(1780). *A General Dictionary of the English Language*. London.

(1781). *A Rhetorical Grammar of the English Language*. Dublin.

(1786). *Elements of English*. London.

Sherrard, Nicholas (1997). 'Questions of priorities: an introductory overview of Optimality Theory in phonology'. In Roca, Iggy (ed.). *Derivations and Constraints in Phonology*. Oxford, Clarendon Press: 43–89.

Siegel, Dorothy (1974). *Topics in English Morphology*. New York, Garland Press.

(1980). 'Why there is no = boundary'. In Aronoff, Mark and Mary-Louise Kean (eds.). *Juncture*. Saratoga, Calif., Anma Libri: 131–4.

Smith, N.V. (1989). *The Twitter Machine*. Oxford, Blackwell.

Spencer, Andrew (1988). 'Morpholexical rules and lexical representations'. *Linguistics* 26: 619–40.

Sproat, Richard (1985). *On Deriving the Lexicon*. Unpublished PhD Dissertation, Department of Linguistics, MIT.

Stanley, R. (1967). 'Redundancy rules in phonology'. *Language* 43: 393–436.

Stemberger, J.B. (1992). 'Radical underspecification in language production'. *Phonology* 8: 73–112.

Steriade, Donca (1979). 'Vowel harmony in Khalkha Mongolian'. *MIT Working Papers in Linguistics* 1: 25–50.

(1995). 'Underspecification and markedness'. In Goldsmith, John (ed.). *The Handbook of Phonological Theory*. Oxford, Blackwell: 114–74.

Stockwell, Robert P. (1990). 'On the evidence for bimoraic vowels in Early English'. Paper presented at the 6th International Conference on English Historical Linguistics, Helsinki.

Stockwell, Robert P. and Donka Minkova (1990) 'The Early Modern English vowels, more O'Lass'. *Diachronica* 7: 199–214.

Strang, Barbara M.H. (1970). *A History of English*. London, Methuen.

Strauss, S. (1979). 'Against boundary distinctions in English morphology'. *Linguistic Analysis* 5: 387–419.

(1982). 'On the theory of word-formation and its role in phonological analysis'. *Linguistic Analysis* 9: 253–76.

Sullivan, Anthea E. (1992). *Sound Change in Progress*. University of Exeter Press.

Sweet, Henry (1881). *The Elementary Sounds of English*. London.

Szpyra, Jolanta (1989). *The Phonology–Morphology Interface: Cycles, Levels and Words*. London, Routledge.

Thomas, A.R. (1967). 'Generative phonology in dialectology'. *Transactions of the Philological Society*: 179–203.

Tollfree, Laura F. (1995). *Modelling Phonological Variation and Change: Evidence from English Consonants*. Unpublished PhD Dissertation, Department of Linguistics, University of Cambridge.

Trudgill, Peter (1974). *The Social Differentiation of English in Norwich*. Cambridge University Press.

Tucker, Abraham (1773). *Vocal Sounds*. Facsimile Alston, R.C. (ed.), *English Linguistics 1500–1800*, Volume 165. Menston, Scolar Press.

Vachek, Josef (1966). *The Linguistic School of Prague.* Bloomington, Ind., Indiana University Press.

(1972). 'On the interplay of external and internal factors in the development of language'. In Malmberg, Bertil (ed.). *Readings in Modern Linguistics.* Stockholm, Mouton: 209–23.

(1976). *Selected Writings in English and General Linguistics.* Prague, Academia.

(1983). 'Remarks on the dynamism of the system of language'. In Vachek, Josef (ed.). *Praguiana: Some Basic and Less-Known Aspects of the Prague Linguistic School.* Prague, Academia: 241–54.

Vaiana Taylor, Mary (1974). 'The great southern Scots conspiracy: patterns in the development of Northern English'. In Anderson, John M. and Charles Jones (eds.). *Historical Linguistics II: Theory and Description in Phonology.* Amsterdam, North Holland.

Vennemann, Theo (1972). 'Rule inversion'. *Lingua* 29: 209–42.

(1974). 'Topics, subjects and word order: from SXV to SVX via TVX'. In Anderson, John M. and Charles Jones (eds.). *Historical Linguistics.* Volume I. Amsterdam, North Holland: 339–76.

Viëtor, W. (1904 5th edn.). *Elemente der Phonetik.* Leipzig.

Walker, J. (1791). *A Critical Pronouncing Dictionary.* Facsimile, Alston, R.C. (ed.). *English Linguistics 1500–1800,* Volume 117. Menston, Scolar Press.

Wang, H.S. (1985). *On the Productivity of Vowel Shift Alternations in English: An experimental study.* Unpublished PhD Dissertation, University of Alberta.

Wang, H. S. and Bruce Derwing (1986). 'More on English vowel shift: the back vowel question'. *Phonology Yearbook* 3: 99–116.

Wang, William S-Y. (1969). 'Competing changes as a cause of residue'. *Language* 45: 9–25.

(ed.). (1977). *The Lexicon in Phonological Change.* The Hague, Mouton.

Watson, G. (1923). *The Roxburghshire Word Book.* Cambridge University Press.

Weinreich, Uriel, William Labov and Marvin I. Herzog (1968). 'Empirical foundations for a theory of language change'. In Lehmann, W.P. and Yakov Malkiel (eds.). *Directions for Historical Linguistics.* Austin, University of Texas Press: 95–195.

Wells, John (1982). *Accents of English.* Cambridge University Press.

Wettstein, P. (1942). *The Phonology of a Berwickshire Dialect.* Zurich, Schuler.

Wiese, Richard (ed.). (1994). *Recent Developments in Lexical Phonology.* Düsseldorf, Heinrich Heine Universität.

(1996). 'Phonological versus morphological rules: on German Umlaut and Ablaut'. *Journal of Linguistics* 32: 113–35.

Wiik, K. (1965). *Finnish and English Vowels.* University of Turku Press.

Winston, M. (1970). *Some Aspects of the Pronunciation of Educated Scots.* Unpublished PhD Dissertation, Department of English Language, University of Edinburgh.

Wood, S. (1975). 'Tense and lax vowels – degree of constriction or pharyngeal volume?' *Lund University Phonetics Laboratory Working Papers* 11: 109–33.

Wurzel, Wolfgang U. (1989). *Inflectional Morphology and Naturalness.* Dordrecht, Kluwer.

Zai, R. (1942). *The Phonology of the Morebattle Dialect*. Lucerne, Raeber.

Zimmerman, S. and S. Sapon (1958). 'Notes on vowel duration seen cross-linguistically'. *Journal of the Acoustical Society of America* 30: 152–3.

Zsiga, Elizabeth C. (1993). *Features, Gestures and the Temporal Aspects of Phonological Organization*. Unpublished PhD Dissertation, Department of Linguistics, Yale University.

(1997). 'Features, gestures and Igbo vowels: an approach to the phonology–phonetics interface'. *Language* 73: 227–74.

Zwicky, Arnold M. (1970). 'The free-ride principle and two rules of complete assimilation in English'. *Papers from the Sixth Regional Meeting of the Chicago Linguistics Society*: 579–88.

(1974). 'Homing in: on arguing for remote representations'. *Journal of Linguistics* 10: 55–69.

(1985). 'Heads'. *Journal of Linguistics* 21: 1–29.

Index